PENGUIN BOOKS

TO THE BALTIC WITH BOB

Griff Rhys Jones was born in 1953. He was educated at Brentwood
school and Cambridge University. On the way to becoming a writer, he
worked as a security guard, a petrol-pump attendant and a television star.

To the Baltic with Bob

GRIFF RHYS JONES

PENGUIN BOOKS

PENGUIN BOOKS

Published by the Penguin Group
Penguin Books Ltd, 80 Strand, London WC2R ORL, England
Penguin Group (USA) Inc., 375 Hudson Street, New York, New York 10014, USA
Penguin Books Australia Ltd, 250 Camberwell Road, Camberwell, Victoria 3124, Australia
Penguin Books Canada Ltd, 10 Alcorn Avenue, Toronto, Ontario, Canada M4V 3B2
Penguin Books India (P) Ltd, 11 Community Centre, Panchsheel Park, New Delhi – 110 017, India
Penguin Group (NZ), cnr Airborne and Rosedale Roads, Albany, Auckland 1310, New Zealand
Penguin Books (South Africa) (Pty) Ltd, 24 Sturdee Avenue, Rosebank 2196, South Africa

Penguin Books Ltd, Registered Offices: 80 Strand, London WC2R ORL, England

www.penguin.com

Published by Michael Joseph 2003
Published in Penguin Books 2005
1

Copyright © Griff Rhys Jones, 2003
All rights reserved

The moral right of the author has been asserted

Printed in England by Clays Ltd, St Ives plc

For Jo

The
Baltic
Voyage

NORWAY

Oslo

Göta
Canal

Trollhätten

Skagerrak

Kattegat

Gothenburg

NORTH
SEA

DENMARK

Copenhagen

Malmö

ENGLAND

London

Borkum

Kiel

Brunsbüttel

Lübeck

Cuxhaven

Elbe

Weser

Ems

Hamburg

Amsterdam

HOLLAND

Vlissingen

GERMANY

BELGIUM

0   100   200 miles

0   100   200   300 kilometres

Peter McClure

SWEDEN

Gulf of Bothnia

FINLAND

A maze of islands

Åland   Turku   Helsinki

Hanko   Gulf of Finland   St Petersburg

Vormsi

Lake Vänern   Stockholm   Tallinn
Motala   Daloro   Port Montu
L. Roxen   Hiiumaa   Haapsalu   RUSSIA

Lake Vättern   Söderköping   Saaremaa   ESTONIA

Visby   Fårö   Kuressaare
Gotland   Gulf of Riga

Kalmar   Borgholm   Ventspils   Riga
Öland

Baltic Sea   LATVIA

Karlskrona

Bornholm   LITHUANIA

POLAND

Kattegat

Helsingør   Helsingborg

miles
0   20   40   60

0 20 40 60 80
kilometres

Copenhagen   Malmö

Kolding   Korsør
Arøsund   Odense   Skælskør
Abenrå   Svendborg
Sønderborg
Flensburg

Kiel Canal   Kiel

Baltic Sea

Acknowledgements

Thanks to Louise, David, Ness, Claire, Robert, Cat, John and Jo.

Contents

Prologue

It was half past ten and it was eventually, even reluctantly, getting dark in Kent. Hulks, rusting engines, trailers, plastic barrels, half-finished cement boats and a 900-year-old tractor – all the dwarfing, ghastly litter of a boatyard melded into a shadow of impenetrable gloom. On the other side of the sea wall, some way below us now, bizarrely, we could see the beckoning light of the only pub for 5 miles. 'Come back, don't go. Look! Beer!'

Bob lit a cigarette. He sucked. The red glow briefly rimmed his bald cranium. 'A neap tide actually means that the water comes to the highest level. Just like springs,' he said.

'Oh. Really?' I replied.

'Mmm.'

It didn't sound right to me. I shifted on the hard cockpit bench and went on sorting out ropes. Surely neap tides meant the water didn't go all the way down the plug.

The darkness hid the dirty mud-grey water, which was now flooding in all around us. Hid the flecks of poisonous-looking yellow foam that always accompanied the rising waters on the east coast. There was a slight movement, a tip of the deck, as Baines walked across it. We were floating.

'Can you switch on the instrument lights?'

Baines's bearded face, tinged scarlet by the navigation light, appeared briefly in the hatch. There was a click. 'There you go.'

Night is the only time to set off in a boat. 'And the engine.'

Baines switched the key in the ignition and another light glowed red. He depressed one of the two black corrugated rubber buttons on the control console and held it for ten seconds. He let go and pressed both together. The engine coughed and chugged into life. Steam and exhaust smoke rose up through the glow of the stern light in the unseasonably cold June night.

'I want to warp her round,' I said. The others looked at me.
Baines nodded.

'Rick, could you let off the stern rope?'

'What, completely?'

'Yuh.'

'OK.'

He fumbled with the ropes on the fishing smack's foredeck.

'Just give the stern a push away.'

He did, with his foot. There was a moment of hiatus while the
incoming tide caught the back end of the boat and 14½ tons of
wood and metal swung slowly out into the channel. As long as the
forward rope was tied in place, *Undina* would simply pivot on it,
wouldn't she?

She did. The last of the flood tide carried her round.

'Hold out the bow.' I didn't want the new paintwork to bang
against our host. She bumped back against the side of the smack,
and ended up facing the other way, out towards the Swale and the
mouth of the Thames and the North Sea.

1. Chromium

The plan was to go to the Baltic for the summer of 2002.

Michael, the boat builder, had originally promised to return me my boat, *Undina*, at the beginning of May. I telephoned him in the middle of March. 'So, anyway, Michael, as I was saying, it would probably be a good idea to take her up to Harwich for some sort of sea trials and then we can go across to Holland.'

'Yup. And when were you planning this then?'

'Early May.'

'Early May!' He sounded astonished.

'Yes. You said early May.'

'Well, she won't be ready by then.' There was a distinct admonitory tone to his voice.

'Well, yes, as I said, I'll have finished this very important radio project that I'm working on and then I'm free. Free! Free of everything. I really have to do this thing. And it's up anchor and away.'

'Yes, but not in early May. Dear me, no.'

'No. OK. When, then?'

There was a noise like a lorry going round a corner. 'Eeeeeeeeeee . . .' Michael gave a heavy sigh. He grunted. He made little chicken cluckings in the back of his mouth.

'For safety, say the end of the second week in May, say.'

'Yes . . . yes . . . that's fine.' It made no odds. I wouldn't have finished the very important radio project until then. Not that it was that important really. It was perfectly sound. It had won a Sony award. The authorities were so enthused by having something funny on the radio that they had almost considered the possibility of another series. But it could all wait. I didn't care. As long as I got to the Baltic by June.

Six months earlier, on a freezing December day, Michael and I had driven down to Cowes to look at *Josephine*, the sister ship to *Undina*. She was a near clone, but we were immediately impressed by her fittings.

'Yes, we had them chromed,' *Josephine*'s owner said.

'They were bronze, though.'

'Yes. But they would have been chromed originally.' And he took us below to show us his varnished floor and lavatory arrangements. But my eyes kept returning to the gleaming silver finish.

'Busy at the moment?' he asked.

'What? Yes. Just finished a play.'

'Any good?'

'Well the first three hours were excellent. But then the interval came . . .'

Both boats had been built in the 1950s. There were seven altogether. They were designed by Philip Rhodes, an American, and made of wood by European yards, which must have been cheaper in the immediate post-war period. They were yachting icons of their time – fast, modern, not wooden for sentimental reasons but because wood was light and strong and fibre-glass was still an experiment. They were the Chippendales of boats, neglected as they became unfashionable, but now redolent of the period and era. Dead classy. Though the thought often occurred to me, if you owned a Chippendale escritoire, would you sensibly toss it in the sea?

From the beginning, for me, the relationship was almost wholly one of aesthetics. I was stricken with the boat. I couldn't walk up a jetty towards it without pausing to admire it. West End musicals, radio series, new translations of creaky French farces, television clip show career opportunities, the finding of another two million for the Hackney Empire (after the builders lost it), the sitcom I had written (which the BBC sports supremo suggested a woman should write), a seat on the committee to decide on the European City of Culture, they all seemed so blisteringly unimportant.

In motor-car terms, the 45-foot boats were like 1950s Maseratis: sleek, low and streamlined. And now there was this chrome. It was a revelation. It defined their classic origins and the slight American raffish glamour. On *Josephine* that morning, the new covering reflected back a distorted, envious Mr Toad, as I leered admiringly into it.

So we had to have ours chromed. Every stanchion, every cleat, every screw-bolt on the deck was laboriously undone and sent to a man in Romford, who was apparently surprised to find we wanted them back in less than a year. I was surprised, in my turn, at his initial quote.

'Six thousand pounds!'

'It's the polishing. You can have any amount of dipping, it's the polishing that takes the man hours.'

'Well yes, but . . .'

'How much do you want to spend?' I hadn't been asked a question like that since I was in the 'Carpet Museum' in Marrakesh. 'Five thousand, four . . . ?'

'Yes, four is more like what I had in mind.'

'We'll say four, then.'

'OK.' Clearly, I had been rash to interject at four. Who knows, he might have gone on down to a quid. Or done it for nothing, if he'd been in a generous mood. I'd never had my fittings chromed before. It was new. It was a new experience. I wasn't a boat builder, I was a would-be fantasy yachtsman.

'So why would you be coming down on Monday anyway?' Michael had asked in late May.

'To pick up the boat, Michael, as discussed.'

'Oh I don't think that's possible, because we won't have the chrome back by then . . .'

'But that's outrageous.'

'We did ring. But he said he'll hurry it up and it will be scheduled for next week.'

'No, Michael. Look, this is nearly June, and we have to be in Flensburg in Germany by the eighth of June. I just have to go.'

'Do you want me to cancel it, then?'

'Yes. Er . . . yes. We'll forget the chroming.'

'He's got them all chemicalized and coated with the stuff, he says. It's just a question of putting them in the tank.'

'So if we get them back they'll all be covered with chemical coating?'

'I suppose they could wash it off.'

'What's the latest you can pick them up?'

Michael made a noise like a small electric drill. 'Eeeee . . .' It was agreed that if we could get a lorry to take delivery of the missing parts, if they all fitted, if we scooted straight up the Dutch coast, if the weather improved, we could get my love to this classic yacht regatta, where I wanted to pimp her around, with at least an hour to spare. It was not the leisurely exploration of the Benelux countries that I had originally planned. It was not the drift into an alternative existence, free of the petty concerns of media trash that I had originally sought, but Michael would have a go.

Two weeks later we spoke again.

'Well, we do have the chrome bits all back now . . .' Michael paused. He had the patient concern of a talking dray horse in his telephone manner again.

'Right, yes . . .'

'. . . but these fittings were built with imperial measures, not metric. So we can't source screws to get them back in.'

'I see.' I could almost see the pursed lips and the nodding at the other end of the telephone. Was that a bridle jangling? 'What about the screws that you took out?'

'They were all too corroded.'

'Yes, but couldn't we use them temporarily?'

'We threw them away. It can all be done, but I think it will take another two weeks, so . . .'

I walked away from the phone and paced the room, idly tossing the letter offering a tour of *As You Like It* 'including Bath' into the wastepaper bin. I was beginning to get the impression that Michael didn't actually want to give me back my boat. I knew what this was. He had fallen in love with her himself and was intending to kidnap her and imprison her in his tin shed.

'It doesn't seem very likely. He's doing what he can.' Bob was sympathetic. 'But you want to take her this month?'

'Yes.'

'Right. This month.'

'Well, when did you think we'd be leaving?'

'I assumed the regatta was in July.'

'No, no, that's the whole point. The regatta in Germany is on the weekend of the fourteenth of June.'

'But that's only a couple of weeks away.'

'I know. Are you saying you can't make it?'

'No, no. I've put the whole summer aside. I'm up for it. Don't worry about me.'

'So you can make the departure on Friday? It's tight.'

'No, wait a minute. Next Friday?'

'Michael's getting a crane and a low-loader and after the chrome stuff is all fitted back on, putting the boat back in the water on the Friday. And then we leave on the Saturday. I told you all this.'

'No, all I remember is you told me the regatta was going to be in July.'

'June!'

'June, then. But if the boat isn't going to be ready, don't you think we should wait until the regatta in July.'

'There isn't a regatta in July. They don't have a regatta every month. I've booked us in and we have to be there.'

'But what about the weather?'

I had looked up the long-range forecast and the weather was stable. It was continuously bad. So far, May and June had been notable for being the wettest and coldest May and June for as long as anybody could remember, though, naturally enough, the meteorology office would announce to a shivering, damp nation at the end of the month that the weather had been perfectly normal and not much wetter or colder than the average May or June.

'It's fine.'

Bob didn't sound convinced. In fact he didn't sound anything. But I took his silence to mean that he wasn't convinced.

'If the weather is bad, all we have to do is nip across the Channel, twenty miles from Ramsgate, and then get into the inland waterways and we can get up to Flensburg without ever going out to sea again.' Neither of us wanted to go out to sea in anything rough. He seemed partially reassured. 'But we could do with someone to go with us for that bit. I mean I was hoping that George and his mates would come . . .' I said.

'And?'

'Well it's his half-term. He's decided to go drinking in Whitehall instead.'

My son George was seventeen. I thought the trip would toughen him up, but he was already tough enough to refuse to go. I was now reliant on Bob. 'Didn't you say that you had a couple of friends who . . .'

'Oh yeah. Yes. That's no problem. There are loads of people.'

A week later, Bob rang me back. He'd arranged for a mate, Baines, to get working on the electrics of the boat as quickly as possible, but Baines had contacted the yard and been told he had the whole weekend or as long as he wanted.

'No, I don't think so, we're leaving on the Saturday.'

'That's not what Michael told me.'

'What?'

Michael was apologetic when I phoned.

'It's the Jubilee weekend, Griff.'

Dear me, I had forgotten entirely.

'We can't get the driver of the crane to come out over the weekend. The earliest he can do is Monday.'

'What's the problem? He's a monarchist?'

'No, he's booked for something else.'

There was nothing to be done. The schedule was, at least, being sort of set down, you know, subject to alteration, of course. Trundle the boat out of the yard on the Monday, stick it in the water on the Tuesday, rig the mast and bend on the sails during the day and leave on the high tide on Tuesday evening: leaving – what? – five days to shoot up the Channel and whisk into the Baltic.

I raged around my study. 'No, no, I've got a better idea. He can deliver it. I'll just fly up to Flensburg and wait for it.'

Bob was mollifying. 'But that's the whole point of the journey, to sail there.'

'The whole point of the journey is to wander gently through Dutch inland seas and explore the Friesian Islands on a leisurely cruise and sit in reedy shallows smoking pipes.'

Bob and I were cowardly sailors. He, partly because of a limitless inexperience of any practical use and me, because I was a coward. On the telephone the week before, he had become irritatingly confident about the weather. 'We'll be all right in June. Should be lovely.'

'No, no.'

'No?'

Why did I have to knock back Bob's infuriating insouciance?

'June can be terrible!'

Bob raised his eyebrows. Since he was extremely difficult to disconcert, I felt it was my job to lie and exaggerate. An hysteric can't stand cool people being cool about important and life-threatening things (most things), so tend to lean on the fuel supply in order to induce A PROPER SENSE OF RESPONSIBILITY. This seldom works, but it makes us feel better.

'June can be TERRIBLE. There was this bloke, this journalist from the *Daily Telegraph*. Did you read about him?' This was a safe, if redundant question. Bob rarely read anything. Not even the instructions on the packet. Especially not the instructions on the packet. 'He was planning to sail round Britain a couple of summers ago.' I was conscious that had once been one of our plans, so this would impress him. 'And he ended up WRECKED, totally SWAMPED in a storm, in mid-June, off the Shetland Islands.'

'Oh, right.'

'So the weather will be VITAL. June is NOTORIOUS.' Perhaps I'd gone too far. Bob was looking suspicious now. Was he worried about the whole trip? 'But, you know, we'll get the long-range weather forecast and keep an eye on things and anyway we're only going to hop across the Channel.'

'Yess . . .'

★

Bob arranged for his choice of crew, Baines and Rick, to come to a sort of meet-and-greet at the 'Welsh Embassy' (my house), in central London, and then phoned to tell me he would be late himself. This was wholly expected.

The doorbell rang.

Rick!

'Come on in, Rick. Bob's not here . . .'

'Ha ha. Yeah, well . . .' (He obviously knows Bob quite well, then.)

Rick was wearing a leather motorbike caterpillar suit, which he peeled off and left in the hall. He liked my furniture (his uncle ran some sort of furniture restoration business). Rick rolled spectacularly thin cigarettes and would have a glass of wine.

The doorbell rang again.

'Come on in, Baines. Rick's here, Baines, but Bob . . .'

'Oh ho!' Baines knows the form too.

Baines was weedy, bearded and thoroughly affable. He was just called Baines. I wanted to call him Baines something or something Baines. But it was just Baines. He did have a real name, and I tried to elicit it, but he was reluctant to give it, not because he was on a witness protection scheme, but because he had been Baines since he was a baby. He had been born in Kenya and, on the way home from the hospital, the doctor had managed to run over his grandmother's pet ocelot, in the driveway to her farm. The ocelot had been called Baines and the baby was instantly christened Baines by the grandmother and, eventually, by everybody else too.

Even before Bob himself bothered to arrive, I had gathered that neither Rick nor Baines seemed sporty, clubby or, worst of all, in Bob's estimation, 'straight'. We talked. Naturally enough, since he wasn't there, we talked about Bob, and then about Bob's planned visit to Glastonbury. Both of them were ardent fans of the Glastonbury Festival, as I was myself, of course. Though I hadn't actually been there since the very first one, when I had hitch-hiked down to Somerset after A-levels to watch fat girls with no clothes on roll about in the mud: the pinnacle of freak-out sophistication in 1971.

While we waited for Bob, I invited Baines, who I knew was waiting to fix our electrics, to examine our collection of boxes. The week before Bob and I had been on a trip to a basement shop opposite the Saudi Embassy in Mayfair, where I had been overwhelmed by a heady mixture of power, innocence and desperation.

'OK . . . right. Obviously I've got to have some sort of new GPS system.'

'Right, OK.' The salesman nodded slowly.

'And we thought we should have some sort of iridium phone.'

'Mmm. Yes.'

Retrospectively I realize that he was thinking, 'Well that's two grand already.' But he gave nothing away, except to adopt the look of a man trying hard to give nothing away.

Come to think of it, he'd probably been through this before. He probably thought that we were going to walk out with a catalogue and a cleaning kit. After all that's what we'd done to three separate salesmen at the Boat Show in January. But that was January. Now, I was leaving in three days. I was frightened he might not take me seriously.

'I do need these things quite quickly.'

'I am confident that can be arranged.'

By the time I left, I'd added a hi-fi set, a German radio and a complete electronic charting system. He was extremely quick to return my calls from then on, and even took back an inverter large enough to power an electric submarine, which I had been convinced I would need, but which turned out to be pure hallucination on my part.

Baines stood in my front room and looked approvingly at my shopping.

'Yes, well, I wanted to make sure we had the right equipment, you know, for the whole journey. Safety has to be a high priority.'

'Yes,' said Baines. 'Of course. This is a car stereo, isn't it?'

'Yes. Well we'll probably want some music too, won't we?'

'I should jolly well hope so,' said Baines. 'Well done.'

Rick immediately focused on what I was later to discover was his particular and, some might say, all-consuming interest.

'And charts?'

'Yes, well, I've ordered a computer. It's a special rugged computer, designed, I believe, for the US army, with a gel thingie inside it that compensates for vibration, and a special waterproof specification, which can run C map, so we'll have electronic charts . . .' Rick's eyes flickered slightly. '. . . but I do, of course, have paper charts,' I added quickly. Of course. No sailor worth his salt, or at least one who read any yachting magazine, manual, handbook, pamphlet or prominently displayed notice, would ever rely on electric charts, alone. That word 'alone' was the crucial consideration here. Charts could be personally beamed down from a cartographer, licensed by the Royal Hydrographer, hovering in a space capsule directly above your boat, but the proper mariner would always unfold a vast piece of cartridge paper the size of a volleyball field, and set to with bits of see-through plastic and a pair of dividers. God knows, I knew this was sacred law. In fact, I first went on boats when there was no other choice. (Mind you, then, the only affordable way of finding out the depth was throwing a lump of lead on a rope with knots in it over the side, and I've done that too.) But having returned to the business of sailing my own boat, after a ten-year lay-off, I was shocked by how easy it had become.

The GPS system is linked to a clutch of satellites, owned and run by the American military. They orbit the earth and beam down directions to anyone with a receiver. It's the same system that allows an irritating woman to direct mini-cabs down back alleys. In fact, it's so damn good that everybody is scared to death of it. Barely a week goes by without the yachting press running gruesome fright-stories of boats grounding in the Caribbean or warning that at any moment the United States might go to alert red and switch the lot off. Thunderstorms, electrical interferences, wonky antennae, misreadings and mistaken entries will lead inexorably to maritime disaster. So I had proper charts and a pencil too.

I showed them to Rick. He nodded approvingly.

It was the doorbell.

'Ah, Bob.'

Bob sauntered in to join Rick, Baines and myself, lit a fag and slumped into a chair in my study. He was full of two things.

The first was a thoroughly irritating smugness. I knew where this was coming from. Bob was a fixer. He had dedicated his life to fixing things so that he had, himself, to do as little as possible, apart, that is, from breed parrots, which had turned into a lucrative if complex pastime. His flat used to be full of cockatoos and macaws and at some point a monkey, which bit off visitors' ears. But having midwifed several enormous and colourful birds into life in Clapham, he had emerged from nursing eggs in warm flannels to discover that Chelsea had moved across the river towards him. His poky flat was worth a fortune, even more than the cockatoos, which were valued at several thousand pounds each, so he'd loaned his aviary to a parrot farm in Northamptonshire and his flat to a yuppy. He'd moved himself and his huge collection of failed projects (plaster dogs on a wall mount, miniature models of the cast of *Coronation Street*, sepia-tinted photographs printed on pull-down blinds, garden seats made out of the Chelsea North Stand, dozens of hand-made cds of his band 'The Long Horns' and his collection of chicken suits and wigs) up the road and into an empty space above Kebab House.

'It sounds good, Kebab House, like Badminton or Mansion House, I thought.'

And now he'd fixed two keen and willing members of crew to help us cross the Channel. Clearly, in his eyes, it was at least the equal of getting a boat, charts and a trip organized. So he was sitting, lounging even, drawing hard on his cigarette, smiling broadly and literally putting his feet up.

'Not on the new electrical equipment please!'

He twisted round and reached into his back pocket. 'I managed to get this, by the way, from Stanford's in Covent Garden.' He pulled out what looked like a street map from his back pocket and began to unfold it. 'It was ten quid. I was amazed. Ten quid.'

'What is it?'

'It's a chart of the Dutch and Belgian canal system.'

We put it on the floor and laid it out. This was the other thing he was full of. Baines and Rick looked over our shoulders. 'Yeah . . .' I started. 'The general thing is that we don't have a lot of time to get to Flensburg, so we're going to have to press on. Obviously, if the weather turns bad we won't want to go out into the German Bight in June . . .'

'It can be very stormy in June,' said Bob. 'There was this editor of the *Sunday Times* who was drowned in a hurricane . . .'

'Yes, yes. But look, you see . . .' I produced a big Admiralty chart of the English Channel and unfolded that too. 'Whatever the conditions, we can cross here . . .' pointing to the narrow area north of the Straits of Dover '. . . get over to, say, Ostend, and swoosh up into the Dutch canal system here . . . here.' My finger waved uncertainly over the map. 'Well definitely here anyway.' I finally found a way in, through all the dykes and sea walls that had been erected in the last fifty years to effectively close off all but the major port entrances to the Low Countries. 'And the best way in is certainly almost straight ahead. Vlissingen, or Flushing, barely fifty miles from England, is at the mouth of a huge estuary.'

We transferred our attentions back to Bob's little map. The estuary was joined to the heartland of Holland by any number of canals. We could have been looking at a road map of the Midlands. Thick blue lines snaked off in every direction. It seemed there was a bewildering choice of land-locked routes. First, we could head north through industrial Holland. Then cross the northernmost bulges of western continental Europe safely inland, passing through Groningen to the Ems, the river that separated the Netherlands from Germany and then . . . Bob's map ran out.

We turned to the AA Road Atlas of Europe.

'This is only temporary,' I reassured Rick and Baines. 'We'll get more detailed maps before we go.'

'Or up there in Holland somewhere,' added Bob. He knew that every chandler and shop we had been to so far only had maps and charts of the Solent and routes south. Everybody wanted to head to the sun. It was one of the reasons that Bob and I had decided to go the other way. The other was because we'd done a little of the route already and realized that this was easily the best direction for cowards.

At the end of the season, the year before, Bob and I had set out on our first independent trip in *Undina*. We sailed the 6 miles down the River Orwell from Ipswich and found ourselves facing the sea at Harwich. By my calculations, our least complicated destination was Holland. You took a ruler and drew a pencil line from Harwich to Ijmuiden and then you sailed along it. Going south was a different matter.

The Thames is a deceptively huge river. It comes as a shock to those who have travelled for several months on Network South-East to discover that they are still in the Thames Estuary. The estuary runs right up the Essex coast and into Suffolk and has dug channels and deposited sandbanks all the way up to Harwich. It's a tricky business working your way through the Wallet Gut or the Goodwin Channel towards France, particularly at night in an unfamiliar boat.

So a year ago, we had simply avoided the Thames Estuary. We'd sailed straight across the North Sea and popped into Holland down a handy canal (before any change in the weather could challenge our seafaring abilities). And there, at the end of the canal, we'd discovered Amsterdam and tied up behind the railway station.

The prospect of taking a floating bedsit to one of the seamiest cities in the world had an enormous appeal for Bob and myself. In 'yachtsmen's harbours', the marina is the main event. It is like spending a couple of days anchored in a park-and-ride facility. By contrast, the Sixhaven in Amsterdam was next to the Shell petroleum headquarters. It was a marina in someone's back garden. There were geraniums on the pontoons. A ferry (a metal platform, half bus, half bridge) ran continuously across the Nordzee Canal. We crossed with dozens of bicycles to walk straight into the equivalent of Oxford Street, still dressed in oilskins. The hippy population of Amsterdam probably assumed we were protesting about chemical waste.

The next day we left the brown cafés behind and, about ten minutes from the centre, passed through a narrow lock and out into the muddy brown waters of the Ijsselmeer, with its medieval ports, now cut off from direct contact with the sea. We nearly reached the long, low, flat, sandy, barely visible line of grassy banks that line the north-west coast of Europe and run in a chain out towards the Elbe: the Friesian Islands. They lay just a day's sail to the north. *Riddle of the Sands* country.

In 1897 Erskine Childers and his brother had discovered almost exactly the same thing as us. They got to the end of the Nordzee Canal in their boat *Vixen* and decided that if the wind blew south they'd go home, if it blew north they'd explore the Friesian Islands. It blew north and, as a result, Childers wrote his one novel, *The Riddle of the Sands*, A MOST IMPORTANT BOOK for the small boat sailor. The paranoid story about German naval intentions is a little preposterous, but the boating descriptions are excellent.

But why stop there? I remember peering at our charts and thinking how simple it would be to go on further. I liked sailing in coastal inlets and shallow waters. The boat had its protective centreboard. The shoals held no particular fear for us. Hamburg, Lübeck and Copenhagen were up there somewhere. Real cities with sex shows and crazy nightlife. Not simply whitewashed holiday destinations, but proper ancient ports and, surely, we could slip behind those islands, couldn't we? We need never venture far from shelter.

Closer examination revealed more islands and more hidden passages. I had never taken the trouble to think about the Baltic. But even the most cursory examination showed you could island-hop through Denmark. It was an archipelago.

The coast of Sweden looked boring to begin with, but, beyond Öland, there were more archipelagos. Uncountable separate dots of land covered the chart for hundreds of miles and, up there, beyond Sweden, beyond Helsinki, right at the top of the Gulf of Finland, where the map takes a right turn into a narrowing funnel, there was St Petersburg. St Petersburg: a place so romantic, so utterly remote, so exotic and yet so potentially packed with live sex shows that it seemed incredible that it was possible to visit it by boat from England, and by a route that would only require only two 30-mile crossings.

I was hardly the first person to notice this. Cumbersome lighters called cogs had been transporting furs, illegal immigrants and Russian dolls down through the river systems for centuries. The Vikings had set up trading posts which had developed into towns, now ancient and impressively preserved, like Tallinn or Visby. This was all based on the sensible principle of getting south without going out into the cold and blowy North Sea. With careful planning we could head out into the far Nordic regions without ever really getting wet.

Mind you, it wasn't strictly fear of the high waves that influenced us. We were far more terrified by the prospect of boredom. Tracy Edwards and Sir Francis Chichester notwithstanding, the only time anything actually happens on a long sea passage is when something goes disastrously wrong. That's why the hairy-arsed bohos who sail from Rio to Portsmouth love it when the mast snaps in two and they have to make a new one out of a spare oar and a tea towel. Otherwise it's just sea. It can be big sea. Huge sea sometimes. Sometimes a flat, sullen, miserable, grey, gently rolling slab of a sea. But mostly just an ordinary stretch of water and a course that consists of an imaginary line, as straight as possible, right through the tedious middle of it.

For us, the shore was the attraction. We could enter the system at Delft. Explore Utrecht. Take a detour to The Hague. Linger in Amsterdam. Sit and listen to the curlew in a ditch near Groningen. It became an ambition to make a real escape into a timeless world of petty incident.

2. Mast-up

Back at my house, Bob smoothed the map. He reached over and twisted the desk light round towards him. It came off in his hands.

'Just put it down over there.' I switched another light on. Bob took a pencil and began to trace a series of loops and tailbacks, twisting across the Netherlands.

'It's not entirely straightforward,' he said. 'We have to go through locks.'

'And under bridges.'

'There must be a mast-up route,' Bob said.

'Why?' I asked.

Bob was a Panglossian optimist. He was convinced that most obstacles could be overcome and, if not, would probably dissolve at his approach. 'They must have a route that allows boats to get through.'

'That's ridiculous.' I countered. I was an Eeyorean pessimist. Obstacles would rise up and stop us whatever happened. 'Maybe they don't make provisions for sailing boats to drive through the middle of Utrecht.'

'It's easy,' Bob continued. This was the sort of statement that was guaranteed to irritate me. 'You just go up here . . .' He was marking the route with a blunt pencil, which was obliterating most of the chart information. 'ooops . . . can't get through there . . .' he traced a loop which took us roughly back to the beginning. '. . . round the outside of there . . .' Now we were heading 20 miles inland. '. . . and back through this way.' He sat back and admired his work. We would certainly comprehensively explore most of the hinterland of the Benelux countries, and visit Alsace too.

'Just a minute . . .' Rick took up the pencil. He leaned in closely. 'Look just here.' He pointed. 'Is that part of the name or a swing bridge?'

'A bridge, I should think.'

'You're not even looking at it, Bob.'

'It'll be fine.'

'We can't just go wandering all over the canal system looking for high enough bridges.'

'Hold on,' Rick was applying himself. He twisted the map round. 'We could get through that way, couldn't we?' He started to trace an alternative route, taking us further north. It was becoming like a maze in a puzzle book.

'Yes, but what's the significance of the smaller blue lines?'

Bob lit another cigarette. 'What lines?'

'Well some of them are thick and some of them are narrow.'

Baines was leaning in now. He turned the map over. There was a box explaining the symbols on the back.

'There's an explanation of symbols here.'

'Good.'

'It's in Dutch.' Bob exhaled through his nose.

'Dutch or not we can probably make sense of it.' There was a pause. 'Well, some are . . . do you think *bruckke* means bridge?'

'Probably.'

'So what's a *brikke*?'

I reached for the bigger chart. 'I mean with the best will in the world, we'll have to allow a day for the Kiel Canal and then another day from Kiel to Flensburg.'

Bob looked perplexed. 'I don't think as much as that.'

'It's another fifty or so miles up the coast.'

'Is it? Where is it then, Flensburg?'

'It's here!' I stabbed at the map. 'On the border between Germany and Denmark.'

'But that's up in the Baltic!'

'Yes! That's where we're going.'

Bob was staring at the chart with renewed interest.

'I didn't think we got that far that early. That's Denmark there, is it?'

'Yes!'

'Oh, I thought we were trying to get down here somewhere.'

Bob waved an index finger over the lower Friesian Islands and then nodded sagely. I noticed Rick had pursed his lips and was frowning slightly. Was Bob quite the navigator that he claimed? The same thought had occurred to me several times.

The next morning my mother wanted to know about the plans. She couldn't remember how far up towards Amsterdam my father had taken his boat on our family holidays and neither could I.

'You go into these locks with these huge barges and you have to be quick about it . . .'

'Yes, yes, I know.'

'Your father used to get so cross.'

'Yes. We must have gone via Williamstad into the Maas.'

'Well, it was all so long ago.'

'But did you go into the canal system at Dordrecht?'

'Oh now. Dordrecht. Yes. I remember Dordrecht. We spent most of the afternoon waiting for some man to come and open the railway bridge. And you know what your father was like. Are you going to go through the canals, then?'

'Yes.' I was only half listening. If it took six hours to negotiate one set of bridges, we might get about as far as Rotterdam by the time we were intending to be in Flensburg. 'But only if the weather makes it absolutely necessary.'

'Well, it's not very good at the moment.'

It wasn't. It was dreadful. Squadrons of low-pressure system bombers had been sweeping across England, dropping payloads on a demoralized population. There were gales and high winds creeping across the Atlantic even as we spoke.

Later that afternoon, I drove three times around the one-way system in Limehouse Docks, trying to get to the Cruising Association clubhouse, missing turnings because of the water sluicing down around me, my windscreen wipers thrashing in a frenzy of ineffectuality.

I parked my car in a small pond. I sat brooding. The whole vehicle drummed and rocked under the onslaught of the monsoon. Bad weather always irritates me. It always seems absurd. It might as well be good weather as bad weather. It might as well stop. Eventually, I gave up waiting and gingerly stepped out. It was dusk-dark at five in the afternoon. The raindrops smashed into the pavement and threw up a hedge of water. My shoes filled instantly. I capered down the road, leaping through torrents of water streaming off the bridge. It was like running through a car wash.

I sheltered, sopping, under the porch of the Cruising Association's latest London base. My father had been a member. I had joined about a week ago. I had nurtured the memory of a long, low, wood-panelled room lit by yellow lamps; of polished mahogany; of discreet desks and book-filled walls; of ship models and sepia photographs of distinguished members with big moustaches like Arthur Ransome. All that had gone. The new headquarters looked like a hall of residence at Essex University. The scuffed vestibule was hung with notice boards announcing courses in weather watching and competent crew certificates.

The library was on the first floor. Steaming slightly, I approached the desk. 'I'm looking for details on European inland waterways.'

'Righto.' The librarian looked the sort of bloke who enjoyed a challenge. I wish I'd been able to ask him about navigating the lakes of the Andes. Now he led me down the room and up to a bulging stack. 'Which area in particular?'

'Um, Holland, Belgium and the North German regions.'

'OK.' He tensed in front of the shelf and suddenly shot out an arm. His fingers whisked out a bulging file and with a practised swing he cradled it into the palm of the other hand. 'This should help.' I turned the marbled grey cardboard cover. It was a loose-leaf binder. Hundreds of papers and letters had been holed and slipped into place. Some were complete logs, some just warnings and advice. Some were typed on old yellowing paper in the undulations of ancient typewriters, some were scrawled in an annotated fashion.

'I don't know if this might be of any use.' The librarian put a folded map beside my file. It was a complete chart of the Northern European waterways and on it was marked, in lurid pink, the mast-up route. It followed exactly the same route that we had so painstakingly worked out on our own map.

Scrabbling around in the flimsies I finally discovered advice from some other helpful coward who had been coming back the other way. If stuck in Hamburg and scared to death of the north-westerlies that habitually lashed this coast, you could get to the Dutch canals via Hanover. You had to take down the mast and drive about a hundred miles inland, but you need never actually see the grim North Sea at all until you finally debouched opposite Ramsgate.

If we were that desperate, we could stick the boat on the back of a lorry and drive the whole way to St Petersburg. Had I become so terrified of the sea that I needed to go by land? At some point we would have to face the German Ocean. If the weather was that bad then we weren't going to make it anyway.

3. Fraught

I thought I had been patient with Michael, the boat builder. Some long silences, perhaps, on the telephone. A heavy sigh, now and again. But I understood where he was coming from. He just had craftsman's warp. Craftsmen don't notice time passing. This is the basis of basket weaving and vegetable patch therapy, after all. It was what I wanted to discover for myself: to drift into timelessness, to float back into an unscheduled adolescence of the early 1970s.

But I was not feeling totally calm when I finally stood on the quay and looked down at the boat. The chrome was in place. The hull was beautifully smooth and freshly painted. The boot top line, the scarlet flash just above the waterline, was neatly done. The name had been painted across the stern in gold paint. But the deck tops were unpainted. The varnish work, on the dog-house sides, was the same varnish work that had been there last year.

'I don't understand.'

The boat looked half-finished. Everything was yellow and peeling.

'Well, I can see you're disappointed. Yes, we haven't done the varnish. Yes, the interiors haven't been painted. Yes, we haven't dealt with the cabin roof.'

'Have you fitted the anemometer?'

'Yes, we haven't fitted the anemometer, but we have done all the important work.'

'You haven't varnished the cabin sole.'

'But we've replaced the broken boards.' By the navigation station there was one freshly varnished, spanking new set of floorboards, mocking the tired, foot-worn look of the others. I stood and glared at my boat. I was taking this boat to a regatta in Germany, which had been especially convened so that the owners of classic boats could show off their bright-work to each other.

Michael avoided my eye. I sighed.

'Well, we'll leave on the high tide. It's at eleven isn't it?'

'Yes, but . . .' He made a wry face.

'What? We can leave?'

'Well . . .' He shrugged now. Obviously I should have been aware of this. '. . . it's neaps.'

'So . . .' I knew the answer.

'So . . .' He looked hopeful on my behalf. 'She may float.' And he cocked his head to one side. 'It depends on whether there's an on-shore wind or not.'

Time and tide wait for no man. It also, apparently, makes an appearance and does its wet, floating stuff for no man, neither. The creek where the boatyard lay was a muddy gut at the far end of a tidal system, miles inland.

'I've arranged for the local tug to turn out,' Michael said. 'She may be able to pull her off, through the mud and into the deep channel. But . . .' He looked mournfully down the river where a couple of Thames barges sat, up to their lee boards in the soft stinking grey fudge. '. . . I'm not very hopeful.'

I gritted my teeth. 'OK, well let me tell you,' I found myself saying. 'I intend to leave tomorrow, Michael! As soon as she floats at midday! We will drag her off, and we will leave.' It was the sort of announcement a hysterical thirteen-year-old midshipman might make to his bosun, when left in charge of a battlecruiser – utterly mad.

Michael looked for some sort of inspiration in the dust. He scratched his beard. 'We won't have fitted the sails by then.'

'You won't have fitted the sails . . .' Good Lord, I was actively spluttering. 'Well fit them, then!'

Michael turned and looked at the boat sitting in the mud below us. 'To what?' he asked.

Undina's mast lay on a couple of trestles in the shed. First thing in the morning, the crane would be employed to lower the 18½-metre wooden spar into the boat. The rigger would rig the stays and the shrouds, and then in the afternoon the sail maker would bend on her new mainsail. The sun would rise, the night would come, the tide would ebb, birds would fly south and Michael's boatyard would do things in the proper order dictated by tradition and tea-breaks. And I would grind my teeth in impotent frustration.

'I need to fill her up with diesel. Is there a pump?'

There was the sound of laughter somewhere in the shed. 'Pump?'

I was directed to a petrol station 2 miles away. I went off to buy some big plastic jerry cans.

There was no point in stumping up and down the quayside in a bad mood. I could be in a bad mood in the supermarket, amongst the refugee asylum seekers, buying boxes of tinned food, in a bad mood in the chandlers buying rope and torches, I could be in a bad mood just sitting in the back of the car tapping my fingers and waiting to see if the sea would grace us with an appearance.

I had to hand it to Michael. Throughout all this, he retained a calm and blissful imperturbability and an apparent pride in a job well done. There was a good reason for this. It was a job well done.

I was blind to his achievements. Just forward of the main cabin, to take an example from many, he had built a beautiful wooden cabinet to hold the gas bottles. It was minor thing, a box, but folded to the line of the dog house and so beautifully made that, later, I had to get used to other visiting wooden boat owners nodding and jutting a protuberant bottom lip, as they caressed the slight curve to the lids and the beautiful dove-tailed joints. It was perfectly in keeping, so were the new anchor chain arrangements, the mahogany lockers (panelled with interlocking rattan fronts) and the refashioned cockpit locker lids with teak-planked panels.

The hull had been repaired and cosseted until it was a mirror-smooth dark blue. The deck brought up to russet perfection. I just couldn't see it, because I wanted the whole thing finished, and now I was late. I was incapable of seeing that I was, paradoxically, late for the experience that was intended to make lateness and punctuality and clock-watching utterly redundant, but perhaps that would come later.

By half past ten the following morning the waters had risen quite considerably around the boat, and a small, black, period tug came chugging around the corner.

'Righto lads.'

For the time being, a tow-rope was triumphantly produced from a back locker, tied around the mast, the strongest point on the boat, and then everybody went for tea. I stood goggle-eyed, the townie aghast, the man in the Bateman cartoon, fuming helplessly. Tea! Tea! At a time like this! My mouth was opening and shutting, wordlessly. After a while, I noticed that the tug captain was waving at me.

'I think that's about the height of the tide,' he shouted. 'She's going out now.'

'They've all gone for tea!' I called back.

'Well I'd better give her a pull now anyway.'

I ran shouting towards the shed. Michael and his men came running out, clutching their mugs and we leaped down on to the deck. Tugboat Ted leaned into his little cabin and there was a dirty churning at his stern. The tow-rope tightened and without a murmur *Undina* slid straight out into the channel.

For a moment, everyone – the tugboat captain, Michael, the gnomes of the shed, Baines, Rick, a passer-by with a bald dog and myself – stood transfixed. There was silence, apart from the warm tick-over of the tug's engine. The muddy waters lapped at the mini-cliffs of the saltings.

'Well that was nice and smooth,' said Michael.

I waved over at the tugboat and started *Undina*'s engine, holding her in the centre of the channel.

Michael made a face. 'I don't know where you're going to put her, exactly.'

Now there were men running excitedly along the wharf, shouting at us. A short fat man in a black corduroy hat cupped his hands. 'I haven't got a berth for you along here,' he yelled.

'Thanks,' I muttered. 'Great. We're not even permitted to tie ourselves up.'

'You might be able to go alongside the barge,' Michael said, pointing ahead.

'No, no. I thought you said we could go round to the other yard, Tester's was it, if the boat got off.'

'Yes, but I didn't ring him.'

Michael had never thought we'd get afloat. But now we were: triumphantly, literally buoyant, fluting over the water, as the engine gathered speed. I pushed forward, and *Undina* began to surge down the narrow creek at 4, 5, and then 6 knots. The water gurgled. The bow wave curled up. We were high on the full tide and could see over the sea walls to low fields and saltings. Cows posed for Dutch paintings. The rush of the ebb was adding to our speed. A lone heron rose up and raggedly flapped away across the ditches and out into a landscape littered with the scattered pylons and random industrial hutches with which the British like to decorate their coastal scenery. The channel was marked by withies. Michael stood near me as we slewed on down the creek.

'Just take her out beyond this boat here . . . don't get too close to the bank as you come round the bend. There's a spit reaching out there.'

But nothing was going to stop us. After ten minutes we slowed down, as the creek met the Swale, a marginally bigger cut in the land. And there were larger boats jumbled up against the bank. We swung out and around a moored dinghy and came alongside the fishing smack with a bare minimum of shouting.

Rick brought the car. We all sat up on the deck and made another cup of tea. If I felt calmer, I wasn't about to show it. We had kidnapped the boat. Michael was clearly disconcerted. For the first time he seemed to become aware of our intention to leave.

'Is she ready to go?' Rick asked him.

'Oh yes,' he replied. 'She's ready. I'm not sure Griff is, though.'

I was inside, muttering. I had wanted to create a gentleman's club of varnished wood, gleaming fittings and glowing lamps. I squeezed my way around the cabin in a daze, picking up objects and opening cupboards, grimly taking stock: the mess, the shavings all over the deck, the unfinished work. The paintwork was mouldy. The holes where the original gas fittings had been removed were plugged with what looked like black chewing gum. The cracked veneer, broken seats and split ventilation cowls, with paint applied directly over the masking tape, were still exactly as they had been at the end of last season.

'You didn't move the table then?'

'No, we didn't get around to that.'

Michael was fixing the life raft to the stern of the boat. A single one of his workers was helping him. Baines was running wires underneath the cockpit seats to attach the antenna for the electrical navigation system.

'And the storm jib?'

'We had a look at that. There's no way we could attach a stay to the mast without designing a special fitting.'

'Michael . . .'

He must have noticed the dark tone in my voice. 'Yes . . .'

'Tell me something. Isn't there anybody else in your employ who could be possibly giving us a hand getting ready now?'

'No. No.' He shook his head mournfully. 'They're at the yard and we are all the way over here now.'

'I see.'

I heaved up a container of bottled fizzy water and opened a cockpit locker. I pulled open a box and vainly tried to stuff them into the available space, losing control over my senses and starting to rave.

'Fucking hell. Fuck me.'

I was emotional, I could tell. So could most people within half a mile.

'Right that's it!' Up on deck there was the noise of a man downing tools. If you have never heard this famous sound of the 1970s it is a dull clunk and rattle as a wrench is thrown on to a hard surface. 'I'm not working another minute for this bad-tempered bastard!' I looked out in time to catch the back of a short, overalled figure stumping off the boat, and the startled face of Baines poking up through a hole.

'Oh, no! Look what you've done now.' Michael rolled his eyes. 'Dave gets all worked up about things. We'll never get him back now.'

Otherwise, he was largely unabashed. 'Look, I'm sorry we haven't done the work you wanted. I am genuinely. I tried to hire extra people before Christmas, but they weren't up to the job, and that's the truth. Let's have a cup of tea.'

So we had a cup of tea. Baines chased the fuming carpenter down the sea wall and persuaded him that I was an hysterical actor. A car was sent to the yard and arrived back with a boy with a brush who swept up some of the shavings. The life raft was fixed to its cradle. The anchor was set into its locking pins. The mainsail arrived and was attached to the mast and boom. The furling jib was hauled up and set. The new iridium phone was screwed into a spare place on the battered Navigation bulkhead. Tins of ham and packets of soup were stuffed into lockers and cupboards. By five-thirty the ground crew were standing back on the shore. It was an awkward farewell.

'It looks like the weather will hold off,' Michael observed.

'Yes. Well . . . we'll probably head for Ostend and then go up the Belgian and Dutch coast.'

'If you're going straight over, you'd probably be better going for Flushing. Ostend would take you a bit further south than you need to go.'

'Yes.'

And he turned away and left us alone, as the waters began to rise around us.

The banks faded. It got dark.

At eleven-thirty that night, we warped her around. The tide reached its full height. We undid our ropes, and slowly moved out into the stream. We could finally escape. The solid spokes of the American-style steering wheel were in my hands now. The deck was beneath my new, ridiculously priced sea boots. I relished the smooth swing of a heavy boat. It was cold. It was dark. I shivered the shiver of a leg at the edge of a bed sheet on a windy night when you're warm, but the corners are cold.

In Whitby once I watched as a tiny freighter slipped quietly out through the swing bridge and into the North Sea in the snow. How many times have I seen the boats sliding down from Ipswich on a similar journey, their navigation lights pricking through the dark as they slip away on the black river. Departure by boat at night is the essence of voyaging, the eyes searching ahead for shadows or obstacles, the darkness almost palpably slipping past. The Waester-baeke diesel was purring, muffled in its padded cell beneath our feet, as we moved away and down the creek and, about a hundred yards from the jetty, we went aground.

4. The London River

It was not a remotely serious grounding. That, naturally, was to come later. We had hardly made speed anyway. We were still nosing our way out of the creek. We happened to nose our way on to a mud bank.

'I don't think we're moving forward any more.'

The others stopped talking and looked around. I stuck the engine in reverse.

'Get the centreboard handle.'

An old boat has a museum collection of tools and accessories: heavy brass original handles from disused winches, kept, 'just in case', by some previous owner; flat, pronged handles, chipped and green, like some forgotten gardening tool. There was the handle from a defunct monster bilge pump which sat proudly in the middle of the deck but was connected to nothing. Baines stood there, holding them up one by one, while I craned round backwards to try and guide the boat.

'This one?'

'No, it's a fat one.'

'This one?'

'It's got a sort of square end.'

But, by now, the boat was screwing backwards with a trajectory peculiar to older boats with long hulls, into deeper water.

Undina had been built to sail in the shallow waters of Bermuda and therefore possessed this handy retractable fin, which had just sliced soundlessly into the Brie-like mud. By going backwards, we simply pulled it back out.

'This one?' Baines finally had a carefully repaired, greeny bronze lump weighing 3 or 4 pounds in his hand.

'Yeah.'

'Shall I pull it up?'

He was inserting the handle in the slot and running his eye over the mechanism.

'No, no, it's OK. Leave it down now.'

'Aren't we going to be in shallow waters?' He wanted, as he did with every mechanical device we were to encounter over the next four months, from owl alarm-clock to canal hand-bridge, to have a go with it.

'It's safest if we leave it as a sort of sounding board.' Baines looked disappointed.

'But you could raise it up . . . a little bit.'

Perhaps we shouldn't have set to sea in total darkness without a comprehensive course in boat-management for my new crew. And, who knows, one in anger-management for myself. But the details of sailing this particular boat, the winches, handles, storage, could be picked up as we went along. Bob had been before. Baines had crewed on racing boats. Rick had worked as a mate to a delivery skipper. They were all quite capable of pretending to be more qualified than I was, and I had spent half my life on the east-coast rivers. The most pressing problem was whether we could make it to Flensburg by next Thursday, our planned date of arrival, but there was no anxiety. This was the period of release. We were up and chatty.

Even in the darkness I could feel the creek was opening out. We had to get out of the Swale and into the main channel of the Thames. There were denser shadows ahead, where boats were moored. I steered towards them.

Rick was up on deck and close to me. 'There are boats up there ahead,' he said knowingly.

'Yup.' I reassured him that I had seen them.

'Shouldn't we be well over there, then?' He pointed over to the side of the channel.

'Er . . .' Gosh, that was an odd thought. 'No, no. I don't think so, Rick.' The boats were anchored in the middle of the fairway, in the deepest water. 'They're big fishing boats,' I pointed out, 'floating in the tideway. So there'll be plenty of water all around them.' I steered the boats close under the bows, aware that they were lying calmly to the outgoing tide, following their line from one dark shadow to the next, as the channel deepened and flowed out towards bigger waters.

I could feel Rick standing at my side. He peered intently through the darkness at the ships we passed, then at the shore and astern. He frowned and scrambled down through the hatch.

I called after him. 'There's a red light above your head. If you kill the bright lights it will make it easier to see out here.' In the night-club glow that followed, I could just make him out, hunkered diligently over the charts with a divider and protractor in hand.

There was hardly a ripple in the water, apart from the ones that we were causing ourselves. Bob was making a boogie-man scarecrow of himself, pulling his plastic jacket over his head. It was already getting cold. Baines was flopping up the portable fenders, untying them from the guard rail and passing them back to the cockpit.

The obstructions were passing behind, the green winking light of the first buoy in the Swale could be seen ahead, and there was clear deep water up to it. I was vaguely aware of Rick standing in the hatchway holding the chart.

'Shut up while I'm talking!'

'Rick . . . sorry, yes?' I said.

He came out with the chart and shone a torch on to it, so that I could see it. He pointed a finger. 'I reckon we're about here,' he said firmly. I peered. His finger was on the creek.

'Good, excellent,' I replied. The chart was already covered with little pencilled crosses, tracking our half-inch passage away from the dock and down the Swale. During the early evening, I had drawn a course to the Thames and then the Knock buoy about 20 miles ahead.

Now, having gained attention, Rick solemnly gave me his compass course and I confirmed back to him that it was the same as the course already entered. I showed him the new electronic system with its full-colour map of the estuary, and its magical capability of locating us to within a few metres: a child-like, black, flashing representation of a boat, slowly moving across an illuminated chart, like a computer game. 'That's us,' I told Rick. He seemed impressed. 'There's the starboard-hand channel buoy, I think, isn't it?' I pointed. He peered ahead. A tiny green light was flashing way ahead in the darkness. 'Three flashes every ten seconds, isn't it?' He looked down at the chart.

'Yeah.'

The little black ship was moving well into the deeper water in the middle. 'Does anybody want to make some coffee?'

Baines went below to light the stove. Rick went to mark a new position on the chart.

The Swale joins the Thames estuary half-way down the humped back of Kent. And with an outgoing tide we sluiced down through a cloudy night to the black expanse of the London River. Opposite us, invisible to the north, lay the edge of the Essex marshes, the forgotten country of Foulness, a low-lying waste of mud and sand that gradually flattened out to sea, where London had for centuries dumped its power stations and gun ranges. Conrad always seemed to have found this place, 'a waterway leading to uttermost ends of the earth', as gloomy and frightening as any heathen shore. 'And this also,' says Marlowe suddenly (in *Heart of Darkness*), 'has been one of the dark places of the earth.' In the *Mirror of the Sea* he compares the sheds of Southend to African huts.

Exotic Whitstable and the first hills of savage Kent were below us and to the south, and we stayed within a few miles of that dismal shore, creeping out and away to the centre of the channel. Once the river mouth would have been crowded with ships, 'a great stir of lights', but the port was finished. Cargo vessels still went up to Tilbury, but the tessellation of buoyed channels and seaways that runs out into the North Sea was no longer thronged with the trade of all nations. The big ships loaded with containers went further north to Felixstowe, where they tied up at a blank wharf in a deep channel and were unloaded within hours.

There were ships about. On a clear night, such as this, near to a populated shore and big ports, the waters seemed alive with light. Far off, against the slight, dark hump of the shore, were confusing pricks and necklaces of white and yellow: the sodium glow of streetlights or garages. Away in the distance were clusters and brighter galaxies, the oil refineries or chemical storage depots of the lower Thames. To the right of them a dull jaundiced glow rose up from Southend. And, this close to the massive centres of population, there were patches of far-off, hazy, upward yellow marking towns and cities, beyond the curvature of the earth and out of vision themselves but sending their sickly glare up into the clouds. Radio towers contributed vertical stands, pricking out red danger signals.

The night never fully closed in. The whole messy shit of the south-east's permanent largest brown site and dumping ground pulsed and glowed with an impossible glamour. Nowhere is more alluring and fairy-like than an industrial complex at night. On a still night, like tonight, the water darkened to a glistening, satin, reflective black.

And in front of, and between, this Milky Way of distant shore lights, headlights, shop signs, warnings and illuminations the shadowy forms of large ships passed along their routes, marked themselves by winking, blinking, flickering beacons, some of which blared through the dark, others merely blushing, confusing our sense of distance and proportion. Sometimes, the fainter light was closer than the brighter. Sometimes a small and distant light would suddenly rush upon you and pass close by, the light itself rocking on what was now a black cone, speeding by a few yards away and back into the night. Sometimes the light that had begun to worry you, seemingly hovering aboard an obstacle and about to collide, gradually resolved itself into a star, millions of miles away and hanging low in the sky.

So at night, on a boat, you stare. You stare ahead, opening your eyelids wider, frowning hard, like a villain in a silent movie, pop-eyed, peering into the black. After a while, your forehead hurts and your eyeballs ache and the back of your neck goes tense. And, you remember the chilling fact that a large boat can charge up from its hidden place on the other side of the horizon to be on top of you in seven minutes.

'You've seen that one over there?'

'Yes, yes.'

Baines was pointing to a red light far off on the starboard.

'It's going down the channel, isn't it?'

A ship, even a big one, only puts on five lights when it gets dark. On its aft mast a single white light, on its forward mast another white light. At its back a stern light and on either side of its body a couple of lights, red for port (port wine) green for starboard. From these useful and distinguishing marks it was our job to work out which way it was going.

'Just beyond that there's another one.'

'Oh, yeah. Got it.'

'Hold on.'

I could almost hear Baines's brow furrowing. Was that rubbery creaking just his impressive new sailor suit or the furious puckering of his face? And that wet elasticated stretching must be his eyeballs protruding from his head.

'What's that one doing?'

'I can see the green. Just there.'

Just to add to the general state of disorientation, most cargo ships leave their sidelights, standard lamps and table lights on too, and never draw the curtains. Far from resembling the neat children's drawings of big round green lights and big round red lights against a plain black background in the manuals, the reality is a tiny prick of green in a disco.

'Look at it sideways.'

'Eh?'

'I read it in a book when I was a boy. If you can't see in the darkness, try looking for it out of the corner of your eye. You see it better, apparently.'

'My eye doesn't have any corners.'

'Well, just, you know, look to one side of where you're supposed to be looking.'

'How do I know where I'm supposed to be looking?' Baines had a strangled tone. His neck creaked round, his brow furrowed some more and his eyeballs rolled in their sockets.

But the lights were moving across the other boat, way to the north of us, in another channel altogether. It would have had to be a pretty crazy captain anyway who brought his ship over to where we were.

'It's a good idea. Keep the boat where small boats go. That way you won't meet any big boats unless they're already aground.'

'Yeah. Which they might be. Like a wreck or something.'

Bob and I took the first watch and entertained ourselves with mindless lists of music from the early 1970s.

'"Quicksilver Messenger Service". "It's a Beautiful Day". "Quintessence".'

'The Steve Miller Band.'

'Yes. Edgar Broughton.'

'Out Demons Out.'

'Indeed.'

'Is that the sun going down still?'

To the north-east, above the scraggy clouds, the night sky was lightening and pinkish grey.

'It could be some sort of town glowing.'

But there weren't any towns out to sea in that direction. It was two-thirty. We had been sailing for about three hours and it was already getting light. We settled back. In half an hour the scariness of the blinking lights and unidentified floating Christmas trees would resolve into a blank, pallid dawn and an open, gently adjusting patio of sea.

5. Dawn Over Kent

Dawn at sea can be a profoundly uninspiring event. It may come up like thunder on the road to Mandalay, but off Margate it arrived like a slow Polaroid.

'I can see the front of the boat,' I told Bob.

'I can't. I can't see anything without my glasses.'

'But it's definitely getting light.'

And five, ten minutes later, it was still definitely getting light, without a point where you could say that it actually was light. Turning from looking ahead, I realized that I could clearly see the North Downs to one side. The lights from buoys, ships and zealous town councils were overwhelmed. But by what? By the most generalized, grey, wishy-washy half-illumination possible. Clearly, no one had switched them off, but just as clearly, they were gone. It became a typical, cloudy, wet June morning. But some miles ahead, a dull red sliver hovered on the horizon and then seemed to heave itself bodily upwards: a perfect orange ball.

'It's the sun,' I said to Bob. And for a few moments, we both stared at it. Through the mist and the cold it seemed a powerless pallid blob, quite unrelated to the same sun that regularly drops out of sight with a loud red shout. Above it, though, there was a wash of pink in the sky, and behind that, the first tinge of blue. Within half an hour, our first morning at sea had turned into a gorgeous, sunny, cloudless, advert-skied day. *Undina* ploughed eastwards through a balmy sea, and a fresh south-easterly breeze.

It was all a pleasant surprise, with no reason why it should have been any sort of surprise at all. The good weather had been forecast. It had been forecast from about six different sources. The television had emphatically told us this, but shortly after we had set off, refusing to trust to sun lounger concerns, we had gathered around

Rick's impressive short-wave radio to listen to the late-night ship-ping forecast.

We were in 'Thames', just above 'Dover', below 'Humber' and some way to the west of 'German Bight'. At this time of year, the differences in temperature between the Arctic regions, the big continental land masses and the hot, hot seas (warmed up all the time by the sun sliding upwards on the gradually tipping globe) meant that big areas of low pressure, dollops of swirling cold air and clouds, are dislodged from the far north and sent wobbling south. Most weather forecasting is based on predicting their move-ments. Most horrible summer weather in England is based on their arrival over the furthest outlying bits of the land: us.

We knew that there were several of these monsters swirling up the Atlantic from the Azores, but we appeared to have wandered into a gap in the dance floor. Weather systems were pirouetting away and round to the south, but currently dodging us. Of course, they had a habit of blundering out of the formation, so we sat, heads bowed, with the solemn attention of the Maquis listening to SOE radio messages telling them that the 'hat is green with gold feathers', while Rick cradled his radio in his arms and wrote down every single area forecast, hoping to extract some pattern of his own.

I sympathized with Rick and Bob's urge to second-guess the weather forecast. After all, the professionals were fallible. In Honolulu recently it was calculated that they were only correct 83 per cent of the time. This sounds good, but Honolulu is in-variably sunny. If they had just said, 'It will be sunny tomorrow,' they would have been correct 85 per cent of the time. But since we were still within 50 miles of the meteorologists' head office, where ranks of paid experts were sweating over their isobars, I thought we could accept their generally favourable assessments for the time being.

Bob went below and started to balance frying pans on the stove. It is one of his character traits that he likes to surround himself with his own shit. I sat at the helm, my face gradually turning into a

Japanese Kabuki mask of horror, as he settled himself into a corner of the boat and began to colonize it. First, he emptied his pockets. Lighters, cigarettes, a plastic toy or two, one sailing glove, several unpaid parking tickets, three or four stolen pats of butter from a hotel, two or three napkins, scraps of torn-up cardboard with phone numbers and a large quantity of sweets.

Humming now, and lighting a cigarette, he warmed to the task of getting his ingredients sorted. There were sausages as well as bacon and, despite the kitchen equipment to hand, Bob preferred to use the boat's cutting-down-the-rigging-and-severing-knots knife. It was in a sort of square wooden bucket built into the side of the cabin and to reach it Bob needed first to remove the torch and the binoculars and several clothes pegs. Needing potatoes, he opened the impressive chest fridge and took out most of the contents which he laid on the floor. Putting the sandwiches to one side, on top of the engine casing, and helping himself to a can of Coke, which he placed at his elbow, on a pillow, he focused for a while on the possibilities now presented. He had bacon and eggs and tomatoes already. Now he had potatoes. Noticing sausages, he added them to the morning fry-up menu. He also added cucumbers, bits of ham, some old cheese and the contents of a small jar of capers. The wet plastic from the bacon was pushed to one side, scrunched up a bit and used as an ashtray while Bob pricked sausages and reached across to light a second cigarette with his other hand, commandeering a spare cup to use as a secondary ashtray. He moved across to the stove and the sink area, took the torches, binoculars and more clothes pegs he had deposited there, and corralled them into little piles. Nothing was stowed, stored or lockered. Nothing was ever thrown away. Everything that Bob touched had to remain visible and handy. Old cigarette butts, pulled corks, packaging, pencils, unused food, used food. Something inside him preferred his immediate environment to bear his mark. His territory was defined, like some wild bear, by the limits and extent of his detritus. His urban sprawl disfigured my mahogany uplands and pristine virgin bedding. It demanded use of my green belt and spilled over into my rural areas. And it was all done with a steady, remorseless and deliberate energy. Within minutes the interior of the cabin looked like his own extraordinary home.

I have since had time to reflect on my intensely anal reaction to this behaviour. I was vain about my boat. I was a control freak. I needed order to make up for my own mental deficiency. I wanted to control the space myself. I was over-potty-trained as a child. But who cares? I didn't want to set off to sea in some fourteen-year-old's bedroom.

The 'main saloon' is a grotesque term to describe our shared accommodation. Those of you who think, 'Oh yes, yachting! You rich, boaty bastards!' have no idea of the privations we endured. When we went down the ladder in *Undina* we stepped over the engine casing to find ourselves wedged into a small upper area about 3 feet square. We could turn to our left, and, with difficulty (because the sides curved up to disastrously tilt the floor), fold and double back our legs, push them under a sloping desk and face the navigation instruments bolted on to a bulkhead. But beyond this bulkhead, all space immediately in front of us was occupied by the (admittedly magnificent) stove and sink arrangement. Another step brought us to the galley floor area, which was equally restricted. Turn and we banged into the table. This had two flaps, easily raised to eat, but there wasn't enough space to continue forward in the boat unless these flaps were lowered. Even when lowered, we could only get over to sit on the narrow bench on the left-hand side of the boat by crouching into a sitting position and progressing flat-footed, and shaped like a question mark until our arses made contact with the upholstery. There were two berths, on either side of the boat, above these benches, at shoulder height. The deck came down to within a foot of their mattresses, and getting into them at all required a limbo-dancer's dexterity.

The whole saloon most resembled a third-class sleeping compartment in a pre-war railway carriage, with about a third of the space. Two people could not pass each other in any part of the interior. The shape of the boat dictated that the floor, or cabin sole, was defined by the curvature of the bottom. Under the water it quickly descended into a sharp edge, leaving a few planks' width to walk on. And this surface was broken by large and frankly reassuring baulks of wood which, standing proud, indicated where the keel began and the walkway ended. They were topped by bronze nuts of a size and disposition so precise that you were guaranteed to stub your toe on them.

A wooden boat is constructed like a cage, on to which an outer skin of planks is attached. The cage is made of frames and stringers, jointed, tied and bolted together to control movement, but the cage, naturally enough, takes up a good deal of the available space. To create the object of great outward beauty that *Undina* was, the ingenuity of the designer had been brought to bear, giving her extensive overhangs at the front and back. She looked like a Raoul Dufy boat, sweeping, bowed, womanly: a sleek bracket, lying low in the water for extra elegance, and, like Jane Russell's brassiere, a miracle of cantilevered shapeliness. Visitors were often surprised to find that the first 12 feet of the boat were nothing but curve. We could lift up a large bronze manhole and look down into a superbly constructed piece of furniture with a propeller shaft running across it.

So, you see my point. We had set to sea in a poky hut. I had been brought up on small boats. My father ordered me to put things away. He told me how I was expected to live. He instructed me on the dangers of leaving rubbish all around and losing vital pieces of equipment. He taught me to be 'tiddly'. But he was Daddy and I was six.

'Bob . . .'

'Mmm?'

Bob looked up from his intense labours with a glazed look in his eye. I was leaning in from the wheel, sailing the boat and shouting in a stage whisper so as not to wake the others.

'I just wondered . . . we're going to have to be a bit more tidy, I think.'

'What?' Bob looked around him, avoiding my gaze. 'I'm just making breakfast!'

'Good, good. It's just, you know, we seem to have an awful lot of stuff out everywhere.'

Bob looked around again. 'Yes. Well I'll just sort that out a bit. Hold on.'

He pushed some of the potatoes away from him, moved the cans of beans on to the side of the sink, reached out, wrapped his gloves and the bacon wrapper up in a jumper and tried to stuff it into a bag. The bag was full, however, so he took out the clothes, the alarm clock and the wash-bag that were in it and stood, for a moment, cradling the whole lot in his arms. He pushed some of it behind the stove, on top of the sauce bottles and sugar containers, and put the rest on the bunk opposite. Then he turned and carefully arranged half the torn-up cardboard, his bills and his sweets into a pile on one side of the table and the other into a pile on the other side. He surveyed what he had done, took the empty bag and crammed it on top of the wooden bucket. He seemed satisfied and returned to his work.

At first I assumed he would learn. We would all learn. It was a learning experience. Less than an hour later, with the sails up, the breeze was to freshen, the boat would heel into it and there would come a sequence of sliding, clattering and crashing sounds from below.

'Fucking hell! . . . oh fuck . . . shit!'

'Yeah, sorry. Sorry,' I shouted. 'The wind's come up.' As the water under *Undina* gurgled and splashed, there followed a sound like an upended tea tray.

'Bloody fucking hell.'

I stood up and peered below. Bob was holding on to the stove and glaring up at me. I felt an urge to explain, to teach and to instruct.

'You see, Bob, we're bound to hit weather if we're sailing. You've got to keep things tidied away.'

It was clear enough to me: obvious to me. But it became one of the trip's abiding and profound mysteries, something so deep that it began, even in these early hours, to gnaw like a canker at my soul.

No matter how far we travelled, and our log showed a distance covered, in the end, of over 3,000 miles; no matter how long we journeyed together, and four months were to pass before we left

Undina in her winter berth; no matter how many winds were to blow, and we experienced storms, squalls and even gales, every time the gentle forces of nature drove us onwards through the cold northern seas and the boat gently heeled to the breeze, I would hear from below the sound of smashing, breaking, toppling and shattering and the plaintive cry, 'Shit, fuck . . . bloody hell . . . damn! Oh no! Fuck!'

Did it matter? Really, no. Surely I could take the consolation of knowing that it was Bob's own stuff that went flying and disappeared through cracks into the swill of the bilges. It was only a plastic wine glass that he had left balanced on the central table from the night before. It was merely that framed sepia-tinted photograph of an old Estonian farm worker's granny that he had perched on the top of the life jacket locker that had now gone whistling across the cabin and clattered into the engine. But for me, alas, it was something deeper, and a symptom of the terrible truth that was to gradually dawn on me, as we crept further up the Scandinavian latitudes. If Bob was the fourteen-year-old, then I was the Daddy. Over the next thousand miles, as inexorably as the ageing process, as silently as creeping frost, as remorselessly as my new beard sprouting in forks on my chin, I was metamorphosing into my father, the irascible, anti-social Welsh doctor who was always right and permanently in a bad mood because of it.

For the present it was sunny. It was even warm. The morning was blissful and full of hope. Bob pottered in the galley like a stage magician and leaned across to wake Baines in the under-deck berth by singing to him: 'Oh, a cunty piece of bacon in a cunty bacon roll. Mmm.'

There was a breeze now, nothing too strong, and the sea was gently patterned with wavelets. In a spirit of consensus, I offered up a plan, as Bob served breakfast.

'Let's forget crossing to Belgium,' I started. 'This weather looks like it will stay with us for a while. The storm system is passing south beneath us. We could head much further up, cross right across the sea towards Den Helder, and if things change, slip in above Amsterdam into northern Holland.'

Bob looked a little worried. 'Oh.' He glanced at Baines. Baines seemed unsure of the consequences of this anyway and only raised his eyebrows. 'We'd go in the Nordzee Canal,' said Bob.

'I was thinking we'd go a bit further north.'

'But we'll get to Amsterdam?' Rick asked.

The other three were all now looking at me. They had the earnest expressions of fourteen-year-olds threatened with by-passing Alton Towers.

'Oh, yes, yes,' said Bob, casually. He was very quick to reassure the others. I sensed some earlier pact.

'Well, not necessarily,' I said. 'We are under quite a lot of pressure to get on.' In fact with the delays and the hold-ups, it seemed to me that, even travelling the whole way at top speed, we could barely guarantee getting to the regatta on time.

Bob stopped serving up his black pudding.

'Yes. But we would just go there for a day. We can arrive tonight. Leave tomorrow afternoon.'

'Well that would be . . .' I trailed off. I could guess what was going on. Bob had offered up the lure of Amsterdam to the impressed men. And Bob, as usual, had no clear idea of the nature of time. He never really seemed to grasp that time passed and if you had to meet someone at, say, six o'clock then half past eleven was a different sort of time altogether.

'Look. Nothing is set in stone,' I lied as straightforwardly as possible. 'I'm sure we'll be able to fit it in. Visit some brown cafés, a couple of live sex shows and a quick bit of window shopping on the Reepersbahn, as long as we're quick. But how about if we press on for the time being and then take stock, eh?'

Baines and Rick nodded quickly. Bob thought for a moment. And then nodded himself. This outright fabrication seemed to meet with approval. We would head north.

Rick, for his part, was worried about the shipping lanes. So we examined the chart.

The North Sea is one of the busiest shipping routes in the world. Millions of tonnes of extremely large and powerful ships converge and pass both ways through the Channel. Crossing it in a small boat, you are the hedgehog and they are the juggernauts. Stories are told of freighters arriving in port where, to their crew's astonishment, bits of small boat rigging are found hanging off their anchors at the bow, dread evidence of an unnoticed collision. Like a motorway, though, the sea has been marked off into lanes. Ships head south on the English side and north on the continental side. Ferries, of course, make their own way, crashing straight across.

Small boats are required, by law, to cross these lanes at a right angle and not to wander about in the road like old ladies on scooters. If we sailed directly to our new destination we would make a long and obtuse angle across several different lanes and a couple of gyratory systems. Obviously, we should sensibly keep well clear of that.

We decided on a route that would take us up the east coast of England, almost as far as Yarmouth, way out of sight of land, but edging the downward shipping lane. We had to get north of what appeared to be a ships' roundabout, where the shipping from Scotland met the shipping from the Baltic and joined a major trunk shipping lane heading south. Once there, just by the Wash buoy, we would turn right, cross one lane, then a few hours later cross another and then head straight into the Dutch oilfields. Robert and I felt perfectly confident. When we drew up our courses on the chart, a matter of taking a perspex ruler and marking two straight pencil lines, the second part corresponded exactly to the route we had taken the year before.

At five o'clock in the morning we motored up to the Knock buoy, a hollow metal can some 12 feet high, plonked in a waste of open water, lonely and alien and hardly human in its geometric certainty. Buoys are just markers. On the chart they figure hugely, their shape outlined in detail, their name emblazoned across the depth contours, but in reality they arrive with minuscule impact, a black pin prick on the horizon, an insignificant, wavering black shape, until you come closer and realize that they are as big as you are, just about as big as you must seem to others in this empty place.

We set a new course of 30 degrees, and I stepped up with Baines and Rick on to the cabin roof to fight the stiff cloth of our new mainsail, the big triangular sail, up to the top of the mast.

'Bring her round now,' I shouted to Bob.

'What do you mean?' he shouted back.

'Bring her on to the course!'

'Oh. OK.' He stared down at the compass.

'Let out the mainsheet. The big rope to the side of you. Never mind the course for a moment. The one attached to the end of the boom. That's it. That one. You see, it's attached to a cleat, by the side of you. It's tied up. Yes. Untie it. Yes, completely. Let the wind fill the sail. I'll come and do it.'

We let the mainsail out and the wind ballooned out the sail.

'Are we doing thirty degrees, Bob?'

'More or less.'

I pulled back on the rope until the cloth stopped flapping and the pressure of the wind started to translate through the system and down to the boat herself.

'We need to let off the topping lift,' I shouted up at Baines. 'It's the grey rope, running down the mast, attached to that little tackle with the cleat there. Just slacken it off. Let it go. Let it be slack and then reattach it to the cleat. It's just the rope that holds the boom off the cockpit when there's no sail up.'

And the back end of the boom dropped a few inches, tightening the creases out of the sail, making a smooth wing of cloth.

The jib, or foresail, a massive triangle of synthetic white canvas, was furled by a winding mechanism around its own wire support right at the front of the boat.

'Rick, just let that go . . .'

As the wind got into it with a crack, the cloth billowed out and it pulled the rest of its own mass free, flogging, like a flag, in the wind. We tightened the back end to make 'a wing' of this sail too. And as the wind hit the flattened planes, the boat, quite naturally, leaned over. There was a crashing and tinkling sound from below.

'Fuck, shit! Damn!' said Bob.

I reached beyond Bob and, pulling back the lever of the engine, put the motor into neutral.

'Rick, you can stop the engine.'

He turned the key. The engine died. There was a rumbling beneath our feet. I put the engine briefly into reverse. Somewhere beneath our rudder, at the back of our hull, the propeller cunningly folded itself up, and what appeared to be utter silence suddenly descended on the morning.

It wasn't completely quiet, of course. After a while the surge of the sea along the sides of the boat became audible. The rigging and wooden bits of the boat creaked, as they really do. There was a slight drubbing, a powerful vibration from the sails above our heads which translated itself through the whole structure like the pulsing of a living thing, but to begin with, most of all, it's the quiet that you notice. The brain is suddenly released from a noise it has grown so used to that it no longer registers it, but when it stops, the freedom is like stepping out of a printing house, or switching off the mower or smashing the television. It is like stopping holding your breath. It is a religious moment.

'Ahh,' said Baines.

'Now we're sailing,' I added inanely, just as my father might have done.

6. Dutch Approaches

For the next eight hours or so we sailed north, at about 5 miles an hour, not much more than walking pace, really. There was an eerie emptiness. This was the English Channel. But no ships passed. No clouds marred the sky. Off watch, Bob went and slept for his four hours. I tried to, up in the forepeak, attempting to adjust to the rhythm of the light seas, but half-way through the morning went back on deck. It was all too perfect and sunny to stay below.

Baines had already fixed the new GPS and set up the antenna for the iridium telephone. Now he started on the rest of the electrics. Bob and I watched him with the fascinated attention of deficient layabouts. It was like watching a beaver make a dam in a documentary.

Baines never travelled without his equipment. He had brought on board a magnificent tool-box, built of aluminium, which took up more room than he did. It opened to reveal an armoury of carefully graded pliers hung in rows, drill-bits shoved into special pockets and a mass of wires, tapes, screws and fittings.

I had a tool-box myself, of course. I wasn't a fool. I had read in my sailing book that I would need a set of spanners and a wrench or two.

'Can I see it?' Baines asked. I prevaricated. No man likes another man to look in his tool-box, but I opened a locker and humped out my big plastic box. He looked at it.

'It's not really right for the boat,' I explained. 'It's just one of those boxes from Homebase.'

If Baines felt any scorn, as well he might have, he didn't show it. He opened the hopeless plastic bin with a considered, decorous gravity. 'No, no. I see the handle to the right here has gone,' he said thumbing it gently like a wounded pheasant. 'Tch. They make these things so badly.'

I nodded. How nice of him not to point out that it clearly only cost three quid. 'Jolly good hammer,' he went on. I had to be modest about my hammer. It was part of a set of things that had come in a clear extruded plastic mould along with a spanner and drill labelled 'Budget Tool Kit'.

'Oh dear,' he continued. 'These tubs aren't waterproof. That's the main problem.' My tools were rusty, already a disgrace, especially given that some of them were still in their packets. ('Three Spanner Set, Why Pay More?') Baines closed the lid carefully. 'We should build that up a bit.'

I nodded.

'You don't have a drill, then?'

'Yeah, yeah, I do.' I rattled around in the bottom of the box and pulled it out. 'There's a wooden handle bit somewhere that screws in there,' I explained.

'Gosh, an old hand drill!' He took it with reverence. 'I haven't used one of those for years. I meant an electric drill.'

'No.'

'OK, I'll use mine. It's just it's only a battery-operated one, not really very powerful. If I'd known I'd have brought my bigger one.' He opened a green carrying case and took out what appeared to be a machine pistol. 'I'll just fix the sound system,' he said and, using the drill, started to make holes in the sides of the cockpit.

There seemed to me a serious finality about holes, particularly on a wooden boat. But after making six or seven holes, Baines started to join the holes up using his drill like a saw and converted them into one big hole. He measured the speakers for size, used his drill as a file to pare down the edges and opened up a perfect circle into which he plugged the speaker.

And so he continued. To begin with, I followed him around, like an anxious widow with the new lodger. I was humming and bleating. 'There is this other thing which doesn't seem to be working . . . Can I get you a cup of tea? Don't feel you have to do this, of course.'

But Baines seemed to have fallen into a trance-like state of paradisaical calm. To me the mechanisms of the boat smacked of irritating over-complexity, to Baines they were an opportunity – more than an opportunity, a wonderful surprise. He loved to fiddle. Speakers went in. Wires were attached. He opened the locker lids and, instead of taking things out, disappeared into them himself.

Suddenly he popped up. He stood up half in and half out of the cupboard holding a long handle. 'What's this?' he asked.

'It's the handle for the manual bilge pump,' I replied quickly. He wasn't going to catch me out that easily. 'Actually, it does tend to get lost down there . . . I was wondering whether we should fix it to the locker lid.' Baines was already measuring it against the lid itself and looking serious.

Bob lit a cigarette. He dragged on it and exchanged glances with me. Baines was a staggering recruit to the company. I was a little distressed. He certainly drew attention to our deficiencies. Bob couldn't give a damn. For myself, I was paralysed by Flabby Pseudo-Intellectual Syndrome: the conviction that picking up a hammer or drilling a hole would create more work than it would solve, combined with weak resolve and utter ignorance. But this was fantastic. Was there nothing Baines couldn't do? Baines went below to use the head. A few minutes later, he stood in the companion-way.

'Fantastically efficient those vacuum systems, aren't they?'

'Yes. Although it can smell.'

'Really? I worry a little about the pressure build-up. It could almost be enough to crack the self-sealing seat.'

'Could it? It never seems to work quite right.'

'Are you covering the hole?'

'What?'

'I guessed as much.' He took me below and showed me my lavatory. 'You see there's a little hole here,' and he pointed to a nipple protruding above the pipework. I had noticed it before and was only aware that it made a whistling noise when you pumped. 'You put your finger on it you see.' He did so. 'Otherwise you don't create a vacuum.'

'Really?' I was staggered.

He pumped the handle and a great gurgling sound of rushing waters came from the system.

'Bob!' I called. 'I think you'd better come and have a look at this.' I reflected that Bob and I had sailed the boat for a month, the year before, completely unschooled in the basic system for emptying our lavatory. We probably hadn't been listening very carefully when the previous owner explained it, or something. But how did Baines know how the system worked? He pointed to the instructions written on a label stuck to the base of the unit.

'Ah, I see,' I said. 'It might have helped if Robert and I had read the instructions,' I said.

'Not really,' said Baines. 'They're for another type of marine lavatory altogether.'

Over the next few days, Baines fixed antennae, sealed the hatches, rigged the rest of the iridium telephone, took up the entire floor and dismantled the water system, mended the pump for emptying the sink by taking the whole thing apart and putting it back together upside down, rigged gels over the lamps to limit the glare when we were sitting at the table, nurtured the engine and mastered the gas alarm process. He was like a horse trainer or a fire-arms expert on the *Antiques Road Show*. He would lay a sensitive hand on the mechanism to comfort and reassure it. Turn the operative bit gently, raise or lower a handle, press a button, fiddle with a setting. You could tell that he was already silently planning to take it apart.

Gradually it got calmer still and, by three o'clock in the afternoon, the wind had died to almost nothing. The North Sea lay like a lake around us. A solitary black bee blown far from shore circled the mast and dropped down on the deck where it lay exhausted. As if drunk, it staggered around the warm deck and then, after a few minutes, and to our consternation, took off again, determinedly flying west out across a sea of gently heaving shiny planes of water.

Years before, when I first crossed the Channel with my father, he had had to navigate by dead reckoning. There were no electronic aids except radio direction finders and we didn't have one. He had to draw a line on the map, calculate its bearing and follow it by compass, allowing, of course, some degrees for sideways motion caused by the tide sweeping up or down the Channel. He was always an agitated sailor, but never a particularly well-prepared one.

Half-way across we sighted an oil rig. He pointed at it with a quivering finger and rushed to check on his charts. Clearly there were no oil rigs just off Ostend. We were out. Out by a lot. The tide had dragged us further than expected. The compass was useless. His voice began to rise in pitch, his eyes to roll wildly. We had sailed much, much further north than we had ever intended and were now drifting into the oilfields off northern Holland. It was useless to point out that if we'd come that far we must have been travelling at the speed of a small car. He had the evidence in front of his eyes. We were bodily drifting down on the oil rig. However much we pulled in our sails and tried to head south, we seemed to be getting closer to it. We were doomed, doomed. Except that the oil rig, on closer inspection, was moving in our direction. It was under tow. There was a tug some way in front of it, pulling it down the English Channel at a cracking speed. We easily passed behind it. It chugged away into the haze south of us and, some hours later, we came ashore on the coast of Belgium, precisely as he had calculated we should.

Now we too spotted an oil rig. I wasn't going to be fooled a second time. There weren't any oil rigs this far south, except being towed. And there, in front of it, by what seemed half a mile, was indeed its tug, pulling it eastwards this time, towards Great Yarmouth. There was already an oil rig there, anchored off Great Yarmouth by the town council as an attraction. Perhaps it had been so successful they fancied another one.

By three o'clock in the afternoon, we had started the engine again and changed our course to head directly east towards Holland and the shipping lanes. We crossed an imaginary purple dotted line and passed no ships at all. Some hours later we crossed another and we were out of them. We passed three orange bottles tied to something beneath the water, a few birds and that was it. For the rest of the evening, we motored across calm seas into a serene twilight.

Just before nightfall, further into the middle of nowhere, a flight of pigeons suddenly flapped past and banana-ed overhead. They were heading for Holland. One of them came around, circled a bit

and crash-landed on the deck. It was sleek and iridescently feathered. Hardly a town pigeon on a booze cruise, it had a ring on its
leg and the look of pampered existence. After pausing to recover
itself, it shat on the teak deck and started strutting about on the
cabin roof, seemingly indifferent to the fact that its fellow pigeons
had just flown blithely on.

Bob puffed out his own chest, rearranged his own feathers and
started cooing at it.

'Come on boy. That's right. Coo. Cooo.'

'What is this Bob?' I asked. 'Dr Doolittle?'

'He understands me. He's tired. You can tell. He's listless.'

'Cobblers. What about the others? They didn't need a rest.'

'It'll go on and catch up in a minute.'

But it didn't. It hung around. Perhaps its interior homing mechanisms told it that we were heading in the right direction. Perhaps
it figured we were going faster than it could manage by itself, or
that it had clearly lost the race so it might as well take a ride home.

'What are you doing?'

'I have an affinity with birds.'

Bob was turning his head to one side and making gurgling noises
in the back of his throat.

I went below. Minutes later, Baines stuck his head in.

'You'd better look at this.'

The pigeon was sitting on Bob's shoulder: not, I hasten to add,
in Long John Silver mode, upright and attentive; more using his
neck as a spare window ledge. Bob was crouched forward like
Quasimodo, but he did look unconscionably pleased with himself.

'That's nice,' I said. 'Make it say something now.'

The bird stayed. It finally hid under the rubber dinghy, from
where it looked out on the sea, balefully, pecking at the rest of us
and only allowing Bob to come near it. Mind you, since he generally
approached clutching a saucer of milk and bits of expensive biscuit,
it was hardly surprising that they bonded.

'Pity the bee's gone. He could have eaten that.'

It got dark again and we motored on, watch on, watch off,
through a calm evening into our second short night in transit. The

dusk always brought forth a residue of anxiety. The storms were still racing up from the south, but seemed to be swirling inland. The sky was clear, but as the pink wash of the sunset faded, so did any sense of sunny day. The darkness had none of the cavalcade of splendour that the stars routinely give the Mediterranean or the Tropics.

As we neared the shallow waters of the Dutch coast, mysterious objects began to appear out of the sea. Bob and I were on watch when we slowly approached something wobbling and fluctuating and extraordinarily bright. For half an hour it defied analysis. The light kept fluttering and changing shape: now a butterfly or a cone, now a ball.

It turned out to be what we had known it to be all along, a stationary fishing boat. Except that it was not only lit with identifying marks, but was ablaze with white beams of light; powerful searchlights swivelling into the brown sea around and alongside it, as if to tempt squid or some other murky fish to the surface; its crew, busy with wire and derricks, on a gently heaving sea, at one o'clock in the morning: a bright, blinding oasis of frenetic human activity in the middle of nothing. It seemed furtive and no business of ours, something we had stumbled into and now should leave behind. A searchlight momentarily swept in our direction, then back to its task.

Then we passed into the oilfields. Squatting space invaders, speckled with lights, like *Star Wars* death planets, crouched low above the sea, surrounded by guardian flashing buoys. They rose up over the horizon, a rampart of towers to the north of us. Some had flares burning. We could identify support ships anchored between them. We were outriders skirting a futuristic city. Bob and I had gone through here twice before in daylight, when they had all seemed grey and similar, but now, each tower of lights was subtly different, tracing different shapes and possibly different purposes against the darkness.

In the night, particularly, the peculiar working world of the sea seemed to demand our attention. It asserted its difference from the land. It didn't stop. Everything continued to function. And the huge, private, expensively maintained network was paradoxically made more visible.

By the morning we had sailed for thirty-six hours and were approaching Den Helder. The sun was up. There was no wind. We had fuel enough. The weather forecast remained good. We were out of contact with mobile phone masts, so I used our newly installed iridium telephone, linked to a network of satellites, to telephone home and explain that we weren't going to Flushing and there was no need for any concern. We weren't going to Den Helder either. With conditions as they were we could press on and aim for one of the islands up the coast, probably Borkum, but if things got bad there were plenty of other bolt holes on the way. We were entering *Riddle of the Sands* country.

As it happens, it was the only phone call I was ever to make on that equipment.

7. Pornographic Milkmaids

Texel, Vlieland, Terschelling, Ameland and Schiermonnikoog, the Dutch Friesian Islands, passed by to the south-east as a sequence of distant, unattainable glittering dunes on the horizon. By nine in the evening, we were edging around the eastern rim of the last of them, into the estuary at the mouth of the Ems, the border between Germany and Holland, in an exceptionally benign mood. Nothing happened all day. There had been dolphins playing alongside at three o'clock, which were more than likely to be porpoises. But, anyway, I'd been asleep. We had filled the tanks with half of our spare fuel and checked the oil. The rest of the time we'd talked about seventies rock bands. Bob was jigging and singing.

'We're going up the estuaree, and eat a big momma, momma meal from my pant-er-ee.'

Baines put aside his screwdriver. He scratched his beard.

'What are you doing, tucking yourself in like that?'

Bob was hoiking his black jeans up over a black-patterned, baroque print silk shirt. 'It's my belt.'

As well as engineering The Stereophonics, Baines had once run the second-coolest vegetarian mushroom café in Brixton. He owned more than one second-hand Mercedes. He was alert to the unhip, even in the middle of nowhere. 'Bob, you look like that arse on *Pop Idol*.'

'I like high-waisted trousers. In the seventies you had a sort of tube which came right up here. What are these birds about with their jeans hanging over their fannies these days? What's wrong with this?'

'You need to let your shirt dangle over the top.'

'You get a red mark around your waist.'

'What is that thing anyway?'

'I've got at least a dozen with me, from Snivelgoo, a designer with the BBC.'

On closer inspection, the shirt's black and white eighteenth-century toile effect featured pornographic milkmaids on swings. Later, Bob wore pink and green giant alligators, cerise fully rigged sailing ships and blue and yellow mermaids. 'I tried to bring the appropriate ones,' said the snake-skin, cowboy-booted exhibitionist from an 'I love the early seventies' era. Robert had conservative views on dress. He liked to look like an off-duty circus performer.

'Why are you all dressed up anyway?'

'We're nearly there, aren't we?'

Comparatively speaking, we were. But there were still hours ahead; those irritating hours when the destination can be clearly seen and the boat owner discovers that his vessel is actually moving slower than a milk float. We were beginning to head inland. We identified a large red and white middle-ground buoy marking the entrance to the river.

'I think we could head off to the side of the channel now,' I said.

Rick frowned and pointed at the compass. 'The course is eighty-three degrees,' he said.

'Um . . . yes. I know. But we should stay just outside the main buoys here.' I pointed them out on the chart. 'We'll keep well out of the big ships' way, and they won't come after us.'

He pondered this as if I had suggested he wore high-waisted trousers too. 'Well . . .' he said finally. 'The person I used to deliver boats with always insisted that we went in the channel.'

'Well . . .' I said back. 'It is actually illegal for pleasure boats to sail into some shipping lanes. And around here in Germany they actually enforce it, you know, with gun boats and fines and things, so . . .'

He nodded. But it wasn't a very confirmatory nod. It was more of an 'if-you-say-so' nod.

The low sun lit a distant prospect of Borkum: a crest of tall seafront buildings, a white hotel or two, perhaps a touch of esplanade, several striped lighthouse beacons, their flashes already cutting through the slight sea mist. The landward side of the island was almost connected to the mainland every low tide by 30 miles of exposed sand. The whole place was not much more than a high drift on a gigantic shallow beach. To the south, the Ems flowed out close in to the island and, then, bending towards Holland, left a massive bank, just submerged, between it and the North Sea: the Borkum Riff. It had a tarry mariners' tobacco named after it, and it wrecked ships.

Edging inside it, for the first time in forty-eight hours we came within range of the shore. It was already beginning to get dark. It was a shock to look up from the confident, ordered harbour on our electric chart to the gloomy reality that surrounded us. We had come to a big hole in the mud. Even in the semi-darkness, the walls of the place were utterly featureless. There were no trees. Bare ramparts of festering, glistening clay imprisoned a crowded litter of boats, tied to damp wooden pontoons at dripping, telegraph-post piles. It was low tide and the whole contraption – boats, piles and pontoons – had sunk to the very bottom of the pit. It seemed deserted. There were no lights on any of the boats. We paused for a moment in the entrance, hanging in the mist above the murky waters bathed in sodium glow.

'Any spaces?' I called.

Baines pointed to the far pontoons and we motored towards them. We touched the bottom but, with the centreboard pulled up, we got flat in against a narrow floating concrete wharf, hung with rusting metal rings and half-heartedly topped with a metal walkway. When Baines jumped ashore with a rope, it swung wildly. It was eleven o'clock at night, forty-eight hours at sea, and the tackiest landfall imaginable.

Bob lit a cigarette. 'Right. Now what do you think?' he asked. 'It's a bit late to get to Amsterdam, isn't it?'

'What, tonight?'

'Yes. But it is quite a long way away, is it? We could get back by tomorrow afternoon.'

I looked around at the mud walls.

'Well, Bob . . .' This was why he was dressed in his pornographic print-gallery shirt. 'I'm not sure how we'd get there. This is an island some way out into the North Sea . . .' He looked around.

'Oh. OK.'

We all stepped out on to the wobbly pontoon and walked up towards some unlit buildings. Ahead of us, on the ridge of the sea wall, a bus drove up. It was lit, but empty: a country service. It sighed and opened its doors. Bob started running towards it, rocking perilously from side to side in his unsuitable shoes, but long before he got near, the bus sighed again, closed its doors and set off back into the night.

I separated from the others and walked around the marina to where I thought I'd seen lights on a boat. Two men were sitting outside in the darkness.

'Is there much more water over here?' I asked them.

'No. It's shallow here,' they told me. 'You're best where you are.'

'Nothing open?'

They laughed.

The others were standing under the darkened clubhouse eaves. Bob walked around and tried a few doors.

'There are some lights up the back here,' he said.

'But it looks like some sort of house,' said Baines. 'Don't knock, Bob . . . I think it's probably the staff. They'll have gone to bed.'

'How far to the town, do you think?' asked Bob.

I peered into the night. 'It must be about three or four miles,' I said. 'That felt like the last bus. Bob, it's a seaside town in early June on a rugged island in the North Sea. And it's nearly midnight. I very much doubt if there's much going on there. I mean, you know: night-clubs, casinos, restaurants, sex shows, no. You go, if you want. But I'm whacked. I'll probably stay here, I think.'

'Me too,' said Baines quickly.

Bob dragged on his cigarette. Rick stood for a moment. Bob shrugged. 'OK,' he said.

8. Borkum Rift

The next morning there was still no one about, but the clubhouse door was unlocked. I pushed it open on a long, padded bar, an aquarium, potted spider plants and tables made of orange wood. Three fat blokes were hunched over a dangerous bend in the end of the bar. They stared at me. A woman was cleaning things with a rag in the corner.

'Can we get breakfast? . . . *Frühstück*?' I asked.

She looked at me as if I was mad. 'Yes,' she said.

After a shower, we ate fried eggs, looking through the fence of masts and out to sea at a bleak day full of Borkum's healing iodine.

I needed to sort out the next move. We had a hundred or so miles to go around the German coast, passing outside more islands and then into the mouth of the river Elbe en route to Hamburg. But, at the risk of disappointing Bob, before we got to Hamburg, we would leave the river and enter the Kiel Canal, which cut across Schleswig-Holstein to the bottom of the Baltic Sea near Lübeck.

The Elbe was a mammoth river (it ran out for miles through extended shallows in a deep cut in the sands) and like all massive rivers it produced a huge tidal current. To complicate matters, the mouth of the Weser, another river, similarly busy with traffic, though not quite as powerful, had to be crossed before we even got there. The effect of all these rivers, silting up their entrances and crushed by storms, was to make the actual point of entry far out to sea and that entry had to be made in good conditions. It was important to juggle with the tides.

'The pilots all tell us to head for Helgoland,' I explained.

'What's that?'

'It's a huge rock about fifty miles out in the gulf between Denmark and Germany. It was British until the turn of the century, when the Germans swapped it for Swaziland. Then we the British took it back after the war and used it for bombing practice until the mid-1950s.'

The others nodded. It seemed just.

'All the Germans go there on ferries for duty free, but it seems a long way to go out and wait for a tide. I can't see why we can't just pick up the tide as we go up the coast.'

'Yes, but we'd miss the duty free,' said Bob.

'We would, but we're still in a hurry. And anyway we don't need any duty free, Bob.'

Bob shrugged.

I also knew it was strongly advised that nobody should try to get up the Elbe at all if the wind was blowing in from the north-west when the tide was flowing the other way. Steep waves built up which could swallow a coaster. That was why yachts went to Helgoland; to wait for favourable conditions. But I kept that to myself.

The forecast for us was still good. The marina office had a weather chart, taken from the Internet, in its window. The storms were still roaming beneath us, heading across to the Alps. The day before, floods had washed away houses, overturned cars and killed eight people on the upper reaches of the Elbe, but it was quiet in Borkum.

Bob had stuffed his pockets with pats of butter from the club-house, wrapped in paper napkins. He put them in the fridge, next to the half pound of Lurpak. We left the marina and motored around to the harbour, a big, square, sturdy sort of place with a wide gate to the Ems and a number of small commercial vessels, coastguard boats, tugs and fishing vessels moored to its walls. Rick and Baines tied up. Bob wandered off to see about diesel.

He wandered back about five minutes later. 'There's a chandler up the back here. Very nice blokes. "Cheech and Chong". They want to know how much fuel we need, because they deliver it on a trolley.'

The harbour must have been a Second World War stronghold. It had the neatly ordered waste of space that goes with military installations: the place that Carruthers went to spy on in *The Riddle of the Sands*.

Cheech was serving in his own blockhouse. He was an unusual chandler. Shop assistants in boat stores generally look as if they've just stepped out of the galley of a racing boat where they've been helping themselves to the cheesy bites. They wear new polo shirts, chinos and leather deck shoes and gleam, like their brass lamps, with a knowing bonhomie. Cheech and his twin, Chong, looked as though they had stepped off a Malayan pirate ship. They were both short and very hairy. They had the sort of hair that gives no clear indication where hair stops and beard starts. It hung to their waist, was straight and carefully parted. So were their beards. Their feet were encased in Chinese slippers. On his head Cheech wore an embroidered smoking cap. He could have passed as the caterpillar in *Alice Through the Looking Glass*.

Bob had been ferreting around the shop and now placed a collection of jars of mustard, bubble gum and licorice sweets on the counter.

'Heh, heh,' he started up with his new friend. 'We would have thought you two would want to run away from here and start up a brown café in Amsterdam.'

Cheech stared steadily at him. 'What do you mean?'

'Er . . . Well, you know. This is an interesting line of business for a couple of people like you to be in,' he added lamely, waving vaguely at the Ashram outfit.

Cheech looked at Bob quite hard. Bob swallowed. I took some of the pots of jam back to the shelf. 'We are Dutch,' said Cheech eventually.

'Well yes, that figures,' said Bob. Cheech stared flatly back at him.

'We're going to the Kiel Canal,' I explained, changing the subject. 'Do we need to go to Helgoland first?'

Cheech didn't think so. 'It's no big thing if the wind is in this direction. You just need to be careful with the tides, but if you're a big enough boat you can easily do it in one tide.'

Back at the boat I looked over the chart with Rick.

'We should leave at about four,' I said. 'That way we'll catch the end of the outgoing tide.'

He nodded. 'Leave at four, then?' he said, but he looked worried.

Rick was always up for it. He had been enormously diligent loading fuel and water, while Bob meaningfully 'guarded the tap'. Rick had leaped smartly ashore, tied off, roped, hauled and tidied in exemplary fashion. But I sensed unease. Rick obviously liked to work by the book; but which book?

'There's minimal flow along the coasts, you see,' I went on.

Did he see what I was talking about? I couldn't tell.

'Everything all right?' I asked.

Rick smiled. 'Yes, yes. This is very different from the sort of sailing I'm used to. But it's fine.'

'How do you mean exactly?'

'Well the bloke I usually go with runs a tighter boat, you know, expects a much firmer discipline, you know. But this is cool. It's great. I'm having a great time.'

I wasn't sure what he meant by a firmer discipline.

'Well, chatting.'

I tried to excuse us. 'Rick,' I said. 'This isn't a military boat. We are just cruising. We're doing very well.'

'Yes, yes.' He looked away and back at the chart. 'I'm having fun.'

At tea-time, we left Borkum and set off back out to the mouth of the Ems, all the sails up, swimming along. But something was missing. What? Oh, yes. Ominously, the pigeon had jumped ship, just before we left.

Two hours later the tide went slack and the wind went slack too. The sea heaved us about, and we were banging and wallowing. It corresponded though with a chance to turn north and take a short cut straight across the Borkum Riff, through a channel that would cut three or four hours off our journey time. Even at low water there were two or three fathoms along its length. It was obviously maintained to allow boats to get out to sea without having to completely retrace their steps. Back on deck we scanned the waters to the north and Bob spotted a distant, flickering dot of a buoy.

'Here we go,' I said, and we turned through 45 degrees.

There is something very satisfying about taking a by-way over shoals: the back route, the cut-through, cheating the major channels and exploiting your rights as a little boat. Much of *The Riddle of the Sands* is about little else.

Rick was worried because we were almost immediately going to crash on to a sandbank, at least, we were on his chart.

'I think we'd better go back to the main channel, this can't be the route.' He told me. 'We're further north than we should be.'

I looked down at the GPS. 'No, look. The buoys are in different positions on that thing too,' I said. 'They've probably moved the buoys because the sands have shifted in storms and the chart hasn't kept up.'

Rick nodded unhappily and, with his chart rendered obsolete, spent time on deck (a rare thing for him), watching carefully as we jumped across the shallow bank, like riders crossing the desert, from marker to marker, until we reached the German Ocean.

The wind picked up, the sails filled and the boat dug in for the first real, triumphant sail of the journey. *Undina* responded to any slight adjustment to her rig like a surf board surging on in a strong off-shore breeze. We made supper. We put *The Who: Live at Leeds* on the stereo, and charged on; heeling, but not uncomfortably, in a trance of smooth, unruffled power.

'Did you actually wear velvet loon pants?' Despite the earlier waistband lapse, Baines was secretly in awe of Bob's prog-rock credentials.

'I used to sell them,' Bob said. 'Crushed velvet. I think I was the first, joss sticks and little bits of hippy crap, posters and things off a stall at gigs. I had an arrangement with the promoter, Mel Bush. He let me. Probably because I was only sixteen.' Bob had been Wiltshire's earliest hippy entrepreneur, taking wild drives through the night with Lemmy and the rest of Hawkwind. Lemmy had bought him an extra hot curry as a rite of passage. His stall had turned a tidy profit, but meant he kept missing school.

'But what went wrong?' I asked. 'Just up the road, Felix Dennis and Richard Branson were doing the same things and look at them now. You should have ended up with a multinational Maltese jeans business, at the very least.'

'I should have done.' Bob lit a cigarette and stepped into his white, clog-like fold-across shoes. 'But that wasn't the point, was it? Life's too short for all that.'

Big weather was certainly around. We watched the sun set in a perfect box in the low cloud that smudged all over the horizon to the west. Over that way too, something that certainly looked like a waterspout (a wonky grey clay pot, hanging like a trunk from wet, black masses of heaped-up cloud) appeared for a few minutes, and then gradually wiped into the background. We sometimes bowed over to gusts, as a rank of heavy clouds passed overhead, swirling round off the land and marching in a north-westerly direction. But generally the weather seemed to pass to one side or the other. We had the impression we were running up a corridor between rainstorms, although it was a corridor that did seem to be narrowing all the time.

In reality, though, we were in another form of narrows altogether. The Ems–Jade shipping lane is a stretch of marine motorway. It runs just from north to south outside the islands. All the pilot books are straightforward about it. 'Pleasure boats must not enter these lanes.' The German coastguard had apparently become quite firm. I put on my most daddy-like demeanour and attended to the task of impressing Bob with the seriousness of the situation.

'I've read that Germans will seize goods to the value of a probable fine,' I told him. 'We have to stay at least a mile clear of that line of buoys.'

Bob looked suitably concerned. 'What sort of goods?'

'I don't know. Whatever looks valuable.'

He looked around and shrugged. 'The only things we have on board are the radar and the GPS. If they took those we might bang about all over the shop.'

'They might take your shirts,' said Baines.

The lane was marked by a series of aggressively flashing buoys, with no more than a mile separating each one of them; like a line of lamp posts. It stretched ahead the way we were going for sixty miles. At night you could see exactly where you were supposed to be. Only a madman would willingly wander over into the traffic.

But each of us, except, perhaps, Bob, nursed our little anxieties. The threat of German patrol boats and the picturesque clouds added a hint of tension to the evening.

We drew our bearings on the chart and entered electronic marker points on the GPS. We cross-plotted our position and entered it on the other, spare, GPS. We sailed on the bearing. After a short while, I realized that I had misentered it. Tch. Stupidly, I had read the wrong position off the paper chart. I could see that we were heading on a slightly diagonal course that, had we had followed for five hours, without checking, would have taken us straight on to a German nudist beach. But we were continually updating our position. We spotted the mistake quickly. We corrected it. Then we double-checked it. We left it for ten minutes, checked it again, and reassured ourselves. And then we checked it again. There was the shipping lane. There were the islands. We were in the middle. We just checked again. Yes, good.

When we spotted the boat coming towards us, half an hour later, we had our first moment of doubt and pain.

'What's that then?'

Here was what was quite obviously a big boat, with castles and white superstructure, chugging towards us through the dusk.

'We must be in the shipping lane!' Rick was very quick to assume we had got lost.

'No, no. I don't think that's possible,' I said. 'Hold on.'

Rick persevered. 'I think we had better turn east.' He pointed to the shore.

'No, no. We can see it. We're not going to hit it.' Baines started scanning the horizon for fast patrol boats. Bob went below to hide his valuable shirts and shoes.

'No, no, this was preposterous. We were going fast, but not 50 miles an hour. It would have meant that we had been sailing 45 degrees off course.

'Well we haven't had this compass swung,' Bob averred doomily. In moments of crisis, Bob turned to part seven, module two, of his Fulham evening class.

'They might have moved the buoys!' said Rick. I suddenly

regretted saying all that stuff about the little channel across the Riff.

'No, it would be a huge undertaking to shift the entire Ems–Jade shipping lane. Look, hundreds of massive buoys. It would be like uprooting the M6.'

The ship passed by. It was not yet dark. We could see that it was a small coaster. I checked the chart again. We were, in every respect, on track, in position, exactly where we were supposed to be, visually, virtually, electrically, magnetically and on paper. Then, it struck me. It was obvious what he was doing. He was doing exactly what we were doing, only in the other direction.

'He looks big to us, but he's a small craft on the small craft track, outside the main shipping lanes,' I said. 'He doesn't want to cross out into the lanes, for the same reason that we don't, so he's just taking the local by-way, the same one we're on.'

'Yes.'

'That's what I thought,' said Bob.

Bob and I took the first watch of the night, from eight until midnight. Baines and Rick had gone below. It got dark. I was at the helm, and left Bob to potter around. He seemed to be busying himself around the chart and the navigation station. We switched on the radar.

For my part, I was probably enjoying myself too much. This was what I had come for. Here we were off these remote islands in the cusp of the North Sea. We were already passing Germany. The most difficult part of our passage was behind us. After two days of motoring, the wind was in our sails and driving us towards the Baltic. *Undina* was thrashing into the dark. Had the wind been in front of us, we might have been hitting into the waves, but from this angle we scudded across them at the fastest point of sailing. I was exactly where I wanted to be, both literally and metaphorically.

We hit a squall. Some big cloud had crept up on us. As it passed overhead, the wind blew strongly and we leaned over with it. The hull dipped into the sea. We still had a lot of sail up. I called down to Bob.

'Bob. We have to furl the genoa!'

He came on deck. I turned to take the wind out of the sails. They flapped. There was a lot of noise. Bob dithered.

'The jib, Bob, we have to take some of it in! Take the rope! No, not that rope! The furler, there.'

Later I was to realize it was a vain and hopeless dream that Bob would ever learn the ropes. Baines would shake his head in disbelief. 'It's not a learning curve,' he said. 'It's a learning loop de loop.' Four months and 3,500 miles later I would begin the same conversation with 'The furler. That's the rope that pulls in the jib, Bob . . .'

For now, hanging on the wheel, in the middle of a squall, I raised my voice.

'That rope! That one there!!' Bob pulled, but failed to make any impact on it. 'You'll have to use the winch.'

Bob took the rope and, to my accompanying incredulity, started to wrap it on top of the rope that was already around the winch. If he pulled it now, we would have two ropes hopelessly tangled into each other.

'No!' I was bellowing now. (It was very noisy.) Bellowing is when you shout very loudly and give it some extra emphasis by using your chest. Up until then I had merely been shouting. 'Don't do that, you dunderhead!' Bob let go of the furler.

Suddenly Rick shot up on deck in his willing-and-able mode. He pushed Bob to one side, reached for a winch handle and began winding in the jib sheet.

'Not that rope!' I shouted. 'He stared at me and blinked. 'Not that rope!' I leaned past him and released the jib. It flapped furiously again. 'The other rope. Put the other rope around the winch.' He did so. 'Now wind it in.' He wound it in and we shortened sail.

Now, I know I should never have shouted. I should certainly never have bellowed. The yelling was, in retrospect, a mistake. But I blame my father. He shouted all the time, not just at us but everybody. When *Windsong* came into a harbour she did so to a chorus of bellowing. My father at the stern of the boat, my mother (the Bob of the venture) almost in tears, because she couldn't interpret my father's instructions, and me at the front, yelling back at him. 'Get closer to the mooring buoy! You're still miles away.'

'Just reach it with the boat hook! Gwynneth, let the jib sheet go! Not that one, the other one! How many years have you been on this boat?'

'Oh, I wish you'd never bought the damned thing!'

One day my sister gave up on us. I remember her walking off down a long jetty by the side of a canal, somewhere in Belgium, with my father in tears, trotting along beside her, apologizing and promising to mend his ways. He never did, either.

For the present, Rick went back below. I apologized to Bob for calling him a dunderhead. He shrugged and lit a cigarette. (Baines later told me he was impressed. The particular choice of antiquated insult, he felt, indicated the salty nature of the reprimand.) We rushed on. The squall had died down. At least we had less sail up. It was a fine evening, with clear visibility, though now quite dark.

Another hour passed. It was nearly time for the watch to be changed. Rick had clearly not been resting. The speed he had jumped out on deck during the flap showed that he was, in fact, hovering around in the saloon, and now he stayed there, waiting. Bob had also gone below.

A bright red light came up on the starboard quarter.

'I need to identify a light about two o'clock,' I called in a light, unthreatening sing-song. 'It's on a bearing of about eighty degrees. It's a strong red flashing light.'

What happened next was sudden and melodramatic.

Rick came bounding up on deck. I could see that he was considerably agitated. He stared around into the night.

'It's OK,' I said. 'It's still some way off. We just need to work out what it is.' But Rick turned and shouted down the companionway in authoritative tones, 'Baines, put the engine on.'

'No, no. Just a moment . . .' I began.

But Baines had already turned the engine on. 'Get the sails down!' said Rick equally impressively.

I protested, raising my voice (the engine was on). 'I don't really want to get the sails down now.' Baines appeared on deck. Bob was looking up through the hatch.

Rick was clearly in an executive mood. His eyes were gleaming. He was speaking with a clear and determined, if rather spookily soft voice. He had, it would appear, assumed command. Had he been screaming, had he been panicking, then there might have been some justification in throwing a bucket of water over him, bundling him below and ignoring the whole thing, but for the time being Rick gave every appearance of having discovered something that threatened our imminent demise.

'What . . . what's the trouble?' I asked. He continued to ignore me.

'Take the sails down!' he repeated. I didn't see any danger. I think I told him so. He continued to ignore me.

Baines was preparing himself to go up on deck.

'OK. Wait. All right! We'll get the sails down!' I decided to humour him.

But it was quicker and safer to do it myself. I ran forward, hooked my lifeline to the jack-stay, released the brake at the foot of the mast and brought the main down. I wound a couple of ties around it. We slowed down. While I was up there I could hear Rick ordering Baines to take in the jib.

'No! No!' I shouted, clambering aft. 'Just a minute!' I engaged his attention. 'We shouldn't take the jib in, Rick. We are in the middle of a seaway here and I don't want this boat to be without any form of steadying sail, rolling about all over the place. We'll take in a bit of canvas. We've done that.' I seemed to have got his attention. 'What's the matter here?'

Rick was at the wheel. His hair was blown back and his head was lifted to the salty breeze. He lifted an arm and pointed a large forefinger at the red light. 'That is a tow!' he pronounced forcefully. I looked where he was pointing.

'That is not a tow!' I replied equally forcefully. At this point I really had no idea what it was. I wanted to go below and take stock of the charts, but the likelihood of a large oil rig being towed across major shipping lanes in the middle of the night by an unlit tug was remote to say the least. 'Where's the tug?'

He pointed back at the red light. 'That is the tug! And those lights there . . .' He swung around and pointed at the red lights on three radio masts on the shore. 'That is the rig.'

Even Bob was forced to confront his agitated protégé. 'Rick. No. Those are radio masts. We've seen a lot of them in the past. Take my word.'

'We have to stop going forward until we know where we are.'

'I know where I am!' I said, slightly untruthfully.

'There are ships ahead on the radar.'

'If there are, then we certainly can't see them yet. And they are most unlikely to be moving around without lights.'

'They're there!' He pointed at the shore.

'No!' I gaped. 'No, those are the shore lights, there! Those are radio masts there!' I shouted. 'That is the line of the marker buoys for the shipping lane there! I am fully aware of all the lights around us except one. The only unidentified light is that red blinking light, there!'

Well, we could have stood there all night pointing at lights and exclaiming, but Rick wasn't really listening. He was trying to put the engine into gear. Every time he pushed the handle forward the engine raced.

'It won't go into gear,' he told Baines. 'OK.' I had never seen somebody set their jaw before. 'We have to take this boat back to port.'

'Back to port!' This was terrific stuff. 'What port?'

'We have to get back to Borkum and get this seen to. Turn her around.'

'Turn her around?' I said. To get back to a port south-west of here we would have to sail this boat directly into the wind.

'You come up here, and instead of familiarizing yourself with things immediately start shouting . . .'

'I am not shouting,' he said quietly.

No, he wasn't shouting. Damn. He was as eerily self-contained as Steven Seagal in a fire fight, I had to give him that. I had only half registered that Baines had lifted the locker lid and was fiddling with the throttle controls. 'Baines!' I said. 'There's a red button on the side of the throttle handle. It can be depressed to rev the engine without engaging the gears. It's probably got stuck.' Baines looked down and released it. 'Oh yes,' he said. The boat shuddered into gear.

Rick didn't seem to notice anyway. He had taken on the role of coxswain of the Lowestoft lifeboat now. His legs akimbo, the wheel in his meaty paws, he was staring around himself, into the night, and wheeling the boat around in a circle, while he scanned the darkness around him for signs of flying Dutch tow-tugs.

I went below. Bracing myself, while the boat was thrown about as it crossed and recrossed the waves, I finally got to look at the chart. I took a bearing of 80 degrees and ran it as far as I could. The red light was a lighthouse on Wangerooge. It required some searching for, because it was still some ten miles off and located well inland. I turned to the radar. It did, indeed, register a number of blips, some 5 or 6 miles ahead in the mouth of the Weser. I went back to the companion-way and tried to address Rick calmly. I was going to be eerily quiet as well, just to show him. The boat was now going around in a tight circle.

'The light is a lighthouse on the shore and the radar blips you can see are almost undoubtedly buoys in the mouth of the Weser,' I said.

'I don't think we should go on into the estuaries with a lot of traffic at night. We should wait for daylight,' he retorted.

The moment for laying him out with a belaying pin had passed. It was nearly dawn. In an hour it would be light. I sighed.

'OK. You're on watch.'

We had been doing so well. The night had wound us all up. Now we were going around and around in little circles. Precisely what I'd left home to avoid doing in the first place. I went back below, checked and rechecked the chart and went forward to brood.

9. Up the Elbe

I didn't sleep. I lurked in my fore-cabin. I could feel the boat continue to circumnavigate a portion of sea about 30 feet wide. After an hour, we went back on course. It was getting light. I went to check our position a few times and then back up top, three hours later at five o'clock. The wind had died. There was a sluggish sea and a searingly bright sky of flat cloud: a yellow morning.

Rick handed over the helm and we motored across a great pewter slab of water towards the entrance to the Elbe.

The Thames may no longer serve ocean-going vessels, but the Elbe most certainly does. As we moved in towards the narrowing estuary, the land still no more than a smudge at the limit of visibility, the early-morning rush hour swung into life. Container ships, passenger vessels, banana boats and freighters were waiting for the morning tide. Out to the north, other big ships were approaching: high, square-sided blocks, teetering on the meniscus of the sea.

It was slack water in an hour, at six-thirty or thereabouts. For a while, the tidal movement would be stilled beneath us, then, soundlessly, the water would gather itself up and slide towards the invisible river far ahead. The ships, which had assembled in the night, began to wheel very slowly into new positions, delicately arranging themselves into a line, 10 or 20 miles long, to progress like circus elephants, one by one, up the channel.

We had to squeeze between a shallow plateau and the shipping channel.

We pootled across the watery wastes to the first major buoy of the entrance: the Schlüsseltonne. It was a vast, important mark, wallowing in eddies. We were right in the entrance to the Elbe. A light wind had come up. It was blowing from the south-east, not from the north-west, the supposedly dangerous quarter. It was hardly more than a breeze. The tide was at its very final exhalation, running out of power. But even so there was something sinister about this place. All around was flat and featureless and yet, as we motored on into the channel, there was a distinct change in the water. Even this tiny opposition between the feeble tide and the slight wind started to work up sharp indentations in the surface. The water seemed to fall away into steep little troughs, like the wash from a passing boat. We were slapped up and down, audibly banging on the crests with our long, over-hung stern and rocking violently in the middle of calm waters. It passed soon enough. Quite possibly the tide faded and turned. We began to pick up speed.

While we passed through the narrow gap left between the tall beacons dripping with weed and the buoys, rocking now in the incoming tide, the line of boats from Jamaica, from the States, from China rolled by on our left, overtaking us and heading the 30 or so miles up to Hamburg. The line then abruptly ended. The rush hour was over. We were alone again. A fishing boat came the other way down the small boat channel. The wind had freshened and was blowing off the shore, the way we wanted to go. I wanted to put up some sail. There was no reason for motoring in such conditions. Stupidly, this made me nervous. I was conscious that sailing itself seemed to make Rick twitchy.

'I'm going to put out some sail,' I said. Or, at least, I meant to say that. A sort of weak croak came out and I swallowed in the middle of it. This was ludicrous. I was behaving like some sort of learner driver. Why was I telling him anyway? I could do what I liked.

I decided to set the jib myself, pushing the side of my leg against the wheel and slipping the furling rope with both hands. The sail ballooned out. The boat shifted round. Rick darted forward to adjust the helm.

'No, no. It's OK,' I said confidently. 'There's plenty of water here.' I reached behind me and casually swung the wheel to bring us back on course. You see. I could do it on my own. It was a hollow demonstration.

Cuxhaven, like Felixstowe, was little more than a long, extended wharf along one side of the river. It was topped with cranes and warehouses and busy with pilot ships and river traffic.

I crossed to the other side. I could feel Rick tighten.

'You should be on that side,' he told me.

Well, he was utterly wrong. But what the hell.

'That's the starboard side of the river. We should be going in on the starboard side,' he continued, getting more insistent.

'No, Rick, no, we shouldn't.' I was deliberate and quiet. This was good. 'That's the port of Cuxhaven on that side, Rick. It is very much like Felixstowe, where I . . .' – I paused. I was trying to be reasonable but I was beginning to sound silly – '. . . where I have sailed . . .' – another pause – '. . . all my life.' I gulped. 'It would be very unwise to sail in close to that side of the harbour, because, Rick, large vessels may, at any time, be coming and going from the side of that wharf, you see, and the harbour authorities would not like it if we went along there and got in the way. So I think what we'll do is come this side of the river until we are past Cuxhaven and all its ships.'

'Well, OK. If you say so.'

On the town side of the river, a massive dredger, the size and appearance of a floating multi-storey car park, was heading downstream. It started frothing and bubbling at its stern and proceeded to swing itself cumbersomely towards the wharf.

I restrained from pointing to it. I was just grateful that the commander of the behemoth had taken this moment to so comprehensively demonstrate to any passing small boat (us, in other words) the dangers of sticking to the straightforward rules. If Rick understood, he gave no signs. Meanwhile, a coaster had been coming up behind us at speed for some minutes.

'There's a boat coming up behind you,' Rick suddenly said.

'Yes, I know,' I replied. 'I've seen him.'

There was a pause.

'Well, you're going to have to get out of his way.'

I paused myself. 'No. I think he's probably seen us.'

The coaster was coming closer. It was approaching up on our wake. It swung out a bit and sounded a blast on its horn.

'He wants you to get out of the way. You'd better get out of the way! Get over there!'

'No, no, Rick.' I sighed and gripped a spoke more firmly. 'He doesn't want us to get out of the way. He's just telling us he's coming through, like a cab driver or a lorry. He is the overtaking boat, you see. We are both in the correct channel. The last thing we want to do is confuse him by suddenly changing direction.'

Bob looked out. 'I'm coming past on the port side,' he said.

'What?' said Rick.

'It's what that means. One three-second blast.'

'Oh. OK.' He stood, gripping the backstay with his look of studied concern. On the bridge of the coaster a crew member in overalls gave him a cheery wave as his boat chugged past. Rick grinned and waved back.

For a while the river was clear of traffic. We swung around, across the coaster's wake, and crossed to the far side, where the wharf ended and was replaced by a bank of startling green grass, topped by cows. There were even farm roofs.

There were about a dozen sailing boats and motor vessels ahead of us now. It was strange to be amongst other yachts, a reminder that despite the damp and the grey skies this was really the holiday season.

The Kiel Canal was built in the nineteenth century for strategic reasons. Germany wanted to be able to get her battleships into the Baltic. It was designed for, and still took, big ships, but of course the canal was largely redundant now. Real big ships were too big for it in the modern world. In fact real big ships could no longer enter the Baltic at all. The waters of the Kattegat were too shallow for ocean-going bulk carriers to pass through the Danish entrance and the canal was now far too small. The granite blocks and the lock gates had an industrial museum charm, overlooked by enfolding trees.

As we left the final straight of the river and began to cross over towards the far bank, our flotilla of ships increased its speed and dragged down sails. Alongside the high walls, there was a floating pontoon and already there were yachts tied up to the far end, deep inside the lock. I would have preferred to take my time, to sniff around and prepare carefully, but, as with all locks, the gates seemed just about to close. We bustled with the rest, swung in and tied up as graciously as we could.

The lock was a box. We were suddenly sealed up. The blustery June day, all the weather and the tumult and the travel were stilled and left outside. It was like entering a church from a shopping street.

I stepped down on to the pontoon. It wobbled slightly, but the feeling of arrival – of the journey having been possible after all – suddenly rushed in. We had crossed the North Sea in three days. We would make it to the blasted regatta after all. Above me, the glistening walls were hung with weed. The underwater sluices began to rumble like an exploding jacuzzi and we all, very gently, began to rise upwards into north Germany.

The lock disgorged us. The rest of the flotilla hustled up the canal, we turned instead, and nudged into a small marina in Brunsbuttel, just beside the northern gates, where we took one of the last available spaces. There were other boats motoring in and hovering in the clear water looking for somewhere to stay. 'They'll raft up against us,' I told Bob. So he scrawled a note on a piece of cardboard: 'Achtung! Wir gehen aus 4 in the morning, Tommy!' He propped it up against the side of the dinghy on the cabin roof. As we sat in a café we watched it blow off. It was better that it did. Not, I thought, because of its provocative racism, but because it marred my boat's greyhound-sleek excellence.

'God, she does look beautiful,' said Baines. As we had walked away from her along the pontoon towards the shore we had stopped several times to turn and admire her.

I had been horse-riding in Montana the year before. It required little more than getting into a line behind another horse, watching it shit and listening to my own mount groaning and heaving as it walked me up into some of the most spectacular mountain scenery on earth. I have never understood people who like to cuddle horses. They seem nervously powerful and they have big yellow teeth. But after listening to my horse straining with the effort of carrying me,

I felt warm towards it afterwards. I nuzzled up to its neck and patted and congratulated it, even though it still twitched in that nervous, shivery, vein-tightening way that horses do. It had borne me over the precipitous paths and never fallen down the mountain once. Good horse.

And of course we felt very much the same about the boat. We sat, ate ice cream and stared lovingly at her. Good boat. Despite the lack of attention to some of her paintwork she was far and away the prettiest thing in that harbour. She was a gem. We would wow them at the classic boat regatta.

I looked up. 'Oh. . .'

Nosing her way into the little boat park was the loveliest boat it was possible to be. *Undina* was instantly a dog. We were long and low but this boat scarcely stuck out of the water at all. We were lean and narrow but this boat was a floating ironing board, on edge. We were dark blue but this boat was purply blue with a slight matt tinge to her hull and her prow, which appeared to have been honed with a pencil sharpener, was, moreover, sheathed, at the very tip, with a gun-metal cowl, like an arrow head. The decks were almost flush. Two barred hatch covers seemed to be all that broke the smooth surface of her perfect teak-planked decks. She was 60 feet long and her single varnished mast was a totem of dominance.

She slid in, like a barracuda amongst jelly-fish. Six men in close-fitting overalls covered in reflective patches and wearing monkey boots padded around her deck silently passing out warps while a lean grey-haired helmsman held her perfectly still in the water. She had come from Holland. She made *Undina* look disastrously dumpy. She was a '10-metre'. I wandered away from the bill in the café and stood watching as the crew finished tying *Zenia* alongside. After a while I caught the helmsman's eye.

'Are you going to Flensburg, to the regatta?' I asked. He looked me up and down.

'That's right,' he answered and turned away to polish his binnacle.

10. Love

I had never intended to buy a boat really. It was Bob's idea.

My father had owned a sequence of wooden boats. I had been brought up to disdain 'plastic boats' as 'floating caravans', to pity their owners and their unseaworthy, condensation-trapping 'bath tubs'. There were many different divisions of weekend sailor. My father was of the tarry, romantic regiment. He would discard his Marks and Spencer's suit, drag on a filthy pullover and a tattered oil skin, top it off with a jaunty navy blue yachting cap and look every inch the fat doctor playing at sailors.

It was routine when sailing with him to discriminate against lesser yachtsmen and important to admire real boats. Almost any rotting hulk elicited favourable approval, as long as it was wooden and hung with smelly ropes. When he bought *Windsong*, built in 1929 for duck shooting – 'It had racks for the guns down the main saloon, you know' – we got used to strangers standing at the quayside and offering compliments. It was a terrible boat. My brother despised it ('It sails like a cow'). But it looked beautiful.

What was this man doing with this boat? It frightened him almost as much as *Undina* was beginning to frighten me. Part of my adult recklessness was the result of standing watching my father fretting and panicking over his impossible yacht. Now Bob was taking my place as the juvenile delinquent – 'Oh, it's fine. Don't worry. We'll get in there. Put your foot down' – and I, for my part, was becoming over-cautious. But my father had bought his boat as his substitute garden shed. A wooden boat is hard work. He revelled in it.

He had done woodwork at school (something I managed to avoid), and all his adult life he carpentered. He made lockers, shelves, racks for mugs, ingenious holders for pots, all of which got put into the boat. He bought elaborate pieces of equipment. (One year he bought my mother a paraffin stove for her birthday.)

And he loved fitting them. Drilling the holes, gently blowing the sawdust, sanding down and running his thumb along the grain.

Gradually, *Windsong* sank lower and lower in the water, as he bolted, screwed and glued an ever-increasing number of fitments to her insides and added more shackles, pins and screws to his collection of spares.

He would disappear into a chandlery and stand, for what felt like hours to us, transfixed by a peg board hung with galvanized eyes, in a trance before a selection of brass hooks, or seemingly hypnotized by a box of rope offcuts. And we had to wait. Sometimes, on a damp Saturday in May, he would row himself aboard his boat, with me, aged ten, in tow and just sit there. Or so it seemed. Sometimes he would open the engine and kneel in front of it, unscrewing massive nuts, or disassembling pistons, and he would require his children to kneel there with him, like the Arnolfini family, only instead of our hands conjoined in prayer we would be holding spanners or wire, or strange cigarette things, which needed to be lit and inserted into the belly of the engine to get it going on cold days.

Like a surgeon, like, I suppose, the hospital consultant that he was, he needed to have his tools to hand, somebody else's hand preferably, ready to be passed to him at a moment's notice at the critical stage of the operation. Of course, it was always critical. Nothing if not a self-dramatist, he pursued every aspect of his sailing adventures in an atmosphere of tension and recrimination.

And the waste of time! The boat had to come out of the water at the end of the season. This was when his contempt for the namby-pamby, fibre-glass sailor was flourished with real vigour. After all, they had merely to wipe down their bilges with a sponge and forget about her. Forget about *Windsong*? (Or *Dunlin* or *Xara* before her?) Impossible. The real work was just beginning.

Was it every weekend we went down to that freezing West Mersea boat park? Was the entire winter spent in that grim, gravelled patch by the saltings, where boats were propped up on legs and trussed in tarpaulins for the winter? It certainly felt like it then, when time was so precious, and we wanted so desperately to waste it. Instead, the barnacles had to come off the bottom. We had to lie on our backs on a bit of tarpaulin. I can still feel the cold seeping through from the stones beneath my back. With a flat-bladed scraper, we pushed at a crust of tiny conical shells, which crumbled away and spattered down on to our faces. We felt the slight stinging, and feared to breathe in the flakes of the ghastly anti-fouling concoction that had been slapped over the hull and would have to be slapped over the hull again, before we were finished and she could go back in the water. At least all that scraping was vaguely satisfying. Like picking at a scab. On a good day, the skin of dead molluscs would fall away in satisfying strips; on a bad day, we were sand-papering. Black sheets of 'wet and dry' were soaked in buckets of freezing water and rubbed ceaselessly against the acres of pale grey hull until it 'keyed', by going a slightly frothy white, and then back in the bucket to soak off the gunk and more rubbing, rubbing, rubbing.

A wooden boat needs constant maintenance. The manuals recommend that varnish is done twice in a season. That is, rubbed down and several coats applied, not only over winter, but also in the middle of July. I can't recall that we ever did that, but we certainly painted, polished and scrubbed all year long, and for what? For some daft romantic pride.

After the Baltic journey was over, I hosted a party for the members of the Classic Yacht Club.

There were two key men from the exciting world of modern boats present. One was an expert in epoxy resin, the other had made his fortune in carbon fibre. His latest project was trying to produce a carbon fibre that showed its stresses, just like wood. Both men, however, owned and sailed classic wooden boats. 'It was love,' said one. 'I just fell in love with her,' the other echoed. 'Oh, she is so beautiful and the curve of her . . .' Everywhere, these men and women were fervently whispering their intimacies, sharing their affairs, their sweethearts. 'I've chartered. You need the convenience, but ownership, well, that's a different matter . . .'

After supper, Rosemary from the Little Classic Boat Museum on the Isle of Wight showed them old black-and-white footage of

J class boats being launched in the 1930s. Like a Lone Ranger film on a stuttering super-8 projector at a boyhood birthday, the party was stilled, apart from appreciative oohs and aahs.

I suppose I loved my father's boat, and feebly tried to stop him from selling her fifteen years ago.

'Are you going to come with me and sail her?'

'No.'

'Are you going to maintain her?'

'No.'

'Well it's pointless keeping her.' And she was sold. He was ill. He died and his ashes were scattered in the mud in the upper reaches of the Deben. My mother had made no complaint about the sale. Both of them were old. She no longer wanted to be wet and dirty, perhaps she never did. But, oddly, she keeps tabs on *Windsong*.

'She's in Lowestoft now. And they've spent a lot of money on her, restored her original rig. I don't like the colour they've painted her, though.'

So someone else was in the grip of a hopeless infatuation, wasting money on keeping the old tub afloat.

I still wanted to sail as I grew older. Despite the pain, it was bred into me. No other form of occupation really constituted a holiday. When I had money, I chartered. I became an advocate of the rented boat.

'It's the only way to do it,' I told anybody who would listen, and many who weren't listening at all. 'For the money that my father spent just mooring his boat I can have two weeks in the Caribbean on a bigger, faster, more comfortable fibre-glass yacht! I can take friends, sail in warm water, catch fierce fish and then walk away.'

On one holiday the engine failed in the Tobago Keys. We sat for an afternoon, while the skipper ('You rent them for the week. Costs almost nothing and they have to do all the work') contacted the base on the radio and a spare part was ferried out. We didn't sit, in fact. We snorkeled in a natural aquarium on the reef. When the engine had been fixed and we were ready to go, the skipper took me aside. 'Thank you,' he said earnestly.

I was puzzled. 'What for?'

'Thank you for staying. So many would have left.'

'No!' I was shocked. It had never occurred to me that we could.

'Americans would have just insisted on another boat and a sea plane to get them to it.'

'Really?' I made a mental note that next time . . .

Bob had become a fixture on these sprees. What a perfect companion he was. He was one of life's layabouts and always available. I would sometimes ring other, more employed, busy men of the world. 'It's a last-minute thing,' I would tell them. It nearly always was. 'I've got this boat in Turkey for a couple of weeks and we're just going to drift down to Marmaris.'

'What a lovely idea,' they would say. 'Can I come back to you?' But I knew they were really thinking: 'God! He means next week.'

But Bob was a constant. He was the only true committed hedonist I knew. And when we first went, he was like a cockney child taken to the country to see cows for the first time. Bob was a wide-eyed, baptism-seeking convert to the sailing life.

We must have been in the Aegean. Crossing an azure sea one late afternoon from some smudgy violet rock to another, I remember glancing at Bob, who was sitting holding on to the wheel. He had an odd look in his eye. He was gazing around him appreciatively. He had a fag on. He was wearing something comfortable and colourful. The sun was shining. He was eating a Greek sweetie. He smiled and nodded to himself. And then he cackled. Some people get it. Others never do.

Paul, by contrast, was a busy man. When he came with us, he sat in mute admiration as we busied ourselves for leaving the port. 'Look at you. Gosh. I never knew you had all these skills. It's like watching a different person. Ha, ha.' He was full of intelligent and searching questions as we negotiated the harbour exit and raised our sails. And then, when the course was set and we settled back to sail our distance, he sat with a fixed smile of anticipation. 'What now?' he asked.

'Well, we just sail,' I explained.

'Mmm.' He smiled brightly. After a while, he started drumming his fingers. 'What time do we get in, then?'

'Oh, I don't know . . . about four hours.'

'Right.' He shifted on the hard bench. The smile hardened. 'Can I do anything?'

'No, no. You're fine.'

'Right.' And he nodded.

Paul is the sort of person who sits aboard a sailing boat and watches a motor launch roar past with a quiver of barely suppressed envy.

'Oh, that looks like fun.'

'That isn't a lovely boat. That's a ghastly, vulgar piece of shit, Paul.' Vainly, I told Paul that sitting on that boat is like sitting on a washing machine after it's been thrown down a hill, that the noise and the bumping are moronic, that inside it has all the taste and dignity of a footballer's bathroom. His eyes remained fixed on it until it thrashed over the horizon. And he imagined it tied up outside some bar while we were still wallowing along at walking pace.

'Would it be a good idea to put the engine on, perhaps?' he offered, finally.

Of course, he never came again. He was probably sea-sick at some point. He probably injured himself and had difficulty sleeping, but that wasn't the real reason. He just didn't see the point.

Bob, however, embraced the delusion of sailing straight away. He found little difficulty in adapting to a life of doing nothing at all while appearing to progress to something or somewhere.

I was shocked when I discovered he was secretly going on sailing courses. He signed on to become a 'competent crew' with a company in the Solent and went for a long weekend on a 30-foot sailing boat.

'The instructor was a bit of a Nigel,' Bob thought. 'No sense of humour. Heh, heh.' He'd put a stuffed cat on Nigel's bed, and for a satisfying moment Nigel had thought it was real and lost his rag, but Bob wasn't sure that Nigel really appreciated his easy-going approach. 'At one point he said that he wasn't going to be able to give me the certificate. I don't know what all that was about.'

Nonetheless, officially, Bob became a competent crew. Then he went to evening classes in Fulham. This was in preparation for his 'day skipper' certificate. 'To be quite honest,' Bob told me, 'the instructor was a bit of a granny.'

'In what way?' I asked.

'Oh, I don't know. I made some joke and he wasn't up for it, but we got along quite well in the end.' Bob's renowned ability to smooch anybody meant that he sailed through the course on good terms with his teacher, who 'took it all a bit seriously'.

Bob came out the other end of the winter with a dedication to sextants and the science of positioning from the sun, a sketchy but committed knowledge of the movement of tropical storms, an urge to do his own weather forecasting and an irritating emphasis on safety procedures and compass swinging. He still couldn't untie a rope from a cleat in less than three minutes, had no firm grasp of the principles of sailing and couldn't tell the difference between a sheet and a halyard, but give him half an hour and the right book and he could tell you what the lights on an approaching vessel might mean.

He didn't actually have his certificate as yet. That was only awarded when the theoretical knowledge, which Bob was swiftly forgetting, was matched by his actual experience. So the journey we were to undertake was now an important part of the whole scheme. Quite where the whole scheme was heading remained a mystery. But he needed to get several thousand miles under his belt.

Of course, I was merely envious. I was irritated as well, but more because my incompetent crew had become an incompetent crew who now, apparently, knew a lot more about sailing than I did.

'Now, Griff, just before we actually leave the dock,' he suddenly announced, as I was trying to manoeuvre the boat out of Ipswich wet dock to take her on the Orwell for the first time, 'I must just ask you: what is your man-overboard procedure?'

'My what?'

'Your rescue procedures in the event of a member of your crew falling overboard.'

'Falling or being pushed?'

'Whatever.'

'Well, Bob,' I replied, 'at sea, my preferred method is to mark the GPS, set a man on deck to point out the missing person, throw a dan-buoy overboard, followed by other detritus to mark our way back to them, turn around, take down any sails and approach them from the windward side. But in this river I would probably shout at them to stand up and walk to the bank.'

Bob considered this. 'Hmmm,' he said. 'Well, I suppose that's one way of doing it.'

I was lazy too. I knew at some point I would have to overcome my indomitable pomposity and try to swallow my annoyance at the whole system's emphasis on arcane knowledge over practical skills. I would have to get a certificate myself.

Secretly, I thought it was quite handy that Bob had various bits of paper. It was always my intention, should we get stopped by any authority whatsoever on the way to St Petersburg, simply to indicate Bob and tell them that he was the skipper. Bob would produce his documents and we would go on our way. It was especially useful that he had got his radio operator's licence.

In the event, we never got stopped by anyone. The boat looked too serious.

11. Possession

Baines told me he had once seen a sign in the back of an old Porsche: 'He who has the most toys wins.' Oh dear. But what about the gun in the newsagent's shop in Epping? I must have been eight. We all had guns in Epping. You couldn't visit a friend for an afternoon's digging mud without transporting an IRA-sized cache of weaponry. We sat on the sofa, watching cowboy films on the telly, surrounded by pistols and plastic machine-guns blasting at the baddies. 'Pchew! Pchew!' All small boys were required by law to be able to imitate explosions and at least six different kinds of gun-fire, from the straight-spitting 'ccceeeyow' with the extra fading whine of ricochet, through the windy, gobbish 'pcchh, pcchh' of an automatic, part-silenced machine-pistol, to the back-of-the-throat-spitting-up-a-fishbone 'acch, acch, acch' of a sten gun. And everybody knew that a gun required two fingers held up; only girls threatened people with fake guns made of one index finger pointed feebly in your direction. 'Bang!' What sort of gun sound was that?

And then one day in the window of a newsagent at the far end of Epping High Street (newsagents being part-time toy shops and replica gun merchants in those days) there appeared an object so redolent of sophisticated menace that I stood transfixed before it. It was a silver automatic pistol, by 'Lone Star', I think. It had a black grip on its squarish handle and unlike those cowboy guns with old-fashioned revolving bits, it bore a striking resemblance to the sort of gun that gangsters used. It looked real. But that was only the half of it. This gun was in a case. It was laid into a velvet-lined cut-out. But also cut out were two little compartments to take ammunition and, I shiver at the memory, a bottle of gun oil! It might seem that it would be impossible to better these accoutrements. Some wily executive at a creative meeting at Lone Star had been given a direct line of communication to the psychology of the eight-year-old boy in Epping. 'Let's add a little bottle of oil to the package. It won't cost us much, but it will get them, believe me.' He went on: 'And then we can put another smaller gun into the same case, a sort of matching mini-weapon, which the murderously inclined pre-adolescent will want to stuff down his sock when he goes to one of those extended mock gang battles on the building site round the bottom of Kendal Avenue.'

Every day I walked the length of Epping High Street, past Church's the Pork Butcher, past Mr Pelosi's Brunchi Bar, past the seven or eight shoe shops that seemed to comprise the rest of Epping's shopping requirements to stare in the newsagent's window, to check that the case was still there, to dream of the possibility of ownership. What if some other boy had a birthday before me? Could it ever really be mine? But do I remember the moment it actually was? Because my mother bought it for me, as I requested. It was my 'big present' that year. I vaguely recall the little red seal around the bottle of oil. It had a cork and a pin of metal in the cork with which it was possible to take a drop and transfer the oil to the mechanism of the gun, which, I also recall, was a grey anodized thing inside. I must have taken it in a trembling hand and plugged Richard Everett with it. 'Pchew, pchew, pchew.' But I really can't, no matter how much I dig around in old files in my computer brain, recall any details of the actual ownership of the thing. It simply wasn't as emotionally imprinting as the wanting.

One evening in Suffolk, in late January, forty years later, Bob sidled across the garden. 'Griffule, actually I was thinking, just, you know, what with the course, not that I've finished it . . .' he scratched at his pate, 'but I was thinking of buying myself a boat.'

I reeled. 'Don't do it.' It was an instantaneous response. I rehearsed the familiar negatives, the hassle, the weather, the ties. 'We're happy chartering.' But he knew as well as I did that we'd both started looking in the back pages of the yachting magazines. Just for fun, you understand. There were always copies of *Boats and Planes For Sale* around, even when it still included the planes. Nowadays it was just boats, and we had fantasized over some of the bargains thrown up by the end of the Cold War. We used to speculate on whether the regularly advertised ex-minesweeper, with its wooden hull, 250-foot length and accommodation for fifty, might prove to be a liability in the long run. Even if the £200,000-odd price tag did seem an incredible bargain for such a huge, floating, sod-you thing. So what about the German navy motor torpedo boats, instead? More practical *and* more sexy, they would cause a stir with the village Boat Owners Association. Bob had a friend of a friend who had something similar, though. The major problem was that it used up 300 gallons of fuel an hour. 'But only if you go at top speed,' Bob told me. 'I mean you'd only want to do that once in a while. We could get to Amsterdam in a few hours.'

After all, we already had two boats. They were only little boats, one an open dinghy, the other an 18-foot-long family day sailor called a Drascombe Lugger, which I kept in the creek at the bottom of the garden in Suffolk. At one point I became convinced that we should buy an old wooden MFV, or Motorized Fishing Vessel, and use the derricks at the back to haul the open boats aboard. 'That way we could chug all over the place and do a bit of sailing when we got there.' The advantage of the MFV was that it was A PROPER BOAT. It was built of wood. It even had a sort of rig for steadying sails. 'And they are dead cheap. They actually have to burn them up north in order to get their compensation money. I always thought it would make a fantastic opening to one of those rugged Ken Loach downtrodden working-class films . . .'

'Burn them?'

'Yes, because they have to prove that they aren't going to be used for fishing again.'

'Why?'

'Well they are having to reduce the fishing fleet in the North Sea, to save stocks of fish.'

'Are they?'

We even went aboard a lovely Scottish example moored in the Orwell. We were time-wasters, I suppose, but she was 50 feet long and had a magnificent crew's cabin with box berths for six all piled one above the other on either side of a table and stove in the stern. And she was very glamorous, with black sides and a varnished top. God knows what we were supposed to do with her vast hold, pitch dark and still smelling of fish. Turn it into a disco or something.

In retrospect, I wonder whether Bob's strategy that January was more calculating than it seemed. He put his hand in his back pocket and brought out a picture of a dilapidated flying saucer.

'She's very cheap,' he told me.

'Yes. Well, that figures. It must be the original fibre-glass boat, from the seventies. Is it?'

'Yes. Twenty-six foot long, though.'

'Mm. You might find that it suffers from osmosis. And it wouldn't be terribly nice inside, I shouldn't think.' It wasn't terribly nice outside, but that wasn't bothering Bob very much.

'No, but you would be able to take this boat across the North Sea, or down to the Med, wouldn't you? You see, I have to get four thousand miles of sea-passages done to get the certificate.'

I felt the need to be diplomatic. 'Well, I mean, you know, people have sailed around the world in smaller boats than that.'

'As small as this one.'

He produced another yacht broker's photograph. The glare of a photoflash reflected off a sad-looking hulk in the corner of a dismal yard. Incredibly, it was even uglier than the first, with a bulbous cabin, riveted black plastic windows and a bilge keel.

'This one I could afford now.'

'Bob, Bob,' I found myself saying. 'Honestly, don't. Don't buy one of these. They're too depressing. What the hell, I'll buy a boat. I was going to buy a boat myself . . .'

Was I really? Was I? I know that I was bored by the Drascombe Lugger people-carrier. I was middle-aged and I wanted the soft-top, sporty, river-hog sloop that went soaring past us one windy afternoon.

But I had no idea what sort of boat I was really after when I first went looking. In my weaker moments, I try to imagine myself as a used boat salesman. What, I wonder, would be my reaction if some vague lally came into my overheated office (a portakabin to one side of a mud hole full of moored yachts) and answered my questions as follows?

'What length?'

'Not sure. Could be big but, maybe, if it's nice, small. Or medium, of course.'

'You're looking for an old boat?'

'Possibly. I mean I might buy a state-of-the-art modern boat, you know, for some exciting sailing. If it was small then I could keep it in the creek. But I might buy a 250-foot minesweeper, if I liked it. Big, small? Not sure.'

The bloke with the silly moustache and the Scooby Doo flaps for hair wondered openly whether it was actually necessary for him to get off his arse and go out into the damp January fog.

'There are quite a lot of boats out there. Feel free to wander around and give them a look over. I'll be here if you need me.' He went back to his paper.

I persuaded him that I was a serious enough customer for him to venture outside. He showed us some sad-looking boats and then added, 'I mean if you're looking for a wooden boat, there is this rather lovely thing that has just come on the market.'

He took us down a pontoon. There was a long, dark object tied up to the side of it. I hesitated. Oh dear. This was a different sort of boat altogether. She had these dorades like a liner. She had wide decks like a proper classic boat. She sat very low in the water. She looked powerful. She was dark blue, wooden and she was about three times the price and the size that I had been intending to get. But I sat inside her. I sat inside her for a long time. I opened all the drawers and laid fingers on the catches and the butterfly screws, I opened the teak-topped lockers, I admired the hatch covers and I turned the wheel. I nodded slightly as silly moustache told me all about her. I ran fingers along the surfaces and caressed the mahogany cabin sides. I should have poked knives in the hull, asked searching questions about her keel bolts and kicked the deck, but for the time being it was just a gentle thing, you know, a sort of tender affection, a sort of wanting to get to know and be with her . . . I pulled myself together.

We went and looked at a really horrible five-year-old racing boat too. I mean, I looked. I didn't actually touch it. Or in fact go aboard at all. I was too busy glancing back over my shoulder. Something had happened. The notion of a fast modern sailing boat for the river was receding into the mist. The shade of my father was lurking at my side. A plastic boat was all very well to rent, but to own? I kept seeing myself at the helm of this rather magnificent yacht cresting a wave (in black and white, funnily enough), sealed in a nostalgic bubble of stylish yesteryear. I wanted to be Humphrey Bogart or John Kennedy. This glistening possession, demonstrating to the world my individuality, taste and discretion, would be my equivalent of a plasma television, wouldn't it? It was pathetic.

I got Bob to come up to Suffolk. 'Look,' I explained. 'There's no point in me buying something sensible.' I fancied this would strike the right note with him. He instantly agreed. 'Bob, the point is, we sail sensible family-sized boats when we charter. I have decided,' I announced magisterially, 'that if I buy, I must buy a wholly impractical and unnecessary boat.' Bob nodded and took a long drag on his cigarette.

'The minesweeper, you mean.'

'No, no. I mean something that is just there to be admired and look glamorous and be a head-turner. Something we want to be seen in, otherwise, with all the other distractions, it will just end up on a mooring and we'll never go to it.'

I was thinking of the Drascombe Lugger. Just the act of getting aboard it last summer had meant washing off 3,000 pounds of guano and rolling up a carpet of green slime. We had only used it once in the year. In fact, I'd left it out on the mooring the whole winter. Wiser counsels might have pointed out that failing to look after one boat is not a sound basis for getting a bigger boat, to fail to look after. Bob was many things, but he was not a wise counsel. 'But that's the point, Bob, we really have to love this boat or we'll get tired of her,' I told him. He agreed.

It was time, we decided, to look at every impractical wooden boat for sale on the entire east coast.

In Levington we were taken out by the owner. He was clearly a desperate man. His boat was very pretty. He had spent a fortune on her. He worked as a carpenter anyway and had managed to do a lot of the work himself, although he was concerned that he'd had to take the day off work to show us the boat, because she was on a swinging mooring some way from the marina, and the brokers weren't prepared to row us all the way out there, but, candidly, this was the second year of trying to sell her, so he was quite open to offers, because the yearly costs were quite steep, not that steep you understand, perfectly manageable in fact, and she was a great sailing boat, great, but she was wooden and not many people appreciated the quality of a wooden boat these days . . .

We let him ramble on. It was obviously therapy for him. He was like a man with the responsibility for a very ancient parent trying to get them into a nursing home.

Our working knowledge of wooden boats was expanding. Owners and brokers probably thought they were extolling virtues, but wiser counsels, of which there were none available at all, might have pointed out that they were adept at lobbing in off-putting hints. The 50-foot Robert Clarke *Cinnamon* we saw next had all the lines of a pre-war classic, and a pre-war damp interior as well. She wasn't advertised in a yacht sales office. She was just tied up in Ipswich Dock, but when I went to look at her, blow me, she was for sale as well.

Ronnie, who owned her, described himself as a professional explorer. He'd had several expeditions in her, including one supported by the Prince of Wales looking for interesting new plants in the Azores. Off the African coast coming back from South Africa, he got into a storm and lost her mast.

'It was our first trip.' He had a haunted look in his eye. 'We drifted for thirty days living on spam.'

I was intrigued. My father had always stocked his boats with plentiful supplies of spam.

'We hated the stuff,' Ronnie explained. 'But luckily we'd been sponsored by them.'

One advertisement in *Boats For Sale* took me back to Maylandsea in Essex, a mud town where my father had kept his boat when I was young, and where I'd first learned to run across ooze without sinking.

The yard took us out in their aluminium work boat to *Ariadne*, a 6-metre gaff-rigged racing boat, originally built to represent Spain in the 1936 Olympics. She was the hobby of a carpenter at the yard. She was 30 feet long on the immaculate deck, and only about 5 or 6 feet wide at her widest point. It was possible to straddle her with one's legs akimbo. It was necessary to straddle her with legs akimbo. She was like a planked large canoe.

'Are you going up to the bow? I'll just move back a bit, we can pass just by the mast. Hold on to the rigging. No, don't hold on to me.'

Beneath us, our feet, in their heavy shore shoes, clumped around on the exquisite, thin, holly-trimmed teak planking. It was like walking on an expensive Italian mandolin.

'He takes part in all the old gaffers' races,' said the carpenter's girlfriend. 'He's so quick that he usually comes in several hours before everybody else and has to sit around waiting for them to turn up so he can get his trophy and come home.'

This was exactly what I wanted to hear. I would eat up the bosomy opposition in my new sliver of a racing skiff, and I began to picture myself at the helm, with a pipe and a Basque hat. She did look, when all was said and done, superbly impractical.

Bob confirmed this. 'Look down here,' he squawked suddenly. He had stuck his head down the hatch and was looking below decks. 'What's happened to the cabin?'

Below there was nothing but some ribs and shiny copper nail heads.

'Sometimes he does put out a lilo,' said his girlfriend, 'but he didn't want to fit her out. It would slow him down.'

Mike was a raffish lawyer. His boat was a perfect Holman, beautifully maintained and about 35 feet long. He was charming, good company and took me for a sail down the Orwell in the early summer. She sailed beautifully. He was very proud of her. Nobody could fail to be impressed by this little ship. And we were getting on so well. His girlfriend made me a lovely bacon sandwich. He was so enamoured of his boat that he was obviously utterly convinced that I was going to buy it.

'Ah,' he said, 'she's a grand thing. She needs a little work. I was planning to attend to the coamings. The engine has been reconditioned. Take the helm.' It was love. He wanted me to love her too. Like an older man offering up his mistress. 'Feel that.' He was listing all her attractions and abilities. She was supple, smooth and willing.

But as we sailed down the river, God forgive me, I was thinking of another boat altogether. Concentrate. Concentrate. I took the tiller. Of course *Undina* had that lovely wheel, didn't she.

'It's a nice roomy cockpit,' he said.

'And deep so you can get out of the wind,' said his girlfriend.

Roomy? Not really. Deep, yes. Cramped really. We were sitting on top of each other. An extra 10 feet gave *Undina* expansiveness. She had real elegance. She had such lines . . .

'It is a marvellous cockpit,' I said, shamefully.

'And down below, we find her very comfortable.'

'Mind you, there are just the two of us,' said his girlfriend.

'She is very comfortable,' I said. Well she wasn't really. Like a lot of British boats she was too narrow and deep. When you descended the ladder you ended up in a railway carriage with the windows in the roof. The American designer of *Undina*, Philip Rhodes, had been an early advocate of width. *Undina* had a huge stern and, so, was flatter down below, and that extra length . . .

'Another sandwich?'

'I won't be able to keep *Tabitha* on, so I've got to say goodbye to her. And I want her to go to someone who really appreciates her and is going to look after her.'

He meant me. He was looking at me when he said it.

'And . . .' – he leaned forward – '. . . I can see you love her.'

No, no, I didn't really. I was just being nice.

'Yes, she's very practical, isn't she.'

'Oh yes, that's one of her strongest points.'

'We're just going to sail down the Stour as far as Manningtree.

You have a house down there, don't you? Then we can turn around and go back to Ipswich.'

'Yes, and actually I'd better get back to the house. I mean, I did say I would do something with my wife this afternoon.'

'What was that?'

'Something important. I've just remembered.'

'Well, I suppose we could drop you off over at the pier in front of Shotley.'

'Yes.'

'I'm not sure it's easy to get ashore there.'

'Yes it is. It's easy. I'm just ringing my wife on the mobile phone. She'll come and pick me up, don't worry.'

So we picked up a mooring with great difficulty and his charming son, who had been aboard to help sail the boat, launched the cumbersome rubber dinghy and rowed me, with two silly little paddles that make you row like a speeded-up film except that you progress like a slowed-down film, especially if you've got a passenger weighing down the back, across to the dank pier in front of the pub.

'Thank you so much for showing me her . . . She looks so lovely from here . . . I certainly will be thinking seriously about her . . . No, no, don't worry about me. My wife is on the way.'

We came to rest some 5 feet from the muddy shore. I leaped, the rubber dinghy moved backwards and my foot plunged through the water and into the black stinking mud, half-way up my ankle. I skipped forward. The other foot plunged in.

'Are you all right?' asked Mike's son.

'Yes. Yes. I'll just get my shoes off. Ouch. Ow! Quite a lot of shells. No, I'm fine!'

I got to the bank and waved the two leather mud balls off my feet at Mike.

'Thanks for the trip! I'll be in touch.'

Shortly afterwards I made an offer on *Undina*.

12. By Canal to the Ostsee

Back in Brunsbuttel that night, Baines, Bob and I sat in a pizza house. I had drunk ten double espresso coffees in a variety of cafés. Now, instead of being very, very tired, I was very, very tired and hugely agitated at the same time. Rick had gone back to the boat to sleep. In fact, he had kept out of the way for most of the day. The owner of the pizza house put menus in front of us.

'We've got to get rid of him,' I announced.

'Well, the trouble is, he thinks he saved our lives,' said Bob.

'Yes,' said Baines. He was, as ever, anxious to be fair and solicitous for my welfare too. This made me even more agitated. Another cup of espresso arrived. 'But Griff, you have to be honest: you did give in to him.'

'It wasn't a question of giving in. It was like being with a man at the edge of a pavement on a dark night when there's no traffic to be seen in any direction who refuses to cross the road in case something comes. What was I supposed to do? Knock him out? Was there any traffic when you crossed the entrance to the Jade?'

Baines looked thoughtful. 'No, no. There was nothing, no. We didn't see any ships until just before you came on deck.'

'It's these courses! It's these fucking courses!'

'No, no.' Bob was outraged on behalf of the courses. 'No, I don't think he's been on the courses. That's the point. I think he's doing it entirely off his own bat.'

'Well I'm inclined to give him some cash for a bed and breakfast and point him in the direction of Hamburg.'

'What happens in Hamburg?' asked Bob.

'That's where the plane goes from on Sunday. There's plenty to amuse him in Hamburg. He can spend a couple of days there until the flight leaves.'

'That's not a bad idea,' said Bob. 'How far is Hamburg from here?'

'It's too late to go to Hamburg tonight,' said Baines.

'Is it? Oh. OK,' said Bob. 'Even by train?'

'I think so,' said Baines. Bob shrugged and lit a fag. 'The best thing, the thing that would be most sensible, would be for us all to eat this meal and get some sleep,' Baines said and he called the waiter over. 'Can we order?' he asked.

The waiter looked at his watch. 'No,' he said. 'It is too late!'

'But you gave us the menus.'

'But then you talk.'

'Yes, but we were just filling time waiting for you.'

'The chef has gone.'

Bob got to his feet. 'There's no problem,' he said, 'I've cooked pizzas in this sort of place myself. I can do them.'

'No, no.' He made us three disgusting slices of cardboard covered in red paste. By the time they arrived, I was asleep on the vinyl gingham tablecloth.

We were on to the *Imray Baltic Pilot* now: a guide to the Baltic that crammed the whole of Sweden, Latvia, Lithuania, Estonia, Finland, Poland and Russia into a book the size of a comic annual. It suggested that we visit the British Services Yacht Club in Kiel, so at four o'clock the next afternoon, we motored through a white, dead calm towards our first 'Baltic mooring'.

Common throughout what the Germans call 'the Ostsee', a Baltic mooring is made up of two posts and a jetty. It's a simple proposition. You guide the boat between the posts, loop a rope over them as you pass and then continue towards the jetty, bringing the boat to a stop by reversing the engine or pulling on the ropes, close enough to the jetty, anyway, for a man at the front to step ashore and tie you up, but not so close, obviously, that you hit it with a sickening crunch. It's a delicate matter of judgement, really.

I favoured the boat. I couldn't see the front from where I was, anyway. As soon as we got within 6 or 7 feet of the thing, I put the engine in reverse and expected Bob to leap for the shore. He, on the other hand, favoured the man. He refused to budge from his perch until he could drop with a dainty trip on to the decking. Between us, it was an achievement if we reached land at all.

Later we worked on a system. 'Bob,' I said. 'You must indicate to me how far away from the jetty we are.'

'OK,' said Bob. From then on, as we approached, he stood with his hands stretched wide apart like a crucified scarecrow and gradually brought them together until we hit the jetty with a sickening crunch.

We'd left Brunsbuttel at an itchy seven in the morning, and had hardly expected to get to Kiel so early in the day. But miles of rather pleasant green countryside passed by on either side at a terrific speed. The occasional large ship rumbled through. The canal was deep enough for several thousand tons. It was wide and had big stone banks.

'Bang, crash, smash!'

I was underneath with my head in an interesting hole I had discovered under the pilot berth. 'What's happening?' I started up. The wire that held the centreboard was slack. There was a rumbling and clanking sound from beneath and the boat was juddering.

'I don't know.' Bob was looking around the immediate scenery in a contemplative manner.

'We're touching!'

'Are we? Oh, is that what it is?'

'Pull her out further into the middle of the canal.'

'OK.' He took a drag at his cigarette and steered a little into the canal. 'I thought you'd want us to keep out of the main shipping lane.'

'Well, yes, but stay in the canal. We can't go in the fields.'

'Oh.' He paused to ponder my contradictory instructions. 'OK.'

Baines and I had decided to tidy up the entire boat. I had owned the thing for seven months. Perhaps we should sort out what was in it. The lockers in the cockpit were certainly stuffed with mysterious equipment: not one, but two hand-held syringe-like pumps; a sad-looking dan-buoy; a large pure white soft bimini sunshade (presumably dating from her previous existence in the Bermudas); a heavy black bucket made of recycled car tyres; several lengths of bamboo; a brush with seven remaining bristles. But I was particularly exercised by the ropes and cordage. So I spent most of the journey along the Kiel Canal half-tipped into a hole, pulling out hanks of rope. This is the sort of job that starts as an irritation, becomes absorbing and ends as a glorious obsession. The previous owner shared my predilection for gigantic quantities of not-quite-useful-enough rope.

New rope, in a coil, is seductive, slippery, fresh. It smells good. It feels clean and malleable. In short lengths, it has a heft to it, which is nicely satisfactory. I'd far rather hold a nice big bit of rope than a baby, myself. And look! It's dramatically reduced in price. Yes, it's pink and has green bits woven into it. But, surely, we can make use of an extra 7-metre length of rope, can't we? So it goes back to the boat with all the other amazingly good 'finds', in a mess of aniline spaghetti.

'Crunch, crash, bang, rattle!'

The wire from the centreboard went slack, the boat juddered.

'What's happening now?'

'Search me.'

'Bob, we're going aground again.'

'Are we? I don't see how we can be.'

'But look, we're right close in to the bank again. Ducks are carrying their nests into the trees.'

'We weren't that close. There's a shopping trolley or something back there.'

'Yes. It must have fallen off the *Bismarck*, when it came through here!'

I went on deck, got out my mobile phone and telephoned my office in London.

'We're on the Kiel Canal,' I told them.

'Right.'

'Any messages?'

'No. We didn't even know you were away. What's that noise in the background?'

'Um. It's "God Save the Queen".' It was being played over a loudspeaker system.

'The pilot-book says that it's a tradition,' Baines told us. 'They play the national anthem of every boat that passes through.'

'We've got some courtesy flags,' Bob pointed out. 'We could fly different ones and pass back and forth and get them to play a medley.'

But we were nearly at the end. It started to rain. The big locks to let us out were deserted. We tied up, and while we waited for them to fill, I walked up into an office building and paid our fee at a booth. Five minutes later, we were in the Baltic.

'British Services Yacht Club, British Services Yacht Club, British Services Yacht Club! This is yacht *Undina*, yacht *Undina*, yacht *Undina*.'

Bob was a licensed radio operative. He had a bit of paper to confirm this. The boat had another bit of paper, which told us that we were allowed to have a radio at all, but Bob was the authorized user. He paused. Then he remembered.

'Er . . . over.'

The year before, we had known how to use the radio, in a general sort of a cack-handed way. But since then, Bob had picked up all sorts of prescriptive information and now, frankly, we were scared stiff of the thing. After all, the open channel, channel sixteen, was listened to by all the professional seamen in the area; all the captains, the lock operators, the pilot boats, the coastguards and the police.

'Go on, then,' I said to Bob. 'Give them a squawk or a bell or a "ccccccccch" or whatever.'

'Yes. Very simply done,' said Bob. But I knew. For all his tosh about call signals and frequencies and the correct order, I could see he was rehearsing under his breath. When he finally spoke, he sounded like something out of *In Which We Serve*.

'British Services Yacht Club, British Services Yacht Club, British Services Yacht Club! This is yacht *Undina*, yacht *Undina*, yacht *Undina*. Over.'

I had never heard him talk like this before. He had a radio modulation in his voice. Up and down went the mellifluous tones.

'Oh yeah. Hello. This is the British Services Yacht Club. What's up? Over.'

The voice at the other end was more down-to-earth.

Bob raised the mouthpiece. 'This is yacht *Undina*. Request berth for the night, over.'

Now he had turned into Tony Hancock.

'Yes. OK. No, that's fine. Yeah. Come straight ahead. There's plenty of space.'

'Wilko.'

'Yes, wilko. What name again?'

'*Undina*, over.'

'Can you spell that?'

'Um . . .'

Bob had committed the radio alphabet to memory.

'Uniform . . .' There was a long pause. 'Nurse . . . no, not nurse. Number. Nelson. No. I'll come back to that. N, anyway. India. Yes.' There was another long pause. 'India . . .' The code was stuck up on a piece of paper by the transmitter. I tapped it. He searched it frenziedly. 'Delta!' he whooped. 'India. Nelson . . . Alpha. November! November. Sorry. I'll repeat that. Uniform . . .' He stopped again. 'November. India.'

'OK, *Undina*, come up to the office when you get in. Bye.'

The club was like any other marina, a series of grey posts and walkways. We crunched into our Baltic mooring, next to an expensive racing boat.

The clubhouse was a modern white building, like a social club. There were showers, a large bar and offices run by jolly women. A board, inside the entrance, advertised the club committee. The Commodore, in one of those tightly fitted berets, and even tighter camouflage fatigues, was vaguely recognizable from the First Gulf War television show. The bottom row featured a silhouette, complete with military cap. (We were told it was one of Military Intelligence and he wasn't allowed to actually show his face for security reasons. 'Does he come to committee meetings under a hood?' asked Baines.)

A little bloke with a beard came bustling down the corridor. He had twinkling eyes and a giggle in his voice, and welcomed us effusively. Baz was delighted that we'd come from Kent because he was from Gillingham. He'd grown up near the Swale. 'We didn't have any boats or nothing. We just had old pallets or floating rafts. You know boys. Anything to get afloat. And then I got involved in the sailing business with the army. So when they set this up and I was up for retirement, they said I could be the chief civilian instructor and asked me to set up the training programme.'

The British army is the only army that includes sailing as part of general training for troops. The line of identical sailing boats in the dock was their sail-training flotilla. 'The thing is that it has to be life-threatening in some way,' Baz explained. 'So we have an arrangement where we go whatever happens. Even if it's blowing force nine we have to leave. And most of them have never been on a small boat before in their lives.' He laughed uproariously.

Baz, a civilian now, could find himself in command of a major general or a brigadier or simply a group of squaddies on basic training. That afternoon they were waiting for the paratroopers. 'They've just been in Afghanistan, so they'll be a little bit lively.' Baz laughed and scratched his beard. 'There'll be a bit of a piss-up here tonight.'

We presented our passports and filled in a form. We were free to use the facilities.

'What are you lads going to do with yourselves, then?' Baz giggled.

'How far is it to Hamburg?' Bob asked. 'We were wondering if we could get there by train and then come back late tonight.'

'Ooh-er,' said Baz. 'Well it's possible.' He smirked at us. 'There's quite a big red light district in Kiel, you know. You don't have to go all the way to Hamburg.'

The modern centre of Kiel (its heraldic motif, a nettle leaf) was prosperous and soulless. The bleak pedestrian walkways with their ageing planning solutions were as characterless as their English equivalents. There was no record of the past. It had been wiped away by the war (80 per cent of the city was destroyed and then rebuilt, hence its ugliness). But no sense of an imaginative future either. We tried to get into a beer cellar, and stood for a while amongst crowded tables and upturned barrels, while waitresses carried steins of beer to self-consciously noisy groups. 'Mebbe I didn't luz you, kvite as ozzen as I should hev.' The singer, in a white cowboy hat, worked his way through a couple of country standards before we were finally told that the place was full, and all the tables were reserved.

Back at the British Services Yacht Club the paratroopers themselves seemed to be drinking quietly and purposefully at coffee tables. Archie, one of the instructors, in a tight turquoise polo shirt, was the commander of *Flamingo*.

'I love that boat. I love it,' he told me.

Hermann Goering had loved it too. *Flamingo* was the last remaining of six 10-metre yachts supplied by Hitler for the 1936 Olympics to each of his services. Goering had sat in its polished cabin, when it was owned by the Luftwaffe, and tried to work out a way of getting it for himself, without success. At the end of the Second World War, an enterprising brigadier had come down to the waterside in Kiel and found all six of these beautiful boats tied up against the quay. He promptly requisitioned the lot as war booty, and they were divided up between the occupying British services.

'Eventually, the Germans protested, so a deal was made and we actually paid for them,' said Baz. They were kept at the club along with the private boats of service officers. 'There were a lot more boats here a few years ago, as you can imagine,' he went on. 'We're not far from the border here, you see.'

He meant the border with East Germany. Here, for the first time, we ran into one of the elements that had defined the Baltic over the last fifty years, and would undoubtedly define the next fifty: the maintenance and then the dismantling of the Cold War.

'That's a great place.' Baz pointed to Bornholm on a map on the wall. 'You'll love Denmark. You'll love the Danish people. They're really nice. In fact, I married one.'

He introduced his wife, Maria.

'I have to go back to England for Christmas,' she said. 'And the English are all like the Danish.'

'Oh, that's very true,' said Baz. 'We miss out the Deutschers. We head straight up to Denmark, don't we, darling?'

'Yeshh.' Maria's face squeezed into a rubber ball of smiling, and in a fit of fellow good feeling I invited everybody back to *Undina*.

Bob and Baines were sitting at the cabin table. They had just started a game of backgammon. Rick was bright-eyed.

There were ten of us now in the tiny cabin: six crammed around the table. The rest were wedged in where they could. I sensed, from Bob's and Baines's guarded expressions, that they'd had enough of the military two step, but we made coffee and handed round drinks.

'Oh, aye.' Archie was peering at his cup. 'You've got metal cups.' He winked at his German girlfriend, the other instructor and Baz. 'We don't even have those in the army any more, do we?' Baz chuckled.

I chuckled. 'Oh no. We're pretty basic aboard here.'

'Aye.' He gazed around with the impassive heavy gaze of a man whose brain has been forced through sixteen bottlenecks. Something was just stopping him from saying what he really thought, but only just.

Suddenly, or as suddenly as he could manage, which was pretty ponderously, he turned to his German girlfriend and pointed at me. 'Do you know who this is?' She shook her head. 'Ah, but we all do. But you don't.' She shook her head again. 'Well if you were English, you would know who this person was.'

She looked more bemused. 'I have to work in the morning. I should go.'

The other instructor finished his drink. Baz scooped up Maria and they all left, except Archie. Archie waved a big hand. 'I'll just finish this. I must get to bed.'

I looked across at Bob, who was chuckling like a village idiot.

'Well, Archie, I agree. We've got a bit of an early start in the morning.'

'Me too. I'd better be going myself pretty soon. I had.' His face contorted into a mask of pained concern and he helped himself to another drink which Bob had put on the cabin table in front of him.

'But she's a lovely boat.' He got more emphatic. '*Flamingo* is a lovely boat. But in the end you know . . .' Was this the end? '. . . it's all up to you. You.' He stabbed a finger in my direction and got to his feet. He stood and for a moment ran his hands over the shiny mahogany of the cabin superstructure. He furrowed his brow and looked around like Robert Shaw sniffing for shark in *Jaws*. 'This is the cabin?' he said finally, belched, turned and went forward. Half an hour later we got him off the boat and he staggered away up the pontoon.

At six on the dot, Baz came whistling down the dock and I got the weather forecast. I didn't need to go out. I could hear it being shouted across the pontoons.

'Four, five metres per second,' hollered Baz at the instructors. 'Gusting up to ten in the afternoon.'

Was it only four days since the dark start on the Swale? A single night in Borkum. A night in Brunsbuttel. A night in Kiel. The next leg, drifting around Denmark, would give us time for wasting time. I felt sure of that. But, for now, we started the engine and motored on; out into the grey light of the Kiel Fjord towards a busy traffic of military ships, tugs and yachts. Ahead of us there were two big Baltic traders, working sailing boats 100 feet long and probably 100 years old, with all sails set, heading for Flensburg too. We had to get to the regatta.

13. The German Race

On the back of the March 2002 edition of *Classic Boat* magazine there was a black-and-white photograph of a glamorous yacht, in full sail, next to a prominent picture of a spoon. At first, I had taken it to be an optimistic buck-the-trend promotion for cutlery ('Watches, cars, mortgages: advertisers, these boat owners do have interests other than bilge pumps!'). But an editorial inside made me look more closely. It was for an annual regatta in the Flensburg Fjord, in the Baltic, sponsored by Robbe and Berking, the noted cutlery manufacturers.

'Do you speak English?'

'A little.'

'I am telephoning about your advertisement in *Classic Boat*.'

'Oh, I see. Wait a minute, please. I will connect you to Mr Berking.'

Mr Berking himself! Roger Cook and Michael Moore go about these things the wrong way. The quickest way to reach any managing director is obviously via his hobby.

'Can I just apologize at the start. I don't speak any Danish,' I began.

'OK,' said the voice at the other end. 'Yes, I am sorry. My Danish is not good either.'

'Well, you speak very good English.'

'Thank you. You are Danish?'

'Me? No. I am ringing from England about the regatta. I thought I was telephoning to Denmark.'

'No, no.' There was distinctly less avuncular warmth in the tone. 'Flensburg is in Germany.'

'Oh.' Damn. Flensburg was up the neck of the bit that joined the head of Denmark to the flabby body of the European mainland. I had assumed that that far north, it would be in Denmark. In doing this, I was repeating an error that had led to several wars, countless casualties and some very long and boring history lessons about Schleswig-Holstein. I just hoped that my 'oh' hadn't sounded too disappointed. I sensed that the wounds were still raw.

'We are on the border with Denmark, but we are German.'

'Of course, yes. I was hoping to bring my boat to the regatta in Flensburg.'

'I see.' There was no outward show of enthusiasm for this proposition. Perhaps he'd hoped I was going to order a canteen of cutlery. 'You would have to be invited,' Mr Berking continued flatly.

'*Ach so*. I see.' I didn't mean to say '*ach so*'. It just came out. Years ago, to help me with German O-level, I'd been sent to Wuppertal to see how dull Germany could really be. I stayed with Doris, our old au pair, and her husband Heinz, and in a bid for colloquial chumminess prefaced every remark with '*ach so*', picked up, I suppose, from listening to Second World War films, and not listening to Mr Kidd, the German teacher, although he always maintained a convincing impersonation of a villainous SS officer. Finally Doris had to intervene. 'Plis, plis, plis, Griff!' she suddenly burst out one morning at breakfast, 'we must have less of this "*ach so*".' And now here it was again. Surfacing in the swamp of embarrassment like a bloated corpse.

In Germany, Mr Berking paused for a few seconds.

'Plis, tell me,' he said, 'what sort of a boat do you have?'

'I hope she qualifies. She was built in 1956. By Abeking and Rasmussen. They are German.'

'I know.'

'Yes. She's forty-five feet, that's in metres . . . er . . . eleven, is it? No, three tens are thirty, obviously, so . . .'

'Perhaps you could give your address to my secretary and we will send you all the forms.'

As we sailed up the rocky north German coast through the Kieler Bucht towards the mouth of the Flensburg Fjord, the wind freshening a little with every hour, Baines at the helm, me gently (no really) instructing him on the finer points of sailing to windward, I had time to reflect that we appeared to have made it. Like most achievements it had been a largely insensitive, bludgeoning process. But now we had no more than 15 nautical miles to go to the great regatta. We had time in hand. The festivities started the following day. The race the day after that.

I had never, despite sailing boats since the age of four, taken part in a proper race before. Come to think of it, I rather despised the whole idea. But I had flown out a crack crew to meet us. (I may have despised the whole idea, but I had no intention of losing.) My brother Bill, whose idea of a fulfilling weekend was navigating a 32-foot racing machine across to Dieppe, eating a *croque monsieur* and then hurrying back in a freezing gale, was booked to bully us up. Tim Blackman, the founder of the British Classic Yacht Club, and a previous owner of *Undina*, won every race he entered. My wife was accompanying my mother, who, though no expert on any part of racing at all, but fancying the trip, had come over on the ferry bearing part of a secret weapon.

I had booked them hotels and hired a car. I had to admit to myself, as the wind blew up and we heeled over a little more, that it was quite probably this financial commitment to the Flensburg weekend that had driven me on all along, but no doubt Captain Scott was thinking about those cheques for oil-cloth and ponies when he decided to make his final push to the Pole.

The wind may have been increasing, but the sun was shining. Distant sandstone cliffs were glowing warmly. What we needed was to get across to the other side of the mouth of the fjord, some 3 or 4 miles further on, turn west and then tack up to our destination. And we were blasting up the shore. Looking down into the cabin, in a smug mood, I suddenly became aware that there was a substantial quantity of water sloshing around. And it was inside the boat.

All wooden boats dry out on land. *Undina* had been in a shed for seven months. The planks in her hull had lost their liquid content and consequently shrunk. Inevitably, back in the water, she was prone to leak a bit. But now there was a large splashy puddle rising over the top of the floorboards. We were heeling over into the wind for the first time, of course, the sides had yet to swell up after their time in the shed, I thought, but all the same . . .

'Baines . . .'

'Yeah?'

'Is the pump working?'

The pump usually worked itself, with a little floating electronic contact lever. It was right down at the bottom and centre of the boat. The boat's hull was like a wine glass with a hollow stem. As soon as we put her over on one side, the water ran into the tipped wine bowl and out of reach of the pump in the stem. This was all very well, except that there was now enough water to fill a barrel.

We were crashing into seas now. The waves were sluicing across the deck. 'Oh . . .' I looked again. There was now also a significant amount of liquid coming in from above.

I clambered down. The sea was spraying in and around the boat; through windows, deck-fittings and the sides of the cabin. Gouts of sea were jetting from the seams of the hatches above our heads, which were fully closed, but nonetheless leaking. By the side of the navigation station, next to the horrendously expensive navigation equipment and directly above the staggeringly expensive, newly installed iridium telephone, there appeared to be a dribbling tap of water. Trying to get a foothold on the increasingly slippery floor, I put out my cupped hands to catch it. They overflowed within seconds. And still the water was rising around my feet.

It was only water. I didn't at any point believe that we were going to sink. But things were getting wet: bedding, clothes, books and papers. Perhaps more annoyingly, electrical circuit boards were getting wet. I told myself they were replaceable. When the locker under the sink suddenly flew open and a dozen saucepans went crashing across the floor, it was only a noise. Indeed, it offered an opportunity. I wedged one under the dribbling tap.

No, my sense of growing, gnawing despair was not because of any of this, directly. We all had our problems. Particularly Bob, who later told me that he lost nearly three packets of duty-free cigarettes. But for me, it was the difference between a guest's irritation at a wall falling on his bed and the owner's despair at his house falling down. After all, I had had this boat refitted in Kent . . . It was at this point, or thereabouts, that the squall struck us.

High winds at sea rarely seem to blow continuously. Rough weather is generally a buffeting, constant, noisy clatter. But every now and again, the whole system decides to gather itself up and really whack it out. In this case, what was already a strong wind instantly became a violent and furious wind. The tail end of the massive storms which had been passing across southern Europe below us, now flicked around and whipped across our faces.

The force of the wind knocked *Undina* sideways. The decks on the starboard side went down into the water and white foam charged along, roaring around the bottlenecks of the rigging and surging up on to the afterdeck. This was the only place where there were no leaks. Instead of clearing out back into the sea, the various bung holes and drainage pipes were hardly functioning at all, and the aft deck, like everywhere else in the boat, was suddenly wallowing with water.

'Let her go into the wind!' I shouted to Baines as I scrambled along the vertiginous deck to get back to the helm.

Baines didn't have to help with the wheel very much. The boat had turned of her own accord and, now, the sudden cacophony of the blow was joined by a cracking, banging and jerking of the rig. The wind stopped pushing into the sails and caught them like rags. The huge, heavy boom was flung around like a drumstick. The noise was incredible. The sails flogged and whipped as if in speeded-up motion.

'We have to get some sail in!' I yelled. 'But, Baines, don't let her . . .'

I was too late. We had swung too far. Instead of holding into the wind, she was inexorably turning through 45 degrees. The bow of the boat, rising and falling into the steepening chop of the sea, was circling round. The wind got into the other side of the front sail: 'whoompf', it banged into an exploding bag of cloth.

Glancing down, I caught sight of a tidal wave of knee-high water rushing across the cabin as we leaned the other way. Looking up, and across what was still a bright, sunny bay, I saw one of the

100-foot Baltic traders, with all sails set, heeling right over, at an absurd angle for such a big boat, and clawing her way round, like us, to head into the wind and mitigate the absurd crash of the gust.

'Bob!'

'Yes?'

'Put down that cigarette and start the engine, will you?'

'Yeah, OK. It's gone out anyway.'

Luckily, we were no more than 5 or 6 miles off the shore. The wind was blowing off it, and the seas, not having a great distance to travel, were not high. They were sharp, though, and unsettled. The engine starting could only just be heard above the racket. But it gave us enough way to head into the wind, and the roaring, flogging and whipping started again.

'Furl in the foresail!' I yelled.

Rick and Baines hauled on the rope that wound the forward sail up.

'It doesn't seem to be coming.'

'Oh, fucking hell!' Did everything have to fail?

'Pull yourself together,' laughed Baines. 'Worse things happen at sea!'

The water from the top of the waves was being blown across the surface in a sheet of spray. It was impossible to put a head above the shelter of the cabin roof and see through the drenching spume. It was as if two special effects men with buckets and a hose were standing just ahead of us, relentlessly drenching water over anyone silly enough to stand up. And still the sun shone.

'Can we get the hand-pump operating?'

Baines reached into the locker and brought out the handle of the 'whale' pump. He fitted it into a socket in the side of the cockpit and began pumping. It could lift half a bucket with each pump, but now seemed to be hopelessly weak.

'Bob, take the helm. Just keep her pointing ahead towards the shore.'

In the cabin I lifted the floorboards and lay down in the water slopping about the floor. Taking a breath, I put my head side down in the water, reached down into the guts of the boat and scrabbled around, trying to find the end of the suction tube. My freezing fingers fumbled in amongst the wooden frames, the wires and little chains that were designed to saw back and forth and free drainage holes. My forehead throbbed with the cold of the sea water. My knuckles scraped over the heads of nuts and finally closed on the boxy filter at the end of the pipe. I heaved it up and dragged for breath.

Sawdust! The box was choked with sawdust. The residue of the woodwork in the lockers and the toilet and, presumably, the deck had lain there, undisturbed, through most of the journey, but the bashing as we sailed up the coast, and the consequent incoming flood, had washed it all down to the lowest part of the boat. I scraped off the red, clogging paste and flung it in the sink. Then I leaned down and started clearing handfuls of the stuff. Up top, Baines continued to pull. The pump started drawing and eventually we heard an empty milkshake-carton sucking, signalling that we had emptied the bilge. The sea would continue to come in, but we could now equalize it.

I slid across the heaving cabin to look at the soggy chart and came up on deck. The three others were huddled down. The special effects team were still hard at work. The world was screaming.

'I think we'll try and get into Sønderborg, for the time being!' I yelled. I was miserable with a sense of failure. Flensburg was some 12 miles up the fjord, but that would be 12 miles of thumping directly into this crazy wind. Sønderborg, to the north-east, was closer and more protected.

We pounded on, taking, as it were, the right-hand fork of the channel and skirting a buoyed outcrop of rock to our left. For fifteen minutes, I crouched down, an ice-hockey goalkeeper in a fire hose, as we crunched the steep vindictive waves, bunching the wind a little in the mainsail to stop it thrashing, gradually taking the measure of the continuous howling, whipping gale. As I calmed down, I realized that the original route to Flensburg would undoubtedly settle.

The fjord was not my idea of a fjord. Years ago I had been to

Norway by sea and I recalled a giant crack in the mountains that miniaturized the liner as we edged our way in, but this Danish inlet, though cut out by the same ice-age, was a flat, estuarine thing. The banks were swelling hills of fields and woods. The waterway, a seething shower tray at the moment, snaked its way up to the German town at its head. Out here now, we were exposed. Further in, we would be sheltered.

In the bucking saloon, Rick was still hunched over the chart, still adding crosses to his already well-plotted course. He looked at me fervently. I put my hands on his powerful shoulders, moved him gently to one side and studied the chart.

'Here's a new bearing!' I bellowed up to the others. I drew the course on the chart. 'We'll head into the lee of the land up ahead. The wind will be less fierce there. We can cut through and get up to Flensburg that way.'

Rick's eyes were shiny and glazed with determination. I recognized the look. 'I need to talk to you.' He came in quite close. 'If you do this you will kill us.'

This proposition was so tremendous I gathered I would have to be careful.

'No, it's all right. I don't think that's going to happen.'

'Oh. You don't think so!'

'We'll get into the lee of the land and then cross safely to the other side.'

'You have to go back, and straight across to the channel.' He had the chart cradled in his hands. He was staring unblinkingly at me, presumably willing me to see the error of my decision, and speaking quietly. But even that was rattling. 'You see those figures there?'

He looked at me with widened eyes, as if to fix my attention. I nodded and swallowed. He was pointing to the soundings on the chart of the route I was going to take. They read 6.7 and 7.5 and so on. 'You know what those figures mean, do you?' With each question he edged his face further forward into my face. We were slightly in danger of rubbing noses.

'Yes, Rick,' I whispered, 'they indicate the depth of water.' I quite shocked myself by staying moderately calm myself. Now we were having a 'who can stay the most calm competition'. 'Even with the centreboard fully down we draw less than three metres. There is plenty of water.'

'There are two figures there. The first indicates the depth of the water. The second the height of the waves.'

'The height of the waves?'

'If you take us there we will be sunk by seven-metre waves.' This was so extraordinarily preposterous that I found myself gazing back vacantly as I tried to think of a way of replying. The two of us stood crouched in the cabin, clutching on, the boat heaving around us, staring at each other.

'No,' I said finally. I decided on simplicity. 'Rick, if that were the case, then these figures here just next to it, they would indicate that there was a one-metre wave, would they?' I pointed to other figures – 6.1, and 5.2.

His huge eyeballs never flickered. 'Have you even heard of a Baltic surge?' he said with impressive gravity.

'Rick, a Baltic surge only happens after a prolonged period of storms with winds blowing in one direction,' I said. 'Honestly, this squall is the first big wind here for weeks and it has only been blowing for the last hour. In my opinion, it is unlikely to have drained the Flensburg Fjord by five metres.'

'In your opinion.'

'Yes.'

'So you take responsibility for doing this.'

'Yes. I do. Yes. I take total responsibility for this.' I had at last become Jack Hawkins in *The Cruel Sea*. I could see closure. 'I have, in fact, taken total responsibility for everything else on this trip. I have heard what you said and, if it's all right with you, I'd prefer to be on deck.'

Rick said nothing by way of reply, but stared hard and breathed deeply and worked his eyeballs some more.

Whimpering, I heaved myself on deck. We motored on. We approached the end of the peninsula ahead. As one would expect, the seas calmed down. The wind itself dropped a little under the shadow of the hills on shore. We crossed over and sailed into calmer waters, over the spit and through the channel, without incident. The depth at one point went down as low as 4½ metres, but the motion was easier. And finally the squall died. It had blown for about two hours. We settled into a well-buoyed channel and were joined by other boats, all making their way up the fjord, some of which waved cheerily at us.

I gave the helm to Bob. Rick joined him on deck. Disconcertingly, he seemed thoroughly bucked by the experience. I went below, pulled off my soaking wet clothes and quivered for a bit.

14. Glowering

Flensburg was only just in Germany. The fjord was the border. The Germans and the Danes had fought over Schleswig-Holstein for years. Palmerston once said only three persons understood the political issues surrounding the area: 'One is Albert the Prince Consort, and he is dead, the other is a German professor, and he is in an asylum, and the third is myself, and I have forgotten it.' I never understood it either during O-level history, but Erskine Childers probably thought he did. *The Riddle of the Sands* started here, and there are dark hints in the opening chapters about the thousands killed by German aggression, lying in the cemeteries on the northern banks.

Flensburg was preoccupied with period sailing when we arrived. Hundreds of polished masts cluttered the skyline. Authentic rigging flapped blankly in the wind. People made final adjustments to their imitation canvas sails and stood, plates of food wedged on their paunches, staring up at complex, out-of-date tackle above their heads. Large antique vessels, arriving late, tried to lever their polished noses into the gaps between lavishly varnished overhangs and glittering taffrails, or drifted sideways across heritage rat-lines and mahogany boarding ladders. Miracles of sanding and carpentry, piloted by elderly husband-and-wife teams, slunk in under the mooring ropes and tied up in the shallows behind jetties. Then their owners dragged out tiny camping stoves, and erected tents over their fine, over-long booms. The former rum capital of Jutland had become a Vietnamese boat city of classic yachts, in preparation for its regatta.

My wife Jo was waiting for us. She had brought my mother over on the ferry, and they stood on the jetty with a huge bag they had lugged over, containing the 'snuffer' for my new gennaker (the secret weapon). It was a piece of white, opaque plastic shaped like a Florida matron's sun-visor, but about the size of a plastic armchair. The gennaker, which had been made especially for us back in Kent, was a large bag of a sail. It was not quite a spinnaker (the coloured balloon that you see on the front of racing boats) and not quite a genoa (a big triangular sail). It was half-way between the two – a 'gennaker', you see – and it would dramatically increase our speed.

The snuffer, for its part, went to the top of the mast as the sail was unfurled and, when it was time to finish with it, was pulled from underneath to slide down over the massive triangle, gathering it all safely in. We had not had time to try it out and here we were, planning to race with it.

To get to the shore meant clambering across a Bailey Bridge of quality superstructure. Near to the end of the little jetty on which we were moored, a shaven-headed man stuck his head out of his hatch and glowered at us.

Glowering was part of the gamesmanship of this particular event. Everybody's boat was, of course, exceptionally precious. Competition, even for mooring space, was naked and earnest. If not openly warning people against scraping their paintwork, or catching something on their vulnerable equipment, owners lay in hiding, ready to pop up and shoot an inquisitorial glare at anyone who passed.

We had occupied a parking space next to a 20-foot boat filled with young automatons. After a while they jumped on to our boat and started moving our stuff. I realized with a start that they were untying us. I rehearsed my own glower.

'Everything all right?'

'You would be better moved further over.' Another young man with longer hair was releasing our stern line.

'No, thank you. We're OK here.'

He shrugged theatrically towards his companions. I assumed a puzzled scowl of disgruntlement. We were beginning to fit in.

I needed to check out the form for tomorrow's race and made my way to the organizers' hut. It was a ferry cabin, sliced off at the bottom and deposited on the dockside, and there was a queue of yachtsmen in front of me. Each was being given a set of charts, a document of some kind and their wimple – a natty linen burgee with the name of the race on it, to be flown as an identifying mark. When it was my turn, I approached the woman at the desk, and explained in halting German who we were.

'It's all right.' She stopped me mid-flow. 'I speak English. But it is quite impossible for me to deal with you now. You must come back in the afternoon.' She turned to the next person in the queue, who looked properly serious, and issued him with his details.

'They don't seem very pleased to see us,' I said. Back at the boat, Tim Blackman and Baines were bonding by dismantling the water system together. Baines was half in the bilges pulling up bits of piping.

'Look at this.' Baines held up a hand happily. There was a pile of white sludge dropping through his fingers. 'The entire fresh-water system is blocked.'

Tim chuckled expansively. 'And at some point we'll need to pressure-flush the entire fresh-water system. But we'll get it back working for now.' I stopped and glowered at the plumbing for a change.

I had booked a hotel for everyone (except Bob) – a modest lodge just across the main road. It had a smoked glass bar. The rooms were smothered with an alarming pastel-pink upholstery (even up the walls). There were folded pamphlets parked on every level surface, multi-patterned fitted furniture and an aquamarine nylon rug. It had no difficulty becoming the most comfortable and luxurious hotel I had ever stayed in.

The room was impossibly snug. The heat was even and serene. It was a miracle of sealed privacy. I stood and absorbed its shelter. The bed. The bed! The cheap coverlet was dry and smooth under my touch. The duvet was clean and fresh. My feet, chafed and raw with the scrub of sea water, found the smooth edges of the sheets. I lay and stretched out my back. Slipping gently into that ordinary hotel bed was arguably the most sublime experience of the entire four-month trip.

But that was still to come. The room had another purpose. Before we left England I knew that we would have to equip ourselves with charts. I had visited an ordinary chandler with the expectation of disappointment and they had obliged me. They had nothing further north than Holland. They had recommended me instead to 'Small Craft Deliveries' in Melton, near Woodbridge in Suffolk.

So, on an industrial estate, surrounded by industrial gardens where no one ever went except the gardeners, I entered a room in 'Small Craft Deliveries' lined, like a baker's, with narrow-shelved drawers. In this cramped space – a prefabricated shed in the corner of a suburb of a small town – was collected the entire documentary evidence of a once-great maritime power. Each tray, or shelf, held dozens of different Admiralty charts. They covered the entire world. Barry, who greeted me, had the attentive resignation of a man with a complex job and dithering customers.

'Is there a general book or package for the Baltic, at all?'

'Not really.'

'So I have to buy each sheet separately.'

'Yes.'

He handed me a pamphlet. I studied the list of available charts and tried to work out a pattern. Each sheet cost £15. I started to reel off the names and numbers: '2469, the Kiel Canal, 2116, Fyn etc., 2364, Lübeck etc., 2360, Kaseborg/Borgholm.' No sooner had I spoken than a sheet of paper the size of a desktop came wobbling across the room towards me.

The owner of 'Small Craft Deliveries', Mr Clarke, had, as you might expect, been a delivery skipper, in the days when Suffolk ship building had still produced small ferries and supply ships. He had originally had the charts for his own use and, as the orders faded away, he had turned to selling them to others. As a further service, he handled corrections to the charts as they were issued – and they were issued weekly.

A buoy might be moved in the entrance to the Orinoco. A sandbank could shift in Chesapeake Bay. He and his assistants went through every one of the thousands of maps they had in stock and laboriously pencilled in the information they received. For particular clients, stocks of charts were brought up to date and passed on to ships at sea. Fifteen quid was a bargain.

'Will you need the coast up to Århus?'

I paused and examined the heap in front of me. Ten, eleven, twelve, that's thirty-six threes . . . that's £180 there already . . . 'Well, I don't know if we'll manage to get that far up . . .' I murmured. 'No, no. We won't.'

We were planning to go about 3,000 miles. Adequately supplied with detailed paper charts for any eventuality, the costs would be gargantuan. But never mind the costs. What were we proposing to do? Tow a container ship full of maps behind us? Where on earth would we put all this paper?

Barry took me into a corner and held my sweating hand. I would have all the important paper charts, for the big seas and the long distances, but for the actual close work, like Bob Dylan before me, I would forgo the folksy certainties of the old ways and go electric. The detail would be stored on a computer.

'You must have paper back-up!'

'I understand.'

'After all, electricity and water are not happy companions.'

'No, indeed.'

I left the shed in Melton with over a thousand pounds' worth of exquisite maps, rolled up in cardboard tubes.

By the time we got to Flensburg, I still hadn't managed to get my computer working, but, naturally, I had managed to ruin my precious, cartridge-paper cargo. Despite my care (I had taken them from their cardboard tubes and laid them flat under the mattresses), there had been that leak. A thousand pounds' worth of paper was now in danger of turning into blue and cream papier-mâché. (And this on top of Bob's duty-free cigarettes.)

Jo and I wrapped them in towels and cradled them along the quay, where the tideless Baltic lapped against the landing steps, over the disused railway that ran alongside the dock, across the busy road and into the hotel room. We laid some on the beds themselves. Some were dangled carefully over the towel heater. We draped a particularly beautiful, blue and cream tessellated pattern of Finnish islands over the shower curtain rail. By the middle of the afternoon, I had to enter the pristine room like a wall-paperer, ducking under '1405, German Bight', tip-toeing in the gap between '1406, Southern North Sea' and sitting on the lavatory under '2297, Stockholm to Turku'.

They dried quickly enough, but most lost their silky finish and become furry and sadly crumpled. In a few places they stuck together and a bit of the Gulf of Bothnia beyond Turku became a white, crumbly tear. Well, that sorted that. We'd just have to avoid going there.

I paid another visit to the cabin-hut. This time we were allowed to register. The woman in charge had been superseded by another woman, who was clearly even more in charge than the first woman. She was blonde and glamorous and sophisticated. Even Bob could see that. From the cavalier way she was handing out forms, it was obviously not her job to hand out forms. It was her job to be the lady of the *Schloss*.

'So where have you come from, then?'

'We have come from Britain, ma'am. From the United Kingdom.'

'Oh, you are from England. But you are going to race in the regatta,' she smirked.

'Yessum.'

'But how did you get your boat here?'

'We have sailed it here, ma'am.'

'You have sailed it across the North Sea!' She shrieked charmingly and widened her eyes for the benefit of the other girls in the cabin. It was our turn to smirk, and so we did.

'I don't believe you,' she went on. Not like 'I don't believe you!' in a sort of expansive, good-humoured American hyperbolic way, meaning 'No, really!', but in a rather curt, meaningful and dismissive way. The atmosphere in the cabin turned a little frosty. Quite how else we might have got our large sailing boat there was not clear. But we took our papers under their watchful eyes, and our 'wimple', and slunk off.

When we got back to the boat, Tim was standing on the shore looking worried.

'I don't know what's going on. But we seem to have been put in class with fifty- and sixty-foot boats.'

There was, it has to be said, a bewildering variety of tonnage seeking to take part in the massive all-comers race. The organizers had divided it up into separate classes, which would start at different times and be awarded different trophies for their achievement.

'We'll never compete with these big buggers. What details did you give?'

It was my fault. There had been a bit on a form somewhere and I had filled it in, in a frankly cavalier fashion. Three feet to a metre. She was 45 feet in length. That was roughly 15 metres, wasn't it? I mean. It was only a bit of fun.

My brother was horrified. 'She's not even fourteen point five metres.'

'She's only thirteen point seven!' Tim had raced this boat before. I could tell that he was disturbed too. 'We might be able to do something about this,' he said, looking determined. The three of us stomped purposefully back to the little cabin. The blonde lady looked suspicious again. My brother and Tim looked grim. A man in a blazer with a bemused half-smile was summoned. He looked frightened.

'There's been a terrible mistake,' began Tim. He showed him the documents and pointed at the boat. Then he pointed at me. The man in the blazer brought another man in a blazer over, and then another. They consulted their lists. With great reluctance they transferred us from the class of big ships with huge crews to the class of smaller cruiser racers with medium-sized crews. It had about sixteen boats in it. I was very pleased. It seemed a result.

'It's a calamity!' said my brother.

'It's not good,' said Tim.

'Oh.'

'I mean, it's better, but some of these boats aren't really old at all. They've got a lot of those what they call "Spirit of Tradition Boats" in the class. They'll have new rigging and carbon spars and should be given a handicap but look, nothing. It's just a straight race.'

'They shouldn't even be in the same class,' said my brother. They both frowned and scanned the blustery horizon. The nervous man in the blazer smiled.

'Well, there we are,' he said. 'But after all. It's only a little bit of fun, isn't it?'

We nodded unsmilingly and marched off.

The blond robots on the small boat next door were beginning to unload stuff. Kettles, anchors, buckets, lengths of chain, spare mooring warps, tins of food, two fire extinguishers.

My brother watched them sallowly.

'They're lightening their boat,' he explained.

Tim was rushing around now. He had a long roll of tape in his hand and was wrapping all our bottle screws and wires in white tape to stop the ropes catching on them.

'Do you want to unload any of our heavy gear?' I said lightly, joshingly, really. Tim and Bill caught each other's eyes and ground their teeth a bit.

'No, no, it's not really worth it for a boat of this size,' said Tim. 'No. No. It would be a lot of trouble.'

Nonetheless he watched the neighbours pile their outboard motor on top of their heap, cover the lot with tarpaulin and tie it up with a length of twine with distinct envy. He swung his gaze around. All along the dock purposeful men with shaggy hair were padding about, hauling on ropes and emptying holds. Some were wielding pliers and fixing shackles. Some were up their masts making tiny adjustments to their standing rigging.

'No, no,' said Tim. 'After all, it's just a bit of fun.'

We needed to buy new blocks. We had rigged our gennaker and the snuffer, but needed to find some way of controlling it from the cockpit. So we went to the chandler on the quayside and examined the options. Here were two snap blocks, made of plastic and metal. They were pulleys. The rope went through and gave the crew member a purchase. They were designed to be 'snapped' open, so that it was unnecessary to laboriously thread the rope through the holes. And they were thirty-eight quid each.

I placed them on the counter, with a couple of Tilley lamps, some screws and a pair of pliers. Other may have been emptying their boats. We were still equipping ours.

15. *Schnell, Schnell*

It was a proper June day for the race: grim, grey, with a yellow, lumpy sea, heavy, rain-sodden clouds cruising at head height and strong gusty winds. The gun was at eleven. By half past nine the harbour was seething with antique vessels, jockeying for space in the water.

Months of poring over the pictures in *Classic Boat*, where *Thenadra* or *Endeavour* thrashed it out, or *Cambria* and *White Wings* charged down to the Niolargue, had convinced me that the most important thing in racing was matching shirts. I had originally thought of entire costumes: given our 1950s pedigree, perhaps stripy matelot pullovers, reefer jackets and white ducks? Or how about blazers and yachting caps with polo necks: Tony Curtis in *Some Like It Hot*? I had glimpsed our larger rivals in the fading evening light and the 12-metres were generally equipped with well-liveried crews: matching pale orange wet-weather gear, booties and baseball caps. Some had natty, dark navy fleeces with crisp Nehru collars. One team went to sea in overalls, the budget option, like a gang of house-painters out for a spin.

So I had skulked in the Matalan equivalents in the Kiel shopping centre and browsed thrift shops in the Flensburg pedestrianized precinct. I was tempted by Day-Glo green and yellow fleeces, decorated with images of the Incredible Hulk, but they seemed a little inappropriate.

I was giving up the whole idea, when, the evening before the race, I caught sight of a flash of colour on a bargain rack, in the impromptu market that had sprouted around the dockside. It was a blue and red, laterally striped, long-sleeved tee: a sort of French look, but matching the principal colours of the boat. They would give us an identity. We could proudly go forth, as the sole representatives of British seafaring might, in a natty, uniform costume.

The next morning, as we reversed out of the berth and, caught by a sudden gust, were blown sideways into a raft of moored boats, I doubted whether the effect was quite what I had had in mind. The owners of the moored boats rushed forth, leaping to their sterns, shielding their ensign staffs and push-pits, to find our crew, smartly turned out in what appeared to be blue and red striped cocktail dresses.

Baines, a thin figure, straining to push off against the wind, seemed to be wrapped in twenty or so square metres of woolly frock. My brother Bill, a large man anyway, had compensated for excess size by wearing several layers of pullover and a couple of extra-fleecy fleeces underneath and waddled about like a pregnant budgie toy wrapped in a curtain. Bob was wearing his on his head in a Carmen Miranda turban.

We bounced off, got into forward gear and scraped the hull once or twice against the barnacled posts of our former berth. Amidst a chorus of shouting from the shore, from our own boat and from every other vessel in the harbour, I managed to haul *Undina* around and out into the narrow seaway, now thronged with boats hurrying out towards the start line some way down the fjord, all frantically pulling up sails and taking in fenders.

Motor boats crowded with spectators threaded through the fleet. Our dramatically lightened neighbour slid past on the outside, his spinnaker already set. The wind was directly behind us, blowing up the course. And the whole armada was gathering speed as it headed away from Flensburg.

We struggled with our new gennaker. A great length of yellow string seemed to be heaped on the foredeck. A sausage of white sail came out of a blue bag. Tim, Baines and Bill ran ropes up through the new blocks, round the outside of the rigging, outside the forestay and on to the clew at the back of the sail. They snapped the shiny new shackle at the head and fixed up the opaque sun-visor in its place. Then they pulled it up. With a bang, the sail filled. We increased our speed and jillied out towards the start.

I didn't want to join the yacht-racing fraternity. It seemed too dangerous. You ran the risk of turning into a man with a small head and big body who makes laborious statements of the obvious. I had made a pact with Tim. 'You helm,' I told him. 'I'll just get her out.' But as we sped down the fjord we began to pass other boats and I found I was gripping the wheel protectively.

Each section of the race was due to start at a different time. I knew the principle. We had to get ourselves into the best position for the opening shot, time backwards to calculate the speed of approach and make sure that we didn't pass over the line before the gun had sounded. The line was marked by a buoy at one end and, at the other, a committee boat, stuffed with men in blazers.

Matters were complicated by the fact that everybody else in the race wanted to achieve the same thing, and they were now all shooting about in a high wind in a confined space. They were joined by other boats, which had arrived early. And thought they might as well tack back and forth until it was their turn. And, even worse, a large number of boats who weren't taking part in any race at all, but were just out for a day's sail and, quite rightly, had no intention of getting out of the way to assist people with small heads and big bodies.

Under these circumstances (and indeed for the rest of the race down to the buoys at the mouth of the fjord and then back up, in a sort of figure of eight, specifically laid out to ensure that the boats would have to sail under every conceivable angle of the wind), the 'collision regulations' became paramount. Who had right of way? Which boat was on the starboard tack? Was it all right to come inside a boat as you were approaching the buoy? If you were both heading on, with the wind full in your sails, and one boat was overtaking the other, which boat was supposed to keep out of the other one's way?

Since the next five hours passed in a blur of near-misses and brinkmanship in frighteningly high winds, my sketchy knowledge of the exact details had to be reinforced by constant reference to my brother. But my brother seemed to have entered a world of his own. As we set off, I glanced across. There was a grim set to his jaw and a glittering look in his eye.

We crossed the line in good order. The gun went bang and,

within seconds, we were over the line and charging down towards the first mark. I looked around. We were in the middle of a fleet of elegant boats, many of a similar appearance to ourselves. This should not have surprised me. We were, in fact, in the middle of our 'class'.

A yachting race from the water is even more confusing than that most tedious of things, a yachting race on the television. On television, the boats creep along, gradually overhauling each other, but apparently doing nothing. It's the equivalent of an organized snail race. But on the water the effect is electrifying and the tension unbearable, and especially (having experienced all of one race now, I can say this with some certainty) *if you are the one doing the overhauling. Undina* sloped into the field with a steady pace that took her immediately straight up the stern of the first boat ahead. The figures in her cockpit turned and glowered at us, but we were now accustomed to Teutonic gurning.

'Just take her outside,' said my brother. 'We'll stall a little, but we're bound to get past her.'

There were other boats close too, bulging with sails like us, booms stretched out, huge balloons of spinnakers, poles swinging outboard like wayward arms.

I was not yet ready to relinquish the helm. I never did. The boat was alive and bucking forward and I wanted to point it. A slight increase in gust or falling of a wave, a tiny manoeuvre would bring a sudden huge pressure into her towering cloths and she would screw rapidly around. At the same time we passed as close to the stern of the overtaking boat as possible. It was all highly gratifying.

Now there was a narrow patch of water between the steadily moving boats away to our starboard and we swung into it. I would need to just shave the edge of the boat in front and they didn't like that. The helmsman was turning his head round to check on us. We were some 15 feet off his tail. His crew were shouting and waving us away.

'Ignore them,' said Bill.

'They're just fussing,' said Tim.

'You'll take them easily,' said Bill, and we did. We danced past them like an underpowered car overtaking a coach on a motorway.

The wind was strong. We were careering along. We had every scrap of sail we possessed strapped to the mast. 'Should we have everything up like this?' I asked.

My brother was scornful. 'With the wind behind us?' he snorted. 'Of course.'

Somewhere to my right, there was a great crack. I turned to look. The brand new thirty-eight-quid block, made of carbon fibre and guaranteed to resist pressures of thousands of tons, gave up resistance and pinged apart. I watched, startled, as, with a mighty twang, the rope flew out of the mangled pulley, jumped across the deck, and, pulled by the weight of the bulging sail, hit against a bronze stanchion – newly chromed – and bent it neatly in half.

'Gosh,' I said – or something like that. I waved a limp hand in its direction.

'Never mind that now,' said my brother. 'It will hold. We'll lose the gennaker at the buoy, anyway. Keep going! We'll deal with it later!'

We had to cross the wind sideways to the next buoy, along with everyone else in the race. Gone was the downwind rush, the easy twisting past opponents, the delicate jillocking for position. Now everybody was slithering across to the same point. Hundreds of boats altogether and several dozen in the immediate vicinity were attempting to squeeze into a single, boat-sized corner.

We were all moving sideways at a different rate, and forward at a different rate too. But those with deeper, stronger keels than us were moving sideways less than we were. It very soon became perfectly clear that we were in severe danger of sliding sideways into the boat close to and a little ahead of us, on our right.

'Pay no attention to him!' barked my brother.

'Right!' I shouted crisply back. We slid further down towards imminent collision. The faces of the rival crew were close enough to see. They were fixed in expressions of horror. 'That's because we have right of way, is it?'

'Certainly not,' replied my brother, 'but we're going to miss him.' And we did, by at least a few inches. I wondered whether I really shared Bill's confidence. I turned despairingly to Tim.

'Keep going, keep going,' said Tim.

There wasn't much we could do to not keep going anyway. The next buoy turned us further up the fjord. The wind got, if anything, a little stronger. And now there were boats: boats which we had never even seen before, zooming directly across our path, and they were on the preferred starboard tack. They had the rule of law on their side. It was our job, our duty, our profound liability to keep out of their way.

'Keep going!' yelled my brother.

We zipped across the bow of one boat.

'Keep going!' yelled Tim.

We dodged between two others. But, ahead, and down to our right was a fourth boat.

'She's lovely,' I said to my brother.

'Never mind that now!'

She was some 60 feet long, a big thing, with a white hull and little portholes and virtually nothing else visible on deck except a couple of deck-hatches. She was probably built in the 1920s. And she was coming on strongly. We were some distance away, but our two courses were converging. We could all see that we were converging and as if to give extra emphasis to the point, her crew, including a large dog, were crawling up on to the windward side, way above their exposed green bottom, to look at us, and then to start waving and gesticulating as usual.

'I'm not going to be able to get in front of her.'

'You'll go behind her. Keep going!'

Tim and Bill meant 'keep a straight course. Don't turn off, don't pull off and go downwind, because then you'll have to try and go upwind to make the mark. If we don't deviate we could make the target. Deviate and we'd lose valuable time. Don't deviate.' That's what they meant.

But all the same. The nose passed in front of us, with seconds to go, but we were charging on. We were charging rather faster, I suspect, than Tim and Bill had expected us to. The green-bottomed boat, old and stately as she was, was going rather more slowly, I suspect, than Tim and Bill were expecting her to. She was not clearing our path and we were hammering down on her. Her first mast was just to the left of our sharp, pointed battering-ram of a prow, but her second mast was obstinately still to the right and creeping past so slowly. We were heading straight for her fat, green-bottomed middle which yawed up, ever more temptingly round and fragile, like a huge white egg waiting to be cracked by our pointed spoon.

'Keep going!'

We heeled and drove forward. No more than 20 feet separated the two boats. Even Bob threw away his cigarette and turned towards me with an interested look in his eye. We were 10 feet away. The boat had still not passed in front. Now Tim, dragging his fixed gaze from the boat growing ever huger in front of us, turned to my brother with a grimace.

'Dump the main! Dump her!' shouted my brother finally.

There are no brakes on a boat. Sometimes, with the engine running, throwing the gear into reverse can slow a forward momentum: sometimes a judiciously heaved chain and anchor will bring a careering vessel to a halt. But under sail, in deep water, the best one can hope for is evasion. Dumping is apparently another option. It helps if you know what it means, of course. I hadn't a clue. I could make an educated guess.

Fortunately, Tim clearly did. At this last-minute intervention from my brother, he let go the mainsail sheet. In fact, he tossed it away in a frenzy, like a man who'd picked up a poisoned snake. The sheet rattled through the blocks, the boom flew out. The sail cracked and flapped and was instantly replaced by a flogging, bouncing wild thing above our heads.

We should have slowed. Perhaps those lightweight fibre-glass 32-foot racing skiffs which my brother had habitually raced would have skidded to a halt. But we were a weighty 14½ tons. The wind had been purposefully driving us on through amenable seas. Taking the wind out of our sails seemed to make not one jot of difference to our bumptious forward momentum; we surged onwards and forwards without the slightest hesitation.

I heaved on the helm, twisting downwards and wheeling it through my hands. The crew of green-bottom were all on their feet now. One was even holding his head in his hands. Some were reaching out. Others, perhaps more sensibly, were scuttling away along the deck rising up in front of us, as we just, miraculously, shaved under the edge of the stern, so close that we could reach out and pat their beautifully maintained taffrail. So close that I could stare into the bulging eyes of their helmsman, and nod encouragingly, as if this was what we had intended to do all along. So close we could distinctly smell the dog.

'Keep going!' bellowed Bill. The next buoy was still a few hundred yards ahead.

Undina heeled over a lot. Then she heeled over some more. We appeared to be sailing the race at a horizontal slope, not necessarily the most efficient angle.

'I can actually see the bottom through the side window,' Baines shouted out from the cabin at one point.

He was exaggerating. Tch! Baines! He couldn't see the bottom. It was far too murky. He could see water, though. He could see water everywhere. Our dried-out sides were still dried out and wet water was coming through them in earnest. As we sailed back up the fjord, tacking up towards the finish line, the boat began to fill up.

'Bill,' said Baines, 'Bill, I think we've got a lot of water here.'

'Never mind that now,' said Bill.

'It doesn't seem to be clearing with the electric pumps,' said Baines.

Bill leaned in and had a look. He let out a little yelp.

'Where's all that coming from?' he asked.

I called Bob down from the roof and sat him at the manual whale pump. 'Pump!' I ordered.

The boat was wallowing. We were heavily laden with sea water and the edges of the deck were now perceptibly digging further down into the waves.

'Does somebody else want to do this?' asked Bob.

'No.'

'I think we're leaned over so far that the pumps are out of the water,' said Baines.

It was an ignominious finish to the race. We let off some of our sheets and spilt wind. The boat lurched upright. The combined efforts of the electric pumps and the dogged Bob finally had their effect and we emptied out a bit, but we had lost most of our panache and nearly all our speed and advantage. We crossed the finish line almost without noticing.

We felt good, though. We had still overhauled just about every boat that had come into sight. We felt powerful. We felt quietly satisfied.

The results of the race were pinned up on the cabin hut door later that evening. It was like finals. A crush of chattering men in freshly donned yachting sweaters pushed forward to study the sheets of paper. They stood on tiptoes. They clambered on each other's shoulders. Bill got there ahead of me. I finally elbowed through and stood beside him.

'We came eighth,' he told me, pointing at the figures.

'Oh.' I was disappointed. 'Out of how many?'

'Fifteen or so.'

I could sense that he was disappointed too. In a sense, it pleased me. Not because he was upset, but because I thought he'd find the race an amateur event compared with what he usually did, something hardly worth bothering with, something just for show. But here he was: concerned.

'Did you think we should have done better?'

He shrugged.

We rejoined Tim. He seemed equally despondent. 'It was won by one of those Spirit of Tradition boats,' he said flatly.

They ordered beer and sat and chewed it over for half an hour. They should have put in another reef. The boat was over-canvassed. With a proper spinnaker instead of the gennaker they might have had the advantage near the beginning.

I sat and watched them and I commiserated, but I admit that I was largely gratified. Gratified they had come and gratified that Tim and Bill seemed to care. It was satisfying that they believed that we could have won. I preferred to think that some mysterious German fiddle had stolen our victory.

'We should do it again,' I said to Bob as we wandered around the dockside that night. There were a number of bars operating out of tents. He had a large German sausage covered in mustard, and he wasn't really listening. A big crowd had gathered to watch a sort of hippy marching band from Hamburg who played free-form jazz variations with extreme vigour and precision. 'It is the only race I've ever done and I loved it. Loved it.'

'My mother says that you can completely ruin a trumpeter's performance simply by standing next to them and sucking on a lemon,' Bob said.

'I'm going to look up and see if there are any other regattas we could get to. There must be somewhere in Sweden or Finland. What's the word for when you take something and race it at different meetings?'

'I'm looking for a lemon now.'

'Campaigning. We could campaign her . . . Why do you want to ruin his performance?'

'I don't. I just want to see if it's true.'

Bob stayed up all night. He didn't find a lemon. He finally managed to put off their chief soloist by standing very close and filming up the bell of his saxophone. Worn out by racing fantasies, I went back to the hotel room, where the damp charts were still gently swaying in the air conditioning, and slept.

16. Back to Unreality

On the plane back to London, for a few days of catching up, Rick was becoming an increasingly remote figure. When Baines had fought off all the other exasperated passengers to gain his hold on a row of seats, he only tried to get three. Rick was gradually absenting himself.

It was the clearest summer day.

'See there, we must have come past that. What's that?'

A benign coast twinkled in the sunlight. There were river indents and long moles below.

'Is that Den Helder?'

'It's Rotterdam and Amsterdam. The stewardess told me.' Bob was winking and gurning up the aisle.

'Oh.' We were satisfied, even though they were miles apart. But there was the Hook of Holland. And from up here, the water was taupe and the land was beige even in the sun. The North Sea seldom gets to be blue. It has a muddy, river-like, dreary quality all the time.

When I looked again, an unidentifiable edge of England was passing underneath. A great river system swirled into creeks and inlets. There was none of the neatness of a chart, or the simple straightforwardness that defines a city. Even the most chaotic bits of west London look planned and coordinated from the air. It's the true map of civilization. I hope politicians look down, like me, and marvel at the brilliant fragility of it all. But this was a primeval swamp of unformed banks and shallows.

'It must be the Walton Backwaters,' I murmured. But it wasn't. It was the Blackwater: the forgotten Essex estuary where I had spent virtually every weekend of my adolescence trapped on my father's boat.

I began to sort it out. There was the great lozenge of Mersea

Island and soon Osea, the alcoholic's mudbank, where nineteenth-century dipsomaniacs were marooned to dry out like the causeway that linked them to the land. But the creeks that writhed away from the main channel seemed impossibly wide and tortured. Too shallow to explore all those years ago, their reality mocked the acrylic colours and the strict definitions of a chart. They blended and shimmered from ochre to grey and fawn. They merged and mixed with a land the colour of rotting hay bales. I strained to spot the unvisited Northey Island, where the Battle of Maldon took place, but it was gone and the fluorescent green of lovely north Essex, Betjeman's favourite county, shone in the first scorcher of summer.

Baines had carried our damaged electrical circuit boards back to London. He offered to dry them out and try to get them working again, but he warned me that the water had in all probability massacred the interiors.

'As quickly as that?'

He showed me. The circuit boards had been dunked in the water for no more than a few seconds, but had instantly fused. They were encrusted with a yellow goo. The little metal squiggles seemed to have blended together. They looked bust to me.

Everything about the trip so far had convinced me that we needed a third, practical, person aboard and Baines was the ideal. He was technically proficient (Bob knew less than me, which was almost an achievement in itself). He was tireless (Bob had demonstrated his unerring ability to keep out of the way during any work experience). He was small (there wasn't a lot of room). And he liked to go to chandlers'. And Rick? Well, Rick had gone.

Sitting in a Costa's café at the bottom of Albemarle Street, I decided to recruit Baines over the drinking yoghurt.

'Are you up for coming back next week?'

Baines had a job. He was sound engineer on films and pop videos. It was freelance, but it meant that he worked odd days with little notice. The other pressing reason why I needed him was that Bob had decided to go to Glastonbury.

This Glastonbury was particularly special to Bob because he was taking Jack, who was thirteen. It was Bob's equivalent of a camping holiday in the woods.

I offered Baines money. It seemed only fair. I promised that, at some point, I would square it all with Bob.

'Are you going to pay him?'

'Well . . .' This was altering the entire nature of the journey. After all, Baines was an electrical wizard. He knew how to dismantle a porthole. He could scramble down a hole and mend the propeller shaft WHILE THE ENGINE WAS RUNNING. Bob, by contrast . . . Well, I was certain that he'd understand. When I brought it up. Which would have to be after Glastonbury anyway: some time in the future.

Before we left for Germany, I went down to John Fairey's pick-your-own-fruit farm in Suffolk. I wanted to pick John Fairey's brain. He'd taken a small boat to the Baltic and come back.

'Oh, it was all a long time ago.'

He handed me some punnets and I crawled along under the strawberry bushes, helpfully plucking and hulling, hoping to prompt some useful wrinkle.

'We were only allowed to take fifty pounds out of the country by the Ted Heath government, so we had to sail everywhere. Try and leave the hulls in the strawberries if you can, they keep longer. The Danes are lovely people. We arrived at one lovely island, a gorgeous place . . .'

I opened my mental notebook.

'Svaetob . . . Svetling . . . Shillting . . . something like that, I forget.'

I closed it.

'They loved the English. A delightful couple came down and invited us in for tea. He was a champion long jumper.'

I had plucked another huge ripe strawberry. The hull was dangling on the plant. I didn't know whether to eat it or throw it away.

'Then of course, the Russians had invaded Czechoslovakia.'

I hid it under the heap.

'It was quite a tense time. The Swedes were terrified of the Russians. In those days they had put, what's the word, you know, depth-charges under all the entrances to the archipelago, so that they could blow up the lot if they invaded and they thought they were probably next. And that's where we were sailing.'

'It's a bit calmer now.'

He looked rueful. 'Yes . . . I suppose so. These are lovely strawberries.'

'Yes.'

He shuffled on. 'I remember we got into a fog. Dead calm, just drifting. And a radar plane came down and circled over us and went away. Thirty minutes later a patrol boat emerged out of the mist and just lay there looking at us. We waved and hallooed, but they said nothing and went away. I'm not sure about the Swedes. Not so friendly: a lot of lovely girls taking off all their clothes and that on the beaches, though. The Danes are lovely.'

We had filled two large boxes with punnets. The weather had been wet and was now, in early June, unexpectedly hot. His farm was full of families picking away.

'I must say,' he went on, 'she's a lovely boat, though. I was quite surprised when I saw you had her.'

He must have seen me on one of my few trips out on the Orwell the year before.

'Oh. Why?'

He smiled. 'Well, you know, I didn't think you were the sort of person with the time and the patience for that sort of boat.'

'Oh.' Was I really worthy enough to have charge of this vessel? It was like applying to adopt in Brent. What did they think I was going to do? Beat her? Teach her to smoke? Leave her with a boaticidal aunt?

17. Danish Blues

On our return, Flensburg felt like the day after a party. Every vestige of the regatta had been bundled away. We paid the Captain Haddock harbour master and the professional electrician who had fitted a new battery charger and motored off down the fjord to a rendezvous with Jochen Dumker, the local wooden boat expert.

We were leaving Germany, but only just. The northern side of the estuary was Danish. The long flat land was deep green. My wife Jo had come as well as Baines. She was joining for the next two weeks and I wanted this to be a sylvan idyll.

People marry for various reasons. They take on the vicissitudes of another person's career. They share a bed and get used to unforeseen habits. But nobody should be forced to endure their spouse's return to infantile escapism. I had promised Jo a summer cruise through a wonderland of fjords. It had all looked so promising. But towering explosions of dank, grey, atmospheric bulk were loping menacingly across the emptiness. There were Danish flags flying in every garden and farmstead, but they seemed like matchsticks against all this hugeness. It was as if the processes of nature were simply an irrigation machine made to pick up water, billow it into sponges of cloud, and then dump the lot on Denmark. The decks were slippery. The gathered sail filled with water and gouts periodically sloshed on to our heads. Fingers became baggy and red. And the boat leaked.

The entrance to the little port was crossed by a swing bridge. We waited and, on the hour, it opened. It was shallow inside and we tied up where a man had been waving us in. 'You are very welcome here,' he said and hurried below.

We were moored to the private sailing jetty of a transit company in an industrial estate lined with chain link fences. Like all industrial estates there never seemed to be any industry. Nobody was around.

There were a few grey cars, parked on big car parks. It was still raining.

Jo and I walked out through a security gate into a boatyard. It was deserted too. All Denmark was shutting up, apparently, for the annual holiday, which was about to start, or had just started, depending on who you talked to. We peered into empty sheds and, at the back of a hangar, found a neat office with a glass door. Someone was on the telephone. We knocked and stood respectfully aside while he finished his call. His eyes had a haunted expression. His face was haggard. His English was not good.

'You go there. I wave,' he said morosely. 'You must go where the old boats are. Here.' He pointed down at his own quay. There were several wooden boats tied to it.

'Yes.' I apologized carefully. He looked as if he had recently suffered some terrible bereavement. 'We didn't know where to go, so we just followed the man.'

He nodded sadly.

'We have a few repairs . . .'

He looked at me with tearful eyes. 'I have been in my shed all night. I have no sleep. To finish.'

He had been getting all the Danish boats into the water for the beginning of the holiday. We were not going to persuade him to do anything to *Undina*.

'Tomorrow I take holiday. I have four children. I never take holiday in five years. We are taking a tent to Germany.'

Perhaps this was why he seemed so beaten. A tent in this weather seemed an improbable rest-cure.

'No. No. We quite understand.'

It seemed the only real help we could give him would be to go away and not torture him with the possibility of missing work. 'We were in a race . . .' I began. His eyes flashed with pain. He recoiled slightly. '. . . and I think we might have pulled the stem with these strong winds. Because the screws have moved a little.'

'It's OK.'

'It's OK. You'll look at it?'

He winced. 'No. That is a strong boat. The stem is OK. It's OK.'

'No. Fine. Good. Well you hurry along. Would you like us to lock up for you?'

He smiled wanly and we escorted him to his car. I don't know why, but I instantly felt reassured by his analysis. He must have known what he was talking about, even though his assessment had been done from 200 yards.

We took a taxi back to Germany, where we had left a rented car. This seemed a little retrogressive, but we'd needed it as an umbilical link to real, dry life.

Since the Schwengen agreement the border posts had fallen into disuse. They were still there, but you drove straight through. The Customs guards and their dogs had gone. Only a few hotels and a row of sex shops remained.

'There used to be a difference,' the taxi driver explained. 'In Germany no porn. In Denmark a lot of porn. So the Germans came here to get porn. But then they got tired of it and got their own porn. Now there are only these few shops. There were many more.'

This sounded encouraging. The initial porn frenzy quickly had given way to satiety. The tide of filth had simply run out of oomph.

Baines and I stopped the taxi at the border and got out to have a look. 'It's for research,' we told Jo, who elected to stay in the car.

Men in sex shops wear bomber jackets. There he was, loafing and leafing in the corner. The assistant had long hair and looked like someone with a temporary job. Nothing out of the ordinary there. We swaggered in as loudly as we dared.

Anal sex? A little too commonplace, sir. How about farm animals? How about men tied up with electrical wires and apparently in the throes of being throttled to death? How about men with hundreds of clothes pegs clipped all over them? Not really torture, but certainly painful. For my part, I'm as curious as the next man (who seemed to be burying his head further in his magazine), but I didn't want to look. It was about as sexually stimulating as an operation.

Oh no! Don't say that! Look over there! Operations!

The man with the long hair behind the desk was peering round a stack of 'piggy fun' to get a better look at me. Was I giving the impression that I didn't know what I wanted? Amongst such choice? Or was it that I was wearing yellow oilskins, and he wondered if I wanted a peek at his wet-weather collection.

I had been prepared for some healthy lesbo-horny-housewife-super-stud action; but with one-legged women? Oh dear. Very old men, who looked like Norman Tebbit, having sex, with each other? I couldn't look. Or the fat pink men eating what appeared to be human excrement. They were most horrible of all. Or perhaps not. I turned away and found myself looking at a grainy photograph of a woman who had turned her pudenda into a curtain rail. I looked away again and fixed my eyes on a red and hairy fleshy organ. It was Baines. He pulled a face.

'Perhaps if we ask him he'll take us round the back and show us some normal sex pictures,' he said. 'You know, under-the-counter stuff.' We brushed past the man with the bomber jacket and stood for a moment, gasping for breath, on the tarmac outside the fishing tackle shop next door.

We drove on, back into Flensburg in silence. The Saturday afternoon shopping streets were crowded with prosperous burghers. Many of them were wearing bomber jackets and perhaps thinking of one-legged elderly ladies with no clothes on covered in clothes pegs.

It would take the population of a medium-sized town like Flensburg to supply enough fat, ugly men and one-legged women to pose and photograph and staple the collection, let alone supply the market.

'It's definitely finished,' said the taxi driver.

18. Cats and Dogs

I plunked the Tilley lamps out of an oblong locker above the engine. I rattled them. They needed filling with my miniature steel funnel. It needed holding. This left only one hand to control the polythene bottle, which always caved in and blobbed a flat slick of paraffin on to the mahogany fridge-box top. (It was part of the ritual to soak it into a sideways-applied, reeking absorbent wipe, leaving an iridescent smear behind.) The lamps were from a variety of Pacific Rim manufacturers with 'spot the difference' individual design features, but they were all made of sheet tin. Even the screw top of the fuel tank was a tiny miracle of metal origami, with its twisted, indented fitting pressed out of a single plate.

I always forgot whether twisting the handle in or out brought up the wick. But with patience the flat-weave mantle wobbled up through the ovoid, down-turned bulb mouth of the cowl. The glass shade could be yanked up into the crossed wires, by its just-strong-enough metal lever. A match could be applied and a yellow crab-claw horn of light would flare, sootily, and then after a moment get screwed back to a steady warming glow.

We loved these lamps. We hung them in rows from the cabin roof, so that every time somebody got to their feet they banged their head on one. We balanced them on the cabin table and away to one side by the galley. There was one on the locker top to the forward end, one up by the stove and one hanging over the companion-way.

If it was cold, as it was in Denmark, we could put a heater on and a blast of warm air would shoot along at ankle height. There were red fleece blankets. We bought cushions and wedged ourselves into our womb of glowing reddish brown mahogany and flickering light.

'What was that?'

'What?'

'I felt a drip.'

'No it's all right. It doesn't matter.' Jo moved herself along the bunk a bit. But I got to my feet.

'Damn.'

'Mind the lamp.'

'Oh, no,' I moaned. The boat already felt like a big wet Japanese bath. The wood underfoot was slippery with humidity from the near-sinking in the race. But now there were rivulets running across it. 'This hatch is leaking!' I ran my fingers along the inside cowling. The tips glistened with water.

'Look there.' Baines pointed to the corner where a steadily bulging droplet was growing. It swelled and fell with a plish. Then a little stream, then a run of plops. Then it began to swell again. I went banging around for a torch.

'It doesn't matter.'

'Of course it matters.'

'It's only going on the floor.'

'Yes, but it makes the whole place slippery and hopeless.'

I shone the torch into the darker corners. The hatch had a central skylight. It was a solid varnished mahogany lid that fitted over a raised wooden edge. I ran my fingers over the pane and they came back wet. But it was impossible to tell whether this was from condensation or the rain.

There was another run of driblets.

'It's dripping off the other corner now.'

I took a few leaves of kitchen roll and carefully wiped the underside of the hatch, dabbing into the corners and running it along the underside of the fitting, where a perished rubber gasket was supposed to seal it. Then I stared at the edges, willing the water to seep through from a single, pluggable hole. Nothing was visible, but, already, a chain of pearly drops was forming on the underside of the fitting. A large globule fell with a sloosh.

Baines and I took the kitchen roll and rolled it into twists. 'One sheet should absorb an entire puppy's bladder,' he said.

Twelve or thirteen sheets later, we had equipped the seams of the hatch with a caulking of super-absorbent, double-quilted tissue. We used a screwdriver to tamp it into place. It ran all around the inside of the join.

'That's holding it.'

We sat down again.

'Mind the light.'

I pulled the blanket back around me and reached for my book.

'Plosh.'

A stream of dribble fell from the corner.

'No!'

'Watch the lamp!'

'Calm down. What are you doing?'

'I can deal with this.' I went up into the cockpit and leaned into a locker. The rain poured down on my back. Jo called to me from the cabin.

'You should at least wear a waterproof.'

'Never mind that now.'

I pulled out the diesel cans and the toolbox and felt down in the recess until I grabbed a roll of blue builder's rubble bags. I hoiked it up, took one, and with a knife slashed along two sides. I took the now flat piece of plastic up on the slippery roof, cleared the boat-hooks and boom gallows to one side and laid the plastic over the top of the hatch. Then, reaching round for any heavy weights on deck, weighted it down at the corners and sides.

Now completely soaking wet, I clambered back down into the cabin.

'Well you're certainly wet now. Keep away from me. Mind the light.'

I sat for a few minutes, streaming slightly. My eyes were fixed on the hatch.

'Relax.'

I hunched forward. I drummed fingers.

'Plop.'

'Christ!'

'Well it's less than before. It will stop soon.'

It did stop. In half an hour of steady observation, the drips gradually became less frequent. The little beads appeared more slowly. The muscles in the back of my neck unknotted.

'It's definitely stopping,' said Baines.

I began to breathe less stertorously.

'Yes.'

'Oh dear.'

I turned to Jo.

'What?'

'I think it's dripping in our cabin too.'

In our bunk that night, in the pitch dark and the damp air, eyes stuck open, unable to sleep, we lay waiting for the inevitable icy trickle; a sudden spattering in the face, or the spreading damp on the toes of the sleeping bag, or a clammy moisture sliding down the side of the hull to touch us with its cold fingers.

For the next few days, as we gently progressed further north, towards Kolding, where we had promised Bob we'd pick him up, we slithered about on deck, swathing the bottom of the mast in plastic masking tape, covering hatches in ripped plastic bags. Baines got out his tool-kit and completely disassembled the portholes. He produced a mastic gun and squeezed blobs of rubber around the existing perished gaskets. We sliced engine protection seals up into lengths and glued them to the underside of the hatches.

We rang Michael in England.

'You want to get hold of Captain Tolley's Creeping Crack Cure,' he told us. 'It's a liquid. You dribble it in; it works its way into the invisible openings and sets hard.'

So we tramped around more chandlers', inquiring after Captain Tolley's elixir, but nobody had it; nobody on the entire trip. One place in Sweden had once had it, but all their stocks were gone.

It became a holy grail. We longed for a sighting of this mysterious panacea. No town was too small, no capital too grand, no boat store too distantly glimpsed across a desolate marina, but we would cross to get to it: in search of a glimpse, a smell, perhaps, an empty tin of the fabled Crack Cure. Did Captain Tolley's bewhiskered mug smile reassuringly from his packaging? Was it a great can or a tiny bottle? Was it a clear liquid or a smooth paste? Who knows? We continued to leak like a wet sock every time it rained.

For a few minutes in Sønderborg it became greyish: a wan sun flickered through black clouds and lit the long wharf, the castle and the woods beyond, but it was a mere outbreak. 'It sunned,' but maybe only twice in five days. This was not a heavy, tropical long-expected downpour. It was wet, English, holiday rain.

We sailed north up past the Sønderborg Bridge and through a channel into the next fjord. The winds were light. It was better to be at sea. The rain was part of the experience. There was something magnificent about standing in a downpour, sailing down towards the massive smoking power station that marked the head of the inlet. But the aimlessness of the journey seemed to overpower me here.

The windy streets of Åbenrå were deserted. A lurid pink paver smothered all individuality. There was no road and no pavement, there was only this seamless river of puce walkway, running between ancient houses that had once been hovels and now glittered with produce and shone with new paint, as if the building crew had just popped off out of the shower.

And the statues? Just by a bicycle stand lay a carelessly discarded, large stone egg. Round the corner in a square there was a special arrangement of cut triangles, like a badly segmented cheese. On a roundabout, child-sized mannequins with outstretched hands held aloft a model of the world.

'It must be something to do with budget dumping,' Baines said. 'You know, they get to the end of the season and blow the lot on another one. "I thought we needed something to symbolize World Peace." "Didn't we get that last year?" "Yes, but this is a dove in black granite carrying a symbol of hope to the young people of the world." "OK, stick it in front of the fire station."'

But amongst the incessant drippage, one thing offered hope. On this short leg of the journey I made a critical discovery. Half-way down the fjord, tacking into the wind, still blowing from the south-west, in gentle conditions, I had opened the locker while on the port tack and stopped to stare down, mesmerized by the quantity of water pouring in through the hull.

The side of the boat pressing down into the sea was squeezing gouts of water through the planks. Every time we leaned over, another gallon poured through the seam. Sluiced, not dripped, but rushed, like a waterfall, down the smooth inside and into the bilges. It had a crest, for Christ's sake. Turning on to the other tack to get the leaking side up out of the water, I leaned over and felt along the hull with my hands. The plank was sprung. I could feel the ridge of it where it failed to join with the plank below it.

'I think I've found our leak,' I announced eventually.

The following day I woke at seven to see the Haven Kontor. He was like an English vicar with several parishes to serve: a seven-harbour man, or a five-harbour, one-marina and three-Baltic-posts man, but he was sympathetic. He wrote down the name and telephone number of the nearest wooden boat builder in Arøsund, 10 miles further along the coast.

The other thing on my immediate list was more problematical.

'You must check the rigging, after the heavy sail,' Michael had told me, sombrely, when I phoned him about the leaks.

'Got a bosun's chair?' asked Baines.

'Oh, yes.' We had. I had seen it, but never used it. 'It's very simple,' I told Baines as we stood in the drizzle, holding an arrangement of belts and webbing. 'We sit in this . . . somehow . . . and attach it to the main halyard.' The mainsail was hauled aloft by a wire. It descended from the mast top to an ancient winch with a drum brake. Release it and the sail fell quickly; a human being, of course, even more quickly.

Baines volunteered to go up in the 'chair'. He had to pull it on like a pair of trunks and struggled to insert himself, yanking feebly at some luggage-strap plastic fittings, and then hanked himself to the big rope. He nodded. I wound the winch. He lurched slowly up over the boom to the first crosstrees. I stopped.

'OK?'

'Yes.'

'There are some screws there.'

'Are there? Oh . . . yes.'

I wound him up some more.

'Just a minute.' He spoke suddenly. There was a pause. 'Let me down a bit, will you?'

I released the brake and gripped the handle fiercely, conscious that it was just a square hole that fitted over a square bolt. But Baines was a skinny runt. I let it rotate the other way several turns. He was no weight. There was another pause. 'Everything all right?'

'Er, no.'

'Oh.'

'Just a bit of vertigo. You'd better let me down, I think.'

'Oh. OK.'

I lowered him down carefully back to the mainsail, badly bagged and obstructing his easy descent. Then he got to the deck.

'I was fine, until after the crosstrees,' said Baines, panting a little. 'Then it seemed a long way down. Um . . .'

'Yes.' I had to go myself. The rigging couldn't suddenly not need doing, could it? 'I quite understand.' I was already stepping into the blue nappy.

'You can't seem to get your arse right into it.'

He was right, but it looked simple. I sort of hitched myself back a bit.

'You have to get your back right against it.'

'Yeah, yeah.'

'But you can't, that's the trouble, you feel insecure.'

No, you couldn't. I yanked it about a bit and settled my cheeks on to the edge and heaved, but I wasn't going to be able to get any further into the thing.

'I'll haul you up then.'

'What? Oh yes. Of course!'

Pish. It was my boat. I had to go up. But because it was my boat, I was the only one who really knew how the winch worked, wasn't I? But I was already being dragged up over the badly bagged mainsail, where I had to get my feet free of the running jack-stays and then sort of widen my legs to accommodate the metal bits that stick out at hurtful angles. But doing that made me acutely aware that I was hanging in mid-air in a bag with holes in it, only I wasn't really sitting, I was perched on the lip of it.

I quite liked hugging the mast. I could just get my arms and legs around it.

'Let go of the mast.'

'What?'

'You're at the crosstrees. Everything OK?'

'Yes.' I saw what he meant. I was already surprisingly high.

'Shall I keep winding?'

'Yes. Don't let go!'

'I won't let go.'

'No, don't.' He was quite right when he said it got more difficult after the crosstrees. The mast was just a big, slippery yellow pole.

He kept turning the winch. Now there were two bits of cable-like wire, jutting down diagonally to join the crosstrees, and I had to get my feet out from under them, hugging the mast in a grizzly-bear embrace at the same time, and while I did this, I felt strangely detached, not from myself, you understand, but from the mast or any other form of tangible support. I swung above the narrowing deck. I was slipping further out of the backside supporter and forward on to the flimsy-looking bright yellow webbing, which tightened around my crutch, and was held together only by those plastic clips that never seem to hold the overnight bag in place. As we got over the vertical tightropes of the stays, my shoes caught underneath them. Baines was remorselessly yanking me higher and higher.

'Yeah, yeah. Hold on a moment!' I looked down.

The boat had shrunk to a pear-shaped pear, about the size of an actual pear. She was scarcely bigger than my stuck feet. How on earth had she become so insubstantial? The mast must be enormous. If the mast was so tall and the boat so small, then my weight at the top of it must topple the whole thing sideways into the water, mustn't it? No, no. This was plainly impossible, but, strangely, that doesn't stop you thinking it, especially when you're gradually slipping out of a navy blue nappy 10 metres above a wooden deck with sharp things sticking out of it.

I was near enough at the top now.

'OK,' I croaked. I dandled a while at the wind's caprice.

'Everything all right?'

'Yes!' I clutched a bottle screw avidly. 'Yes, fine . . .' I paused for about thirty seconds, breathing heavily. 'Yes, right, I think I'll come down now.'

Baines lowered me with a professional lowerer's application. I began to enjoy the view, over the petrol station roof, towards the power station. Within a few minutes I was back on the deck. I struggled out of the bosun's chair.

'Everything OK?'

'It was tight around the crutch. It seems very badly designed.'

'No. I mean the rigging.'

'The rigging? Oh, the rigging . . . Yes. Er, fine.'

And we left it at that.

Another damp passage brought us up to Arøsund, no more than an ugly nineteenth-century hotel by a ferry stop; a shop, a couple of cafés, a big car park and a few grey houses hidden behind sopping gardens. Sometimes big lorries wheezed to a halt and lingered amongst the acres of puddles, for the flat car-ferry to Arø, a lurid green hump, half a mile away across a puke-coloured channel. Walk a hundred yards in either direction and that was it. You were in eye-poppingly green fields. Somewhere to the south was a campsite. A few holidaymakers in plastic coveralls peered out through smeared wet patches in the condensation on the café windows. We were in a Danish limbo. Neither holiday nor working week, and still the rain fell steadily.

When we pulled in to the marina, the carpenter family I had telephoned from Åbenrå were waiting for us. Mother did the books and spoke English. She was there to ensure no nonsense. Her husband and her daughter, Bernadette, who wore matching blue overalls, were the woodworkers, and they examined the boat with tender fingers and exclamations of distress. I pointed to the damaged paintwork and the peeling varnish and, over coffee, demonstrated how the hatches let in water. The mother translated to her husband, who nodded his curly grey head and pointed to bits of the interior. They exchanged looks.

'We can do all this work for you,' she said, 'but we cannot do it now. Will you leave your boat with us and we will do it in a few weeks. It is the holiday season now.'

'Yes, yes, we know.' I explained our journey and our schedule: how we meant to pick up our new crew in Svendborg and boasted about our ultimate destination in the frozen north. She ruefully asked whether we couldn't come back to them after Copenhagen and, because they were dedicated and they loved my boat, I wished we could have said yes. Their little yard was out of Vermeer. Two ancient sheds heated by antique stoves, and filled with the smell of wood shavings, opened on to a courtyard formed by a wooden fence. Inside it there were neat stacks of lumber, a half-built, wooden rowing boat and heaps of chain and mooring buoys. But I said no.

The next morning we tied up at a nearby pontoon. They lowered a floating platform and Bernadette settled herself on to it, and began poking at the seams. We found the 'bimini top', our canvas sunshade, and, pulling the boom across the pontoon, rigged it to protect Bernadette from the rain, while she pulled out the caulking and bolted the plank back to its frame.

In the corner of a field, a little beyond the edge of the marina, there was a large tent. While we waited, I peered at a poster in the café.

'Is this a circus?' I asked.

'Yes, but it has finished. Yesterday. Gone.'

It hadn't. Unsurprisingly, given the local population's indifference, that night's performance was sparsely attended. At seven, a sprinkling of camping families shuffled into the medium-sized top and, clad in a lurid selection of spattered polythene, rather better wrapped up against the muggy cold than we were, perched on rickety seats to watch the dampest show on earth.

It was the sort of circus you ran away from to work in a shop. Towards the end of a chilly first half, largely featuring household pets which fetched things, and after a rather large, Amazonian, dark-haired woman had managed the seemingly impossible task of working up a sweat by heaving her partner around in a slapstick battle of the sexes, a collie dog and a pair of small horses ran on and tried to bite their handler. The dogs jumped through hoops and with a flourish the ringmaster waved a brand and set the hoops alight. As one, the audience leaned forward. Could they possibly warm themselves slightly by the flickering glow of the flaming metal circles? But, alas, the collies jumped through, the two-man band oom-pahhed, and the only source of heat in the tent was instantly extinguished.

During the interval, I volunteered to cross a field to a Swiss-chalet fish restaurant, mainly, I have to confess, to try to get warm. The owner looked worried when I asked if we could eat after the circus.

'What circus?' she asked.

I pointed across the field. She registered the tent without comment.

'It will be finished in an hour.'

She looked at her watch. 'No. This is impossible. The chef is finished now.'

It was just after eight.

19. Maybe, Yes, Bob

We were concerned for Bob. He came back from Glastonbury a fan of Roger Waters.

'No, it was great lying in the dark. All proper guitar stuff, you know. None of this modern rubbish.'

'I was at the first Glastonbury,' I told Baines.

'So was I,' said Bob.

'I'm surprised you didn't meet,' said Baines.

'We probably did,' said Bob. 'Did you roll naked in the mud?'

'No, but I watched carefully.' The difference was that one Glastonbury had been quite enough for me.

Baines went below and put on The Stereophonics.

It was just as grey and damp in the next marina. The town was just as comfortable and neat and featureless. The buses were just as regular. So we went to Odense for the night to see *Star Wars: Attack of the Clones*. The bus trip into the second city of Denmark, past signs to 'So Bad' and 'Off Toilet'. The sweet shops selling British newspapers. The Irish bar where the barman showed us his T-shirt, which read 'Odense' and got him shouted at when he went back to Dublin ('Hey, Mr O'Dense!'). The noxious tourist restaurant where he recommended we eat. And the subtitled film, where we were left wondering why the incomprehensible gibberish of the evil leader of the Federation, he of the crocodile eyes and lengthy dewlaps, could be subtitled to gales of laughter. (It was subtitled in the original.) It made for a bland visit.

Odense is someone's future vision of a town. The poor slum, which Hans Christian Andersen escaped, was now prettified and carefully preserved. (Who chooses the lovely colours? Green shutters and grey walls, then pale red with blue windows, then brown and Prussian blue.) The municipal concert hall, modern, big, a celebration of Nielsen, the native composer, was benign, comfortable and anodyne. We were shocked by the sound of a police siren. It was so long since we had heard one. (In Flensburg, every few minutes had been punctuated by the self-advertising clamour.) In the cinema, the only graffiti in the loo was a single line, in black marker, carefully drawn along the grouting. A couple sauntered past in matching purple nylon anoraks. On the corner, an entire family stood with their bicycles wearing red lightweight parkas and matching red shorts. Of course! Denmark was *en fête*. These were holidaymakers: trapped between the closing of the museums and the opening of the restaurants, waiting in this form-less, airbrushed city for something to happen.

We woke in a grey mist of fine drizzle. The hedges of pink roses sheltered a stand of sopping poppies at the side of a grey wooden walkway. There was not a breath of wind. It was like being suspended in wetness.

We motored out from the harbour. The sky was dove grey, the sea a pewter mirror. Porpoises plunged through the glassy water. We saw a seal, had lunch and took it in turns to get completely drenched by stair-rod rain. And then we rounded a cape and headed south to the gargantuan new bridge that straddles the shipping lanes connecting the Baltic to the North Sea and the rest of the world.

Suddenly the radio crackled into Danish: 'A fledder, harrty brsihkop . . . gale warning . . .'

'Wasn't that a gale warning?' asked Jo.

'Erm, yes. Yes that sounded like a gale warning. Yes. In the navigation channels.'

There were several enormous cargo vessels chugging along to the east of us, some going up, some coming down. This was definitely a navigation channel, and the warning was broadcast from somewhere quite close. Half an hour ago it had been dead calm. Soon it was blowing breezily. In a short while, it was, unexpectedly, a force seven or eight: whistling wind, flapping sails, choppy seas, a heeling and bucking boat, and us, trying to pass under a huge bridge, between a big pylon and the buoyed channel.

The huge green beacons, which, moments before, had seemed like tiny dots on the horizon, suddenly bounced up in front of us, and I clambered between the cabin and the deck, studying the charts, and confirming that the big green post with a green hat on was exactly the post I had expected to come across.

I was half-way up the companion-way ladder when the VHF radio crackled again. 'English sailing ship . . . English sailing ship. Contact traffic control on channel eleven.'

We looked foolishly at one another. *Undina* was bucking, as the mainsail stole the following wind from the foresail and then filled it again with a series of mighty claps. I turned and looked around, there was no other sailing ship visible.

'Do you think they mean us, then?' said Baines.

Like a mini starship travelling at warp speed and hurtling towards a mystery planet, we heard for the first time a message from intelligent life attempting to contact us. It was a moment worthy of a space shanty from the pen of Robert A. Heinlein.

I grasped the radio handset in my trembling hand. 'This is English yacht *Undina* . . . this is English yacht *Undina* calling bridge . . . calling bridge.' The boat pitched up on a stern-breaking roller. 'This is yacht *Undina*. Did you have an inquiry? Over.'

'Yes. What are your intentions?'

What did he think we were about to do? Crash our sailboat into his pylon and bring down the bridge?

'We intend to pass under the bridge to the west of the starboard hand buoys and proceed for about a mile before turning across the channel for . . .' Damn. I had been doing very well too. I took my finger off the handset. 'What's the name of the bloody place we're going?'

'Korsør!'

'Korsør.'

'OK, watch for southbound traffic.' And then he was gone. No 'over and out', not even the customary click as the handset was switched off. I switched off my own.

It was a small exchange, but a strangely comforting one. We had established our little place in the traffic of the Sjaelborg Sound. As we drove under the bridge at 7 knots we looked up at the giant 'H' masts towering against the rushing atmosphere, three great halogen lamps on each of them, flashing intermittently through the gathering gloom, and tried to work out where he might be, this traffic policeman, watching all the ships pass back and forth under his roadway, but the bridge was smooth and impersonal and gave nothing away. In a few moments we were underneath, and rushing down to the far buoys and our turning point; to make a run across the lanes, and into port, ahead of the gathering storm.

The harbour, when we finally spotted it in the confused grey smudge ahead, was marked by a mole: a heap of blackened rocks piled into a barrier against the waves, and as we sluiced over towards it we could see that the seas were swelling up and falling back in a broken rush at the entrance. At the last second, we swung the helm around and shot through the narrow gap into the marina. A party of ducks was crouched down, sheltering from the wind on a little spit of sand just inside and below the mole. We turned into an empty berth in the lee of a fishing boat. Bob threw a line to a man stooping against the wind on the pontoon, who promptly dropped it. Our bow, caught by the wind, swung out across the berth. Bob threw again. The man caught it this time and he and a companion, and Bob, hauled the bow of the boat round against what was now a furious blast, struggling hard until they got the rope around a bollard.

Our helper was a stout, pop-eyed man with a beard and close-cropped head. 'We saw you coming in and thought hey! Yeah, you were rocking in the entrance, yes?'

We tried to look as if we came into small harbours with a following storm every day. 'It was pretty blowy,' we shouted back.

'Yes. We saw another boat come in about an hour ago and thought that was the last.'

In fact, we weren't the last either. Another, smaller, boat came in when the dark really fell, and we could see her mast-head light waggling obscenely back and forth, as she bounded through the mole. But by then we were sitting in the restaurant in the marina, chatting to Yvonne, and eating authentic Danish food (a national cuisine seemingly invented after a late night in the pub): meat balls, and a mess of beef cubes and fried potatoes with a fried egg on top. Yvonne was married to an Englishman.

'He won't eat any of this stuff,' she told us.

'*Het my fet*,' Bob said to her.

She looked at him. 'What?'

'It's Danish, isn't it?'

She laughed. 'No.'

'Oh, yes,' said Bob. 'It means "you show me".'

'How do you know?'

'It was in *Star Wars*.'

She shook her head. She spoke excellent English. Bob pointed this out.

'I have to. My husband won't learn any Danish and still can't understand what my friends are saying.'

'When did you meet him?'

'We got married nine years ago,' she said. And she pronounced the nine 'noin'. Her husband was from Norwich and had come over to work on the bridge.

'Ah.' Baines leaned in with a look of patriotic pride. 'So the bridge was actually built by the English.'

She laughed. 'English, Germans, Italians. Most of them were Dutch.'

The next morning in the harbour master's office, as I paid nothing for our berth, I noticed there was something peculiar about the day. The wind was still fresh but the puddles were shining. Denmark was glistening, under the bright, hard, unfamiliar glare of the sun.

20. Mast Height

The sun managed to turn the northern straightforwardness of these neat little brick towns into something reasonably strange and somewhat wonderful. We sailed back across to Fyn, in a good mood, into a looping, narrow channel that led to Svendborg.

'You'll need to head up to the southern side of the channel,' I told Bob.

'Yes, I'm just heading for the buoy.'

'Well, you're not.'

'I am.'

'No, Bob, you'll get blown sideways. You have to come up to the buoy more.'

'I am coming up to the buoy.'

He was pointing directly at the buoy, but I knew that we would make leeway down on to the shore unless we pointed more into the wind. So we went on arguing.

Svendborg was once a Viking stronghold. 'Vik' means inlet. It was from this port, and others tucked away in amongst the islands, that the longboats had originally come. And, in this land-enclosed and intricate waterway, curving round to an island-studded bay, it was easy to imagine how early civilizations felt the need to explore the world and beat it up a bit.

'If anything, it feels like a current could be pushing us off the shore,' Bob said now.

'No, no.'

'Well it's quite possible.'

'No, not really. It's entirely impossible.'

Bob was behaving like a fourteen-year-old. I like his grandfather. (He would have paid more attention to his father.) I explained that his forward straight line was an illusion. That he was in fact following a banana route to the buoy. He was on an ellipse. I drew him a diagram. If he continued on this course we would be turning ever more until we were pointing directly into the wind.

'I'm pointing at the buoy.'

'Oh, for Christ's sake.'

In the end, I asked him to steer directly across the channel to the port buoy, so he did, and made up to it easily. This meant that I hadn't proved anything. And he thought he'd been right all along. He refused to learn. I refused to teach. I thought it was all obvious. So did he.

We gently turned in to Svendborg's inner harbour. There were not many places we could stick ourselves. It really was the holiday season, after all. The local yachtsmen, sensible sailors in their sensible boats, seemed to know that you got to Svendborg long before seven o'clock in the evening if you wanted somewhere to park. Their sensible crews sat, with smug expressions of indifference on their faces, watching us fuss around.

When I was fourteen, I would gradually bury my face in my hands as my father dithered and then laboriously tried to turn his boat around. Now, as I did exactly the same thing, I was aware of Baines and Bob sighing and rolling their eyes. I feigned indifference. I chuntered into reverse and forward again, in a perfect 92-point turn, until *Undina* eventually swung round to face back the way she had come.

The harbour master bicycled round and took us back into the big dock, to tie up just behind a super-tug and a fire tender, against a massive wall of granite. All marinas are the same, but all docks are different. This one had a little café set into the edge of a corrugated iron warehouse, which was so grimy, and peopled by such weary dipsomaniacs, that we decided to congratulate ourselves on being a long way from the tidy yachting set and their sensible boats.

We picked up our new visitors, Rebecca, the former cultural attaché to the Australian Embassy, tall, beautiful and blonde and, incidentally, a friend of Barry Humphries (who cannot have based Les Patterson on her, except as an extreme joke), and Matthew, her husband and a writer.

During the next afternoon, we swung back across the sound,

and around the top of a couple of off-shore islands, and made the hidden entrance to a remote, twisting channel by evening.

It was slightly misty. For several miles we ghosted between the banks and past the deserted fields. Ducks and swans shifted out of our path, carefully, as if anxious not to disturb the dropping calm. The water was limpid and still. This is when it 'chuckles' and gurgles under the bow. The wake folds away across the plane of water in a great widening 'v': an ephemeral record of your passing. It is only possible in waters of complete stillness and, then, seemingly only at dawn or dusk. The dying light magnifies and allows the tiny things to feature large.

And finally, at the head of a mere, we reached the end of the fjord and a little town; a church on a bluff, a nineteenth-century sugar-beet factory and close streets of red brick houses: Skaelskor.

We pulled up next to some fishing boats on the far wall. On the opposite wharf, in a marquee, a folk-rock festival was plunking along, but we were already too late for it. The occasional plaintive twang issued from the tent and, sometimes, a bearded man, with a glass of beer, who lay on one elbow on the grass. It was a Sunday evening. Even the boys who hung around the bridge at the bottom of the high street conversed in whispers, and muffled their mopeds.

We were crowded on the boat. I was like some fake Greek shipping nabob. Rebecca and Matthew were my Charles and Camilla, with the obvious disadvantage that there was no room for them. They took our fore-cabin. Jo slept in the quarter berth, I on the saloon bench. We became fairly quiet ourselves; playing out a courtly minuet around the interior, whispering politenesses, as we stepped out of each other's way, or over prostrate bodies, or excused ourselves, reaching for bags, hanging up clothes, or just scratching. Finally, we settled in the dark: six bodies, breathing and sighing and turning over with exaggerated care, rustling loudly in sleeping bags, during an utterly sleepless night.

'This is what sailing is all about,' Rebecca told me the next morning, when I apologized. I nodded. 'No, I really understand it now.' She and Matthew had no yachting pretensions. When we were travelling, they sat in the cockpit like wary children, perched on the edge of the seat with expressions of alertness, ready to throw themselves bodily out of the way, if anything needed to be done.

'The truth is,' Matthew said gallantly, 'you are pretty cramped, even on the largest boats.' Rebecca owned an art gallery and she had danced attendance on a number of multi-millionaires. 'We used to go on a German yacht with this very nice chap, who had inherited a fortune and was somewhat insecure, like so many of these very rich people.' Matthew looked around him. 'It was a little bit bigger than this boat, perhaps. We had a cabin to ourselves, with a porthole, and a bathroom of sorts . . .' He continued hastily, 'But it does seem that, even on the biggest boat, you experience . . . a certain level of privation.' I agreed. Both Rebecca and Matthew were exceptionally tall. There wasn't actually room in our cabin for them to lie at full stretch.

'But we love this boat,' added Rebecca. 'Isn't the cabin just so beautiful? Aren't the lights marvellous? It's all just like a Tracey Emin installation.' Luckily, the nights were short and the days long, and, thank God, now sunny.

For something to do, Rebecca began to time our urinations. 'You took thirty seconds,' she told Bob, when Bob walked forward to piss over the side, rather than struggle with the plumbing below. 'That's longer than Baines. He gets going in twenty. But that's still quite a long time.'

'Maybe it's because you're watching me, Rebecca.'

'I'm not watching you, Bob, but I can't help noticing. All of you seem to be taking longer and longer to pee. I think you may have prostate problems.'

Rebecca's father was a Scottish doctor in Australia. 'He used to reach over with a scalpel and just chop off any moles or anything after dinner. You don't want that developing into a melanoma, he'd say.'

Bob got worried about his prostate.

'It's the biggest single killer of middle-aged men after a heart attack,' Rebecca told him. Next time he pissed over the side he took sixty seconds to get going. 'It really inhibits your bladder. It's one of the symptoms. In America they check people over forty as a matter of course. How old are you, Bob?'

'I'm not going to tell you.'

'Well Baines is not yet forty, but he's having trouble peeing already.'

'Some men can't piss in public at all, Rebecca.'

'Especially in a pub when it's a bit grungy and some big fat bloke comes and stands in the stall next to you and farts and belches while he pisses.'

'Or there's a tall Australian woman timing you.'

But Bob brooded on the possibilities. We all did, for the week that Rebecca sailed with us, and for another week after that when she had gone.

'I'm definitely going to have the test when I get back,' said Bob.

'It's stupid not to,' I agreed. 'My father died of prostate cancer.'

'Well it runs genetically.'

As soon as Rebecca had left we started pissing normally again. And, because we all felt fine and the worry had gone, none of us bothered to look into it, or get somebody else to look into it and, no doubt, we will all die of it soon enough.

The route ahead took us inside the islands and therefore under bridges. The charts were helpful. Each bridge was marked with two figures. One, placed between two vertical lines, gave the width of the span, not usually a problem for us, and the other, between two horizontal lines, its height. Looking ahead, I noticed that the first bridge, a railway bridge, crossed the sound at a height of 25 metres.

'That shouldn't be any trouble.'

'How tall is the mast?'

'Well Michael told us twenty metres.'

'Is that from the deck?'

'I don't know. He just said that we would manage twenty metres.'

'The bridge after that is nineteen.'

'Oh, that's OK. We'll get under that,' said Bob.

'I reeled back. 'What?'

'He's bound to have left a margin for error.'

'What if he hasn't?'

Matthew leaned in politely. 'But if we can't get under,' he asked, 'do we have to go a different route?'

I frowned at the chart. 'Yes. We'd have to completely retrace our steps.'

There were strong arguments for risking the bridge. It would take a full day to get back out the way we had come and that would add an extra day to the journey as well.

'We can ask at the next place,' said Bob.

'Ask what?'

'They must have dozens of boats going on by the short route and they'll know the height restrictions.'

'Who? The mast-measuring men? We know the height restrictions. Nineteen metres.'

'No. They say nineteen but they're making allowances for the highest state of the tide.'

'There isn't any tide.'

'But there are these surge things. They must allow for that. It's probably twenty-two or twenty-three metres really.'

We passed under the first bridge playing Wagner loudly, for confidence. Even with 5 metres' clearance, there was a tense moment as we came up to the arch. It looked, from below, as if the mast was bound to hit the bridge, but we swept underneath.

'See,' said Bob.

'We knew we were going to pass under that. It was the twenty-five-metre bridge.'

'Yes, but we must have had ten clear metres.'

'Don't be ridiculous.'

We tied up on the outside of a mess of pleasure boats, but all of them were smaller than us. We had the tallest mast in the marina, only by a few feet. 'But, Bob, it's a crucial few feet!' And anyway we had a radio aerial and a weather vane and some other bits of wire sticking out above the actual wood.

Bob and Baines went up on deck to measure the mast.

They came back five minutes later.

'You're fine,' said Bob. He sat down and lit a cigarette.

'What does that mean?'

'You've got plenty of room.'

'So, what's the height of the mast?'

'Seventeen and a half.'

'Seventeen and a half. That's much lower than we thought.'

'Seventeen and a half, eighteen and a half, something like that.'

I gripped the side of the saloon table.

'Like what?'

'It's not possible to be completely accurate. You have to include the depth of the boat above the water line. I mean there's the mast to the top of the cabin – that's about sixteen and a half – and then, how much?' He spread his hands. 'About this much. What's that? No more than two metres anyway. You've got plenty of room.' He took a drag on his cigarette, pulled on a shirt covered in ladybirds and went to have dinner in the yacht club. It was a Chinese restaurant. Bob took the opportunity to practise his Cantonese.

'*Hakky Yang To.*'

.The waitress laughed.

'It means "I am bald",' he told us. Bob spoke the international language of the hairless. He could draw attention to his trichological deficiencies in seven or eight different languages.

'This boat . . .' he waggled his hands in the direction of *Undina*, lodged at the end of the jetty. 'This boat is high mast.' He mimed the mast. The girls giggled. 'Will we get under the bridge? Bridge!' he made a bridge with his hands. They giggled again.

'Bob.' Why did I feel an obligation to point it out? 'These girls don't know anything about the size of the bridge.'

'They might do.'

'Bob, even if we asked the captain of the bridge-building and maintenance team, he'd only be able to look at us and say, "Probably", or, "How the hell should I know?"'

We walked up to the town and explored the romantic ruins of

the castle by floodlight. In the middle of the hump of a keep was a magnificent twelfth-century round tower with a hooded roof.

Bob stood and looked down a hole. 'What's this do you think? A swimming pool or something?'

Matthew looked down too. 'I think you'll find it's a recent excavation pit.'

'Right.'

The next morning we left at seven. We had a long way to go. At half past six, Jo and I hoisted a rope to the top of the mast, tied a knot in it and measured the result. We dropped a line over the side and measured from the water line to the top of the cabin roof. We arrived at a total of 17½ metres. The bits poking up might add another half a metre. Bob and Baines came up on deck and smirked. We passed under the bridge without incident.

The long day's sail followed narrow channels in wide bays, through a maze of waterways and islands.

'You'll have to look out for the reeds,' a Dutch yachtsman had warned me. 'It's a lovely sail but if you don't mind the reeds.' I imagined *Undina* like the *African Queen*, doggedly looking for open water in a waste of tall grass, but, apart from one moment, when I looked down and saw some long, streaky things in the water, we never encountered reeds. We had clear water to Køge and the gateway to Copenhagen.

21. Denmark for Beginners

Some years ago I made a commercial for Danish television and cinema. It just came through the post. Things did from Denmark, where *Smith and Jones* was an imported television favourite. I proposed myself as the director and then read the scripts. They featured two lawyers debating the value of sugar. One continuously pointed out the demerits, the fact that it rotted teeth and impoverished farmers, the other made surreal points in return. 'Flies like cheese as well as sugar.' 'Sugar will kill you if enough of it falls on top of you.' And so on.

Karsten, who was the copy-writer, flew over from Denmark and I sat with him in a basement room and fished for a few director's guidelines. 'First of all, Karsten, these advertisements are paid for by the sugar manufacturers, are they?'

Karsten had long blond hair. He was part Swedish. He looked like a rock star and spoke with a slight American accent. 'Yeah, sure. They are for Danisco.'

'Right. But they read a bit, actually, how shall I put this . . . sort of anti-sugar.'

'That's true, yes.'

'They're supposed to be anti-sugar?'

'Sort of. You see in Denmark everybody is taught that sugar is bad for you, yes? And so the sugar company wants to make sure that they are being fair. They are just putting the arguments and then we have the strap line, you see.'

I looked down. 'Sugar. You decide.'

'Yes.'

Karsten seemed pleased with the resulting films. Danisco asked for extra rights to show them in Danish cinemas and they won awards at the International Advertising Festival in Cannes. I assumed they had successfully depressed the sales of sugar throughout

Denmark. Now, ten years later, Karsten drove down to see us and took me for a tour of Copenhagen in his battered old Volkswagen, to explain the Danes.

He pointed across the roofscape of the old town.

'See there,' he said, 'on top of that building where the crane is. That is my new office.'

He was now, partly on the strength of his bold stance with Danisco, recognized as one of the leading copy-writers in Denmark and, like his English counterparts, had immediately left his agency to set up on his own, taking, I trusted, some of his clients with him.

'Business is excellent. But you see my car over there?'

'Yes.'

'Why do you think, Griff, that I drive that battered old thing?'

I shrugged.

'I shall tell you. Because I would not have my clients if I didn't. Here, in Denmark, I could not be seen driving in a top-of-the-range Porsche or Ferrari, even though I could easily afford one. Danish people don't like anybody to show off.' We were eating in a café near the royal palace. 'Our Queen is a designer,' Karsten explained. 'We love her. When it is her birthday everybody comes into the square here and they shout for her to appear and she will come out on the balcony, but mostly she is too busy with her work.'

Later, he invited me to try and spot a Rolls Royce or a Bentley as we drove north through the waterside suburbs. 'Look here. There are plenty of successful people living here, and these houses are expensive but they are very careful, you know . . .'

'Discreet.'

'Yes, exactly.' Karsten was as well placed as anyone to examine the Danish psyche. He made a living doing it. I asked him about the pristine state of the houses we had passed so far. 'Nobody makes them paint the houses,' he said. 'They will just do it, because they want the town to look good. I was in London in the slum area along by the Thames . . .'

He didn't mean Chiswick. '. . . the East End?'

'Yeah. And I thought, how can this happen? How can the people here let themselves live in a place which has become so bad? I don't mean the government. I mean the people themselves. Don't they have any pride?'

The Danes do have an enormous social conscience and they pay massive taxes to support it. It is part of the fabric of their society. After the Napoleonic Wars, when they backed the wrong side and were mercilessly punished, losing Norway, bombed by Congreve rockets and shot to pieces by Admiral Nelson, the Danes became a small nation and the conscience of Europe. When the *Daily Mail* salutes the Danes for their robust attitude to the European Community, they should bear in mind that the Danes are not John Redwood.

'No, no, you see, the problem for many people in Denmark is that the EU want us to make laws that we do not want.'

'Well, that is similar.'

But Karsten meant that the EU's laws were too reactionary for the cooperative, tolerant Danes. They already have a minimum wage far above that demanded by the EU. Denmark has stricter safety regulations and more regulated work practices. Karsten regarded the EU as retrogressive. 'Pride. That is the secret. The Danes are very proud of their tolerant history,' Karsten told me. Hence the flags, and the patriotism.

Some time in the 1960s, alongside bobbed hair with swept-up ends and tight, red plastic mackintoshes, Denmark became synonymous with bare-wooded design values. What was not French cookery-ware at Habitat was expected to come from Denmark: chicken bricks, plain coffee tables in blond wood, shapely stacking chairs, shelving units, thick glasses and angular lights. The Danes were clean (all that laundry) and effortlessly tasteful in a puritanical kind of way. Spare, modern, practical and uncomfortable, that was Danish: nothing frilly or ornamental, please.

I had my own experience of Danish design, when, at the age of twelve, I signed up for a school trip to Denmark. God knows why I went; probably because Jimpson did. We were billeted in a bed and breakfast hotel and shared rooms where we lounged around waiting for our Danish supper, comparing pen-knives and reading improving comics.

Above the bed in my room was a Danish light. It was a metal lantern with a wide shade in chocolate, which was a fashionable colour then, and it had a raising and lowering device built into a unit half-way up the cable. At some point I reached up and lowered the light. I just pulled it. That was it. It came down. Having satisfied myself, I lifted it up again, but it wouldn't go back up. The cable just hung there in a flaccid, unsupportive loop. Jimpson explained that the principle was undoubtedly that of a roller blind. You had to pull it a little further down, the spring action would take up the slack. So I tried pulling it down a bit further, but, somehow, I failed to let it go at the right moment and the spring didn't take up the slack. In fact we had more slack hanging down than before. In fact, the light was now lying on the bed.

I gave it a hard pull, a yank even. There was an audible crack. The lamp, the cable, the rising and falling unit, the little cone of beige plastic that attached it to the ceiling and a lump of the ceiling itself came away and fell on to the duvet.

We considered the matter gravely. It was beyond repair and, being in a foreign country and at the mercy of two gym masters, we decided that the only course of action was to take the light, which was broken anyway, stuff it into a plastic bag and throw it into the middle of the lake. It flopped on to the surface and slowly sank and nobody mentioned it again, not even the management of the hotel, who must have noticed. Perhaps they were glad to get rid of it.

The Danish Design Centre in the middle of Copenhagen had a special exhibition of student work, which still reflected the valuable nostrums of the 1960s, plus a few extra socially aware twiddles. (There was a strong emphasis on provision for the disabled.) But the director of the centre was convinced that the design ethos was a product of the Danish character, and nothing to do with modernism or sixties magazines.

'It has more to do with a certain modesty.'

'Like the Shakers.'

'Exactly.'

Karsten had used this word modesty too. It was an important

part of the Danish character. In the mid-1920s a writer, Aksel Sandemose, had made up a satirical set of regulations called the *Jante Love*, or the laws of modesty, in *En Flyktning krysser sitt sport* (*A Refugee Crosses His Tracks*). They were based on the prevailing attitudes of his neighbouring Jutlanders. He found the whole 'you're no better than you ought to be' way of life oppressive, and left Denmark altogether. But a large number of Danes missed the irony altogether and believed that the laws were real.

'It means that nobody should think themselves better than anybody else. You should know your place. Don't show off, or do something remarkable, because your neighbours will only point to the trouble it will bring.'

And the director of the Design Centre saw this counsel of asperity reflected in his furniture. 'Something that is well made, suited to its job, content, perhaps, to be a table.'

There were four of us sitting around that over-laden table in the Design Centre. The head of the Tourist Board, who had kindly arranged the meeting, his assistant and the director himself. The others were already nodding in agreement and I realized that even these liberal, university-educated people, who knew that the *Jante Love* were made in a spirit of sarcasm, believed in their established truth. In fact, they were rather proud of them.

Oddly, the Danes had no false modesty about being Danish. It was my first introduction to the pecking order of the Baltic. The Danes are immensely proud of Denmark. This is because they are the most sophisticated of the Baltic nations. I was told this not only by the Danish, but also in Estonia, Sweden and Finland, without a trace of irony. Nobody said, 'They think they're the most sophisticated', as we British might about the French. It was taken as a matter of course. Denmark looked south. A Finnish sound engineer solemnly told me that the Danish had much more in common with Italy than the Arctic circle. 'They even drink more espresso coffee.'

The Danes felt no affinity whatsoever with Russia and the north. Up there was still as remote and pagan as the missionary bishops of northern Germany had found it, when they first launched the German Knights on the heathen, at the beginning of the last millennium. 'But doesn't this exemplary restraint lead to conformity?' I asked my panel at the Design Institute, 'Name me a Danish hero. A contemporary hero.'

There was silence. 'Well we have a footballer who plays for an English team,' the design chief started, 'but he's only admired, really.'

The head of the Tourist Board raised his eyebrows. 'We do have flamboyant, crazy people. There is one figure, yes all right he was a pornographer, but he was very much larger than life . . .'

'Oh, no,' said the assistant, shutting him up. 'No. He was just a big show-off.' There was a pause. Perhaps the head of the Tourist Board had got above himself.

'So, no David Beckham, no John Lennon, no Stephen Hawking . . .'

They shook their heads and stared at the well-made table. 'No.' they said mournfully, at last.

No Volvo, no Saab, no Nobel, no Eriksson and no Abba either, and yet the Danes pity the Swedes, despite being able to lay claim, themselves, to little more than Danish blue cheese (difficult to get hold of and just as horrible in Denmark as it is in England), the Danish open sandwich (which we tramped around Copenhagen trying unsuccessfully to sample) and Danish pastries (which are anyway an American marketing convenience).

But, remember, the last and final law is: 'Thou shalt not laugh at us.'

'So what,' I said after all this undemonstrative restraint, 'am I to make of Tivoli?'

The Design Centre director laughed. 'Yes,' he said. 'Well, that's the Danes on holiday.' And then he stopped and looked serious. 'But actually I do know one of the lighting designers there and he does do some excellent work.'

As I stood in the middle of the Tivoli Gardens, the combined fairground and pleasure park in the middle of Copenhagen, later that evening, trotting after Bob and Baines, Rebecca and Matthew and Jo, I wondered which lighting this designer might have been responsible for. Was it the red, green and yellow pulsating mushrooms that rose and fell in time to the music? Or the flashing red lights on the fake, immodest Chinese pagodas? Or maybe some of the 100,000 special soft-glow bulbs in the chains of twinkling fairy lights littering every tree?

At first, Tivoli seems to represent Denmark off the leash, but a short walk teaches you that it is, in fact, Denmark at its most house-trained and obedient. It's expensive, but it isn't ruthless like Disney World. We shot at tin ducks (Baines was top shot). We launched rubber chickens with mallets. We were twisted and swung upside down, which got Bob's wallet out of his pocket for a short time, if only into the machinery of the Mighty Waltzer. But the best part of the summer night was just walking under the trees, admiring the fairy lights and the carefully tended Victorian flower borders. The restaurants are even more expensive inside Tivoli than they are in hugely expensive Copenhagen, but they're good, proper restaurants, served by waiters dressed as waiters and not mice or dogs. And it's no seedy Goose Fair either. There aren't gangs of youths charging about, barging you out of the way, as there would have to be, by some sort of social ordinance, in England.

'I still go, once a year, maybe with guests,' The director of the Design Centre told me with pride. And of course he would. It's a little, sealed packet of outdated charm, a home-decorated Christmas tree with all its family quirks rather than a Christmas tree stuck on a department store. It was established in 1843 with the blessing of King Christian VIII as a way of neutering the dog of civil unrest. 'When people amuse themselves, they forget politics,' the King is alleged to have remarked. It used to be owned by Carlsberg. They resisted attempts from Disney and from Michael Jackson to buy it and then sold it to the Scandinavian Tobacco Company. Perhaps it was a good choice, No one could be more sensitive to their image in the modern world than the death-dealing fag merchants. God knows how self-lacerating their Danish advertising must be.

22. Back to Denmark the Hard Way

Staring into space, like a bad actor, whenever the queue stopped for a moment, the woman behind me in the check-in line nudged me in the back of the legs with her luggage trolley. As I bent to pick up my bags, whack. When I stopped to drop them again, whack. After moving forward six inches, a slight rattle, and the neatly blunted three-inch leading edge of the full weight of her excess baggage went right into the bony bit just below my shin muscle.

I was going back to Denmark alone. Bob and Baines would be out in a couple of days. My son, George, and his friend Chas were joining us.

There was nothing to keep me in London at the moment. The others wanted to pick up their lives for a few days. I had picked up my clothes, turned down a request to go to Australia to play an avuncular shopkeeper in a children's sweetie-fantasy, and scurried out of the house again.

Baking in the sun, Stansted airport, continually seeking to extend its flight capacity, was failing, in its usual cack-handed manner, to deal with its current quota of passengers at the security check. Half an hour later, I reached my gate. There was an announcement. 'In anticipation to boarding the plane . . .,' it began, gnomically, and then collapsed into silence. In fact there was no anticipation to boarding the plane at all. The flight was going to be delayed for four hours, because of 'operational difficulties'.

It was twenty minutes after the scheduled departure that they managed to find a bus. We shuffled towards it. They checked our boarding passes to make sure, I supposed, that nobody was trying to smuggle themselves back to the departure lounge. ('I'm not going on my flight, the lure of a free refreshment voucher was simply too much.') And, on the hottest day of the year so far, we

stood on the bus for five minutes, shifting and listless in the swelter-
ing heat, while our camp orderly tidied his papers and sauntered
across to the driver for a little badinage. The latter climbed aboard,
started the engine, closed the doors with a hiss and drove us twenty
yards or so, back to the main terminal.

I was surrounded by men with expensive haircuts in matching
polo shirts. They were a football team. About half were tall and
athletic. The other half, fat and bloated, were the coaches.

'What do they call this airline? Go, isn't it?'

'It should be called Stop.'

'Yeah, that's it, that's my point, it shouldn't be called Go.'

'Well, it's not going anywhere.'

'No.'

The joke did for the next ten minutes. It was passed back, forth,
back again, until it worked its way round to the man who first
thought of it.

Despite mutinies, anxieties and the lack of duty-free shopping
opportunities, I was struck by the advantages of travelling to Denmark by small boat. It was definitely quicker. I was now becalmed
in the departure lounge for longer than I had ever been in the
Channel. So I trawled the mall. The gift shops sold a range of
travellers' junk: straps, wallets for passports, plug adaptors, mosquito
repellents, inflatable corkscrews, air socks and padlocks, but, mysteriously, no padlocks with cables. 'My sister bought me a cable
thing, a retractable cable in a plastic container once . . .' I started.

'Stephanie' stopped me. 'Yes, yes,' she said, 'I know the ones
you mean. I'm afraid since September 11th, they've been classified
as a potentially lethal weapon and we're not allowed to sell them.'

'Thanks.' And I shuffled away. What sort of terrorist were we at
war with, then? The terrorist who got as far as the departure lounge
and then remembered that he had left his lethal weapon in the taxi?

I sat in a dreary coffee shop and read a boat magazine. Recently,
I'd got into the habit of talking to myself. When I managed to catch
myself at it, I fell into a little pit of despair. This was just more
genetic imprinting. My father had conducted entire seminars with
his own counsel all his adult life. Now I was doing the same.

Muttering to yourself, walking along, that's bad, but muttering, sat down with a cup of coffee in front of you, that's clearly insane.

Finally, the tannoy crackled. 'We owe you an explanation of why you have been delayed so long, and since you have been inconvenienced you will undoubtedly want to know why. The airplane had to wait in Copenhagen because of a technical fault.' And with everything comprehensively cleared up, we started on our way.

Earlier, I had telephoned Peter Heller, the boatyard owner in whose care I'd left the boat, just to let him know I was coming. 'After the storm, is everything all right?'

'Oh, sure, yeah.'

'Good, because I heard it was bad in Hamburg.'

'Planes were blown about in Copenhagen airport.'

'Wow. But the boat's OK?'

'Well, just a little damage, you know.'

'A little damage?' I tensed.

'I'm joking, she's fine.'

They were trying to mend the leaky hatches and doing some emergency work on the stem head.

Back in Denmark, I checked into a hotel to let them finish in peace, before wandering off into Copenhagen, a city wrapped in summer. I took a trip to Louisiana, a few miles up the coast, to look at the art gallery and admire the disabled lift.

'It's a disabled lift,' the attendant pointed out.

'Yes, yes, I know that,' I explained, 'I've just never seen one so beautifully integrated into the design of a place.' It was more interesting than the art.

On the way back from the gallery, I jumped aboard a fabulous alien spaceship of a train. The steps emerged from the side automatically. There were plastic bag dispensers for my rubbish and the announcements were made in English as well as Danish. Further down I could see families sitting in carriages designed specifically to accommodate all their bicycles and prams.

I moved away from a screaming baby and took a seat opposite a woman of about fifty in very tight clothes. She was swaying back and forth and grinning. I knew what this was. It was the third time I'd seen it. It was *Hygge*, the Danish inclination to publicly enjoy yourself. Only this time it was *Hygge* as a life option.

An emaciated man in schoolboy shorts and a Mohican haircut was perched opposite her. He was a bit Hygged-up too. She looked at me for a long time and then showed me a bottle of wine. 'We're having some wine,' she said, 'but we don't have any glasses.'

'Me neither,' I answered, patting my pockets inanely. She sighed, wheezily. This was obviously an unexpected disappointment. Her friend got up and moved up the carriage. He returned with a couple of plastic cups.

'We're drinking out of coffee cups now,' said the woman with a familiar Danish drinking grin: a naughty five-year-old's gurning conspiracy. She pushed the bottle under my nose. 'Have some.'

'No, no, thanks, that's really kind, but not now for me,' I apologized carefully. Later, she leered in my direction. 'Will you watch my bags?'

'Yeah sure.'

'Because we're going to the toilet together and I can't leave them.' She indicated her cardboard box and embroidered cloth shoulder bag and a couple of plastic bags spread across three seats. I nodded and smiled. They moved off up the train and out of sight.

A few moments later I heard shouting. Some other man was remonstrating in Danish. My recent acquaintance started screaming in shrill, angry tones, and I noticed, with a start, that she was now standing on the platform outside, smiling generally, skipping a little and waving drunkenly at someone further up the train. Her bags were still lying on the seats opposite me. The train pulled out.

A guard came past. There was a look of exasperation on his face. He took my ticket. I was about to speak and then thought better of it. After a minute or so, though, when the guard had moved on, the mohican skeleton came creeping back. He tidied up the luggage, winked at me and, two stops later, got off him-self, taking everything with him. The modern, antiseptic Danish train went on without them.

23. Cabin Fever

Baines and I sat in my little cabin.

'Ooh, it's intimate up here,' said Baines. He rubbed his hands together. (I'm not making this up. Baines liked theatrical gestures: hand-rubbing, holding up one digit in order to emphasize a point, exaggerated shrugs of a Gallic nature, that sort of thing. In fact, there was a way he stood in front of any big technical job that was marvellously studied. He'd slouch his frame forward a little, one shoulder slightly higher than the other and inclining the head, fag on, squint and lift the eyes towards the object, sizing it up like a mid-west cowboy. 'Oil rigger number two,' Bob called it.)

'Very snug,' he continued.

'Yes, yes.' I sort of agreed, in an Arthur Lowe manner. I didn't want, obviously, to give him the impression that my accommodation was any better than anyone else's: his for example. 'Yours is nice and snug too,' I ventured.

The 'Bainesarium' was one of the quarter berths in the main saloon. Robert and Baines amused themselves, in a determinedly juvenile way, if you ask me, playing at being animal-keepers. 'Bainesgoo' was sometimes fed like a bird by his 'keeper', Robert the Parrot-plucker. Quite.

'No, no, it's very, very comfortable, my bunk. I love it,' reassured Baines, 'but you've got everything to hand up here.'

I certainly had. The first moment I saw *Undina* I decided that the fore-cabin would be my little cabin. I'd been on too many charter yachts not to recognize the advantages of secluded bolt holes and that useful aid to privacy, the door.

Baines was opening and closing the lockers with professional interest.

'I had all those put in, you see,' I explained.

'Michael's done a marvellous job here.' The lockers ran down one side of the hull in an inverted 'v'. They had woven rattan doors like the ones in the saloon.

'Yes. And the whole bathroom was moved forward. It used to come back to here.' Baines was an excellent audience for this sort of stuff. 'Of course, we lost the opening window in the head, but we get this extra space here,' I went on, indicating where my feet went. 'Then we shortened the locker here and added this little seat.' I lifted the cushion. 'And look!' I showed Baines my little under-seat locker.

'Excellent.'

'But to tell you the truth,' I went on, sniffing about for potential DIY assistance, 'we lie up the sharp end with our feet splaying out in a v down here, but here, of course, the feet drop down on the seat.'

'Yes, but you can prop it up with a cushion, surely.'

'Yes, yes, we do. But I was thinking,' and here, I felt, I should open up to the handyman in Baines, 'actually it might be possible to design a fold-down affair, so that it cantilevered up and crossed over to this side and folded back up here . . .'

Baines frowned and chewed his bottom lip. 'Mmm,' he said ruminatively. For the next half an hour we sat and planned a fold-down seat extension which might even open out into a mini-desk, a clothing rack doubling as a medicine cabinet and a special descending television screen that would allow me to lie in my bunk and follow our progress on the chart, or watch *Evil Dead III*, depending on the circumstances.

This was all before the discovery that the front of the boat was a sock in a barrel and leaked like a salad strainer. Maybe this was why, up until now, it had been used to store sails. In the opinion of one boat builder, the bow area was bound to leak: 'If the seams weren't opening and closing a little up there, then it wouldn't be a proper, living boat.' It was a silly place to try to populate.

And God, it was uncomfortable. It was particularly uncomfortable in a big sea. My head was at the very extreme of a see-saw. I floated in mid-air most of the time, and bounced down on the bunk the rest. I only slept in the Bainesarium once, on passage, and what a well-thought-out berth that was by comparison. It was right at the centre of gravity. It didn't swoop around or roll you off. It sat, steady as a duck, gently rising and falling in the midst of the tempest.

My berth was hugely uncomfortable when it rained. Water dripped in through every crack. It was uncomfortable when it got cold. The heater only reached into the saloon. It was uncomfortable going to bed and it was uncomfortable getting up, and, after a few weeks, it began to smell.

You remember those camps in the airing cupboard you used to build out of an ironing board and a blanket, or those tree houses you could crawl into but scraped yourself trying to reverse out of? My cabin was like that. Hugely exciting, to begin with, in a frankly puerile way, but an unsavoury tip after that.

Mind you, it taught me patience. It could take me ten minutes to lever off my waterproof bootees. Sometimes the door to the cabin would fall open of its own accord and Bob and Baines would look up, startled, to see a middle-aged man with a red face apparently trying to strangle his foot while lying upside down in a cupboard.

I would take off vest, shirt and pullover in one heave, if possible. But every night when I went to my cosy cabin, I would stand for a moment, breathing stertorously, sizing up the situation, planning, in the freezing cold, the best campaign for undressing and getting into bed. Sit here to get off the shoes. Put the shoes over here. Get up. Loosen trousers. Take off upper clothing carefully, watching out for knuckles on the ceiling and the portholes. Sit. Take shoes from under arse where I have sat on them. Lean back and roll upwards with the legs in the air. Pull down trousers. Sit up. Bang head. Fold trousers. Rearrange sleeping bag so that the zip won't work its way underneath me in the middle of the night and the useless hood attachment won't smother me at three in the morning. Crawl forward on top of the sleeping bag. Turn over. Lie flat out. Raise legs and pull slithery freezing cold sleeping bag over nether limbs. Shiver with disgust. Realize I have left the light by the door of the cabin on. Crawl forward, trying to stay in the sleeping bag, like articulated, blue caterpillar. Reach to switch off light. Crawl back up the bunk, cursing quietly. Find out that I am lying on zip. Get smothered at three in the morning.

Is it any wonder that, upon waking, I would lie morosely in my bunk, trying to summon the energy to do the whole thing again in reverse, sometimes for hours at a time? The deck a foot above my head was painted a hideous cream. It was caked with several coats.

If I let my eyes wander a little, from where I lay, I could see into the gaps in the dark corners where the frame came up and the hull started down and the paintbrush couldn't reach, which seemed to be filled with a dark and disgusting dusty grunge. More than that, I could poke my fingers into the gap, if I wanted to. So I did, and discovered that it was compounded partly of boat-hold dust and partly of green mould.

If I slipped a little further forward I could engage in a spot of instant weather forecasting. The hatch had a windowpane let into the middle of it. I could see nothing but sky. It was one of the reasons I woke early, most mornings. It woke me. It often looked grey and changed gradually to blue, but wiggling further forward I could see the mast and the courtesy flags flying from the cross trees some 20 feet above me. I could take an instant reading on the state of the wind. I could see clouds or fog. But that was it: sky, flags, wind. It was usually tedious enough to drive me out of bed to check on the real state of the day and, to do that, I had to reverse my procedures. I have never dressed with so much care. It felt like a preview of senility.

Just before we left Denmark, Baines was up with me in my cabin discussing the leaks. He called Bob, who was cooking.

'Bring the computer and show Griff the horrible videos,' he said. 'Have you seen these?' he asked me. 'They're really horrible, ghastly. You'll have nightmares. They're utterly, utterly revolting.'

'What are they?'

'They're his MA course-work.'

Bob came scrambling up to the fore-cabin lugging his Apple Macintosh laptop. 'Very snug,' he said.

'I thought so too,' said Baines. 'Look, we can all get up here, keep each other warm.' Bob pushed himself up beside us, squeezing his long form into the limited space. 'Good isn't it?' The three of us now lay like prairie dogs, crammed into a cupboard. Bob balanced his laptop on his crutch so that we could all see.

'I've shown you these, haven't I?' he said.

'I don't know,' I said.

He started searching through his files. Some three years ago Bob had startled those who knew him well by deciding to get an MA. He'd gone along to a major London art school and applied to be a mature student on a computer graphics course.

'What's your background?' asked the professor who interviewed him.

Bob swivelled in his chair and looked at the wall behind him. 'Well it's a sort of tangerine colour,' he said. According to Bob, this answer so amused the professor that he was instantly enrolled on the course, therefore qualifying for a large and useful grant and access to several hundred thousand pounds' worth of expensive graphics equipment. This last he used to make a sleeve for a cd of his tuneless country dirges, a lot of pictures of himself dressed in a chicken suit running around in a field and a series of shots of my dog transposed on to luxurious interiors for a charity book, which didn't sell any copies. These qualified as homework. If he was up in town and able to meet at Nick the Basque's, it was usually because he was 'attending a lecture' or registering for a tutorial. The last few weeks before we sailed had been a difficult time for him, academically. He had already taken his exams, or rather he had taken some exams. He was annoyed because somehow they had been a bit vague in their instructions, something to do with his not being there enough, or something, and he'd sort of turned up on the wrong day, and indeed sat the wrong exams, but one thing was certain, he had to finish his course-work. All the time we were attempting to spring the boat from Michael's boatyard, Bob had been in London trying to finish his course-work. In fact, the months from the beginning of May onwards, whenever I met him – at parties, playing poker, going out to eat, hanging around the Groucho Club, up for the weekend – he had been trying to finish his course-work. He had, to my certain knowledge, stayed up all night five or six days in a row and still not finished it. Truth to tell, he hadn't actually started it and the staying up all night hadn't been a great help in that direction. 'They wanted it presented in a certain specific manner.'

'What, by the end of April?'

'No, in written form.'

Now I was to see the project. He'd finally finished it and handed it in on the afternoon we left. He wasn't going to bother showing us the whole thesis, including the writing that he'd been forced rather unhelpfully to do, but the broad thrust of it was that these Internet messages that he'd collected were a new art form.

'What Internet messages?'

'They're clip-ons. Little video messages that people pass around to each other. I'm collecting them. Is this the German? I think it is.'

A grainy video started to jump about.

'It's the best quality I can get on this machine.'

'Oh dear,' said Baines. A man on the video had shaken a bottle of beer until it was fit to explode and in one deft movement stuck it up the bum of a woman with no clothes on. The subsequent 'accident' would have been much better left to the imagination, although it might have been difficult to imagine the rapture with which the results were greeted by the beer-swiller.

Bob was rolling around with laughter. 'Want to see it again?'

'Not much.'

'That's one of the mildest,' said Baines. He wasn't exaggerating. Bob was opening another file. A man with an enormous erect penis, the size of a small horse, had both his hands inserted in a woman's rectum.

'I had to go and see somebody before I showed it to them,' Bob said.

What the man was doing now beggared belief.

'That was one of the reasons it took so long. Because I wanted to check, you know, before I submitted it, if it was possible for a course-work thesis to be prosecuted under the obscenity laws.'

'Well, it's a better excuse than "the dog ate my homework",' said Baines.

We'd moved on now to a priapic baboon. Bob was laughing with the glee of a collector and searching out more files.

'Not the finger,' said Baines.

'Oh, you have to see the finger,' said Bob.

In the end, I didn't. I watched until the man got out the chisel and the disinfectant, but at the moment when he applied the chisel to the end of his middle finger, I covered my eyes.

'Is it fake?' I croaked from behind my own fingers.

'No, no,' said Bob, 'Heh, heh, heh. You can see it all. Ouch. He gets some sort of sexual kick out of it.'

I wondered if you could award marks to a dissertation you couldn't even look at. It was just one more reason why I didn't particularly want to have to explain ourselves to any zealous coast-guards.

'It's very cramped up here, though, isn't it?' Bob said.

From then on, my cabin was a box of intermittent nightmares featuring digit-less baboons drinking beer.

24. Sweden as a Smudge

After fiddling around in semi-darkness, I had managed to set the alarm on my mobile phone, put it to one side, and had then lain awake all night, waiting for it to ring. It did, eventually, an hour after I wanted it to, still set to English time.

I threaded my way out past the sleeping yobs; stepping over Chas's arm, tripping over George's bag, kicking through empty tins from late-night drinking. As I slunk past Bob, now in the pilot berth, I touched him on his shoulder. He was just about awake. They were all just about awake, but pretending to be asleep, throwing in the odd fake snore or bogus twitch for good measure. Bob rolled over like a ham actor.

I was in a foul mood anyway. On deck, I gathered in warps and took off the shore cable and stood for a few moments, letting my face fall and wallowing in the energy-less pre-cup-of-coffee torpor of six in the morning.

Then, as I walked back towards the stern to prepare to motor off, it occurred to me that, in order to start the engine, I would need the key. In fact, it would be useful if we had the keys to the boat door too, wouldn't it, which hung on the same fob? It further occurred to me that these keys had been entrusted to Peter Heller the, at first, off-hand and then embarrassingly confidential boatyard owner.

Baines and I had been to meet with him to pay him his money yesterday. And we had bought yet more junk, filler and spare screws and paint which we would never get round to using, hadn't we? We had done everything to waste time in his company, but we had never once thought to ask him for that key, had we? So now, before we could go anywhere, I would have to wait until Peter Heller started on his day's work, in about, what, three hours' time? And the worst thing was, I was up. An hour ago I could have turned over theatrically myself and gone back to sleep.

On the return to Copenhagen with Bob and Baines in tow, and dragging my seventeen-year-old son George and his mate Chas along too, I had realized that I wasn't the Daddy on this great jaunt at all. I was the Mummy. I was the one who tried to get them to stuff the discarded polyester python skins of their sleeping bags into their impossibly small covers. I was the one on my hands and knees with a dustpan and brush after the crisp and bread crumbs. I was the one with the duster trying to polish the salt off the new chrome fittings, already beginning to look like that old bicycle left to rot in the shed. I was the one who sent them to bed, got up first, made lunch, cleared the cabin and doled out money. Well, OK, if I was going to be Mummy I would start behaving like Mummy. No, you can't go by taxi. Take the bus. We're not eating out every single meal. Except that I was the one who wanted to go by taxi and eat out every night and avoid the bus. I had become the hermaphrodite mater-paterfamilias.

In the end, Peter Heller, who had been servicing *Undina*, arrived for work at eight, promptly, with the keys, but then he just stood around for a bit. I think it was that love thing again.

'Well, we must be going.'

'Yes.' But he showed no sign of leaving the cockpit. It was the smile, the endearments, the general implacability. He was giving us little nuggets of advice. 'You can leave the flares inside.' 'You'll be fine crossing from Gotland to Latvia in this boat. What's the worry?' Eventually, I had to point out that it was time for us to leave and he went ashore, but slunk off down the pontoon rather miserably. I was wondering whether I had been expansive enough. He was a big bloke and they like expansive gestures, so, as he sat in his van watching us, I waved a cheery wave and he waved back.

Relieved that we hadn't depressed him to the point of suicide, we reversed out of the berth and drifted back and forth in the harbour, turning to get out. He was back on the pontoon in an instant, shouting about the engine and the lock on the rudder. I made some feeble gestures, but he was now summoning us back to the pontoon. Scarcely believing myself, I brought the boat back in to him. He jumped aboard and took over the engine.

Using the highest of revs and the fullest of locks he turned her on herself, swung her around in several tight circles, steered her backwards in a straight line and as, a final touch, sideways up to the dock again. I stood there, nodding, with a stiff expression. Bob and Baines watched in silence.

Now, I have to say that there are many people I can think of, relatives, or work colleagues, for example, teachers, or mentors even, who might have taken this opportunity to point out that I had continuously laid down dogmatic principles about piloting our long-keeled vessel, which had included her intractability under motor, the impossibility of steering her in a straight line backwards and the fatuity of assuming that you could achieve anything by revving the engine. And now here was this red-headed boat builder demonstrating to the entire harbour that, on the contrary, *Undina* could be stopped on a five-pence piece and turned on a washer. And yet, neither Bob nor Baines said anything. They kept their own fixed expressions of interest and, when Mr Heller was safely on shore, satisfied, if once again a touch emotional, and the boat proceeding out of the harbour into the glazed Copenhagen morning, they changed the subject. It was decent of them, really.

The row of windmills marking the entrance to the harbour slid out of view behind us, and we threaded our way down the sound, towards the south-eastern shores of Sweden. The Öresund bridge to Malmö rose up out of the flattened sea and faded away again into a mist.

There was no wind, as we turned, five starboard hand buoys later, and motored across the shipping channel, dodging behind a ferry, already accelerating up to its 17 knots for the journey to Bornholm.

We clattered on along the Swedish coast, to the limits of our Danish maps, with no Swedish money, no Swedish language, and, seemingly, no Swedish charts. There was a gap in my ordering sequence, which left us in Terra Incognita.

'And we're in the Baltic proper now,' I said.

'Yeah,' said Bob. 'But we dipped our toe in its foot as we came out of Kiel.'

'I remember noticing that we actually sailed across the "B" of Baltic Sea,' added Baines. Had we been expecting this? This flat, sloppy waste of water, filled with green trails of slimy weed, the mists and faint green hilly shores? 'It's Suffolk again,' said Bob, but it seemed a long way to come to get to Suffolk.

We chose a port for the evening called Skerrige. We had been about to motor past the insignificant dot on the horizon, but *The Rough Guide to Sweden* told us that, tiny though it was, it had two of the best fish restaurants in Sweden so we screwed a left turn. As it was, we ate well in one, and wondered what the other was like.

I was feeling hyper-critical as I walked into the village. How could Sweden compare with Denmark? I wanted to absorb Denmark, live Denmark, become Danish, but we'd had to move on to Sweden, because I'd said we'd get to St Petersburg by the end of summer and, to get there, we had to go through Sweden.

The girls were less pretty in Sweden. Except that they weren't girls in the village supermarket at all, but middle-aged women with German-looking faces. Denmark had been full of girls, attentive and girly and giggling. In the pizza restaurant in the Tivoli the waitress had been gorgeous. And she loved us. We could tell. Even when Bob wanted her to explain the pizzas backwards, she still loved us. The girl on the checkout in Skerrige was only interested in the price of my bread rolls.

Bob had enjoyed Denmark too. On the day of his return to the boat from England, when Baines and I had been busy settling with Peter Heller, Bob had disappeared into Copenhagen. He wanted to take another look at the 'Free State of Christiana', which had been established in 1971 in an old army barracks on a seventeenth-century redoubt at the edge of the city. The barrack walls had been put to use in reverse: 'to isolate a liberated environment of freedom and anarchy from a more formal universe, like'. As we approached, across canals crowded with increasingly dilapidated yachts, the number of out-of-date haircuts and floppy trousers increased, and

Bob grew visibly more intrigued. We went through a crumbling gate, alongside bunches of tourists on guided tours, into a hippy wonderland.

Years ago I went to see Ken Campbell's production of *The Warp* at the Roundhouse in London. It was twenty-four hours long. Although it was the mid-1970s, the 'alternative', counter-culture, freak vibe of the gig (how the old waffle comes back) seemed to give a last poke to the ashes of the hippy movement. 'Alternative London' brought their dogs and their blankets and lay in a smelly heap, 'to get into it'.

The tangled soap opera combined all the mystical religions and half-baked conspiracy theories into a long moan of protest against the 'straight' world. The crowd was too cool, and too exhausted, I think, to get very excited by it, but the climaxes of the piece seemed to involve a confrontation between a hippy hero and a 'norm'. Whenever this happened, the heap of rabbit fur (granny coats were cool and foxes were just vermin) would stir itself, a selection of beards and round glasses would start nodding, 'Yeahhh. Hey. Yeah,' and a murmur of appreciation would go up around the room. And here it all was again, carefully preserved in Copenhagen, in a would-be city. Right up Bob's street in fact. And mine, to be honest.

As Christiana's neighbours pointed out, they took the water and the electricity but refused to pay the rent. Or at least they did until 1991, when Christiana finally cut a deal with the authorities. The authorities had, like all authorities, been mostly worried about drugs. Christiana declared itself in favour of soft drugs and against hard drugs, so that was all right then. An uneasy compromise was reached. The thousand people who live there pay rent now and chill out amongst the badly drawn graffiti and dogs rolling in the dust.

We were hardly surprised that Bob went back there to wallow in the spirit of Glastonbury made permanent, but after five or six hours we began to wonder where he was.

Baines telephoned him on his mobile. 'Are you still there?' he asked.

'Yes, I am,' said Bob.

'Well, we thought we might be meeting up.'

'I can't leave,' Bob explained. 'Because I'm in the Christiana Information Office. It's a sort of tourist kiosk, and I've just been made the head of information.'

'Bob,' Baines protested, 'you know nothing about Christiana.'

'Well that's not quite true,' said Bob. 'I've been on quite a tour and seen the very impressive houses that some people have built over by the canal. In fact, I've been shown the lot, and, not only that, but I certainly know a lot more about it than the current information officer, who seems, er, to be a bit the worse for wear at present.'

Twenty-four hours later, in Skerrige, Bob and I sat in the light of a street lamp on the quay, and he showed me his haul from Christiana.

'What do you think of that?' he said.

He had a lighter in his hand. He fiddled with it and took the bottom out. 'See, a secret compartment.'

'Yes.' There was a bit of a pause. Baines, George and Chas had heard music coming from a tent and had gone off to investigate. We were alone.

'You could get quite a lot of diamonds in there,' Bob said, peering into the recess.

'Diamonds?' Distant alarm bells rang.

'Yes. Aren't diamonds sort of what you can get in Russia?'

'I have heard that.'

'So what do you think? We could get some in St Petersburg? And they might be worth a lot more in Hatton Garden.'

'I don't know.'

'It's just, this would come in useful.' He flourished the lighter.

'Right . . . Bob, I just worry on two counts. One, if you get caught then they tend to take this sort of thing really seriously in Russia, you know. Six years in a Russian prison is a miserable thing, so I've been told. And two, the authorities in Russia are probably quite up on the hidden compartment in the lighter thing.'

'What, you think they might have seen them?'

'Bob, you can buy them in London. I've got these tins of Carlsberg at home, just for fun, you know, the tops screw off.'

'Oh.' There was a touch of disappointment in his voice. 'Like these, you mean.' He held up a tin of coke and can of beer.

'Yes.'

'So I suppose the first thing they do is go around and check all the tins of beer.'

'Something like that.'

He pursed his lips thoughtfully.

The boys came back. 'It was just ten middle-aged men on stage playing electric guitars all at once,' Chas said dismissively.

Bob nodded. 'Sounds our sort of gig,' he said.

The long southern coast of Sweden had few landmarks. And, anyway, now we crossed a great bay and headed out to sea, so the shore, which had been a distant, low thing since Denmark, faded down to a smudge and then disappeared somewhere to the west of us.

We were trying to get into the Kalmarsund, a channel that led up behind the island of Öland, an 80-mile-long lozenge alongside the coast. It would shelter us from the big ocean until we popped up at the top of it, and crossed the 30 miles of open water to the mythical granite island of Gotland, bang in the middle of the Baltic. But a full day's sailing would still only get us near to the bottom of Öland. We would have to stay a further night in Karlskrona, where we planned to meet up with the rest of the family, who were flying out to join us for a summer holiday.

My daughter Catherine, who was fifteen, was not keen on boats. Boats were my idea of a holiday, apparently, but I had been told that Gotland was the 'Ibiza of the Baltic' and, though I was pretty sure she only had the sketchiest notion of Ibiza, dangled the prospect in front of her. 'Oh, I'm going to Ibiza,' I sang, and pranced around the living room a bit. It seemed to work. She rolled her eyes and gave in.

Gotland was the preferred destination for the Stockholm clubbing set. It was also the preferred destination for the bicycling set, and the gin and tonic set (or vodka and tonic set) and the retiree set. For the Swedes, Gotland was 'holidays'. The climate was sunnier than mainland Stockholm. Everybody who could get on to a ferry went there in July. At the beginning of August they all dressed up in wimples and hose and ponced about for a special Medieval Week. We had booked rooms in a hotel.

But as we plodded towards our fantasy island, I began to wonder whether Captain Bob, the Long John Silver of the voyage, was entirely the right companion to foist on my impressionable off-spring. He and Baines were both heavy smokers. The dummy sat and watched them with one eyebrow raised.

'Baines, what are you doing?' I asked.

'What?'

'Can't you use an ashtray?'

Baines, who was sitting at the wheel, was periodically tipping his cigarette vaguely in the direction of the sea. The ash fell, unerringly, on to the deck. If I looked down into the cabin, I could see Bob, lying semi-comatose in his bunk. He was smoking too, and had arranged himself at a sort of 90-degree angle, so the ash could fall off the end of his cigarette directly on to the floor. This was without him even having to make the effort of flicking his fingers.

'Bob!'

'What?'

'Look at the ash.'

Bob looked up over the edge of his bunk. 'Sorry.'

He reached out with a foot and smeared the ash into the planks.

'Thanks.'

'That's OK.'

I clambered down into the cabin, kicked Bob, and got an ashtray. As I brought it up to Baines, a gust of wind caught the contents and blew them all over the deck.

Karlskrona marked a subtle change in the landscape. Instead of the Suffolk green swelling fields, we sailed into a world of granite; the beginnings of the lumpy, bouldered, wooded landscape of the north. Singled out by Karl Gustav for development as an ice-free harbour, it was constructed in such a regimented manner that it now qualified as an UNESCO site. The navy yards had been turned into monuments and a huge maritime museum had been stuck at the mouth of the port.

We slipped in, ignoring Bob's suggestions that we cut the corner and wreck ourselves, and took note of our first introduction to the increasingly complex submarine landscape. Unlike the silted bottom of the south, the bits beyond the channels were not gently shelving mud, but pinnacles of stone and outcrops of rock. From now on, we would regularly spot boiling water on semi-submerged obstacles.

Taking advantage of the jolly efficient Swedish railways, Jo arrived in Karlskrona the following afternoon, with Bob's son Jack, Catherine and Catherine's friend Lara. Luckily, there were too many to sleep on the boat, so I got another night in a hotel. But, once I was safely ashore, Bob smirked at the youngsters and suggested a game of poker. 'Ooh, yes please,' they said. Over the next twenty minutes, cackling inanely, Bob separated the boys from their ten-pound stakes. Then he went to the head, returned and rubbed his hands. 'Up for some more?' he asked. The two seventeen-year-olds nodded glumly and counted the rest of their holiday money out on the mahogany table.

'Aha, lambs to the slaughter.' He allowed himself one final vulpine grin before losing £96 to George.

'I warned you,' I told Bob the next morning. 'In fact, I ordered George specifically not to ruin you.'

'Well, they won the money and then refused to continue playing,' Bob whined.

'You're very lucky,' I said.

The next morning, Jo and the girls took the bus to the next stop, Kalmar, and the rest of us sailed out of the harbour, down the long road that marked the approaches, straight into a strong breeze, surging through these dark waters capped with white horses with a steady bounding motion. Bob was at the helm. In his flappy hat and semi-beard, he looked like a Polish camp trusty on a seaside outing.

It was excellent, damp sailing. But lumpy clouds were passing overhead, some rushing like puffs of smoke, low and seemingly trying to touch the mast, others building up high in towering, colourless heaps. Öland gradually appeared ahead and, like all landfalls around here, it was signalled by rows of windmills, built on banks out to sea in an enterprising, unwitnessed engineering feat.

Down below, near the centre of gravity, there was no slipping or sliding. *Undina* seemed confident and buoyant. Baines and I pored over the Navtext. This new bit of equipment took messages from nearby navigational stations and printed them up on a small screen. Each forecast promised gales: gales out in the Skaggerrak, gales in the Belts, gales in the southern Baltic, all arriving with increasing ferocity throughout the coming day. We were, fortunately, in the south-eastern Baltic. At least we hoped so.

The gusts we were experiencing now were a potential 18 metres per second. We still had 40 or so miles to sail. We were making excellent progress, but I wanted to get to Kalmar before the gales did.

Bob was still at the wheel. He reacted badly when I told him to 'mind the jibe'. We were about to turn into the entrance of the Kalmarsund.

'I don't mean you in particular. It's just an expression.'

'It sounds like an expression. *You* mind the jibe.'

'I am minding the jibe. It's just . . .' I broke off suddenly. 'Mind the jibe!' I shouted more loudly.

Few boats are completely comfortable with the wind directly behind them because the sails have to be let out to a maximum to catch it. Rolling down steep seas, there is always a danger that the boat will twist, the wind will slip around on the other side of the sail and the entire rig will come crashing across as a result. This is called a jibe. The boom, the heavy wooden spar at the bottom of the sail, whips across the top of the cockpit, and in strong winds it will do so without warning, in an instant, with devastating effect. In really strong winds, in an uncontrolled state, the spar, or the rigging itself, can be smashed by the sheer force of the sudden explosion of wind in the sail, but, more usually, the danger lies in the possible contact between this length of solid wood, the size of a small tree, and a crew member's head. So the Daddy, or the

Mummy or the Dummy of the trip, with three novice teenage boys on board, and two more as a permanent crew masquerading as men, spent his whole time warning people to look out.

'Careful, careful. Don't stand up . . .'

'I'm fine.'

'No, please, don't. We could jibe any second . . .'

And we did. We corkscrewed off the crest of a sloppy wave and, wallop, the boom came crashing across, jerking at all the blocks, juddering the sheets and tackles, cracking the sail and swinging the whole boat into the wind.

'What was that?' said Bob.

'That was the jibe you were supposed to mind,' I said. Bob was leaning on the wheel, turning the spokes to try and get control. The boat was across the seas now and heeling more. Bob was trying to work out where he was.

'Mind the jibe!' I bellowed again.

'I have.'

'No, not you . . .' I was shouting to try and warn the others. Bob had overcompensated and I ducked down because it was obvious we were about to do the whole thing again, only in reverse. 'Heads!' I shouted, but Bob thought I was shouting at him again and got irritated; even more so when, with an almighty crash, the whole caboose whipped overhead again, in the other direction, and a second shuddering, jarring impact shook the boat.

'Shall I take her for just a while?' I asked, sweetly.

'OK. All right. You try and deal with it,' Bob replied and stalked off.

'Mind the jibe,' I yelled at him.

Sitting in Kalmar harbour that evening, tied up for the night in elegant isolation at a jetty built for a tourist ferry boat, it was the motion that stayed with us. Not just the swaying that made us grip the sides of tables in cafés, but the memory of each stage of the journey, expressed in the aching muscles that had braced us against the elements. The shocking and banging of the first passage out against the wind, the swooping and diving of the reach across to the channel and then the uneasy wobbling surges of the long final run.

It had been a race against a weather system. All the conflicting weather reports had finally fought themselves down to one clear message. With 10 miles to go, the weather station at Borgholm had simply announced 'gale imminent'.

'Where's Borgholm?' Baines asked.

'It's about twenty miles up there,' I told him, pointing ahead.

'Here, then, as far as the gale is concerned,' said Baines.

'I suppose so,' I said and looked around at the scudding clouds like engine smoke above our heads. I caught a glimpse of Bob sitting on the poop behind me.

'Mind the jibe,' I said. He flicked his ash on the deck.

25. They Went to Sea in a Sieve

Two days later the gales were still roaming around. All night, the wind had continued to bang about the harbour. I'd lain there listening to it, thinking about big waves, but just as I fretted myself to sleep, I heard whispers outside the cabin and the whizzy, clicking noise of a walkie-talkie.

They were back already. We were going to cross the Baltic to Visby. We had to start early, before dawn, in order to cover the 30 miles up the side of the island of Öland and then out into the deep for a further 30 miles, to Gotland, plonked half-way between Sweden and Latvia in the middle of the Baltic Sea. And we were ludicrously overcrowded: two fifteen-year-old girls, Bob and Baines, George, Jo, Jack and myself. Chas had returned to England. There wasn't space for all of us to sleep on board, and the hotels were full.

'This is what we'll do.' I had outlined my hot-bunking shift system to everyone over dinner the night before, in what must have been the northernmost Spanish restaurant in the world. 'Jo and I will take the boat out at five in the morning. So we'll sleep first. The children . . .' I cannily included Bob and Baines in this, '. . . will sleep later and stay up late.'

There was a shining look in Catherine's and Lara's eyes. Bob was looking pretty excited too.

'How late?'

'Till dawn.'

'Cool.'

I had suspected it would be. We ate that Spanish staple, pizza, and went our separate ways. Bob and Baines took the kids to rip up night-time Borgholm. They watched Abba impersonators. They climbed trees in the waterside park. They buried Bob as a mermaid on the beach. They played walkie-talkie hide and seek. And now, at three, they were back on board. It was ludicrous to try and sleep any more, anyway. I clambered out of my cabin, falling head-first over Catherine's liner trunk, and found them all, bag-faced; the enthusiasm for staying up all night having evaporated by two o'clock. George was already asleep in a corner of the main saloon, crashed out, with his mouth open.

Outside, it was still dark, but there were streaks in the western and north-eastern sky. While they climbed into bunks, I hauled myself out on deck into the cold, took in the starboard fenders, fiddled with a piece of manky rope and undid the forward warp, leaving the boat hanging on a single stern line. Jo took in the electric shore cable, put on the kettle and made a cup of vile, black coffee.

We had got into Borgholm early the day before, after an overnight in Kalmar. They were uninteresting towns, holiday towns, although Bob had been taken with Kalmar's Russian submarine attraction, guarded by a man from Gateshead in a woolly hat. 'I don't know how it got here, to be honest,' he told Bob, 'I think it had to be towed.'

'But it was bought in Russia?'

'Oh, aye. There was a lot of them going cheap after the Salt disarmament things, you know.'

Down below, it was barely possible for two people to pass each other along its entire length. Unsettling hanks of tubing and wires, like the arteries and blood vessels of a metal creature, had snaked through the machinery. The crew must have been aware that they were only the soft, organic bit of a purpose-built war-robot. Only a few fold-away cots even acknowledged their presence.

Bob's eyes glistened in the semi-darkness. 'Do you think they still have any of these for sale?' he asked.

When I had returned to the boat, the following day, for the few short miles to Borgholm, I had half expected to find Bob standing proudly holding the painter of a Russian submarine, asking me to tow it home. Instead, he had a large wooden box.

'It's a Russian sextant,' he told me. 'I bargained him down.'

'The bloke from Gateshead?'

'Yeah.' Bob had opened the box and taken out the grey-painted sextant. 'He wanted two hundred, but I got it for a hundred and twenty. We need one, really.'

'Well, not really, Bob. I mean, we'll only be out of sight of land for about half an hour.'

'Yeah, yeah. But you never know.' And the 18-inch square cube of the box had gone on the floor, so I could trip over it every three hours, for the next two months. 'I could let you have it for a couple of hundred,' Bob offered, after a while.

Borgholm had been a disappointment. It was famous because the Swedish royal family had a summer retreat there. 'Do you think they chose it because it was so convenient for Matti Olsen's hamburger bar?' Baines asked. 'Or was it the other way around?'

Now the sea was a lichen-grey-green at daybreak. There were a few white horses. It had a purposeful feel under us, like a fast river. We were doing about 6 miles an hour, steady enough, sluicing forward under just one sail.

Two terns twisted past us, mewing pathetically, and a guillemot, like a puffin with a black and white beak, flew alongside. It was not really bright. A low, pink sun was wobbling up over the horizon, turning very red as it rose. Out here, on the sea, there was a wide ceiling of stretched cloud, reaching over towards a distant, low, dark, pine-clad shore. A mounded, misted island lay far ahead and, sitting just below the horizon to port, lay the Swedish mainland, marked by three giant chimneys, wafting white streaks high into the air from a hidden power station, beyond the edge of these bland grey waters, poppling under us.

It must have been about midday before the kids woke and came on deck. We reached the northern tip of Öland and turned due east towards Gotland, but this took us out of the shelter of the island. There were 30 miles of open water to cross. Luckily, the gales that had crashed across in the last few days had, indeed, largely blown themselves out. But they left behind a steep, choppy sea with tall, uncertain waves. Nobody wanted to be below in the lurching pendulum motion, so we wedged ourselves into the meagre shelter on deck, tied up with safety lines, and pitched and tossed together in a fairground gondola.

I started counting down the hours. I wanted to make sure we got home before any more surprise storms came whistling out of the north. The Vikings insisted, in their rules of engagement, that no one was allowed to express fear or give vent to fearful words, no matter how bad the situation got. And with four hours still to go I kept hopelessly cheery.

'This is fun, isn't it? Whoops, here comes a big one.' The slight anxiety, combined with the need to reassure everybody, rendered me completely inarticulate, like my father. 'Ha, ha. You'll need to whotsit the doodah, Baines!'

'Eh?'

'The er . . . just pull the thingie in a tad.'

'Oh, the sheet!'

'That's the ticket! Don't turn her round the oojmaphlip too much, though! Ha, ha. This is great, isn't it?'

Even the catch-all names were unimaginative. By the time Gotland arrived on the horizon I'd driven the rest of them half-crazy with my relentless jauntiness and incoherent instructions. They were as relieved to get there as I was.

The island was no sandy, duney Friesian, low-lying sort of island. It was a redoubt. It was a keep. Huge grey granite cliffs faced us, crumbling and marblized and the colour of galvanized metal.

We saw the town rising ahead. We saw boats and towers and then, gradually, a still strikingly medieval city. Since it was the main port on the island, it had a thoroughgoing, busy port life too: ferries were coming and going. There were pilot boats, pleasure boats and cruisers.

Catherine took the wheel and sailed us down towards the entrance. The boat pitched and yawed towards the seemingly blank walls of the harbour. 'I can see it,' someone shouted, and we watched as the tiny slit became a gap, the gap widened to become a gate, the gate became a gaping mouth and, finally, we sloshed on through; carried in by a bounding sea to the safety of the wide harbour, to be disconcerted, as always, by how flat and harmless the water suddenly became.

26. Half Holiday

The vision of a timeless sandy interval on a laid-back paradise-island evaporated, as we squeezed into Visby harbour. There was a gap for us in the cacophonous boat-park, just up the end of the evil-smelling furthest leg of the marina. It was between a four-storey game-fishing boat, juddering as it pumped out the Bee Gees at full volume, and a chartered 40-foot Bavaria yacht (smothered in drying towels) playing Death Metal at slightly fuller volume.

Mary Wollstonecraft observed that the Scandinavians loved music. Indeed, no hamlet on our odyssey had seemed too small to host its own folk festival, usually featuring Peps Blom (a bloke with a big beard, round glasses and that peculiar look of fierce concentration needed for a tiny fret-board), but Visby was a Disco of Babel. There was an afternoon vibe, with fat, Swedish, rapping DJs, over on the quay. Continuous rockabilly ground out of the travelling fairground on the promenade. Several large motorboats posed as mobile groove-parties, where chubby boys, with no shirts and red gypsy bandannas, swung vigorously to the 'Theme from Fame'. A short stumble down the pontoon, a group of wan girls jiggled about on an Alcopop Palace to extracts from *Grease*. I moored with a concentrated expression of peeved stoicism on my face.

'Cool!' Catherine said.

'This looks all right,' Bob agreed.

Just opposite the harbour was an Internet café. I climbed to the first floor, to the offices of a web design company, where Martin met me at the door. He was plump and middle-aged, and wore the sort of interesting footwear that marked him out as a cyber merchant. 'I moved my whole business here from Stockholm,' he explained. 'We design web pages.'

'For people in Gotland?'

'No, no,' he laughed. 'For banks and businesses on the mainland. We don't have to base ourselves anywhere, so we based ourselves here. It is a wonderful island.' He was getting misty-eyed about Gotland. All Swedes were said to suffer from this affliction. Outside his open window, Elvis was crooning 'Love Letters Straight from Your Heart'. Martin summoned a twenty-year-old with long hair, who looked at my mobile telephone and shook his head.

'This is not really our line of business,' he explained.

Martin furrowed his brow. 'There is a shop in the new town. Can you find the number, Per? You know, these are some of the finest medieval walls in the whole of Northern Europe.' I did know. I'd read the guide book. 'The walls weren't really built to keep foreigners out. They were built to keep the local population out. The sheep farmers!' He waved vaguely in the direction of some imaginary yokels.

Sheep were still a big thing on Gotland. There were warehouses selling special Gotland sheepskins, a sort of tight astrakhan grey twist, made into everything from hats to extremely comfortable-looking bicycle saddle covers. (Mmm.) But the Hanseatic merchants had long gone, though Martin and his like had, in a sense, replaced them. 'In their day, the boats came here laden with furs and made the merchants very rich,' he said, with a slightly different misty look in his eye. 'Just one boat from Visby was worth the whole of the value of the English exchequer, in the time of your Henry VIII. This is why you'll find such wonderful medieval buildings here.'

And we did. The warehouses of the Hanseatic merchants were five or six storeys high with crow-stepped gables. Rows of them ran down the cobbled streets. Suffolk was supposed to be wealthy in the middle ages, but a town like, say, Lavenham had nothing on this place. This was wealth to rival the Medicis, with palaces grouped around squares, a brace of old abbeys and a mixed assortment of magnificent ruined churches.

It was our first sight of the rewards that came to the trading nations of the south. Led by the marauding Vikings, they went to colonize what was then the last wild outback of the medieval world.

At the beginning of the last millennium, the woods and bogs of Pomerania cut off the wildernesses of Estonia and Latvia. There was no settled government up there. The fjords and bays were populated by individual pagan tribes. Russian hunters had come out of the east, via Byzantium, working their way to Novgorod. The Vikings came from the west by boat. Close behind them, the Teutonic Knights roved up from the south. These particular, ruthless crusaders helped establish trading posts, and a dominant class of expatriate merchants to rule them, but outside their walls it remained every man for himself. It was a lawless wild west of northern Europe. The Russians, the Germans and the Swedes have fought for control of the area ever since. Estonia and Latvia achieved their independence only in 1991.

That night, in one of the medieval merchant houses that lined the medieval main street in Visby, we went for a medieval banquet. A sturdy wench came and took our order, sitting astride the bench next to us. 'We'll be back in time for Medieval Week, apparently,' I told Bob and Baines. Baines was leaving us to our family holiday and flying back to England to work. He would rejoin us for the rest of the journey when the kids had gone home.

Medieval Week celebrated the arrival of the Danes in Gotland in 1423. They had laid siege to the city and extracted a tribute. In honour of this dismal defeat, the entire town dressed up in woolly tights, capered about and played Elvis Presley on lutes.

The wench banged some wooden platters of smoked ham and apples on the table. 'Cool,' said the kids. For my part, I had been rather hoping the medieval people had managed to invent hot food. Cushions too.

'That would be fun,' said Baines. 'Shall we dress up, then?'

'Yeah,' said Bob. 'Lepers would be good. You know. I've got some artificial hands we could drop in restaurants.'

'We could come as English sailors. I could be the captain and you two could be a crew,' I said.

Bob looked at me steadily. 'What do you mean, crew?'

We were interrupted by a furious banging. Our waitress trotted out and started stretching herself like an athlete preparing for an

Olympic event. She threw back a leg, arched her back and, with a commendable enthusiasm, gobbed a gout of yellow flame up into the roof space. Singed or not, we all applauded.

'What exactly is she blowing, then?' asked Baines.

'Fire,' said Bob, helpfully.

'Yes, but how come there are always fire eaters at medieval banquets, even in all the films, but they only discovered petrol in the Victorian era?'

Bob spent the rest of the evening trying to catch the waiters out.

'Do you take credit cards?'

'Yes.'

'But how can you take credit cards, surely this is a medieval banquet? Can we pay in groats?'

'No, I'm afraid not.'

'Surely,' Bob continued, 'this meal we're eating here, if this were really medieval times, would cost us less than a penny.' We crept away and left him to it.

Over the next week we settled into an uncertain island life. Away from the harbour and the taxi rank and the cruising 1950s American limousines, Gotland was the Martha's Vineyard of Sweden. The dreamy semi-bucolic life of the town seemed a *House and Garden* magazine fantasy, available down every lane and on every pebbly beach. The manicured farms and the carefully restored houses were the holiday homes of the rich and successful from Stockholm. Glimpses of the luxury interiors, through home-made lace curtain windows, the shaggy dogs trotting across back lanes, the four by fours, with their backs open and the cold boxes being unloaded, the children running down the hills and the bicycles leaning against the flint walls, all spoke of continuity and settled opulence. We felt excluded from it all, tourist ghosts, looking in at the feast but never joining the table. The children quite wanted to go to a club, but they were too young for that.

So we left Visby and went exploring Gotland by car. Out of the town, past the airport and through the fir woods, we dropped into a placid agricultural community with horses and red barns and fields of crops. The sun had begun to shine. The low had moved on.

Scandinavia was now in the grip of an extraordinary high. It would last from the middle of July until the end of September. With one or two exceptions, there was hardly a day of cloud. Travelling around this magical green island became a transcendent experience.

We went off to a place which reputedly served the best cakes in Sweden. The cakes were so-so, but just opposite the café there was a little yard sale: a collection of junk in an open garage. Bob sauntered across the road to have a look and came back in a mild state of excitement. He'd found a picture of a capercaillie in a wood. He took me back to show me. It was rather badly painted, I thought, and I told him so.

'Well, it would go for about £50,000 if it were painted by somebody else.'

'Somebody who could paint, you mean, Bob.'

The stall was run by that rural cliché, an osteopath. 'Do you speak English?' Bob asked him.

'A little.'

'That's good, so do I.'

Another man standing by looked very surprised. 'You only speak a little?' he asked.

'Yes,' said Bob.

'So where are you from? You don't have an accent.'

'Oh, I'm from London,' said Bob.

'But you only speak a little English?'

'I'm sorry, it's just a silly English joke.'

The man looked at Bob for a while. 'That's not silly, it's stupid.' Bob agreed.

Finally he came back to the car. He didn't bring the orange-painted sticks, which he'd rather liked. ('They mark my car park,' the osteopath vendor had told him. 'Yes,' said Bob, 'but are they for sale?' 'No, I'm afraid not.') And he didn't bring the grouse daub. ('He wanted too much,' Bob told me.) But he did bring a small porcelain statue of Heidi in a green dress and button shoes. It was added to Bob's pillage, which included an unexpected variety of china bibelots.

We ventured on to a Baltic beach, down through a stand of

young ash, across dunes, to white sand, glowing bright sun and a freezing sea. The air was sharp and clear and the nearby wooden houses looked nicely Swedish; etched in light and shade. The bathers seemed to jump in, have some sort of epileptic spasm, and come straight back out again. It didn't encourage us. A black Land Rover was parked amongst the dunes. It was connected by a large orange cable to a hut in the trees and sported two huge speakers on the roof rack. Red Bull keeps you awake and slightly irritable, so I suppose it was appropriate that their promotional wagon did the same. I wondered, though, as the kids jumped about and played volleyball, and families watched over their toddlers, if they had the faintest idea what was actually being said by the Niggaz With Attitude: 'Smoke weed every day, somebody here gonna fuck, the bitch jumped off my truck,' went the rap and the kids skipped in a circle. 'All these fine bitches say yes to me, they all just taken Ecstasy, no idea what the side effect would be, oh lady, let's get high.'

We made a hopeless journey to try and find a horse fair in the interior of the island and, having driven for miles around tiny lanes, always getting closer to our destination, but never quite making it, finally gave up and took a diversion to a place called 'Catlans' near Gottlinbro.

It was a fortified farm, dating from the early middle ages. Nobody else was around. The air hummed in the heat. We put money in a box and climbed upwards until we came to a plain, grey room with deal floorboards and, in the middle of it, a crooked table. There was no clutter. It was human habitation without any humans to muck it up, allowing us to insert our own fantasies into the place. No clothes, books or chairs. Only a vase of cornflowers and tansy, standing on an oval table: the sole pure colour in the room. Everything else was bleached and grey. A solitary fly lazily explored his exit. Through the windows the overwhelming green of the fields and trees was sharpened by an early-evening sun. Next door we could see a bedroom with a tiled stove and an old painted cupboard. The house had been there for 800 years and we stayed for nearly half an hour.

Back in Visby, the people up in the town recommended by

Martin the cyber merchant couldn't help me with my mobile phone. I spent an afternoon in my hotel room waiting to get through to a help line in Ireland, who were useless too. Then, the next day, I lost it altogether.

I was tempted to walk away, let the thing go, rely on Bob's instant weather forecasting, but I knew the mobile phone must be in a taxi and I even knew which taxi, because it had been an inappropriate, long, black and ancient 1980s stretch-limo Mercedes, with two fold-down seats, and just me in the back. The phone must have fallen out of my jacket pocket as I lounged in it.

There were only two taxi firms on Gotland: Taxi 44 44 44 44 and Island Taxis. Neither had any sort of exotic cars on their books, certainly not a stretch limousine. I found this puzzling. They'd never heard of it? Maybe I'd been picked up by some sort of Jim Jarmusch figure? Perhaps he was some manifestation of Ingmar Bergman, the famous film director, who lived on Gotland: the 'death taxi', come to collect me. I would search and he would find me and we would stretch off to infinity together.

I decided the only way to find out was via another taxi. I hailed one, jumped in and explained my plight. Swedes generally apologize for their poor English by saying things like: 'Forgive me my disappointingly feeble linguistic skills.' After a while, you assume that everyone speaks English like a United Nations diplomat. But this driver didn't know any English at all, except 'I don't really speak English', which was delivered with sincerity and a slight Wiltshire accent. I explained again slowly about the taxi and, as I had expected from the outset, he instantly recognized my description. At the two-sheds-and-a-conveyor-belt-airport, my driver jumped out and came back in a few minutes. 'Your phone is in the police station,' he told me.

Behind medieval Visby, which creeps up the side of the cliff with narrow streets and cobbled gutters, beyond the walls, which once kept the yokels out and now keep the tourists in, is a new town of near-suburbs, tacked on to the old one. The police station was like a modern school reception building. Several women sat surrounded by computers. I explained my mission and the receptionist fumbled around in a pile of lost keys, lost watches and mobile phones.

'OK,' she said finally, 'is this yours?'

'Yes, that's mine.'

'What make?'

'Siemens!' I said, moderately confidently, given that I could see it had Siemens stamped on it where she held it in her hand. And that was that.

Except that, as I headed back to my taxi, I noticed that there was a beautiful garden opposite the police station. It was big, stretching at least four blocks in one direction and a block in the other. There were great banks of flowers, apple trees, paths, wallflowers, hollyhocks, flowering onions, daisies and, everywhere, brightly painted mini-sheds, but each decorously ornamented and carefully maintained, in the middle of these fantastic explosions of flowers. It was some sort of an allotment.

I went back the following day. Alice, the person in charge, was a retired scientist who had originally come with her husband to work at the agrarian institute for the Gotland government, to supervise the introduction of new crops. She led us up and down the incredibly neat paths and past the well-tended beds. 'It's a question of the community,' she explained. 'We have been given this land by the community and we must keep it well, because otherwise the community will take it back.'

'It's so beautiful,' I said. There was no yellowing turf, no cabbages, no old sticks. It was as fresh and ordered as the Chelsea Flower Show.

'We have rules. We must keep to the rules.'

I sensed that the orderliness went deeper than the rows of red hot pokers.

'Some people want perhaps to put up a different kind of little house, but we cannot have it.'

'I see. They all have to be the same.'

'No, not the same. But you cannot have glass roofs or bigger little houses. We must each do our turn to clean the walking places.'

'What if you don't?'

'You must. The town will take it away if we do not.'

'And if, for example, somebody lets their place fall down.'

'No, this is impossible. Sometimes, there was one family and the father he died and the children took over the garden, but they didn't keep it up. We tell them they must look after the garden, or off they fuck. They must fuck off. Fuck off, we said.'

Bob raised an eyebrow. I sensed that Alice, like the families on the beach, might not be fully aware of the ramifications of the phrase that she must have heard so often in Hollywood films. But then again, on second thoughts, perhaps she was.

The last days in Gotland passed in a haze: wild flowers, lilac hedges and girls with large breasts and their tongues between their teeth, manoeuvring ancient Volvos out of beach parking places, twisting roads through fading grass meadows, flag-posts, flocks of swans, red barns with corrugated roofs and, always, the white-flecked blue sea, in the gaps beyond the slatted sloping fences and the granite-grey cliffs.

The Raukers are standing stones: mammoth natural henges plopped down on the edge of bluffs, worn down by the wind, with narrow bases and big bodies. On our last afternoon I decided to walk up to one of these things, which we could see from a pebbled beach where we were sitting. My path took me through coastal pines, an arthritic Japanese wood, broken and stooped with age, past harebells, rowans, junipers, myrtle berries, wild roses and banks of moss. Above, out of sight, seagulls were crying.

I crossed a bridge across a watercourse that had dried up in the August heat. The stream bed was stone and the natural flagging had formed a series of levels that usually carried the water down, but now stepped up like a staircase through the forest floor.

This was why Scandinavians believed in trolls. Troll steps, troll seats, troll gardens. The little wood by the sea was full of disconcerting, half-human details. The standing stone was in a little clearing on a hillock. It was a majestic and towering lichen-covered rock, an outcrop of some ancient outburst of the earth's energy. A dragonfly buzzed up. The period between the stone's formation and my sitting there was no more than that dragonfly's wingbeat in time, but it was still quite impossible to conceive of the process of gradual erosion that had created this troll Henry Moore.

We took the ferry to Stockholm to catch our flights back to the UK. The family holiday was over. We had to start at five o'clock in the morning. I'd warned everyone on the boat to be ready. It was another bloody early dawn and, this time, for somebody else's boat.

Jo went ahead with the girls. Wrapping all our luggage around me, hanging one bag over my neck, which bounced uncomfortably against my thighs, draping another on each shoulder, and grasping one in each fist, I left the hotel where we had been staying and trudged like a Peruvian gold-miner down to the harbour where Bob and the boys had been sleeping on the boat. It was beginning to rain. The continental blaze had temporarily disappeared. I arrived, wet and aching. Rivulets were dripping down my face. 'Where are the boys?' I asked.

Bob was standing under the hatch, peering out at me. He looked puzzled.

'Oh, just gone to the loo.'

'I'm late. We've got a taxi.'

'A taxi?'

'For the bags.'

'Oh, right. I was just going up into the town to get some bread.'

'Bread? We haven't really got time.'

'I was just going up to get breakfast, have a last stroll around the ancient walls.'

He's doing this deliberately. He's trying to turn me into an old woman. I'm sprouting pink hair and comfortable shoes. 'No, come on, Robert, come on, get out.'

'I've just got to do the fridge,' he says.

I can't believe it, he hasn't done the fridge. Now I have to don a pinafore too. Bob will hoard food. In the medieval restaurant I had had to stop him carrying away all the apples. Now he loaded old cheese, a melon, two already opened packs of sliced ham, a smoked eel, two smoked flounders and a packet of stuff that smelled like herring, into a bag. I offered to carry it for him, and as soon as we got up on the quay, threw the lot in a bin.

We walked across to the car park, around the huge puddles and arrived at the desk. 'Where's the bag of food?' said Bob.

'I chucked it,' I told him.

'But we could have used that on the journey.'

'Never mind.'

'Well, it's nothing to carry,' he said, standing, looking at me there, laden down with our fifteen bags.

The others were waiting at the check-in desk for the ferry. The main bags were taken off me and stuffed in a cage on wheels. We passed through several barriers and sat on some award-winning seating units. There was an announcement in Swedish. 'Does that mean us?' I asked an attendant.

'Yes, the bus is downstairs,' he replied.

We gathered. Everybody else gathered and went to the bus. Everybody except Bob, who had disappeared. The attendant went to shut the doors. 'No, no.' I lunged forward. 'No, wait.' He looked bemused. 'We're just waiting for one of our number.' George disappeared and came back moments later, having hustled Bob out of a loo.

Bob looked puzzled. 'What's the hurry?' he asked.

'We're boarding,' I told him.

He pulled a face that registered absolute astonishment, looked at his watch and shook his head in disbelief. 'There's plenty of time,' he said.

27. The Middle Ages

On the train back to London from Stansted, I had decided to give Bob a cheque for his 'expenses'. He was coming for the entire summer, after all. Yes, I paid for his air fares, all the food on the boat, all the food off the boat, all the taxis, all the hotel bills when we stayed in them, the bus fares and, well, everything that needed money, really. But he was the crew. That was the score. And, as he said, there were extra costs, like his cigarettes, that I didn't pay for, so I wrote a cheque and handed it to him. He looked at it and snorted.

'Is there a problem?'

'Well, no. Hm. Yes. That's great. That's great, that is. That's how things stand is it? I see.' He babbled on for a while longer and then sat brooding under the luggage rack.

It was a long time since I could remember him getting quite so agitated. Bob was, by nature, unflappable. Indeed, it was an unresolved ambition of mine to try to get him to be more flappable. How many times had we approached a concrete pier with a following wind, when I had wanted him to stir himself to some sort of genuine concern, like putting out a foot or something. For myself, of course, by contrast, the most innocent slight could result in apoplectic outrage.

'What's the matter?' I asked, darkly.

'Well, I just think it's a bit much.'

'I'm beginning to think pretty much the same thing myself.'

'Just, if I had to add together all the bits I've actually had to pay for, they would come to more than this.'

'Well, I was rather hoping they might. Do you think I should be giving you more, then?'

'You can't possibly expect me to take less than Baines!'

I narrowed my eyes meaningfully.

★

'Bob just accidentally found the cheques you had given me as last week's wages,' Baines told me later, unconvincingly. I spent quite a lot of the four days I was back in England ringing him and gnashing my teeth down the phone. Baines thought that there should be some level of equality. Bob was outraged by how much I was paying Baines. And I was annoyed at being outmanoeuvred.

'Bob,' I said. 'Don't you see it? I had always assumed that we were the gentlemen yachtsman on this jaunt and Baines was the hired hand.'

He didn't see it.

'You should count yourself lucky I don't send you a bill for your share of the costs of employing him.'

Bob was unmoved.

In vain, I pointed out that Baines was the only one who knew how to unblock the water system, that Baines had linked up the mysterious aerials for the navigation systems. That Baines was the one who went down the sewer when neither of us even knew it was called the sewer. As far as Bob was concerned, he was the one who had supplied Baines. It wasn't the dosh. It was the status.

I offered a solution. That I pay them both and then they paid a third of their wages each to hire me and then we would all be equal. Ha, ha! But neither of them admired this quiddity as much as I did. So now our relationship was to undergo a subtle change from which it never quite recovered. I didn't regret the money, I just found it unforgivable that they had outwitted me.

Charlie seemed an excellent way of redressing the balance. I rang him somewhere in Hampshire. He had worked for Talkback as a runner and like all runners in the media was superbly overqualified for the jobs he was in between at the time. Besides, I thought it might discompose the other two if he was sprung on them, so I bought him a ticket for the same plane and instructed him to make himself known to Bob and Baines on the way out.

Four days later I flew back into Gotland, fired up at the thought of medieval frolics. 'So, it's Medieval Week,' I said to the taxi driver.

'Is it?' he said, 'Well I suppose so, yes.'

'Is everybody in town dressed in medieval stuff?'

'Yes, well, the kids, you know.' He wasn't wearing medieval stuff himself. He laughed. 'I suppose you want to be picked up on a horse, do you?'

'So, what goes on? Is there jousting?'

'I have no idea,' he said, 'Oh, yeah, there is a tournament, yesterday, I think, and maybe later in the week.' He shrugged.

In the second form, I had been in Mr Smart's musical production of *The Boy with the Cart*, by Christopher Fry. ('Boy with the cart, where are you *going* to? Boy with the cart, where *have* you come from?') Now, as I got out of the cab, it seemed like the entire unconvincing rent-ye-crowde in that unconvincing epic had reconvened in Visby, looking almost as self-conscious about it as we 'village folk' had been on the Memorial Hall stage.

I passed a middle-aged couple in their middle-aged gowns. He clearly worked in local government. She, in her wimple, and mother's curtains, was still toting a red mock-leather handbag with gold buckles. The young men who had previously been drunk in red bandannas were running through the gutters, drunk, in jester's hats. Two girls wandered past half-heartedly carolling. They carried a recorder, wore bonnets like inverted boxes and probably read Geography at Uppsala University. They joined me at the end of the large queue of medieval people waiting for the banco-mat.

Two boys in front of me weren't medieval at all, except that they'd drunk quite a bit of mead. 'They fried a whole wild pig,' they said.

'Where was that?' I asked.

'In the marketplace.' They both came from Vilhelmina, 600 kilometres north of Stockholm.

'So it's got mountains?' I was guessing.

'It's good for snowboarding and skiing in the winter and then it gets very hot in the summers too, when it never gets dark. I like that.' This was their first time in Gotland.

There was a far more serious medieval 'wighte' standing next to me. 'Do you speak English?'

'Of course.'

He looked a little hot. He was wearing a thick robe of dark blue fustian with a heavily embroidered cloak and big leather boots. Medievalists always seemed to dress as if they were about to bed down in a ditch in a snowstorm.

'Do you know the stadium?' I asked.

'We were thinking of going there ourselves,' he told me, adjusting his medieval spectacles, the real thing, I noticed, held in place with an interesting piece of thong. He pointed to his wicker basket. 'But we have a lot to carry.' I was impressed that he stopped himself from adding 'stranger!' to the end of his sentence. This was more like it.

The stadium was outside the city walls on a patch of flat ground beyond the lumpy ex-moats. It was surrounded by a 'medieval fayre', which might have been thought up by Kate Bush. There were chairs of a sinuous devising, lengthy velvet robes and velvet cloaks, felt hats of various quirky dimensions and arrows, a lot of arrows, sold by a monk. In fact, there were a number of stalls selling bows, strings and fletches. And people dressed in hessian were looking at them and plucking their weapons in a very serious way indeed.

The tourney was brisk and the knights riding the horses noble and impressive, galloping towards each other at great speed and valorously flouting EU safety regulations. The audience whooped and hollered, but I felt separate from it all, an onlooker, envying their open-hearted commitment to such a footling enterprise, but not really prepared, or able, to join in. Perhaps I should have worn those parti-coloured tights and a jerkin after all. Now I had other things on my mind.

I made my way back to the harbour, too self-conscious to eat in a restaurant, among all the merrie back-slapping, olde-worlde fellowship, and too lazy to bother cooking for myself. I wandered from restaurant to restaurant, nervous that I might be sucked into another medieval banquet. In the end, I went to a street stall to try a *korv*. 'The special', at 25 kroner, was a particularly off-putting technicolor sausage in a bun, with what appeared to be two ice-cream scoops of mashed potato balanced on top of it. I stuck to the straightforward *korv* (hot dog), with *strips* (chips), ketchup and *skrop* (mustard). This last was served from two big hanging sacks. You got hold of an udder, pulled it vigorously and your *skrop* spurted all over your sausage. It was oddly comforting.

As another sun set somewhere over Sweden, I prepared to go over to the ferry to meet the others. I was getting tired of beautiful, over-indulged Visby and Gotland with its model farms and comfortable holiday homes and medieval play-acting. I was eager to cross the rest of the Baltic Sea and get to ugly Latvia and its lack of comforts.

The ferry arrived late. Charlie was delightful. Bob and Baines were chipper. We never mentioned the money again. I just paid it. They just took it.

We went back to the boat and started unpacking.

'Tick-borne encephalitis, apparently, is a big difficulty in these regions,' said Charlie as he laid out an impressive selection of purpose-made travelling kit. 'They recommend tucking your trousers into your socks.' He was reading the Foreign Office warnings about Latvia and Estonia.

'Well,' Baines settled back in the saloon, 'at least that will let them know we're English.'

Bob wondered whether we'd have to go ashore in bee-keeping outfits, like nuclear inspectors or Ebola paramedics.

'What else does it say?'

'Don't go into dark bars with strangers.'

'Especially if you've got your trousers tucked into your socks,' said Baines.

We settled in, with a lot of grunting and heaving, and I produced the new summer-weight duvets I'd bought in the town. Bob and Baines were appreciative. Charlie didn't see what the fuss was about, but he was a new boy. When Mary Wollstonecraft, the mother of Mary Shelley and a prototype Polly Toynbee, journeyed to Sweden, she was disparaging about the peasant backwardness of the natives and particularly disparaging about the sleeping arrangements. She recorded, perhaps for the first time in literature, that Scandinavians slept between two eiderdowns, a practice she thought unsanitary. She obviously never tried a sleeping bag.

Charlie was a competent and knowledgeable sailor. As we pulled out of the harbour into a clear, sweet afternoon the following day, I praised him extravagantly and loudly in front of Bob. Charlie wanted to quiz us a little about our trip so far.

'Did you see any wildlife, for instance?'

We paused and thought about this. 'Well, yes, there were the porpoises,' Baines said, nodding.

'Were they porpoises?' I asked.

'Porpoises, dolphins or pilot whales, we weren't sure, but we saw them. And a seal,' Bob said confidently.

'Did we see a seal?' I asked.

'I thought you saw a seal,' he replied.

'Did I? Yes, probably.'

'Yes, well, there are seals and we've seen a seal, not on this trip, but in the Orwell in Suffolk.'

'I remember. We did see a seal, then, but that was last year.'

'But there was the pigeon which landed. That wasn't really wild, it was a racing pigeon, it had a ring. And there was the bee.'

'Yes,' Charlie said. There was a pause. We had sails up and were creaming along. I had decided to try to do something about our decayed varnish, it was so lovely, and was scrubbing down a hatch with a bit of wet and dry.

'I saw *The Blue Planet*,' Bob said finally.

'Did you?' said Charlie.

'Yes, I saw that too. That had a lot of wildlife in it,' said Baines.

'Yes, did you see that one about the ones that went very fast, the speed? The barracuda does about forty miles an hour, apparently, but the marlin does seventy.'

'That is a lot of speed, isn't it? Going full tilt, a marlin could cross the Atlantic in ten hours.'

'Could he keep it up?' asked Bob.

'Of course, and as a result he's certainly the most deadly thing in the sea.'

'How?'

'Well he has that great long spike on the end of his nose, he comes along at seventy miles an hour and, wallop, he's got a fish on his spike.'

'I see, but how does he get it off?'

'He's got the fish on his spike, but he goes, damn, I forgot, I've got no hands.' Baines made sneezing noises.

We anchored for the night in a little bay called Klinhahn, half-way up Gotland, under the shadow of more standing stones. I went on deck around midnight. The moonlight bathed everything. To the north the headland was a piece of broken cake topped with Christmas trees. To the south the rock and stones stood up at the edge of the forest under the low cliff. Up on deck, pissing, I found the night was cold and glitteringly clear, after an endless sunset which had made puce pools amid the green rocks. The water was green too, and when I had swum in it earlier, it was brackish; not salty exactly, but like a flavoured soup, luridly avocado-tinged.

Yes, I was glad to be moving on again. On our weather monitor, the Navtext, we were now getting warnings and information about the ultimate destination, St Petersburg (details of 'the summer buoys' and the navigation lights) as well as forecasts from the further reaches of the Gulf of Bothnia and 'the Quark', way to the north, and wonderfully remote and mysterious.

We didn't linger in Fårösund at the top of the island, even though it was lying satisfied and tempting in the evening sun. After I had telephoned the Swedish Customs authorities and they had discovered they had no officers available and, apologizing profusely, told us we would have to proceed out of the EU without their stamps, I made a messy Oeuf Arnold Bennett and we set off down the sound at around nine in the evening. The sun set behind us as we sailed out to cross the rest of the Baltic Sea to Latvia.

28. In a Baltic State

Ventspils was a quietly disconcerting port after the drama of Sweden. It lay on a great expanse of blank seaboard with nothing visible to the south or north, except a wide, level coast, stretching away to the horizon.

It took us nearly eighteen hours to make the crossing from Gotland. Eventually, we motored towards giant cranes, past the long arms of the breakwaters in a flat, hot calm, at the very end of the following morning. As we turned into a crumbling dock, dominated by a concrete blockhouse, a man in uniform appeared in a window above us. He waved us on, across the fishing harbour, to the pontoons of a new yacht club. There were three boats in it, and that included us.

I was born at the beginning of the Cold War and brought up on John Le Carré and Len Deighton: propaganda in its own way. 'The grim poverty, the watching eyes, the colourless lives.' It was a cliché of the *Sunday Express* swinging sixties. As we grew older, of course, we grew suspicious of all this. It couldn't be anything but myth, could it? After all, my mate Fischl went to Russia and came back a shagging machine, all on account of his Levi jeans. But I wasn't sure about the alternative either: the woolly-haired, woolly-thinking, fellow-travelling apologists: the Brecht-waving, earnest research fellows at Cambridge in the 1970s.

Only one thing was certain. In the 1960s and 1970s, during my adolescent life, it was as difficult to travel to certain parts of the world, to find out for yourself, as it had been for Marco Polo. Merely declaring Glasnost and tearing down the Berlin Wall couldn't undo that memory. Here, sticking my toe into the waters of the former Soviet Bloc, I never quite lost the sense that we were trespassing into an experiment.

As far as Bob was concerned Latvia was the one that hadn't won the Eurovision Song Contest, and then did. 'But it's always Latvians on that programme *The World's Strongest Man*, isn't it.'

'Is it? I've never watched it.'

'They haul trucks around with their teeth, that sort of thing.'

We were sitting in a fishing harbour by a grass bank, tied up to new pontoons, staring out at a hazy day through drooping eyes. Every new country we reached seemed to jump on us after a night sail. It was only midday, but we'd hardly slept in the last twenty-four hours. We had to make some sort of plan, but that seemed an utter impossibility, so we talked to Albert ('call me Albertina'), the harbour master, and waited while two teenagers in uniforms walked round from the concrete bunker on the far side of the large dock to examine our papers.

'We need money, Albertina, Latvian money.'

'Yes, yes.' He pulled in his stomach. 'I will show you.' Albert had no shirt on, and was about seventy. He used to be in the Russian army and then in the merchant navy, and now, with independence, he had no pension at all, so he'd become the jolly, half-clad dock master of Ventspils.

He ushered us protectively up the bank and into his wooden-fronted offices, holding in his stomach as best he could. We passed some gangster-looking fat men, wearing polo shirts tucked into shiny, crocodile-belted trousers, who were lounging on the grass with the placidity of zoo reptiles. They said something disparaging, in Latvian, to Albert, and pulled faces in the direction of our old wooden boat.

'It's restored, it's restored,' Albert said to them, defensively.

Ventspils had been a favoured Soviet seaside resort. To the south of the harbour was a magnificent shallow, sandy beach, which stretched off and away south, towards Lithuania. But the Russian tourists didn't come any more. They weren't banned. They simply couldn't afford it. The majority of the holidaymakers were Latvian natives.

Later that day we sat on a whitened beached tree trunk and watched the runners and the walkers. The beach is the universal equalizer of the world. The dogs, the elderly couples, the kids on bicycles to-ing and fro-ing in silhouette across the pink vista could have been anywhere: Maine, or France, or Wales. Not England, of course. It was all better presented than that.

'Excellent,' Baines said after a while.

'Mmm.'

'I think it's good to have seen this,' said Bob. 'When people play, you know, "where's your favourite beach in the world?" we listen while they say Ibiza or Southwold or some other cliché, and then we can say, oh, actually, if it's a clean, sweeping huge beach you're after, then it's difficult to beat Ventspils in Latvia.' Then we walked out into the sea, but, after 50 yards, the Baltic had only risen to our pot-bellies and we couldn't bear to prolong the creeping submersion any longer. We plunged under and splashed in the not quite fresh water.

How quickly we fell into seaside holiday torpor, in a place that had the aimlessness of the proper seaside, because there was nothing to do. After Gotland, with its clubs and purposeful holidaymaking, Ventspils seemed the sort of place you got dumped in, and was the more redolent of 'real' childhood holidays because of it.

Half-way through the day, two other boats came into the harbour. They were both small cruisers, some 30 feet long, and had been sailed, single-handedly, in dual convoy, from Gotland by Axel and Ola. Axel was German, but he kept his boat almost permanently in Stockholm, near to Ola's boat. Ola worked in Gothenburg, not Stockholm, where he still lived. They were both charming.

'Are you going to Riga?' Axel asked me.

'Not by boat,' I replied. The Gulf of Riga was a great, wide-mouthed bay some 100 miles long. It would take us two days to sail down into it and then another two days to get back out and we were short of time. But we felt obliged to visit Riga, the capital. So we had decided to leave the boat and go by bus. We would stay overnight and come back the following day. Axel was impressed.

'And can you go by bus easily?' he asked.

'Er . . .' I wasn't sure.

'It takes three hours, so they say, and they run regularly.' Charlie had been to look it up.

'That sounds like a good idea. Yes. Yes. That would certainly save us some time, too.'

Groping for further conversation, we turned to electronic charts. Axel had 'C Map 2'. 'Did you ever manage to stop your boat going north up?' he asked.

'North up? No, no we haven't even managed to link the boat's GPS to the system yet,' I moaned.

'It's hardly worth the bother,' said Axel gloomily.

This depressed me. 'Its manual is written in complicated language. Not complicated seaman's language or complicated computer language, but just complicated writer man's language,' I said.

'Yes, yes.'

I warmed to my rant. It was dangerous and stupid, not properly tested or designed. And, by the way, I had another bit of worthless junk, from Blaupunkt: an all-singing, all-dancing, all-buttons, all-rubbish cd player. But none of these were as bad as the Siemens phone. Hopeless beyond measure in its interactions and back-up and its misinformed catalogue and another sodding German product.

I stopped. Axel's sympathetic smile had become a little varnished. He was German himself, of course. He backed away nodding and agreeing, and scurried back to his boat.

Baines had got hold of his first bit of Soviet loot: a Cuban Romeo y Julietta Number Two cigar – 'incredibly cheap' – and lit up after supper from the oil lamp. 'You're too thin for that,' said Bob. Baines ignored him. He got out his bullet cigar cutter, and prepared himself for a ritual that involved drilling holes, careful peering, smearing the end with saliva and sucking dimples in his cheeks.

'You have to be a big, fat, jowly sort of person,' said Bob.

'Mmm,' said Baines.

'So you don't inhale?' I asked.

'No,' said Baines. The cabinet filled with the characteristic dry dung smell. 'These would cost up to ten quid in London,' he said.

'But what's the point if you don't inhale?'

'It's the taste.'

'Well, it was for Bill Clinton anyway.' Bob had a mate who'd given up cigarettes because he was coughing a bit much and took up Hamlets but started inhaling anyway and then got so addicted he had to roll his spliffs with cigar tobacco. 'How long will that last?' he asked.

'About three hours.'

We grunted resignedly.

'Quite a skill to make them, then, because they have to be the right size otherwise they wouldn't be able to fit them in the tubes.'

'Yes.' Bob lay back and lit a fag himself. 'Just think of that woman sitting there, poor dear, spitting on the leaves, wiping her nose, scratching her pubes and rolling up a cigar.'

'Ah, it's a Number One,' said Baines undeterred. 'Not a Two, that makes it even better.'

'Smells like a number two,' said Bob.

Baines blew out enough smoke to fumigate one of the mattresses and got up to potter around his drawers.

For some reason, possibly the heat, the front of all the drawers had fallen off in unison. Now he had each of them out. Their contents were spread across every surface, and they were glued back together, strapped up with a half-tin of paint to evenly spread the load, waiting to set. Cigar in mouth, Baines went about the cabin, tapping and admiring his workmanship.

Before we left for Riga the next morning, we needed diesel. Albert had gone to his niece's wedding. His friend, in a well-washed and faded T-shirt saying 'Navigator', ushered us across to a Volkswagen van where he introduced us to a dignified, muscular, bullet-headed Russian, in a military singlet, called Sergei Popoff. Sergei immediately loaded our fuel cans into the back of his van and drove us off, pointing to the other side of the harbour at the fishing boats as we left. 'It's no good,' he said. 'Bad service! No oil! Fisherman won't have yachts!' On the other side of the harbour there was a service area with a wooden shack and a hand-pump. About twenty old, dented and bright orange painted-over-rust fishing boats were moored in a higgledy-piggledy mess against the decaying quays. 'It's about ten per cent fishing here, not good,' said Sergei, in the tones of one impatient for improvement in Ventspils, his adopted home. 'The EU limits us.' (The following year, having properly demonstrated that they could restrain their fishermen, Latvia gained acceptance into the Community.)

'The rest is transit. Gasoil' – it was one word – 'from Russia.' He was now pointing at the big commercial cranes. 'Not good.' A black Trabant wisely swerved out of his way. Sergei beeped his horn. 'Chechnya, not good. Here today, three ships, but mostly just one.'

The failures of Russian foreign policy had repercussions in this remote Latvian port. At least here they had a few beaten-up fishing boats in the docks and the cranes were working. The trains came in with carriage-loads of coal to a purpose-built, uniform dock. In Sweden, the dockside would have been beautifully restored with a new maritime museum. In England, a half-arsed council would have scattered a few Millennium bollards around a dock clogged with squeezy bottles. The only reason Latvia retained its huge cranes and trains and wharfs was because it was about thirty years out of date.

Sergei swung the van into a roundabout. 'Chechnya is a big problem for Russia. You have Mussulman in England?'

He meant Moslems. Bob, however, thought he was talking about *The World's Strongest Man*. 'Yes,' said Bob, perking up and hoping to be flattering, 'but you have better.'

Sergei turned in his seat. The car slewed. He punched the steering wheel with his mighty fist. 'No, no!' said Sergei firmly. 'No good.'

'OK, OK,' said Bob, sneaking a raised eyebrow in my direction.

We drove on past wooden houses with laden apple trees in untended gardens.

Sergei was originally from Murmansk on the Barents Sea. 'Many British sailors die there,' he told us, referring to the convoys during the Second World War, which, despite horrific losses, crossed the top of Norway and supplied the Russians after 1941, to the studied indifference of Stalin. He was now a diver with his own company, repairing ships and undertaking salvage, and had married a Latvian wife. He had been in Latvia for the last seventeen years. 'This is not important: Latvia – Russia. I am Latvian,' he said firmly. But his children now had to learn two languages. He pointed to his eight-year-old, who was sliding around amongst the empty cans in the back of the van. 'He doesn't speak English!'

'Well, two languages are enough to learn,' Bob reassured him from his uni-linguistic pinnacle.

We turned into an oasis of highly coloured modernity. After the washed-out town with its few shabby dark shops, the acrylic explosion of the garage was hard on the eyes. It was a mirage of the bright, capitalist EU future that awaited everybody when they owned a car.

We filled up and, on the way back, we passed some gaudily painted fibre-glass cows. Ventspils was, unexpectedly, the latest recipient of this globetrotting street art promotion, scattered disconcertingly amongst the boarded-up buildings. 'Not symbol,' said Sergei solemnly, pointing to them. 'Humour!'

He wouldn't take any money. 'I'm a diver, not a driver,' he said.

'But, it's only one letter different,' said Bob, now into his philological groove.

'Some chocolate for the boy,' said Sergei. I had already surreptitiously slipped the boy some Smarties, when I got out to pay for the diesel. He'd hidden these in his pocket, and now mutely accepted more foreign aid. I gave him a bar of chocolate from the boat and Sergei a pack of Bob's cigarettes.

At ten past one, the one o'clock bus to Riga was still sitting in the bus station in the centre of Ventspils, so we went to a kiosk to get drinks and idly pick through the strange sweeties. (Bob liked to load up with peculiar national confectionery: test-tubes full of sherbet powder, strings of licorice, babies' dummies that you dipped in a bag of green gloop.) We moved back towards the bus in a leisurely fashion.

'I think you'd better get on board,' said Charlie quietly from the door. 'Sergei telephoned ahead. They've actually held the bus up especially for us.'

The bus rumbled off, with a full complement of passengers,

each wearing a slightly pained expression, through a medieval agricultural landscape, fields cut out of forests of pine or birch and unspoilt farmland. The open meadows were dotted with storks. We counted seven in one field.

Half-way to Riga, we stopped at a roadside café. The woman behind me tapped me on the shoulder. 'We are staying here for ten minutes,' she said firmly. I nodded sheepishly.

It was Monday. In the old town of Riga, the churches were all shut and the souvenir shops were open. We visited tourist sights, and everything of note we saw was a relic of some previous occupying power.

Bob was taken with the tawdry decadence of the city that night: the whores working the main square, the money-lenders, the beggars and the whiff of Russian Mafiosi that hung over the centre of the town. He emerged from our hotel in his most highly decorated silk shirt (upside-down parrots and hanging palm fronds) rubbing his hands together. Baines had his mobile phone out. 'I've got the number of a girl I once worked with on a shoot,' he told us. 'She's called Maria.'

'She's working in Riga?'

'She comes from Riga. She's a Latvian supermodel. She might be able to show us round.'

We were impressed, so we arranged to meet. Maria had gone to bed to get her super-beauty sleep when we rang, but offered to get up and show us the action. We stood about at the end of the main drag, managing to be propositioned by every seedy pimp in Latvia, until some of the tawdriness became a little trying even for Bob. When Maria came along, of course, we might well have mistaken her for another hooker, if Baines hadn't stepped quickly forward to kiss her on both cheeks. Not that she looked like a hooker. Maria was a stunning tall blonde and completely vacant.

She led us off to a café to meet up with some jolly friends, Riga's wealthy fashionistas: the model, the Middle Eastern son who owned some sort of speedboat, the photographer and another thin girl, who wanted to be mysterious. Riga's jet-set sat on cane chairs in the warm night, flattering each other for our benefit.

'He is such a good photographer, Willie. He is the best photographer.'

'Oh, you are so funny, Toni. Toni is very funny.'

'I love to sit here in the company of these beautiful girls. These are lovely girls, aren't they?'

'You are a naughty boy. He is naughty but delightful.'

It was difficult to find a point of entry into this dialogue of bald statements. Direct inquiries seemed to be met with startled laughter and wide-eyed surprise.

'This morning? Er, yes. We were making a photo shoot, you know. Toni is so clever. You are so clever, Toni. I love him. He is so sweet.'

Baines gamely inquired after the club scene, the work opportunities and the future of Latvian fashion. What would I contribute? 'Charlie he is so clever with his screwdriver. You are so technical, Baines. Bob, you are so smelly. I love it.' Like Chekhov, with worse dialogue, they lamented that they weren't actually in Paris, Sardinia or the Hamptons and were, obviously, just about to leave to go there, next week, or maybe for the autumn or possibly the spring, certainly next summer.

There was talk of a club. There were constant squeals down mobile phones, but they were bored. They were bored with each other. Bored with Riga. Bored with the café and, pretty quickly, bored with us. So we slipped away and left them peering over each other's shoulders up and down the empty street, because Bob was keen to visit a Latvian casino.

'Oh, Bob, I just want to go to bed . . .'

'Griffule. We can't come all this way . . .' He flapped off determinedly. Unlike Sweden there wasn't any limit to the amount you could lose, or the number of casinos you could lose it in, but a place called the Pirate Club, in a big hotel, had caught Bob's eye. When we got there, Bob was the only one who'd forgotten to bring his passport. He couldn't sign in for membership. Frightened that we'd all desert him, he actually ran all the way back to the hotel and returned five minutes later, sweaty and rather un-international-man-of-mystery-like, ready to play.

It was a brand new casino, packed with gaming tables and run by pirates, but there was not a single customer. Except us, of course. I ordered up £30 worth of chips with the intention of losing them as quickly as possible. Gambling was by now a second-division pleasure. My mind was fixed on my hotel bed with its real sheets and a pillow that smelt of nothing. I assumed it would be inevitable, playing in a deliberately off-hand way, that as soon as I tried to dispose of my cash I would start winning. Except that it wasn't and I didn't. The pile of heavy plastic counters diminished to nothing in less than five minutes. I felt slightly nauseous and left. Charlie and Baines followed. Bob was less concerned about keeping us with him now. We abandoned him, blissfully hunkered down in front of the blackjack table, the only customer in the casino.

I woke early the next day and went to wander around the town. When I came back to the hotel at midday, Bob was sitting in the dining room eating breakfast.

'Where've you been?' I asked.

'Oh, I've just got up,' Bob said.

'Were you at the casino?'

'To begin with, yes. Then this lawyer came in, rather an attractive lawyer, really.'

'A woman.'

'Yes. And she wanted to change some Euros. So you know. I had quite a pile of chips at the time. So I changed them for her.'

'You ended up winning?'

'Eh? Oh no. No. Heh, heh. I lost it all, I think. Anyway, this lawyer invites me back to her flat. And it's right over in the suburbs and I thought I'd quite like to go and have a look. See the real Riga, you know.'

'Research.'

'Yesss. And it's quite different from all this tourist town stuff. She lives in this big tower block, Russian sort of tower block . . .'

'So . . .'

'So I could see that she obviously was a lawyer, because it's pretty run-down, this part of town, and the block of flats, but she's got a big glass coffee table and a lot of leather furniture and a huge television. Doing very nicely. But anyway, she says to me, will I give her a present.'

'What sort of present?'

'That's what I asked. I said. "What, a pair of socks or a box of chocolates?" But she meant money.'

'Well perhaps the legal business wasn't covering her gambling expenses.'

'Obviously, so she wanted me to give her some money.'

'How much?'

'She wouldn't say. She just kept saying, "Oh Bobby, geeve me a present."'

'What this is, she saw you in the casino and thought you were a rich Englishman?'

'She picked the wrong bloke.'

'I can see that.'

'I wasn't going to pay and I went to the lift and left.'

'At when?'

'Oh, six o'clock at least. This had taken a long time. But she wouldn't budge. All the way to the lift she was standing in the door going, "Bobby, don't go. Geeve me a present."'

'Well that's lawyers for you,' I said.

When it's 33 degrees in Riga, the girls get themselves down to a sliver of crimplene apparently sprayed on in a machine shop. Gone was the Swedish plumptiousness. The milky, corn-fed, Ulrika Jonsson look was replaced by a suave spikiness, a high forehead and an angular pelvis. We couldn't help noticing. On an escalator, a full leopard's head, printed on a crimson, stretchy, semi-see-through fabric, wrapped across a grotesquely moulded chest, glared menacingly at me as I rode up towards it. 'Crack of the month' was won by a girl in denim so tight that it looked as if she'd brought a three-year-old's pants and had them twisted on with some pain.

Charlie and I were making our way, via the shopping centres, to the diplomatic quarter. At the beginning of the twentieth century, the city of Riga enjoyed a golden period, before the shitty behaviour of its neighbours shut it down for the rest of the twentieth century. Just beyond the park, where the embassies were, the streets were lined with Art Nouveau buildings. We turned a corner expecting something faintly curvaceous and stood with mouths agape. A sphinx with the head of Penelope Keith guarded the front door of the building in front of us. Above that, the first-floor ledge was covered with heads in Aztec costumes, surrounded by two panting circus strongmen wearing fringed modesty belts and holding up lamps. A few blue tiles led up to a Prince of Wales-feathered South Sea Islander headdress, false tethering rings, some Frank Lloyd Wright spacemen and, finally, at the top of the columns, a row of smug, helmeted women: all in peeling stucco above a quick-print photo-shop. To one side there was a little sign. I bent to look, expecting it to tell me who had designed the house. It said 'Isaiah Berlin lived here: 2a Alberto Ilea'.

We stood back again. 'I once met Isaiah Berlin at a private view of the Venice Exhibition at the Royal Academy organized by Classic FM, you know,' I told Charlie.

'Really?'

'I was introduced to him. Unexpectedly, you know. Isaiah Berlin said "Hello." And if I recall correctly. I said something like. "A great honour."'

'Right.'

'It was just about the naffest thing that could possibly be said to a great philosopher with a silly voice, don't you think?'

'Look at this one,' said Charlie.

At the end of the road there was another mad house. But this had been magnificently restored. It was a wholly inappropriate School of Law: sensuous and distracting, Alphonse Mucha made concrete, a sort of pink and white iced cake. This, in turn, was put to shame by the house next door, which sported a row of half-clad maidens with boat prows for their lower halves, and real galley oars protruding in various directions, as if they were about to row off the side of the block.

'I wonder what the plasterer said when they handed him the plans,' said Charlie.

29. The Wharf

There is a ritual to boat visitation, as larded with unspoken punctiliousness as ambassadorial etiquette. Guests are effectively invited to enter your badger sett. 'You show me yours if I show you mine.' We were back in Ventspils by the early evening, and I asked Ola and Axel, our neighbouring yachtsmen, to 'come and have a look'.

My father deliberately took his boat *Windsong* into the furthest dribbles of estuaries, where the only thing he could meet had wings and ate gastropods. But, of course, he made himself utterly vulnerable to anyone else who did the same thing. Off Stone Point, in the Walton Backwaters, my sister and I would urge him to go and say hello to the only other boat anchored in the reach. 'No, no, they don't want to be disturbed,' he would say, without even looking up.

'But they've got children too.'

'It's much too late now. I have to fix the bilge-cocks tonight.'

Sometimes my mother would prevail and we'd enjoy an evening exchanging stories of engine failures in high winds with another middle-aged couple in pullovers.

Ola was one of the technical directors of the Gothenburg Opera. While he was working for the Stockholm Opera, he had helped design and build a magic £30 million electrical stage system for the show-piece theatre down south, and, as a result, been asked to stay and work on it permanently. But he still based his life in Stockholm, kept his flat there and commuted to Gothenburg 300 miles away on the other side of Sweden. He returned to his Stockholm friends and his boat on the lakes behind the capital every weekend.

'It's incredible,' Axel said, 'Ola keeps his boat on the lake but you know, there are so many separate bays there that he has never explored them all.'

Ola nodded and smiled. 'Yes. This is true,' he said.

Axel had been a management consultant, working all over Europe, but had retired a few years before and now only took freelance work in order to free himself to spend more time on his boat.

'The problem is that Axel is now working more than he did when he was in employment. He is so much in demand,' Ola said.

'Yes, yes, I'm afraid so,' said Axel, nodding and smiling.

Now they stepped up to *Undina*. First they paused, by the dockside, to admire the boat they were about to enter, stare up at the mast, nod their heads meaningfully, that sort of thing. Then, gingerly (and the implied desecration is very important), they stepped up and on to the teak decks, offering as they did so to remove their shoes, in case they inadvertently dragged a stone on board and scratched the surface.

'No, no, don't worry about that,' said Bob, marching ahead in his fake python Chelsea boots.

Axel was especially pleased with the cockpit. He ran his hands over the winches and the cleats. 'This is very fine,' he said. 'And you sit here and you steer the boat with this big wheel.' (Both Axel and Ola's boats were smaller and steered by tillers.)

'There is a good feel about the boat,' he said. 'Don't you think so, Ola?'

'Oh, yes. I think she is very nice,' said Ola in sing-song tones. Sufficient time had now passed for them to go below, where, naturally enough, we had made an effort to get everything tiddly.

'Tidy you mean,' Baines had said when I first used the term.

'No, no. "Tiddly". It means neat and ordered.' It was a word introduced to me by Detective Chief Inspector Derek Wyatt of the Colchester police, one of the few sailing companions of my father. Derek had been in the navy. His boat was very tiddly indeed. Both these men liked their boats to resemble an old lady's cottage. I had inherited the anal fixation.

By the time Ola and Axel came down into the cabin, some tiddliness had been imposed. A blanket had been spread over Bob's air-crash-scene bunk. At least half of his nineteen pairs of shoes had been stuffed away. The wind-proof ashtray scooped out of its impossible-to-reach-in-the-corners ash muck. The red and blue signal flag cushions from the Marine Museum in Kalmar plumped and the brown stain turned to the rear. The six Tilley lamps were spreading a guttering glow, precariously set on every surface. Axel and Ola purred and nodded and squeezed themselves alongside the narrow table. They admired the gleaming mahogany, observed how much smaller below decks she was than modern boats, and then we sat, shoulder to shoulder as if in an overcrowded London taxi, furnished by a Moroccan. And ate a meal with chicken elbows.

They were not heading in quite the same direction as us. The year before they had been to Tallinn via the northern route from Helsinki. This year they wanted to explore the Estonian islands. We needed to press on, to make St Petersburg, but we agreed, on examining the charts we had bought in Riga, that a day's sail could get us as far as Montu. There was a yacht symbol, which indicated an anchorage, but it wasn't an 'official port of entry'. We were now moving from one country to another.

'We can simply say to the Customs that it was not possible to get all the way to the port of entry in one day's sail and we could not enter Kuressaare at night,' Axel proposed.

'Won't they feel a little suspicious if three yachts arrive the same day with exactly the same story?' I asked.

'Well, we are travelling together now,' said Ola simply.

We left Ventspils at about ten o'clock, turning up into a brisk north-easterly, and then across into the notorious straits of the Gulf of Riga; yet another graveyard of ships. The lighthouses on the point, and the beacon in the middle, had witnessed horrible deaths. The Soviets bombed a German hospital ship with 3,000 aboard in 1944. Only a few hundred survived. But the Gulf seemed benign enough now.

After a further four hours, in the glow of a perfect northern sunset, a group of sheds were highlighted pink amongst the fir trees. We sailed closer and a low breakwater came into view.

Montu was little more than this high, dilapidated wharf, which extended from the shore in a dog-leg, sheltering us from any winds from the south, but wide open to all other directions. A moustachioed man and a dog were standing on the top of the cracked and broken quay, staring down at us. In a dream, he moved his fishing sticks as we came alongside a huge black protective tractor tyre, held in place by a rusting chain. It was not a yacht harbour. The quay towered above us. We had to clamber up the tyre and then the chain to get to the top. Beyond the dock were a few vacant sheds and signs of recent building works; beyond them, the gloomy forest.

As we stood there, a military vehicle drove out of the woods and humped along the quay towards us. Two men in uniform got out.

'Yacht *Undina*?'

They had driven from Kuressaare, forty miles away, in order to stamp our papers, and now we felt guilty, but they seemed pleased enough to welcome us to Estonia. One had corporal's stripes and showed the other how to check our documents, issuing us with new forms, which we filled in, in duplicate, on the bonnet of their military Volkswagen in the fading evening light.

'Nice car,' said Baines.

Yachts were new business. Their usual job was to catch illegal immigrants. Just up the road, eighty Kurds had walked up the beach from a shipwreck around Christmas of 1995 and had had to be returned to Latvia.

The bearded junior suddenly grunted and pointed out to the horizon. We all gathered and stared. He pointed again. 'Boat is coming,' he said. We leaned in to follow his finger, but could see nothing. Sure enough, a minute later, on the horizon, we managed to make out two minuscule white dots. It was Axel and Ola, arriving by utter coincidence.

The corporal immediately strode off down the dock and scrambled down a long ladder into a tiny motorboat. His new recruit hurried behind, but was less sure of himself, and the corporal helped him down, placing his feet on the thwarts, reassuring him, and gently leading him to a seat. Then with a roar of their outboard, they bounced off to sea.

I went for a run by the shore along an unmade, white road, surrounded by junipers and wildflowers, towards the pine forest ahead and an overgrown place, like a heath, of coarse plants and scrub. Beyond it I could see, through the trees, the ruin of what had once been a substantial stone house. A car came past, an old Russian squarish thing. It stopped ahead of me. As I ran up, there were two people out in the bay, swimming in the last light, shouting and laughing. But they had finished their dip and gone by my return.

The place seemed lonelier, more moody, as I jogged back, past low stands of very white-barked birches, to where we were moored by the high concrete wharf. It was clear that it had only stopped being a military base quite recently. I had already noticed the rusty watchtowers, but now I could see patches with no vegetation, where huts and encampments had been bulldozed down. Strands of barbed wire were only just overwhelmed by low bushes.

The whole island of Saaremaa had been a restricted area. Foreigners were banned, Estonians themselves were unable to visit most of it. This long, thin peninsula, facing across the Baltic to Sweden, housed missile bases and listening posts. As I got closer to the quay, I nearly stumbled over a low marble monument in the undergrowth. The quay where we were moored had once had a specific purpose. From this spot, most of the people of the Sorve peninsula had been transported into exile during the Second World War. Only a quarter of a population of 6,000 had remained.

The Germans virtually gave the independent Estonia to Russia as part of the Ribbentrop–Molotov Pact of 1939, and the Russians had used the cover of the fall of France to take over the country completely in 1940. They arrested the government, which had been struggling to retain the country's hard-won independence, and took the leaders into captivity. Most of them were to die there some time in the 1950s. This was followed by a purge of Estonian capitalist influences. Ten thousand were dragged from their homes on one single day in 1941 and transported to Siberia. And then the Germans arrived.

The Estonians had greeted the invading Germans in 1941 as liberators, but the Germans had behaved as occupiers. When the Russians eventually returned, behind a 50-mile-wide creeping barrage, and the Germans stood by to make a last stand, they chose to make it on this peninsula, and the population was evacuated from the very concrete wharf where we were tied. The Germans were caught in a withering attack. Twelve thousand troops died in the woods of the peninsula, cut down by shelling before they could get away to sea. For years afterwards, woodmen blunted their saws and axes on the shrapnel splinters that had grown into the trunks of the pine forest that pressed in on the shore where we lay.

In the corner of the harbour, as darkness came, the flame from an oxyacetylene torch in the bowels of a rusting metal hulk sent up sparks and a pretence of activity. It was as if we were glimpsing people from a distance, aware that they were around, but never seeing them. The nearest village was at least 7 miles away.

It was getting dark when we helped Ola and Axel tie up. There was something rather soothing about watching them approach on such a still, calm evening: the only visible boats in the great, grey, wide sea.

'Ola, welcome. This is paradise, isn't it?'

Something whined near my ear.

'What was that?'

'A mosquito?'

'No, no. It was too big for that.'

'There's one, though.'

'That's a model helicopter.'

The air around us was visibly thickening. I looked down at my bare leg. Six or seven brown creatures had settled on it. I became aware that Ola, sitting in his cockpit, was wearing a complete red robot suit. He was almost unrecognizable. He had gloves on. His trousers went down into his boots and came up to meet a jacket with a high shawl-collar which was pulled up to meet his glasses. He had a peaked hood with this suit which was pulled up and tightened around his face. He looked like the invisible man, dressed up. He nodded in my direction.

'Ouch!'

'They are biting you, yeah?' said Ola.

I was slapping at the things, which were now flying into my face and eyes and threatening to start an old-lady-who-swallowed-a-fly domino effect.

With a whirr and a buzz, a row of sodium-yellow street lamps on the quay sputtered into action, and a thick soup of bugs immediately whirled up, threatening to block out their light.

'I think you will need to put some clothing on, Griff,' Ola said with a muffled voice.

'Some boots too,' said Axel. 'And of course, remember that they have tongues which they can stick through the hide of a deer. It is most irritating when they can get through three layers of stockings.'

I ran jumping and hollering back to our boat. Bob was coming on deck swinging his arms around him.

'Where have all these come from?'

'I don't know, but shut the cabin door.'

Too late. The cabin air space was controlled by a squadron of the creatures patrolling the lights. After all, there can't have been that many elk and badgers, squirrels and moles left on the peninsula, and so approximately 17 billion squillion female mosquitoes were dependent on visiting yachtsmen for sustenance.

'It's only the females who suck the blood, you know,' said the authoritative tones of Axel from behind his protective clothing later that evening as the darkness swallowed up the mosquito happy hour.

'Mmm,' I tried to reply from my lump of a face swollen from bites, peering at him through red eyelids smarting from the poisonous repellent which he had loaned me.

'They are incredible creatures, don't you think? So very tiny and yet they can sense the smell of carbon dioxide that you give out from miles away. They must have minuscule brains but they are programmed to survive. They are just so clever at avoiding destruction too.'

That night in my cabin I had time to ponder Axel's words. I lay awake, with a screwed-up plastic rubble bag clutched in my hand. Light but bulky, it could be applied to a big enough area, including the whole electric light, so as to splat the mosquitoes three at a time. Anything smaller than a foot square surface without the relevant pliability allowed the devious insect to flit sideways. But it was a long night.

'You won't be able to sleep until you have killed every one.' Axel's parting words buzzed in my head.

30. Paradise

Axel half-acknowledged the pointlessness of swapping addresses and phone numbers.

'Will you be in London?' we asked.

'Not much these days,' he replied, 'but if you're ever in Badwerten, near Frankfurt, you must look me up.'

We set off in the direction of the mainland, but it was too late and too far. Instead, we turned towards Kuressaare, away to our north, but still on the island of Saaremaa. We tried sailing, but there was no wind, so we started the motor and chugged through a leaden sea.

The harbour was nothing on any chart: two lights on a peninsula and two leading marks on the shore. We crept through little crosses warning of submerged rocks. In places, the chart became a war cemetery of crosses, but as we got closer, buoys emerged to guide us, and a channel led up to two breakwaters and a fishing harbour with boats painted in the Estonian national colours of blue and white. A flat, silver sea, marshes and low wooded headland lay away to starboard. Young boys were swimming off the inner breakwater, diving in, next to a faded orange pilot boat and a tug, in a small, recently built marina with floating pontoons. There was a restaurant, an impressive three-storey harbour master's office and a lot of recently planted trees quietly expiring in the drought. A regular bus service ran from Kuressaare, but there was seldom anybody on it. It was a commercial yacht tourist industry in waiting.

Later that evening, I went and paid our dues. The harbour master, a fit, shaven-headed sixty-year-old, worked for a company that ran three or four marinas in the Estonian region. Earlier in the summer, hundreds of Finnish yachts had passed through. Now it was empty.

He wanted to know where we were going. I told him Haapsalu.

He noted this down, and while I was round the corner trying to identify other possible anchorages, I overheard him talking on the telephone. I made out the name of our yacht and 'Englisher'.

'Have you been telephoning ahead?' I asked him, darkly.

'Yes,' he said. I could see he was slightly agitated, so I hung around. 'Will we stay in Haapsalu, all right?' I asked, dropping as usual into stupid-speak, but wanting to prolong the conversation. He looked at his counter and then suddenly blurted out, 'Haapsalu, young people, too many. Here, Saaremaa, is paradise.'

'For old people?' I asked him lamely.

'Yes, old, young.' He looked at me intently and leaned forward.

'Why do you go on?' he asked. 'You must stay here and see.' He urged me to hire a car and explore his island. He was upset that we were moving on so quickly. There were so many wonderful things to see here in Saaremaa. I smiled and shook my head.

'No, no, it's not possible.'

God knows, I longed to stop. Our journey seemed to have become absurdly attenuated. How could I ever expect to get back here? But in the next two weeks we had to get as far as St Petersburg. The pressure of the unexpectedly good northern late summer was on us now. The local holidays were over and ours were just starting. The winter was approaching faster in these regions than we realized.

We had time for Kuressaare, though, a nesting town, a sweet, slow place with big trees and wooden houses grouped around a curving main road. Round the back of it, in a little market, farmers sat in front of tiny displays of produce: a few mushrooms, a cabbage, two onions, three tomatoes, a pot of basil, a few punnets of blue-berries. There was a fish stall. We bought ourselves another smoked eel from a woman like Maggie Smith, in a straw hat and wearing fifties glasses. The Estonian women were pale and aristocratic, like wan princesses. This was a prosperous town with neatly painted houses. We began to notice that there were banks and automats on every corner, discreet souvenir shops and expensive restaurants. Finns were coming here on holiday in increasing numbers. And apparently it had been quick to adapt. 'Oh, the Estonians were always very bourgeois,' I was told in St Petersburg. There was a hot, heavy, old-fashioned August harvest feel; like an English market town in the 1950s, with a clopping horse or two, and the occasional odd Russian car rumbling about.

We visited the antique shop in search of bric-à-brac and found Ola and Axel, looking at carbide lamps.

'So, you have decided to stay?'

'No, Ola, but we decided we could go a little more slowly.'

The flotsam and jetsam of the Soviet era were stacked up around us: oil-lamps, felt peasant dresses in acid colours, piles of sepia pictures on tin, of square-set Edwardian Estonians in suits, cigarette boxes, powder and patented medicines – some still unopened – packets of soaps, salesmen's samples, bowler hats and uniform caps, baskets of hand-blown Christmas-tree decorations, compasses and barometers in black Bakelite covers from the Soviet era.

Bob bargained, pointing to junk, piling it up on the table, taking it away and opening up more boxes. He left with five Christmas decorations, a plastic cat in a basket and a bad picture of a man in a suit.

We said goodbye again to Axel and Ola, returned to the harbour, fiddled with our mobile phones and did the washing-up. A boiling red sun set between the new bus shelter and an old Russian watchtower. We opened a bottle of wine. Bob set up his sepia picture.

'Nice.'

There was no real urge to go to bed, no energy for cards and no patience for music. So we got out a block of Blau Gotland, a kilo of cheese wrapped in blue wax. It was not, we discovered, blue cheese, it was more like a cheddar.

'This is cheese, good, hard, solid, yes,' I said through mouthfuls. 'Cheddar, Stilton, Cotswold, Emmenthal. What was that stuff we had in Holland?'

'Gruyère.'

'That's Swiss.'

'Well, they sell it in Holland,' said Bob.

When we had had our autumn adventure, the year before, Bob and I had visited Edam. We walked four miles across blank Dutch suburban grassy spaces, past modest, wooden, bungalow dwelling-units, and alongside dead-straight canal ditches before we finally got into the old town.

'We went to a merchant's house and bought mature Edam and a cheese-slice in a specialist shop,' Bob remembered.

'I've got it here, I think,' I said, and banged around in a drawer. We used it to get going on the Gotland Blau.

'I dream of that cheese we had in Edam now,' Bob said wistfully.

'Yes, so piquant, so sharp.'

'This is good,' said Charlie.

'Yes. It's proper cheese,' I said. 'It has the flavour and substance of proper cheese. The whole French cheese industry is just a major marketing con: soft, flabby, milksop rancid butter, that's all the French have. Ammonia-fumed, sour cow-juice cheese.'

Bob told us about his youthful experiments with very strong cheese. He had, in the interests of psychopathic research, eaten huge quantities of extra-strong cheddar in order to bring on nightmares.

'Did it work?' asked Charlie.

'Yes,' said Bob, 'Well, you know, great nightmares.'

'What about?'

'I don't know. You wake up and for two minutes you think that's the scariest thing, must remember that, then you fall asleep again and you forget everything.'

'So how do you know it was a nightmare?'

'Well, you know it was a nightmare because, you know, you're all sweaty.'

'It's apparently better if it's toasted,' says Baines, our voice of technical expertise. 'It's because of the digestion. Cheese takes a long time to digest and it keeps you awake.'

'Well, that would be it then,' says Bob. 'You go to sleep and then it sits there and then at four in the morning, it kicks in.'

Baines cut a slice of Gotland Blau with our Edam cheese slicer. 'Here, have a bit.'

'It's a sliver.'

'Yes, but that's the best way to eat it.' Baines's technical authority extended even to the size of a piece of cheese. 'The entire piece, though thin, releases molecules into the palate.' Baines applied himself to the toasting mechanism with the navigation dividers and made us some toast.

'Yes, yes,' says Bob, 'but you miss the gobful of cloying cheese swallowed down in a suffocating gulp effect.'

I went to bed at three and luckily dreamed of nothing at all.

31. The Wooden Shack

When I was tiny, Arthur Ransome was the staple diet of any middle-class sailing family. His books were handed out with the first lifejacket. His tireless, and tiresome, children, Titty and Roger, were templates. This was what we children were expected to get out of sailing. Like all the most successful children's books, though, adults were banished completely (how unlike real life) and, like a lot of successful children's books, they seem to have been written by a man who, with his pipes and tweed jackets and cosy snuggeries and camping, obviously wanted to avoid adulthood as far as was humanly possible. Barrie, C. S. Lewis, Tolkein and Ransome, come to think of it, all conjure up images of tweed jackets and pipes (entirely off-putting and smelly to most children). I don't think they liked real children. They were jealous of them. They wanted to be children themselves. Anyway, I read Ransome greedily. When my father first took us round the coast of Essex in *Dunlin*, our first, minute cabin-boat, the greatest excitement was that we were heading for 'Secret Water', the Walton Backwaters, a slew of islands in a muddy swamp behind Harwich. Ransome romanticized these into a forbidden archipelago populated by 'Mastodons'. It is still a pleasingly remote area.

I could sort of blame Arthur Ransome for everything if I tried: the wooden boat, the petty explorations, the oil lamps, my bumptious romanticism.

But the first sailing writing Ransome ever published was about the Estonian Islands, and, as we blustered along the sunlit southern coast of Saaremaa the following morning, I was excited all over again to be following once more in Ransome's tracks. In the early 1920s he had a boat built in Riga and sailed it up through the Gulf. Our paths crossed in the superbly named Moon Channel, just east of Moon Island.

His descriptions in *Racundra's First Cruise* exactly mirrored our sailing that morning. 'The pale blue light', the 'glaucous white-splashed water' and the tortuous and utterly engaging doodle of a route had not changed in the last eighty years, except that there was, interestingly, almost a metre less water underneath us than there had been under him.

The sea bed is subject to isostatic recovery. When the last ice-age ended, the weight of millions of tons of ice was lifted off the land, and the whole area is still gradually rising, like a granite mattress regaining its shape. Ransome found it intolerably shallow. It was probably better buoyed by the time we got there, because we didn't touch the bottom until we were almost into the tiny harbour of Haapsalu. We pulled up the centreboard and then spent about an hour in strong winds trying to tie up in an absurd little yacht harbour.

We hired bicycles and rode into the town, through leafy back gardens and on and out on to a reedy bay. Swans were drifting around, herons stalked the shallows and there were steps down to the water on a decayed promenade barely a hundred yards long. In the nineteenth century, Tchaikovsky and Tolstoy had come to bathe in the healing mud of Haapsalu, but there were few signs of magnificence now, apart from the ruins of a German bishop's castle, until we cycled around a corner.

'What's that?' Charlie slithered to a halt. I looked in the guide book. 'It must be the Kursaal,' I said. It was an almost Asiatic-looking pagoda with elaborate barge boards, a sweeping roof and long glass-house-windowed balconies fronting the slimy bay. As we approached it we could see people sitting around in the early-evening sun outside. It was actually open for business. Perhaps we were about to witness some Estonian folk event.

It was better than that. A ten-year-old girl solemnly took our money. We went up the steps and across the wide-boarded entrance platform, into what was a terrifically glamorous church hall, with painted bead and butt walls beneath an elegant hammer-beam roof. The whole of the far side was ablaze with light, because the sun was setting across the bay and shining through the panes of a glazed verandah that stretched right along the wall above the water. And silhouetted against it were the tables of a quite excellent restaurant, like a big tea room, crammed with families out for the Sunday evening concert. We were shown to our own table just near the bar and presented with a menu by a beautiful girl in a short blue gingham dress, just one of the dozens of lovely nippies flitting around the tables. It was as if we had been transported, like weary soldiers in a Powell and Pressburger film, to some vision of tea-shop heaven.

'Look at this,' said Baines, smilingly goofily. 'The menu's in English.' Not only was it in English, it was full of little jokes: 'Hans Off!' for a German ham sandwich. 'Santa Claus's Taxi' for a carpaccio of reindeer. 'Don't spank your child, buy him a pizza!'

Admittedly, a lot of the patrons looked as if they had been at the grand opening in 1886 and the first act had difficulty in getting on to the high stage, because they were in their seventies. But the visiting Dutch choir was followed by Inga from Tallinn. She was some consolation for having missed the 'Ladies of Jazz Festival' the week before. And she sang 'Fly Me to the Moon', while her side man thumped at the piano and periodically lifted his clip-on shades to read the music, like a character in the Muppets. The audience got up and danced beneath a 15-foot-high scalloped shell hanging over the back of the stage. And through the waltzing pensioner couples, the beautiful waitresses carried ice cream-cakes with sparklers fizzing in the fading evening light.

I went ashore to see if I could find any breakfast the next morning, without success, but a girl in the café made me a cup of coffee. Although Estonia had become independent ten years before, she had been seven when it happened, part of a generation for whom the Soviet occupation was already in the past. She only re-membered, she told me, that everyone had had money, but there was nothing in the shops. She had had to ask her mother what a banana was. But she was unexcited by, or perhaps unaware of, any changes. She was off to university to do computer studies. Her father and mother packed fish at the fish-packing factory, but they also had a business selling books. She had had a computer at school, but she didn't have one at home. She identified Estonia with Sweden and not Latvia at all. 'The Latvians think the Estonians are crazy and we think the Finns are crazy. That's what poor people always think about rich people,' she told me.

'We're thinking of going across to the island of Vormsi, today,' I said.

'Oh, Vormsi, yes.'

'What's that like?'

She shrugged and squinted into the sun over her shoulder at the channel that separated the distant wooded hump from the mainland. 'I've never been there,' she said.

32. Vormsi

We hit the ground frequently as we came out of Haapsalu's harbour, bumping along on our centreboard into a strong force 5, making 8 knots, charging over the shallow bays in hot sunshine through a fresh, clean, north wind, trying to make sense of the cardinal marks, with a ferry chasing us all the way. The passage was too narrow for it to pass, so it slowed and ground in behind us, with, I presumed, the captain cursing us from his bridge.

Vormsi had a big, concrete ferry harbour and that was it. We didn't want to tangle with it, so we slipped around the side and found an aluminium boat tied up against the wharf. While we tried to sort out where to moor, we came alongside her. Two large, broad-faced blokes with tough bodies under their T-shirts came out and took ropes. Lett and Max were navigators. They were the Estonian Trinity House.

'Do you survey the depth?' Bob asked.

They looked at him blankly.

'The water.' Bob pointed down and made a gesture with his palms. 'You!'

'No, no,' Max apologized. 'The . . . er . . .' He mimed a big round thing.

'The buoys . . .'

'Yes. The bwoy. Yes we put and make and then . . .' He waved his fingers in little circles around each other.

'. . . You mend. You repair.'

Max nodded. Their boat, shiny and new, was a magnificent lump of metal; essentially a platform, big enough for carrying the biggest buoy. They had two huge water jet engines at the back and could operate in the tiniest of depths. Max wrinkled his brow and smiled.

'I am . . . sorry,' he went on slowly like a man remembering a dream. 'I have . . . learned English many . . . years before . . . in school. But I . . . never speak it before now.'

We were the first British people that Max and Lett had met, and, once they had cranked up the disused machinery of their English, it started spluttering into life. They were keen, as professionals, to see our charts and looked over them with a practised eye. Lett was the superior officer, and, being in charge, had kept a little in the background, allowing Max to make a fool of himself first. But now he put his morning beer aside and stabbed our chart with his thick finger. 'Russian!' he said. Indeed it was. The Russian charts were inkily printed with nineteenth-century typefaces and a piratical spoked-wheel logo in one corner. We realized that they were both a little drunk. It must have been a quiet day.

'Estonian chart. Better.' We showed that we had some Estonian charts for the region and these met with approval. Lett patted and caressed them flat. This wasn't just patriotic chart chauvinism. The Estonians were busy surveying and updating a comprehensive map of their difficult waters. Max and Lett didn't survey themselves, but as they passed back and forth across the shallow plateaus to reach their charges, they left a depth monitor running and it transferred information to their impressive computer.

They showed us the lines of soundings: regular numbers dotted on the blue of the electric map, making order out of the wild formlessness all around us. At the end of the season these soundings were sent off and added to the stock in Tallinn. They showed us on the chart how the channel which the Russians had surveyed in the past was dodgy; told us how boats had been wrecked, how they had helped, although that was not their job.

Max and Lett represented what the Estonians had had to face when independence came. 'The Russians used to do your job?' I asked. Lett nodded. This was why the boat was so new and they were so proud of it. When the Russians left, ten years before, the Estonians had to take over everything. We could conceive of the problems with parliaments and railways, what about this job? Here, in this remote corner, the Estonians had proved that they could do it better than their old masters within a few years. We had hardly touched shore in this country, but the shiny aluminium boat and the powerful computer demonstrated the incredible speed with which the Estonians had become Scandinavians.

'We go soon. Move. You come here.' Lett indicated the dock side. With our customary cumbersome fuss we took *Undina* over to a floating metal yellow pontoon a few yards away, where a large digger was building a new extension to the wharf for visiting yachts. Max and Lett pirouetted their big platform around, pushed the back up against the shore and ran down two ramps. A minute later a small car arrived. It drove straight on to the boat. They waved and, with a great churning of water, skimmed off back towards Haapsalu.

It was marginally easier for us to clamber over the mess of rocks and broken concrete to get ashore than it was to heave ourselves up over the rusting cables and filthy tractor tyres at the side of the wharf, so we stayed where we were and tramped off through the heat towards the island.

Two hundred yards away, across fields of sedge, stood a house. A row of bicycles was stacked up outside, for hire. An eleven-year-old, staying with his granny for the summer, helped ready them for us and then, willingly, took on the duty of watching the boat for the day. Not that there was much he could do if, say, the digger dropped a lump of concrete on to her, or some massive maritime skip wanted its rightful berth, but it was a soporific, lazy late-summer day, the sort of day when it was difficult to imagine that the stillness and the placidity of the island would ever be disturbed. As we mounted and pedalled off along the straight road towards the rustling woods and low cottages ahead, it was hard to conceive that anything much happened here on Vormsi.

Plenty had, of course. Once the island had 3,000 inhabitants: Swedish farmers. Now the population was 300. In between, the Russians had taken over and the island had been off limits to Estonians. The Swedes had fled at the end of the Second World War and, like parts of Salisbury Plain, this perfect place, shimmering in the oven heat, where the piles of logs by the side of the road gave off an overpowering toilet-cleaner tang, where the thatched barns and wooden cottages lay in an unfenced disarray, had been preserved in bucolic dreaminess by the indifference of military occupation.

There was no traffic. The bicycles were perfect, the air was perfect, the scenery was perfect. Only Bob was human.

'What's he doing?' puffed Baines.

'He was the same in Haapsalu,' I complained. 'Hey Bob!' I shouted at his arched back and wiggling legs, fast disappearing ahead. But the legs whirled more furiously. The three of us pumped harder ourselves and, rushing out of the woods, I made slight headway. Corrugated asbestos barns flashed past, and the sagging neglected ruin of a Russian Orthodox church, abandoned in an uncut meadow, but Bob cycled faster. Charlie and Baines fell behind. I pushed into one of the thirteen or so top gears and crept up alongside him. We shot past an old Trabant with Bob cycling like a dervish. Thanks to my punishing running regime, non-smoking, non-alcoholic lifestyle and five years of solid training, I finally managed to overhaul the chain-smoking, addled, unfit slob. I shouted back over my shoulder.

'We'd better wait for the others!'

He screeched to a halt at a crossroads by a village sign. The village was called 'Hullo'.

'Why are you cycling so quickly?' he said.

'Bob, don't be an arse, it's you.'

'I'm not racing, it's just my very well-developed legs.'

'Bob, we're never going to keep up with you if you do this, you don't have to treat the whole bicycle trip around the island like the Tour de France.' The other two arrived. We stood for a moment steaming slightly in the heat.

Hullo was a haphazard hamlet in the trees. There was a shop, which tried to disguise itself as a barn, with a magnificent long mahogany counter. There was a bar behind gnarled, apple-festooned trees. It was dark inside, with gloss green walls and home-made furniture. Beyond there was a startling white church and a pine-needle graveyard. Bob mounted up and shot off again. The black-top road finished, and a rough white track threw up a cloud of dust. We followed him, choking and cursing, through a sepulchral, deserted forest, and half an hour later broke out on the far side of the island, sweating and exhausted, by a shallow sea lapping at a stinking, seaweed-covered shore.

It was the Gulf of Finland, plipping and plopping, like a lake, at our feet. Ahead, beyond the glittering horizon, lay Finland. To the right, some 200 miles away, St Petersburg. To the left, Sweden. We sat on a granite rock, rust-stained and glinting, by a beach of white stones on a lucent, pallid, bathwater-warm, white sea. The wall behind us was breasted with stunted juniper.

We took the bikes back in the early evening. A large woman in a bathing suit locked them away. Her house had been built in two months, she told us. She was a teacher who lived there for two weeks every summer. Her son had built it. It had been a Russian border station, originally, hence the big stones running across the front garden, which had been dumped there to stop anybody attempting to charge the island. She pointed at my beard. 'We have cows with beards like that.'

'Cows?'

'Yes, she is with beard, special cow.'

'Where is she?'

'She is over in the water just now. The mosquitoes, she no like, so many, bit, bit. Then she swim. And his nose is just out of the water.' She stood with her nose up for a moment. Several mosquitoes landed on her cellulite-pickled thighs as we talked, but she ignored them.

'The mosquitoes are bad, then?'

'Very, very bad.'

If the cow couldn't cope, what hope did we have? The sweat had trickled in a damp patch down my back. I could feel probosces being stuck through the weave of my polo shirt even as we talked.

She smiled. 'We not worry after time,' she said.

We walked back to the boat slapping and scratching, jumping and gesticulating, and as we did so, the golden ferry cruised across the golden waters from the mainland past the golden islands to the golden dock and spewed about 400 people on to the island.

One of the mysterious elements of Vormsi was how it sustained itself. We had stood amid the ruins of a manor house, climbed an old Russian watchtower and examined the rails that had carried the missiles out from the rocket station. We had visited a strange pub, with a year's cigarette waste in the copper-hooded fireplace and graffiti on the silver flock wallpaper, which served beer from a fridge and had no water or soft drinks, but had pictures of Spanish ladies in the hall, like a Suffolk rural slum. All these places were clearly built for snow, with small windows and thick-sealed doors, which seemed odd when the air crackled with heat. But what did these people do? There were no crops, just hayfields, but there seemed to be no cows to eat this hay, apart from the one having a quick swim somewhere in the reeds. 'It is a special area, all funded to keep cows,' we had been told.

But now the place came alive. We watched the harbour become a disturbed ant heap. Cars hooted their way past hordes of passengers strolling out with backpacks. A big container lorry was roaring and bellowing, struggling past a parked 1950s American bus. Motorcycles, handcarts, push chairs, mopeds. There were supposed to be about 300 people living on this island. Had all of them gone to the mainland and then suddenly come back? Was this the rush hour?

From behind the ferry a motor yacht now emerged, towering out of the water, white and plastic. It was stuffed with more people, cackling and shouting. Obviously, it could not tie up at the front of the quay. That's where the ferry was going. There was only one other place. It headed straight for where *Undina* was moored. Like a cruiser in the Battle of Jutland, it was accompanied by satellite destroyers, jet skis, noisily careering around it, depth-charging the tranquillity. Revving its engines, the trashy thing bashed into us, and several fat men, with mobile phones clamped to their ears, jumped ashore and started untying our warps.

'Hey! No. Sorry, is this your mooring?' I asked, confused.

'You move along, we come here.'

The pontoon was shorter than our boat. 'No, no, we can't move.

This would be a better place for your boat.' I indicated the wall of the dock with its huge tractor tyres and dented sides.

'No, no, it's not possible.'

I took my warp out of his hands and retied it. The captain looked on. The men in black, with expensive shoes, turned to the boat. A slim bloke in a suit with floppy hair started patronizing us, and waffling on about a bottle of champagne, but the captain, a nervous-looking commander, intervened and decided, instead, that he would raft alongside us. We shook our heads. He was very big. We showed him where the Estonian buoy boat had lain and stood by – I hoped like a salty crew, looking like business, but probably like four grumpy Englishmen, looking like berks. Grudgingly, he squeezed in and we squeezed up a couple of feet. The shaven-headed goons started hurriedly unloading crates of beer on to the shore.

'It's a company party, apparently,' Bob explained. Two women in skimpy tops looked on. More men unloaded crates and baggage.

After an hour they seemed to have revved their last motorbike and crashed their last gear. A few stragglers tottered up the road shouting. The boat was left empty and we sat swatting at mosquitoes as the sun went down.

An August harvest moon rose up across the bay. Two large birds flew off into the west. Bob watched them go. 'Flamingoes,' he said finally. With the weather, I supposed he could be right, but they were probably swans. From now on, though, we would see continuous flights of birds, streaming in great Vs across the sky, and they were all heading south. Perhaps we should be, soon.

Baines struggled across heaped masonry 20 feet high, through a marsh and under a gantry, to disconnect a builder's pump and steal the electrical supply. And then, at last, in Vormsi, everything was tranquillity: reed beds, swans' nests, mosquito-plagued cow bellowing in the distance and the company party way across the island.

I thought everyone had gone, but one man was standing in the shadows looking at the boat. He was leaning on an old bicycle and had bad acne and blond hair tied tight to the back of his head in a

Samurai topknot. He was too downbeat to be with the party. He
just wanted to look at *Undina*, so we invited him on. He took a
drink and sat for a few minutes in a sort of mute fulfilment, like
Baines in an engine room.

Lowri was mute generally. It proved quite difficult to get him to
talk. He had sensitive youth syndrome. On the island he had com-
muned with nature. He had seen several snakes and a wild pig. 'Did
you see the flamingoes?' Bob asked. 'How about the wild Arctic
lichen?' I asked. No, but he had been out on the nearby peninsula,
where it grew. He lived in Tartu and had cycled the 120 kilometres
to the islands in one day. He didn't have a tent, just a sleeping bag.
He was going to the university soon 'to study the physical science'.

'Like biology?' we asked.

'Oh, no, you know, for sport. T'ai chi.'

'Do you sail?'

'No, but I would like to.'

I invited him to come with us the next day. He accepted and we
sat for a while, munching peanuts. I asked him about the Soviets
and the changes of the past ten years. 'Is this a good time for
Estonia?'

'Yes.'

'You feel that there are new opportunities.'

'Yes.'

'Are there many changes?'

He thought for a bit. 'Not really, no.' Then after a while. 'Perhaps
now there's more difference between rich and poor, you can tell
the difference more.'

'And who are the rich people?' He looked puzzled. 'Who are
the people making money? The people you might be jealous of?'

'I don't know, you know, I'm not really interested in this sort
of thing.'

I got up, showed him the hatch immediately above my bed and
told him to knock on it at six in the morning.

'Six?'

'Yes, we have to go early in the morning.' And he went off to
sleep in a ditch or wherever.

It was dark. I sat alone in the cockpit. Baines and Bob were below, rigging up the cabin. Charlie was cooking. After three months' travelling I felt we had reached the zenith of our journey. The pinkish moon was steadily rising into a starry sky. The air was nicely cool. We were miles from anywhere. If escape was what I was searching for, this lonely bay seemed to offer it and . . . my reverie was interrupted by a distant buzzing. I listened but it faded in the velvet night. Good. The water was . . . the buzzing came back. Some sort of two-stroke engine. In fact, several two-stroke engines. No, a convoy of engines was screaming through the night. I stood up and could see a dozen headlights flickering in the blackness. In seconds they reached the dock. Several motorbike engines were revved to the limits of human endurance. An open pick-up truck followed behind and 'the bit of the party that would be fun if we went down by the water and made a lot of noise and things' started.

We sat below like mortified parents at a teenage bash. Girls were continuously flung into the harbour from the quayside. This was in order to hear them scream. If they screamed loudly enough, they were thrown in again. The boat was crushed and walloped against the rusting cement-encrusted contractors' pontoon by the washes from the jet skis. Buggies, scooters and pick-ups came and went on the wharf. Finally, I asked one of the hairy-looking youths, who was wearing a towel around his head as an improvised kepi, what the company that had organized the party did.

I went below. 'OK,' I said to the others. 'You have ten guesses. The company having the party on this island. What do you think it is?'

'An Estonian TV company.'

'No.'

'It's something to do with the Mafia.'

'You've had two.'

Bob, in a party mood himself now, stopped Charlie. 'No, no, that wasn't a proper guess.'

'It was,' I said.

'No, that was just a speculation. It wasn't an official guess.'

'Oh for Christ's sake . . .'

'Fashion!'

'No.'

They weren't club owners, disco people or a travel company. They were folk dancers.

'Dancers?'

'Yes.'

'What, like *Cats*, or in a casino? Exotic dancers?'

'No, no, they're folk dancers.' They were the National Estonian Folk Dancing Company. Their muscles came from their great leaps and cavorting. The girls were pretty, because folk-dancing girls needed to be pretty when they twirled in embroidered dirndl skirts. And they were noisy and arrogant, because folk dancing was still a pretty big deal in Estonia.

The party went away, at about one in the morning. The stars were clear and brilliant, the moon set. It got very dark. The island finally became the lost outpost it was supposed to be.

But, at one-thirty, just as I was dropping off to sleep, lights started flashing at the portholes. I went on the deck, slippery with dew. There was the sound of voices and the white rods of searchlights and a 40-foot racing boat covered with men glided out of the murk. Her decks were swarming with plastic-hooded forms shouting in Estonian. Naturally, they wanted to tie up alongside us. Baines held up his hands and pointed to the wharf our next-door neighbour had disdained. 'That would be better for your boat,' he said, in his technical authority voice. 'Besides, we're leaving at six in the morning.'

'At six in the morning?' It was the decisive factor. They moved on. 'Could you push us?'

We pushed them off.

'Is there enough water?'

'Yes, yes,' we said. I think they went aground at that moment, but an extra shove and they were away, where the water was indeed deeper. We went below, for a few hours.

At six o'clock in the morning it was grey, completely still. The sky was clear, the sun was an orange disc in the east, and the wind no stronger than the smoke extruding from Bob's morning cigarette. Lowri was standing with his bicycle in two bits, and we strapped it to the roof, over a deflated fender and a bit of sponge from a camera case.

We talked in whispers, though we were all awake, unfurled the jib and let go the lines. An exhalation of wind swung the bow away from the pontoon. The stern rope slipped through a rusting hoop. It fell back with a clunk. With a sloppy gurgle *Undina* eased away from the sleeping racing boat and the crude motor yacht into another mauve-tinged day.

33. The Sailing Thing

Everything was clean and fresh that morning: clean, clean, the air was clean, the sky was clean, the morning was clean. The eastern Estonian Islands seemed to float just above the horizon, a little bar of light lifting them off the liquid world. They were clean too. Only we were filthy.

Two distant, shining white blocks meant the ferries were already winding back and forth between Hiiumaa and the mainland. But we would never get to Hiiumaa now, even though the chart's tessellations took us south towards it, to find a way through the rock-strewn waters. At the bottom, by the Island of Pigs, we turned east and, then, ruefully, north and straight into the path of the strengthening wind. The zephyr became a hair-raiser, became a flag-flapper, became a wake-maker. *Undina* surged forward. The sails cracked and filled. For a few hours it was fucking fantastic.

Once in California I went boating with Mel Smith. We hired a yacht and sailed across to the island of Catalina. The passage out took a day. But it was jolly. There were pilot whales bobbing around, pelicans and gannets fishing, and the sun shone – all that stuff. We motored anyway. (Smith took to the water like a chest of drawers.) On the way back, we sailed. And we hit fog and a moderate wind. Half-way across, after several people had been sick, the huge fridge drained all the electricity and we lost power for the navigation lights and the radio, as well as any ability to start the engine. ('You shouldn't have left it on,' the hired hand told us, neatly side-stepping responsibility.)

'Right, that's it,' Mel said decisively, 'we'll go in now.'

The skipper, a boring, bearded delivery crew, looked puzzled. I had to explain to Mel that we were exactly half-way between the island and the mainland. We were at sea.

'Call a helicopter,' he suggested.

'No, no, Mel. Apart from the radio not working, I'm afraid we're not in any danger. We just have to wait. We'll get there eventually.'

And we did. We waited so long that the impossibly huge Marina Del Rey was completely shut at two the next morning when we got there. The chain link gates were locked. There was no one about to help, even when, taking a line ashore, I jumped off the boat, straight into a dock-side Jacuzzi.

But a lot of the sailing thing is waiting: as boring as a Siberian train journey and far less comfortable, living in a yawing box, counting the miles and doing the housekeeping. Later on this day, we were to bash up the coast, frustratingly trying to make a port, any port. But at the beginning, we skipped along. Cutting into the shallow edges, then swinging round, edging up slice by slice, measuring our progress against the rocks and islands. It was bliss.

Baines had gone back to bed. We snatched moments to eat our buns from the island shop. They were stale, so Bob heated them at the stove, muttering and smoking and clutching at handholds. Lowri had brought us a pot of island honey as a gift. Like all honey made from bees living in wild places, it tasted just like any other honey, but it almost made the buns edible. Mawing gooily, we sailed close to deserted shores, more enclosed, curtained forest, no indications of any houses beyond the settlements: no villas, like in Denmark, no grand manors, like in England, no farms, like in Sweden, just the occasional Russian military watchtower, or timber-wharf, to break the unending rank of green.

Finally, almost disappointingly, within throwing distance of a line of glacial boulders, we bounded out into the Gulf of Finland. The breeze got stronger as we walloped into the open sea, and things changed. Out of the shelter of the islands, the sea began to pound us, the water oozed relentlessly through the hatch and the windows and the inaccessible leaking corner, somewhere under the starboard deck, dripped on to my bed, so I put my bedding into polythene bags and started sticking swabs of kitchen roll into the cracks.

Baines was awake, looking for things to fix, turning on his dub selections and fiddling with the bits of machinery that someone else had set up. I fixed a 'way point', a marker to head for, on the electric chart, pressed a few buttons and a line emerged on the screen. 'Marvellous! Just follow that line,' I told Baines and went to curl up on the short side of the boat.

Down below, it yawed and tossed, but, mostly, it leaned. There was no form of stillness whatsoever. Bits of Bob's wardrobe flew across the cabin. Shoes tumbled past. Progress along the cabin floor was a matter of grasping at what was screwed on and trying to avoid what was not. One foot had to go half-way up a side wall to maintain equilibrium. Despite improvised fiddles, charts suddenly slid up and off and on to the floor. Water bubbled up through the floorboards. The steps down to the cabin were useless. They were a man's height and flat, and when we heeled, they were angled at 45 degrees and the bottom wasn't the bottom any more, it was the side.

Suspended in this skewed, rattling, wet, lop-sided world, I tried to sleep. I squeezed a duvet into a polythene bag in the corner and rose and fell on that. My head was on a pillow in another polythene bag. I covered myself in a damp blanket and, in a wheezing pump of soothing, sighing polythene, dozed fitfully until we reached the northern latitude of 57°28'.

We seemed to be half-way to Hanko on the Finnish coast by then. I had promised that we would come about, to make our way east, towards Tallinn, up the Gulf of Finland. 'Good news!' announced Baines, as I stepped into the light. 'The wind has come round to the east.' But it wasn't good news.

'No. We were only going this way to try to get "an offing",' I explained. 'Now that the wind has changed, when we tack, we'll head straight back the way we've come. Damn.' We had had the pleasure. The beat into the wind had lost its skipping, absorbing obstacle-race qualities and had become a thumping, frustrating slog.

Lowri had become increasingly more self-contained. Now, he was suddenly spectacularly sick. Hardly surprising, really, because Bob had given him three raw frankfurters to settle his stomach. He was sick on the wrong side, as well: all over the upside of the deck.

We had to lower a canvas bucket around the swollen bottom of *Undina* to get at the water and swill the dribbly bits away. There was nothing we could do for Lowri, though. Even soothing words are an intolerable intrusion.

It was a perfectly lovely, windy evening. The distant coast with its wild hills was certainly the most seductive we had passed for a while. But with a head wind, we would make little progress, even under motor. I knew we would have to find some place to stay overnight before Tallinn.

I scanned all the charts in our possession. It was impossible. We had no detailed English pilot or guide to all these places. Even the German book which we'd bought in Borkum, a guide to the whole Baltic area, was beginning to run out of ideas. I found myself leafing though a tourist brochure, illustrated with pictogram windmills, castles and milkmaids, in the hope that I might identify some seaside town or fishing port. But there was nothing at all on this huge, wide bay. Distant white villages and towns on the shore had a Mediterranean, civilized glow in the sun. They always do from the sea. When you get close, you realize that you have been pining after a few sheds and a chicken farm. We pressed on to a place called Paldiski.

Even in the darkness that came before we got there, we could see that Paldiski was a wreck. Shadowy, ruined warehouses blanked out the stars. Bent cranes loomed out of the black. On top of the high quay that we tied up to, the concrete was split like ice floes, with crevasses between them, knitted together with rusting cables and wires. But as I climbed up on to the wharf, and stood looking at this devastated facility, I felt in a state of perfect peace. It was the stillest evening. There was a fat August moon. A duck was paddling about in the muddy halo of the red light, gummed up with bugs, which marked the entrance to the harbour. A few bubbles seeped ominously from somewhere deep in the murky water. It was warm and, despite the desolation, as I stood there looking out across the bay, the place seemed to reach out, with a grasp of complete and utter calm.

Some hours later, I was woken by a throbbing sound. It was

daylight. Perhaps six. Too early, anyway. I dragged myself up, peered through the tiny port in my cabin and jerked back as it was blanked by a grey wall sliding across it. I strained around when it had passed and caught a glimpse of a long, low, grey motor torpedo boat slinking up the harbour. Back in my mildewed nest I forgot about it and only clambered out a couple of hours later.

Bob was bounding over the broken, cracked concrete towards me.

'Do you want a shower?'

'Where?'

'On the coastguard boat. It's all arranged. I've had a word and they're extending us the use of their facilities.'

'Nice.'

'I think so.'

'Where's Lowri?'

'He's on there now, having a crap.'

He capered back along the dock.

'Mind the wire! Ah, now, may I present Captain Willi.'

Captain Willi was short and muscular with a crushing handshake. He was wearing a blue uniform shirt. 'Welcome,' he said expansively.

Bob, warming to his fixer role, bent to his task, literally leaning over Captain Willi. 'Now, yes, we go get fuel, yes, with Andreas.' He mimed hefting a can of something and pointed to the boat.

'Yes,' said Willi promptly. 'He come now.' He pointed to a car ponderously galumphing around the shattered dockside in the morning sun.

'Good, good,' said Bob, 'much appreciated, yes.'

Willi gave some firm, military-sounding instructions to Andreas. We got in his car and rocked and rolled around the wrecked harbour, under the pylon cranes, to the entrance.

'That's for sale,' said Bob as we jerked past an amphibious military vehicle. 'Andreas!' He pointed to the 30-foot-long boat with wheels and half tracks. 'How much?'

'Six thousand Euros,' Andreas said.

'Nothing,' said Bob.

At the gate there was a barrier. Two overweight men in camouflage uniforms stopped doing nothing with bad grace and demanded our passports. They were still on *Undina*.

Andreas was very apologetic. 'We have to go back.'

'You're the Customs, though, aren't you?' Bob was confused.

'This is just . . .' Andreas sighed. 'They think they are big men.' He shrugged and smiled, put the car into reverse and we jiggled and wobbled all the way back to the boat, past the amphibious vehicle again. Bob leaned round to gaze. 'They've got one on the Thames, haven't they? Taking tourists.'

'That one works,' I said.

'This one go, Andreas? Brrmmm, Brrm?'

Andreas shrugged. 'Maybe.'

Andreas and Willi worked three weeks on and three weeks off. I was surprised to find that both of them lived inland, near Tatra. Willi had been sent to Campbeltown in Scotland to retrain as a coastguard officer, paid for by the Americans.

They wouldn't have wanted to live in Paldiski, anyway. It was a peeling housing estate that had known better times when it was a Soviet submarine base. The population was largely Russian and unemployment was high. Andreas drove us past the ranks of blocks along untended military roadways, dotted with bronze statues of Russian submariner heroes. There were old men, with the bearing of veterans sitting on the benches in the sun.

'That was the training school,' Andreas said and pointed to a big brick academy between us and the water. The windows were broken. The parade grounds were empty and beginning to follow the docks into a state of crumbling decay.

'We could probably drive it most of the way back,' said Bob distractedly. 'You could take it across the Channel on a good day, couldn't you?'

Back in the harbour, Willi was keen to take us on a tour of his cutter and we clattered around the cream-painted interior, up and down ladders, poking into the galley and meeting the engineer.

Willi's boat used 300 litres an hour at 30 knots. Baines patted the engines. 'That's three hundred and twenty quid an hour at full speed,' he said.

Bob frowned. 'What's the top speed, then?'

'About thirty-five knots,' Willi told us.

'Right,' said Bob. We walked up on the grey-painted stern deck and admired the gun. Bob wrinkled his brow and nodded. 'So, you could get across the Channel in an hour. Not bad. And to get from here would, then, well . . .' He trailed away.

'It would cost you about thirty thousand pounds just to get it to London,' Charlie helped him out.

'But you wouldn't have to go top speed,' said Bob. 'And look at the space.' We were walking past the crew accommodation. 'And you could probably stick that amphibious vehicle on the back easily enough.' He turned to Willi. 'Is this Russian? Russian boat, this?'

Willi smiled and shook his head. 'No, no, we buy from Norway. This was patrol boat.'

'They obviously didn't want to buy from the Finns, because they'd keep meeting the former owners.' Baines said.

'Do you work with Finnish Customs?' I asked Willi.

'Oh, yes.'

'And you arrest yachts?'

'Yachts? No.' He laughed. 'Big boats.' He looked for illegal goods and immigrants. 'Sometimes rescue.'

'But she wasn't built as a patrol boat.'

'No, no. This boat was a war boat. She have rockets. Whoosh. But they are gone.' He noticed Bob's disappointment. 'Here was the rocket launch machine . . . We take away and now . . .' he opened the door with a flourish. 'Here we have sauna.'

We said goodbye to Lowri, who needed to bicycle back to Tartu for the start of term, and set off for Tallinn.

'Well, there we are.' I said. 'We haven't been searched by the coastguards, but we have managed to search them.'

'Not bad,' said Bob.

34. Sex Capital of the North

We motored up to Tallinn, skirting a wide bay and its outlying islands, in a big loop that brought us round to the northern shore of a bow-shaped corniche. The temperature was high. The boats hung sloppily in the water. There were yacht clubs and bare-fronted suburbs on the corniche, and tucked away in its crook was the yacht harbour built for the 1980 Olympics (the one the Americans refused to take part in, as a protest against Russian interference in Afghanistan). We sloped in, behind a long, sandy-coloured breakwater, to a virtually empty dock, below a pile of egg boxes on stilts (former dormitories for the competitors). But our eyes were fixed across the water. A modern road swept round in a great curve. ('Oh you should see it,' Axel had told us, 'all these Estonians charging back and forth in their big modern cars.') It fringed the bay, swooped past a huge Soviet monument (celebrating expanded chests) on towards the city itself, which rose out of the flat plain and the mirror sea in a mound of spires and towers and walls.

Most big, important places tend to creep up, when approached from the sea, as a clutter of litter on a shore, or, if at the head of their own river, with ferry terminals and ragged docks and deserted warehouses. Sydney has its monumental buildings and its famous bridge and its gorgeous bay, but it has flung itself down all over the shop. Rio has its outlying sugarloaf islands and a magnificent tropical background, but lies scraggily in front of its mountain back-drops. Only Manhattan or Toronto had ever matched the promise of Tallinn. Racing into Toronto, along the raised freeway, the city rears up out of a Marvel comic, glittering and modern. Tallinn was the medieval equivalent. It was a front cover of *Conan the Barbarian*.

'We have to be moving on in three days,' I told Bob, Charlie and Baines, as we tied up. The reason lay around us. There were probably sixty or seventy visitors' buoys in the dock and only about six were occupied. They were all Finnish boats.

'Where are you from?' asked a teenage boy squinting at our ensign. 'Australia?'

'England. The red flag is the one that has to be worn by merchant ships,' I explained pathetically. 'What about you?'

They were going home. Everybody else in the harbour was going home. It was already past the end of the season. The Finnish holiday had finished two weeks ago. The schools started up again in a few days. If I looked around, the angular Soviet show buildings in their crumbly concrete overcoats were etched with the brilliant light of early autumn – an alien, worrying gleam. And we were only just setting off to St Petersburg and, as usual, without much of a chart.

The kid was anxious to rope in his dad. He could help us.

Dad sat in our cockpit and fumbled with our sheets of paper. 'You can't go straight, here,' he said. 'You must go to this . . . island, to Kronshtadt first, and there you must speak with the authorities . . .'

'Where should we stop en route?' I asked. We wanted to break the journey overnight. He dragged the chart towards him again and looked at it closely for an excessively long period. I realized that he was quite drunk. 'This is good.' He pointed vaguely at a bit of the coast and looked at it harder.

I asked about the river at the border. This was not good. He and his two friends, who were equally drunk, were all in firm agreement that we should avoid, avoid, avoid the border towns. 'Mafia. Not good.' We all concurred with that.

They had been to St Petersburg, but not this trip. In fact, fewer and fewer Finns were bothering with the journey. It had seemed an adventure when the borders were first opened, but the Russians, it was generally thought, were still living in the stone age. There was nowhere to leave the boat safely. There was a lot of crime and the authorities still treated small boats to the same formalities as they did super-tankers. They would come aboard mob-handed and tape down fridges and drinks cupboards.

On the way back from the harbour master's office, heading for the sauna and shower facilities, laid on in 1980 for the visiting Olympians, I met Baines and Charlie going for a drink. 'We left the boat open,' they told me. 'The Finns next door said they'd look after it.' So, after I had negotiated the labyrinthine corridors of the Olympic dormitories, I was taken aback to find all the next-door neighbours in the sauna.

'Oh, no, the boat will be fine, fine.' They waved at me from the showers, where they were sitting on the floor, rolling in the spray; bright pink and beer-bellied after their sauna. 'Only the Finns can make saunas properly,' they told me. The original sauna was a hole in the ground, with a fire pit in the middle, in which the whole tribe sat and got hot. They all had fire pits of their own now. It was inconceivable that they would not. 'It is my great pleasure,' said the accordion player who had a little wooden motorboat next to ours, not unlike a floating sauna in appearance. 'I go in it every night, in the summer particularly.'

'But for how long?' I had begun, reluctantly, to enjoy the experience. But I rarely lasted more than a few minutes.

'All night. Several hours. Not all the time.' Then, having noticed my expression of dismay: 'I go in, then I have a shower. Cool down. Go back in again.' He was un-selfconsciously dragging a towel back and forth between his legs.

'Aha. But we know you, I think,' a man with a beard, drying his chest hair, was smiling at me. 'You are Jones, yes?'

Alas Smith and Jones had once been big in Finland. We had been their Saturday-night 'Morecombbe and Wysse'. Our programme had been called *Snow in Your Cottage*, which was a proverb, meaning 'subject to foolish bad luck' (just one of many, including 'envy will kill the fish in the sea' and 'behave in the sauna as you would in a church'). I smiled back sheepishly. 'Yes. What, you recognize me now because my hair is wet?'

'No, no. It's a good disguise, but your voice gives you away.'

Tallinn beckoned. Max, the taxi driver, took us in along the banana-shaped road. 'I take you boys to the girlie house.'

'No, we are looking for a traditional restaurant.'

'Yes.' He laughed and dropped us just outside a grim-looking basement. We waited until he'd driven round the corner and ran across a park filled with heroin addicts, into the old town.

We were not the first to discover Tallinn – it had been well colonized by Benetton – but, luckily, it still had some way to go before it became an anonymous, painted 'Euro-stop' harlot like Prague. There were few 'souvenir shops'. This was a serious shopping destination for people who wanted to buy pre-faded jeans, frilly knickers and designer eye-wear. It was difficult to imagine that Paldiski and Tallinn were in the same country. And, despite the rigorous attentions of the Wehrmacht and the Russian army during key military engagements of the twentieth century, the town was a miracle of historical unity. We walked off the main drag up around curving streets and shaded squares past eighteenth-century palaces. Alleys led through to platforms high in the walls, looking over the railway yards and factories of the plain.

Max was waiting to take us back. 'You want to go to girlie house now?'

'No, no. Maybe tomorrow.'

'Don't say that, Bob,' I interjected. But he already had.

The next day we had important business to transact. We were leaving western Europe, so we needed a tourist visa for our visit to Russia. And we had been told that it was easy to get one in Tallinn. But the man with the beard behind the glass screen in the Russian visa office was less sure. The cramped waiting room had a writing shelf along one wall, there were two chairs in a little annexe and at least fifteen men with worried expressions were hunched over long forms, waiting to sit.

'No, it's not possible.' He slid several bulky forms into his tray and passed them under the screen. 'You must have two sponsors.'

I gagged. 'This is not what the Baltic pilot-book said!' He frowned. The others bundled me away, and Bob stepped forward with an innocent expression of mystified amazement on his beaming face.

He discovered we were in the wrong office. The worried men were Estonian Russians looking for a way back home. We just needed a tourist visa. For this we required no sponsors at all, we needed a recommendation from an accredited tour operator. There was one across the road, sharing premises with the 'Red Cat Titty Bar'. Olga was sitting behind a desk. She confirmed that getting visas was incredibly simple. In return for about £100 she could stamp our passports and give us the necessary paperwork in a few hours, but obviously not today. 'We are closing early.'

'Why?'

'It is Independence Day tomorrow.'

'So we should come back tomorrow,' asked Bob a little pointlessly, given Olga's enormous hint.

'No. Tomorrow is Independence Day. And then it is Saturday and then Sunday. We are open in . . .' she counted on her fingers, '. . . four days.'

'But we have to be in St Petersburg by then!'

She smiled wanly. I got to my feet. Bob motioned to Baines, who held me down.

'What if we had the photographs and paid the money now?' 'What if we took you out for lunch?' 'What if we helped fill in the forms ourselves?' She weakened. She was going for lunch in ten minutes. If we got back with the photos by then . . . The passport photograph on my Russian tourist visa shows a sweaty, red-faced man with an expression of exasperated panic, after a 200-yard sprint up a steep hill to Tallinn's central photo-me booth.

We sat on the step outside the Titty Bar. Bob suddenly clucked. 'What about Christophe?' he asked. Chris, a film actor with a lot of work, had managed to find a gap in his schedule and was coming out to join us the next day and gatecrash the zippy bit of the trip. 'He might be a little annoyed to come all the way and not be able to get to St Petersburg.'

Bob telephoned him and left Christophe charging around the suburbs of London, doing pretty much the same as we had, only on a larger scale, while we went for lunch. Here, Bob unwrapped a brown pottery bear, vaguely familiar, with its jaunty step and cheery grin. 'I got three of them in separate places. They're Mischas: souvenirs of the 1980 Olympics.'

'Only another six or seven hundred thousand and you'll have cornered the market,' said Baines.

'What you ought to do, Bob, is try and get something like this,' I said, later. Max, our regular taxi driver, was taking us on a tour and had parked underneath the huge Soviet sculpture on the corniche. 'Or these.' We drove on through the suburbs to the east of the city. Over 300,000 people were housed in giant, rust-coloured concrete blocks on either side of a major motorway, built to house the last burst of Russian colonization in the 1970s. They were the true souvenirs of the occupation.

Max agreed to take us down to the ferry terminals to meet Chris the following morning. I came up on deck, to find a Ben Gunn figure standing on the pontoon. Skinny and impressively bearded, he smiled wetly at me and raised a hand towards the boat.

'English,' he said.

'Yes, yes.' We were in a hurry.

'Wood,' he said.

'Yes,' I replied. We walked off towards the people carrier. Ben Gunn loped alongside. He shook my hand warmly and then produced a photograph of another wooden, clinker-built, heavily varnished boat. He pointed across the harbour. 'My boat,' he said. I nodded encouragingly.

'Mmm,' I said.

'Do you speak English?' asked Bob.

'No. I not speak English.' This made Ben Gunn a rarity. So far in our trip around the Baltic, everybody spoke English. We took it as a matter of course. Bob was not going to back off now.

'We are going to meet our friend who has come from England. He arrives soon. We must go.'

Ben looked at me and back at Bob. He shook his head.

'Bob, he doesn't speak English.'

'Well, you say that, but he can say he doesn't speak English perfectly well.' We had reached the vehicle. 'Max,' said Bob, 'tell him we'll catch him when we get back.'

Max waved the man away and drove us off. He shook his head and turned to us with a turned-down mouth. 'Russian!' he said.

The ferry terminals were new, gleaming with marble and awash with espresso coffee. We found Chris wandering away from them, with his shirt off, dragging his kit towards the lure of the old town above us.

'This is all rather nice,' he said. And it was. It was sunny and breezy. Tallinn looked curious and busy, in fact, much busier than before.

'Who are all these people, then?' he asked. In front of us a swarm of middle-aged Americans in turquoise had halted behind a woman with a ticket on a stick. There were other crocodiles leaving by the side door. The streets were full of these crocodiles, all following sticks.

They were all from cruise ships. Standing on the brow of the citadel, we could look down to the docks, where at least three giant bath-tub toys were tied up. Like some well-planned beach assault, they were still disgorging hordes of pillagers. The more they came, the more this excellent city would succumb. The more horse-drawn carriages they would need. The more the buildings and streets would have to be tidied up into 'historic routes'. All that made Tallinn individual – the smell, the chaos, the guts and the rumble of the city – would have to be subsumed in the greater purpose of serving the tourist machine.

Later, we sat on the deck above the harbour in a tinge of autumn chill. A firm hand slapped down on my shoulder.

'My friend! How are you?'

I turned around. The hand belonged to a man in a stripy matelot shirt beneath a navy reefer. He had a dark navy-cut beard, a navy yachting cap on his head and was called Victor.

'Vassily here. He likes your boat, very much.' He smiled and gestured towards Ben Gunn, who was standing moist-eyed beside him.

'Drink!' said Victor. 'We must "knock some back", of course.'

Victor, who had worked in Liverpool and loved the English, was the owner of the yellow, varnished boat that Vassily, a member of what appeared to be his extended family, had shown me earlier. After drinks and peanuts, they were both anxious to have a look at

Undina, so we took them and another bloke who happened to be a friend, and Victor's twelve-year-old son, and climbed aboard.

Chris waded in. 'So. You're Russian.'

'No,' said Victor.

'Oh. I thought . . .'

'I am Estonian.'

Behind Victor's back, Bob and I made signals at Chris.

'Yes, but you speak Russian.'

'My family is from Russia, but now I am Estonian.'

'Yes, but your country was in occupation here, wasn't it? Don't they want you to go back to Russia now?'

Victor's smile cracked at the edges. 'No. This is my country now. My country. My son he will learn Estonian and Russian at school.'

Chris decided to change the subject. 'And English?'

'Yes.'

'Gosh. That's three languages he has to learn.'

'There are many difficulties here in Estonia. But we must all work together. This is our country.'

Chris nodded vigorously.

On board, Victor and his extended family wanted to see everything. We handed round beers and vodkas. Vassily tenderly stroked the beams and stringers.

'He likes your boat,' Victor said. 'Wood.'

'Wood,' Vassily said and looked passionately around.

Victor was keen that we visited his club. When Max arrived with the taxi for the evening trip into town, Victor walked out with us, pressing a card on me. It was for 'The Mousetrap', a lap-dancing establishment. 'My nephew will look after you there,' he told us. We climbed into the people carrier. Victor barked orders at Max. Max shrugged and protested. Victor leaned in and said something menacing to him. We stared at the carpet.

'It is like you and the Scottish in Scotland,' said Victor by way of farewell. 'We are the ones in charge and they don't like it.'

Max drove off and threw the card out of the window. 'It's a very bad place,' he said. 'I will take you to a good place.' And that, I promise you, is how we ended up in this brothel.

To my certain knowledge, I'd only ever been in a brothel twice before. The first time was in Lisbon. I was seventeen, working as a 'school-office assistant' on an educational cruise ship. My fellow assistants and I found a bodega just outside the dock gates. In a well-lit room with bent-wood furniture and a small bar, a plump, middle-aged woman in a black satin dress waddled over to take our drinks order. Beer was apparently an impossibility. We were puzzled and argued the toss. She laughed gaily and offered us champagne. We didn't want champagne. She leaned over the shoulders of one of the shyer members of our party and started ruffling his hair and caressing his neck. I remember we sat there, looking at this from the other side of the table, in utter amazement. What was she doing? Nobody said anything. Out of the corner of my eye I could see some seedy middle-aged men in suits sitting with their backs to the wall. Now I realized that the woman standing in front of them was gradually lifting her skirt up her thighs. I nudged my friend and he looked across too, while our mate sat in a state of frozen panic as the mistress of the house ran her hands up and down inside his shirt.

We laughed aloud, but only because we were accidental customers. We were laughing at our own naivety. We never found out what we were supposed to do next. Minutes later we were out on the street.

I ended up in the brothel in Hull after performing a show at the university on a stage of crates. The whore-house in the fish-dock was, according to my student guide, the only place to get a drink at four in the morning. Dawn was already coming up. We were the youngest in the premises by some thirty years, and this included 'the girls'. It had a high ceiling with neon lights on chains. Ten or so men, with red faces, were sat around Formica tables, resolutely staring ahead. Each of them had a cup and saucer on the table in front of them. After we had sat for a while, a cup and saucer was put in front of us too and, then, out of a back room, a small man in a suit came weaving across and, surreptitiously, offered us half a bottle of whisky. We took it and sat with the bottle hidden in our laps, adding the spirit to our tea, according to taste. This was to prevent police trouble. I seem to remember two of the 'girls' danced, while women with the ample proportions and drink-sodden, pudding faces of a Degas joined the men from a George Grosz cartoon. These were both brothels from history.

Max's girlie house was through a back door, off a back garden turned car park. It was a semi-detached villa. Inside, the rooms had been converted into bigger spaces by knocking down walls. I felt respect for the entrepreneurial skill of the owners.

I'm not saying it was done well. Perhaps it wasn't built to last, but there was a distinct idea at work here. A complete plywood and upholstery rebuild of the living space, it would have made an excellent Quentin Tarantino set. The whole effect was, well, thoughtful; worth the price of admission itself, which we paid to a charming man behind the bar. He was watched over by three very tall, shy-looking men. We guessed these were Russian. They had the pasty, blank, awkward, oblong faces of Russian military fodder – gawky rather than Gorki, rather innocent and, yes, honest-looking chaps. With their plain-coloured shirts and new leather jackets, they lacked any obvious menace and were probably the more dangerous because of it.

Everybody watched us carefully, like anxious managers in a supermarket, waiting to see how customers responded to a new promotion. Max smiled and winked at us from his place by the bar, where he had, rather too obviously, joined the management side of the enterprise. We sat on the leopardskin banquettes, spread out around the room and now oddly isolated from each other, co-cooned in loud music and nursing our expensive drinks while four 'girls' came across to say hello, and then almost as swiftly went back to their own station on another bench. Clearly, we were not proper sex-tourists. They could tell, almost instantly.

A girl got up and did a pole dance. She wore a sensible black bra and knickers and took some minutes and a great deal of exertion to remove just her bra. It was business-like and entirely unarousing, particularly so when she came and sat on my lap. I remained fully clothed in all my inhibitions and rather wished she'd get off and move along to Baines, but she didn't seem to be able to, and seemed, gradually, to be becoming as self-conscious as me, and I was very self-conscious indeed.

'You have to give me money,' she finally whispered in desperation. I recognized her tone. It was like being on stage. I'd missed my cue, and now everyone was embarrassed and she was prompting me.

'Yes, of course, I'm so sorry,' I said and with some difficulty, because she was straddling my legs, got my hand into my pocket, removed a bundle of notes and, moronically, set about trying to examine their value in the semi-darkness.

I think we were both relieved when the transaction was at an end. She gyrated across to Charlie, who went bright red, and the excruciating evening continued.

We felt we'd exhausted the attractions of the place after a scant half-hour. Max was surprised.

'You want to go now?'

'Yes, Max.'

'Nobody want girl?'

'No Max.'

'I understand. OK. We go to find better girls. These girls . . .' he pulled a face.

Chris agreed. 'Yes, most unattractive.'

'They offered me a go for free,' said Baines.

'Well, there we are,' said Bob. It was true that Baines had at one point been the focus of attention of at least three houris.

'You are very handsome,' said Max. While Max determinedly drove off into the night, we drove around a few bye-ways of our own.

'Do we want to go to another one?'

'Not really. They'll just be the same, won't they?'

'What's the point of this anyway? We're not going to avail ourselves of any commodities on offer.'

'We're here,' said Max.

'OK.' And we all jumped out and trooped in to continue window-shopping.

35. Eels

And now the whole journey began to assume an unreal, over-lit quality. Like an empty travelogue through a deserted, apocalyptic sea.

Vergi was an insignificant stopping place along the blank, pine-covered shore of northern Estonia. We slipped in behind its little breakwater amongst the trees in late evening. It had been an early start from Tallinn. We were barely awake, but the harbour walls were crowded with surprised fishermen. Our last image was of Vassily, his magnificent beard blowing in the morning breeze, hanging in the rigging of a nearby boat and keening after us: 'Woood!'

We passed few ships. A great natural park lay to the south of us. The sky was blue. Chris paraded in his underpants to get a tan. There were 200 miles of the Gulf of Finland ahead of us, as it slowly narrowed towards the swampy marshes of St Petersburg.

When we docked in Gothenburg, at the end of our journey, we met a boat from Banff. Her captain had taken the same route the year before, in August.

'The weather was bizarre,' he told me. 'A tornado came racing down the coast and hit Vergi harbour when we were there. Luckily we were tied up on the right side of the harbour, but others weren't so lucky and whole boats were thrown up on to the wall on the other side. I remember all the electricity went out as far as the Russian border. We had a lot of half-washed clothes in a washing machine.'

Now, though, at the end of August, the weather showed no signs of breaking. There were no clouds in the sky at all. The wind, sometimes fresh, but mostly a fitful, warmish breeze, blew directly in our path. 'Turn around,' it seemed to say. 'Take this wind and blow home. Why are you motoring onwards when everybody else knows the summer is finished?' But it hadn't finished. This was perfect weather: eerie, gleaming, baking weather.

We slid into the tiny harbour on the edge of a wide, swampy bay, choked with reeds and backed by more impenetrable, blank pine forest, and tied up across a pontoon. There were a few visitors' buoys, 'but there won't be any others calling here,' I told the others confidently. I was wrong. During the rest of the evening other sailing boats arrived. And they were all heading back home to Finland.

Pant-boy and I went for a run along a newly tarmaced road, through sweet-smelling pines in the golden dusk, through the wooden village laid out in the woods on undivided plots. We passed a few dogs lying on steps. An old lady waved at us. This was just as neat as any Swedish settlement.

'This is very Russian, though,' said Chris. I didn't know. Chris had been to see an art film about life in a forgotten central Russian village the week before. 'It was just like this,' he panted.

We had stopped in Vergi because we needed to clear Customs. Customs was a military block amongst red-barked pine trees on a peninsula above the dock. The familiar shape of a lookout tower reared up above it. We knocked on a green door. A boy in uniform finally came and I held out our passports and documents. He looked at me with the weary boredom of a conscript. He'd been sent to this deserted corner of the forest to stamp documents for yachts and then been abandoned to fulfil his tour of duty on his own. This building was his house. He kept one hand on the inside door handle. Beyond him, we could see his unmade bed and a half-drunk cup of coffee. He had the bleary-eyed indifference of someone who had nothing to do and, then, when something needed to be done, was overcome by the effort involved to do it. He looked at my documents as if they were examination papers.

'You are in the harbour?' he asked.

I pointed to the boat.

He sighed. 'The harbour master is not here,' he said. 'I will come with him in the morning.'

'Ah, yes.' I prevaricated. 'We are wanting to leave very early.'

He shrugged. 'What time?'

'Just after dawn. We must leave at five-thirty.'

He nodded. 'I will come.' He gave no indication that this news caused him any further distress. It was merely confirmation of his lot.

There was a bar in the elbow of the harbour with a few tables outside. It was dark inside and clad like a ski lodge in yellow timber. There was a pool table in the corner. The master of the hostelry, short, thin and sallow, with hollow cheeks, stood at the bar. He was flanked by three women. One was clearly Mum. The other two were young women, one perhaps his wife, the other her sister. Both were rather beautiful. They stood very still in the gloom, like a picture by Otto Dix. There was a sense of desperation and tension in the room, emphasized by the fact that in front of them, on top of the bar, on a white piece of paper, lay three long smoked eels, smoothly arranged, side by side. I pointed at one of them, hesitantly.

'Ah. Can we buy one of those?'

He nodded slowly and named a price, which was high, but then we were buying the complete fish.

I paid for the eel and also the sauna which he offered to put on for us, so that we could use it at eight o'clock. Having concluded the transaction, he spoke to the silent women, who went off to switch on the sauna and wrap the eel in long lengths of cellophane.

How many eels had we eaten on this trip? I had lost count. We'd lugged greasy fish poles out of Kiel on the bus. In Flensburg we'd stunk out a taxi. We'd hunted them down in Svendborg and Copenhagen. There'd been smoked eels in the hut on the beach at Visby and another in the market in Kuressaare.

In Flensburg, making up lunch, one of our visitors had come across one coiled in a bag in our fridge. 'Euurch. Horrible,' she squealed. I had to disagree and rescued it before she threw it away, in a fit of Freudian revulsion, because smoked eel, as you may have guessed, or known already, is quite delicious. I used to buy them from Hamburger Products in Old Compton Street and once took two to Sussex as a Christmas present for some people who were, luckily, ecstatic to get them. They told me that, in Germany, they used to be hung, twisting, around the Christmas tree. But a lot of people are repulsed by the things, with their improbably tiny heads and sharp mouths full of teeth. A smoked eel is black and stiff. Its skin is edged with a metallic golden colour and peels off after a yank, like an old sock, but a rotten one, because the fatty, greasy gloop gets everywhere. You keep needing to stop and wash your hands, but then the pink and grey flesh can be eased off the bone: satisfying rounded sausages of flaking filet, somewhat like a smoked mackerel but more refined, stronger than smoked salmon and more tasty, best eaten with a little horseradish sauce.

Tom Fort's recent book on the eel filled me with sadness. The need to fill the Japanese Bento box has sent boats to hoover up river-mouths all over the world, and the stocks have dwindled. Worse, the tiny elvers, which might so easily grow into big, delicious eels, particularly since their predators have been fished almost to extinction, have all been sucked up too, for use as fertilizer.

I once met the king of eel suppliers in an eel and pie shop in Walton-on-the-Naze. At one time, his family had owned a chain of jellied eel shops all over London, with show-piece restaurants around Billingsgate. He showed me his trays in the back of the shop stacked one above the other in metal cabinets, each one filled with the long, black, slippery monsters. I immediately ordered a tub of his best and sat in front of my disbelieving children, picking my way through the jelly, the glutinous white flesh and the thousands of bones. It was quite revolting. Typically the English had worked out the least appealing way of serving this delicacy.

He had contacts in Harwich, he told me, where he would meet up with the eel catchers who jealously guarded their trapping sites, and brought him green sea eels from the muddy depths of the Walton Backwaters. This was the setting for *Secret Water*, Arthur Ransome's camping adventure which makes quite a feature of eel fishing.

At the bottom of my garden in Suffolk is a shallow creek and the harbour master, Peter Page, MBE, has an eel trap. He catches them out in the Stour and takes them to his brother-in-law's farm, where they're put in a cage in a brook until they turn grey. I have an old eel tripod, too: once a common way of catching them. The prongs of the tripod are three wide, serrated blades, with a minimal gap between them. The hunter poled along in his punt and plunged it into the neck of the eel, just behind the head, so that the back-bone was caught between the blades. It must have been a tricky business and only possible in the shallow, eel-infested waters of the past.

That evening I fried onions, added boiled potatoes and then, when the potatoes were golden, chucked in lumps of the eel and stirred it up together. This was guess work. The eel is always oily. I assumed it would fry well. As another experiment, I added mustard. Bloody marvellous. It will become my signature dish. I actually enjoyed the fact that the eel had a very strong paraffin taste, presumably from the way it had been smoked. The others weren't so sure. But to me, it all seemed serendipitous: the smell of the paraffin in the lamps and the taste of it in the eels, the connection with where we had sailed from, and the fact that Arthur Ransome had cruised these waters too. We were in a sea which was almost completely composed of fresh water this high up, because the Baltic is formed by the rivers of the far north, and only connects with the North Sea by geological accident, and these green waters have been thick with living things, none more adapted to its half-salt, half-fresh state than the metamorphosing eel. We were linked to these northern lands by water and the water was linked by eels. It was all most apt. I went to bed full up and less worried about the spooky weather.

So far, slipping around Europe, we had rarely communicated with Customs and Immigration. Leaving Gotland, we had spoken to them by telephone, because we were leaving the Schwengen territories. Now, the lonely coastguard arrived at six a.m. with the harbour master, clearly his mentor in all things, riffled through our papers, took crew lists and stamped our passports. As we pulled out into the Gulf for the final haul, a clamour of noisy squawking rose up from what must have been a thousand invisible ducks hidden somewhere in the swamp, and we sailed out into a livid blue early morning, I felt we needed help. We needed someone to ease our way through the potential maelstrom of bureaucracy that awaited us.

My thoughts turned immediately to the British ambassador.

'I know him,' I told Baines. 'It's one of those interesting by-products of sending your child to a London prep school. My son's best friend was the son of the ambassador, or rather he's the ex-ambassador now, but anyway, George was invited to spend a week during the Easter holidays at the Embassy in Moscow, because they live above the shop, you see, in this old sugar merchant's house just across the river from the Kremlin, and we tagged along too.'

'Well, give him a ring,' said Baines.

I was tempted. 'I don't know,' I said. 'I mean, he's retired now. And we are pretty small potatoes.'

Chris agreed with me. 'It's like ringing up Tony Blair to complain about your dustbins.'

'What about your mother's friend in the British Council in Riga?'

'I don't think so,' I said.

'These people in embassies, they'll only come out once you've been arrested.'

'So we might get to meet George's friend's father eventually,' said Charlie.

Four years previously, we had visited Russia under the best circumstances possible. The Embassy compound was still set up for the Cold War. At one point Andrew Wood, the ambassador, asked me if I'd like to see behind the scenes and took me through some unmarked doors on the ground floor, which had real James Bond sliding panels. He stuck his hand into a box, it read his fingerprints and they swept apart; with more of a clank than a hiss, it has to be admitted, but, none the less, a prelude to an exciting MI5-type warren of buzzing lights and dimly lit control rooms, or so I thought. In fact, beyond the security doors everything was strangely familiar: the photocopiers in the corridors, the peg-boards covered with club notices, the cream paint, the 1960s office furniture and the homely men with moustaches and cardigans. 'Gosh,' I said to Andrew. 'It's the BBC.'

I told Andrew's assistant I'd been given a tour and she was very impressed. 'It's top secret in there,' she said. 'I've never been allowed in myself.'

What this brief visit had given me was not only a genuine taste of the Russo-paranoia that still infected relationships, but a glimpse into the 'otherness' that Russia still represents. The history of Russian involvement with the Baltic is the history of Russia's urge to move west, to become European. St Petersburg was built by Peter the Great to modernize his country, to leave the exotic, Boyar Moscow behind, in the past. It was his Harlow New Town, his Canary Wharf. It was his Euro-town. But it only ever became an outpost. The real Russia stretched away across the steppes to the edge of Japan. It had never lost its eastern, Asiatic feel. Estonia, now, firmly faces west, a Scandinavian metropolis, not just because of its well-lit Hennes stores and expensive restaurants, but because its people were bland and dogged and Finnish. Victor and Vassily had already given us a taste of the more exotic, romantic Russian reality.

The people in the Embassy, four years before, had been keen to stress the ordinary, western nature of Russia today. 'We live in a residential diplomatic quarter out in the suburbs,' one told me. 'It used to take us fifteen minutes to drive in. Now everybody has a car. It takes an hour and a half.' Outside the big first-floor windows of the Embassy a continuous stream of traffic rumbled over the bridge into Red Square. We all laughed.

'We had a problem with some British businessman only last week who'd brought a gun with him. God!'

We all laughed again.

'People think this is some kind of wild west town.'

'Actually,' I interrupted, 'talking of cars, we would quite like to hire a car and go exploring around, perhaps into the countryside just outside Moscow. Do you know somewhere we could do that?'

The smiles froze. The laughter turned a little nervous. They exchanged glances. 'We wouldn't be able to recommend that you did that for the present,' said somebody. 'It's not a good idea. Not really, no.' And we left it at that. Later we drove home from a restaurant with the ambassador in a jovial mood. He pointed through the window. 'That's the hotel where that chap was found,' he said.

'What chap?' I asked.

'Some businessman who'd gone drinking in a bar and disappeared for four days. He turned up completely naked in the street in front of that hotel unable to remember a thing about anything.' He chuckled.

No, no, Russia was a different kettle of eels altogether.

36. Vlad the Enabler

The one useful thing I had gleaned from the incoherent Finns was that we had to enter Russia along the main shipping lane. Any other route, they said, would attract the attentions of the sort of authorities we didn't want to attract. So we did as we were told, and slid along as close to the purple-dotted line on our electronic chart as we dared.

We entered Russian waters and a flat, metallic calm descended. It was as if the weather had conspired to make our approach to the final city, the ultimate destination, this fabled northern Byzantium, as still and unnatural and creepy as a funeral procession.

I knew I had once had a plan for getting in there and now I remembered what it was. I went below and came back up into the cockpit brandishing a cardboard hardback book. 'Never mind the ambassador,' I crowed, 'let's contact the Cruising Association Representative.'

The little club I had visited in a downpour, in the last days before we left, produced a handbook for its members. In it, every country and port in the world was listed and, alongside that listing, the name of an official to provide local advice. I picked up my mobile phone with weak fingers.

'Hello, this is Vladimir.'

It was a cultured, polite voice on the other end. When I apologized for the imminence of our arrival, Vladimir expressed no surprise at all. In fact, he was gratified to hear we were coming. He would be delighted to arrange everything for us. He would meet us at the Sea Terminal and telephone to the relevant authorities to ensure that they were expecting us and that we had the right appointments. 'Because they can hold you up a bit if you take them by surprise, you understand.' I did understand. Did we have the right visas? I assured him we did.

'When you get to the island of Kronshtadt, go to the immigration in Fort Constantine and they will stamp you in at once. Then I am afraid you have to go to the Sea Terminal, because the St Petersburg Chief of Police wants to bring the process under his control as well. That's in the city proper. And there you will be stamped in again. And I will meet you there and I shall take you to the marina, where you can stay.'

'Gosh.'

'Looking forward to meeting with you, Griff.'

'And you.'

I ended the call with a moist light shining in my eyes. A sort of miracle had come to pass. I was so overcome by the warm assurance of Vladimir and astounded by the simple efficiency of the Cruising Association's worldwide network, so reassured by this beacon of authority in the waste of rumour and misinformation, that I had completely failed to take note of a single thing he had told me.

I had to ring him again and he good-naturedly took me through it all again.

Vladimir proved to be our blob of Russian anti-matter. Where Russia was inefficient, he was organized. Where it was bombastic, he was modest. Where it was demanding, he was helpful and attentive. He was Ukrainian. Which meant a lot, apparently. He was just marvellous.

There was no wind at all. The sun beat down. The occasional huge boat ground past. The sky was a hot glare, and the water like a badly made mirror. Through the haze ahead I could see a low, grey shape with a high superstructure lying in the water just to the south of our route.

'That's some sort of military boat, isn't it?' I said.

The radio crackled.

'Ruzian coaz-yard. Ruzian coaz-yard. Culling selling sheyup. Selling sheyup. Com yin plez.'

Bob reached for the set.

'Hello, Russian coastguard. This is British yacht *Undina*. Over.'

The radio crackled again. 'Breeteesh Yagt. Vazshoo desy frart deschkyykk. Over.'

'What did he say?'

'I've no idea.'

We were getting closer to the boat and could see its prominent radio aerials and gun. It was a big thing. 'Ask him to repeat it.'

Bob frowned, took a drag, and held the microphone up to his mouth again.

'British yacht *Undina* calling Russian coastguard. Could you repeat the message, please? Over.'

'Breeteesh yagt, Breeteesh yagt. Vazshoodesyfrartdeschkyykk eschbek schbeckyyrrrk. Over.'

It was not immediately apparent whether he was talking English, or Russian, or some hybrid, half way between the two. The 'Over' bit had sounded a little petulant, though.

Bob and I looked at each other. He swallowed and asked for further clarification.

The message came again, more slowly and, this time, with more than an edge of impatience. We still had not the dimmest notion of what was being asked of us, and the ship itself was now only 200 yards off our starboard quarter. It was almost black and utterly menacing, wallowing slightly in the flat swell. No one was visible on deck. This was worse than when I met Princess Margaret and I had to ask her three times to repeat the same inane question. Bob threw his radio manner overboard.

'No, no, we're very sorry. We are English. We can't understand what you are asking of us, I am afraid. I wonder if you could repeat the message very, very slowly indeed, please. Message. Repeat. Very slow. Sorry. Please. Sorry. Slow. Over. Sorry.'

There was a pause.

'Breeteesh Yagt. Breeteesh Yagt. Nim. Nim of yagt.'

'Ah. Russian coastguard. Nim of yagt is *Undina*.'

'Spill.'

We spelt the name. Over the next ten minutes we gave them details of our 'lenk', where we had come from and how long we were going to stay. Each bit of information took place amidst a welter of onboard discussion and guesswork.

'"Porch? Porch?" What does he mean?'

'Port! He wants to know where we've come from. "Yembirech-etshun"? Embarkation!'

By the time we had finished, the vessel was a diminishing insect squatting on the horizon behind us.

Bob put the mouthpiece back on its clip. He was sweating. 'Imagine what it must be like when he gets chatting to the captain of a Greek tanker,' he said.

The 120-mile journey took us eighteen hours. For a short while in the evening, the wind blew and we put up the sails, but it died in the late dusk and we motored on. The night, when it came, hid a thin line of mainland shore, creeping up far to the south. It was 22 August. A magnificent, bulbous, pink harvest moon clambered up ahead of us, even before the sun had finally set in the retreating west. For a while, like Superman on a dying planet, we hung between two red globes in the sky, ghosting along on a licorice sea.

Shore lights twinkled and lighthouses began feverishly messaging from entrances to harbours we would never visit. Perversely, I began to wish we could. There were so many books, films and opinions about St Petersburg it seemed perfectly possible to go there without corporeally visiting it. It was already familiar. But nobody seemed to explore the little settlements in the further reaches of this marshy delta, perhaps for the very sensible reason that you weren't allowed to.

'They'd only be a disappointment anyway,' I said to Baines. We were sharing the watch. Despite the sense of arrival, the others had gone to sleep. 'Everywhere looks glamorous at night, doesn't it? Look over there.' I pointed ahead and to the north at a row of glittering lights. 'It looks like the Riviera, but what is it? Nothing more than a few ugly villas on a muddy shore.'

'What shore?' asked Baines. We examined our chart. The paper Admiralty one had too big a scale. The electronic one showed no major town and the land was still 12 miles away to the north. They should be over the horizon. And yet we were getting closer and closer to these blazing lights. Our course was accurate. We double-checked our bearings, identified nearby markings and peered at the town through binoculars.

It was a city of ships. Dozens of freighters, tankers and ferries, big vessels, were anchored in ranks just to the north of our route. Each of them blazed with light. Portholes, bridges, companionways: every conceivable switch had been thrown.

'Are they having a party?' Baines said. We half expected to hear brass bands playing. But it was utterly quiet. The vessels were only lit to advertise themselves and avoid somebody bumping into them in the night.

Through the binoculars, I could see planes of light moving across each other like sliding screens, as a huge freighter inched through the middle of the fleet and her passing shadow blocked one set of lights and then emerged behind another. Although the moon was hidden by clouds, the night was clear. The cellophane water was laced with jiggling reflections from a fairground armada. We felt like a hostile submarine, or James Bond, slipping past, just out of range, in the blackness.

And just immediately beyond, somewhere in the darkness, was our entrance route. We picked up the first port and starboard buoys with difficulty. They were tiny pin-pricks of red and green, somewhere in the middle of this messy glare.

The wind was coming up again. The sea was getting choppy. Time was against us. We pressed on, turning slightly south towards the yellow glow of a city in the distance.

Ahead was total confusion.

St Petersburg sits in a shallow lagoon, like Venice. It was built by sheer force of character. Peter the Great wanted it there and the foundations of his showpiece city had to be laid in the mud, on a raft of pain and sacrifice. No part of the surrounding land was more than 30 feet above the sea. Most of it was swamp and marsh. It was, and still is, subject to flooding. So, recently, a great plan has been instituted to wall the city from the sea. The twin arms of the barrages meet at the Kronshtadt gate. And now, at midnight, the lights on the construction barges, the cranes and what looked like blocks of flats in Kronshtadt itself competed with these eighteen or so tiny flickering navigation lights ahead of us: one pair every half mile, some of which had failed anyway.

We raced on, ticking off the buoys as they surged towards us, trying to estimate the distances, struggling to work out whether the white light by the green light somewhere ahead was close or miles away. We were surprised, as a buoy we knew was coming suddenly loomed out of the black and its guiding light, which we assumed was still some distance beyond, proved itself to be a flashing green giant, high on a swinging pole, rocking past us in the swirl.

As if to emphasize the confused blackness of it all, Baines pointed ahead. 'You've seen that, have you?'

I hadn't, but I did now. Another sailing boat, about a hundred yards ahead, was coming the other way, passing out into the night, with all sails set. Its identifying lights were feeble, like candles, miserable dots of faint yellow and red, totally invisible until we were almost on her. We passed close enough to see her white sails, pale wings reflecting the glare from the million-watt flotilla behind us, shimmer faintly in the gloom. She was bigger than us.

It was two o'clock in the morning when we breached the Kronshtadt gate, turned to our left and, creeping through unlit buoys, gingerly tied up to an outsize wharf. Charlie and I crawled up the rusty chains and the rotting tractor tyres and scrambled on to the broken concrete quayside above.

In the yellow sodium light of the dead night, we could see the immigration office ahead. It was a white wooden house on a barge up along the waterfront a bit. The door swung easily open. Thousands of bugs were spattered on the white light and the narrow ceiling above. There was a pitted-chrome, swinging half-hoop with a no entry sign on it and beyond that an enclosed stair with a sticky carpet climbing up to the left. We stood for a few moments and half-heartedly called out. The flies buzzed and hummed. We pushed through the turnstile and, quietly, half hopeful we would not disturb anyone at all, called out again.

'There's nobody here,' I whispered to Charlie. He pointed beyond me. A woman was standing at the top of the stairs in a calico dressing gown. 'Come,' she said quietly, and motioned us up the stairs.

She led us into an office on the first floor. I noticed that she had a military shirt under her gown. She was plump and homely with bobbed hair, and seemed more anxious than officious. She took our passports and opened them distractedly.

I apologized for the time of our arrival. She shook her head. 'It's OK.'

In halting English, she explained that we would have to be cleared in St Petersburg too, but she would deal with the papers in the morning, because the office was closed during the night. I explained that we wanted to leave very early, because we had arranged to meet the Customs there at ten o'clock, when they first opened.

She nodded.

'So we must leave at six o'clock in the morning,' I whispered, pointing at the clock. It was essential to my plans. I dreaded missing the earliest opening hour and I dreaded being held up for the rest of the following day, when I knew we could only stay for three days at the most. But I didn't tell her that.

She looked bemused.

'Wouldn't it be better to do this now?' I pointed to the passports. But she was anxious, as the Estonian officials had been, to connect the stamping of our papers with the actual departure of the boat. She indicated that she would deal with it then.

'At six.'

She looked pained. 'Yes.'

We went back to the boat.

'We'll get four hours' sleep, then,' I said to the others back at the boat. 'We're doing all right. So far we seem to have managed to browbeat the officials rather than the other way around, ha, ha.'

'Who's that, then?' said Baines.

'What?'

'There's a bloke on the quay.'

We froze and peered up through the porthole. A big man in fatigues and a uniform coat was standing high above us on the wharf, staring down. '*Yat!*' he said finally in tones of utter contempt. Then he turned on his heel and walked back to the hut on the barge.

Bob lit a cigarette. 'What was all that about, then?' he asked, exhaling.

'He was probably just finding out why his girlfriend wants him to get up at six in the morning,' Charlie said.

We left at six-thirty. The beefy man never bothered to get out of bed and sent his girlfriend out to make phone calls ahead and stamp all the documents for us. We crept out in the grey morning light, past a seagoing, ice-breaking tug and into the dredged canal to St Petersburg, 12 miles ahead. Passing alongside a series of walled harbours in the dawn mist, we joined a traffic flow of lighters and tugs chugging down the narrow buoyed passage across a great bay in the direction of the city, which gradually emerged out of the smog: a monolithic wall of modern housing blocks.

'I wasn't expecting this,' Chris said. The pictures in the guide books showed elegant quays and white palaces, but this looked like Beirut.

When the Marquis de Custine arrived on the steamer *Nicholas I* in July 1839 he had been unwilling to give it the benefit of his doubt. 'The dreariness of the earth, of the sky and the cold tinge of the waters chill the heart of a traveller,' he noted in his journal. 'The best of the days have a bluish tint.' He only escaped from Kronshtadt after being besieged by Customs officials for most of a day and concluded that the Russians had a fatal attraction to bureaucracy. Perhaps, with Glasnost, this was finally diminishing. Here we were, on our way.

We passed two massive, rusting tankers moored to one side of the channel and then, after three hours, the ragged arms of a sea wall: fallen into ruin, broken to the sea in places, covered with vegetation in others. The city closed in. This was what the Thames must have looked like before Rotterdam stole her trade and containerization changed the dockside systems of the West.

The waterway, which narrowed and squirrelled into the city, where it became the Neva River, was like a Paris sidestreet for ships. They were parked up two or three deep in places. Massive ice-breakers, with slab-sided bridge castles, were shoved carelessly into parking spaces too small to take them. Floating docks were banged up against the pavement with entire boats crammed into them. Fountains of welding sparks gushed out of their sides. And we were surrounded by sheet metal, wrapped into elegant forms for the older ships, blocked into box shapes for the newer and teased into absurd mammoth tubby toys for the modern cruise liners, teetering on the water like inflatable steel balloons. Metal gantries and metal-girdered cranes with corrugated metal huts, metal bollards, interlocking metal sides to the wharves, metal cables and metal hawsers. We sat and we gaped. We reached for our cameras but, when we looked back at the snaps, they were just boats. The camera captured none of the dominating, overwhelming presence of this scrapyard of a place.

At first, it seemed paradoxical that all this disordered, exuberant vitality should be the residue of Soviet industrial state control. Shouldn't the organized uniformity of Felixstowe docks, which I passed every weekend, with its faceless quays and matching towers and the steady coming and going of identical ships, be the epitome of the communist ideal? This was crazy metal individualism on the loose. But that was to fail to understand the romanticism at the root of Marxism, which took the industrial work ethic and preserved it in a mid-nineteenth-century jellified trifle, studded with hammers and welders and cranes. Brecht loved the 'Dockyard and the Stock-yard' and its proletarian tang. Physical labour was at the heart of the Soviet ideal. And here it was, still labouring, still raising loads by eighteenth-century cranes, still banging and welding and ham-mering, in a dockyard that was scarcely any different from one Conrad might have recognized. For the first time since we had set out on this trip we were really entering another country. This was where they did things differently.

The Sea Terminal was directly ahead of us. We had to thread our way through a pack of fishermen, who lay like jellyfish all over the water, wrapped in unsuitable hairy coats, wearing pointy hats or furry caps and floating on tiny rubber rafts, or minute plastic boats. Directing worried glances in our direction, they flapped out of our way.

The Sea Terminal, where all visiting boats had to tie up, was built for bigger ones than ours. The dockside was at least 20 feet high and covered in large, round rubber door-stops. Vladimir was standing at the top of it, neatly dressed, modest and polite. 'Welcome,' he called, leaning over the side in a bow-like gesture. 'Do you have your documents? We should go in because we are a little late.' I hauled myself up over the doorstops. He gave me his hand.

'Sorry, yes. It took us longer to get here than we imagined.'

He led me away to the port authority building. Inside, it was vast and brown. We crossed a marble plain. There were glass partitions some miles to the north and on the horizon I could just make out the deserted turnstiles of an empty immigration system.

'The problem is that a big cruise ship has come in,' he explained. 'Everybody has had to go and deal with it. There is only one team here to deal with big ships and little ships like you.'

'Are there many ships like us?'

'This year, no, not really. I have only had one other visitor from Britain and a couple of Swedish boats. Excuse me.'

We had come to a green telephone hanging by a door. The wall and the door were covered in a brown plastic wood-finish veneer. Vladimir dialled and waited. He spoke to someone and put the receiver back.

'No. There is no one who can deal with us at the moment.'

For a moment, Vladimir assumed an expression of failure. I reassured him. We got money from an electric machine which sat, oddly isolated, in the middle of an otherwise vacant parking-lot vestibule and then went to a café in the corner.

The café, like all the human settlements in this mausoleum, was a little protest against the monumentalism of the Sea Terminal. The chairs didn't match. The tables were wonky. There were home-made jars of honey and tins of caviare on the counter. An icon hung on the wall and the miserable old lady who ran the place had surrounded herself with potted plants and toys. No doubt, in a few years' time, her bourgeois individualism will be subsumed in the capitalist regimentation of McDonald's or Costa's.

'Drink?' asked Vladimir.

'Coffee,' I said. I drank four cups and then another two, but, still, when I sat and leaned my back against the concrete, I nearly fell asleep. I had been driven to reach our ultimate destination: start early, press on into the night, sleep for less than four hours. It was barely eleven o'clock and I had been up for six hours.

Eventually we climbed a massive flight of stairs, entered a tiny office and, after some discussion, a man in a pullover with a beard examined and stamped our passports, in his own little nest, with its decayed sofas and coffee table and a television playing in the corner.

There was one more visit to be made: to Immigration. We set off through the labyrinth again to visit a tall man in a silly pale yellow uniform blouson. His office had the most potted plants of all. There was a football match on the television and we all watched it, while distractedly answering questions about the length of stay and the nature of the visit. Neatly arranged on the wall were five plaques from cruise companies (commemorating special visits, first visits and 100th visits). We were small fry indeed. Vladimir then escorted us back to the boat.

I should have fallen on my knees and blessed him. God knows how long we would have wandered the marble halls searching for the secret hidden doors and the distant outcrops of humanity if he hadn't been with us. But Vladimir only apologized for how long it had taken and I apologized in my turn for our late arrival as we unhooked *Undina* from the massive doorstops and, following his instructions, set out to sea again, taking him with us.

The lagoon of St Petersburg is a few feet deep at the most, so channels have been dredged, but not marked particularly carefully. Now we headed right back out into the glistening brown waters, simply in order to go around the corner. It was a sunny morning. There were pleasure boats drifting around. We passed close under the great walls of blocks of flats.

'They have become expensive,' said Vladimir. 'It is fashionable for the new rich to live there.'

After half an hour, we came to a mysterious underwater junction and turned back towards the land, then headed to the north towards Krestovsky Island, where the floodlights of the Kirov Stadium poked up above the trees. At the very seaward tip of the Petrograd Side, the island where St Petersburg was founded, we came to the River Yacht Club.

The marina had been purpose-built, in a bid to host the 1980 Olympic sailing events, but Estonia had won the commission. The River Yacht Club had taken possession instead.

'It is all owned by a trade union,' Vladimir explained as we tied up. 'It was the only way that anybody could sail in the old days, but now they have very little money.' He pointed at the main building. 'They have not been able to repair it since the fire.'

It looked as if we had arrived at some post-apocalyptic remnant in the middle of a small war. The clubhouse was a fine piece of Soviet bus-station brutalism, set in an overgrown park. Blackened timbers poked through the roof and there were black smoke traces around the upper windows, as if a rocket attack had only just been halted. Indeed, smoke from various fires drifted across the scene.

The ground was littered with heaps. There were heaps of metallic rubbish in one bit and heaps of garden rubbish in another. Some tyres had been gathered into a heap in one corner. There was a heap of plastic in the middle of what might have once been a lawn but now had stunted bushes growing out of it. Several old men moved around extremely slowly, making new heaps. They were the heap men.

Some heaps looked as ancient as the city of St Petersburg. They had attracted their own scrubby growth of mini birch trees. Others smoked ominously. The gardens, if they had ever been such, were broken with scrub. The tarmac paths had collapsed into holes in places and risen up into unaccountable mounds in others. There were more abandoned boats under half-hearted tarpaulins propped up on the land and surrounded by weeds than there were in the water. The massive concrete steps up to the building had collapsed. The marina walls had, too, and improvised jetties had been erected to cross the more serious dilapidations. Directly in front of where we moored someone had driven a large metal spike into the tarmac of the jetty for no apparent purpose, other than to trip us up every time we walked to and from the boat.

'You can shower in there,' Vladimir explained, pointing to the ruin.

'We'll form an assault party later,' said Baines.

But it was good to arrive first in a bit of the real St Petersburg. In a few minutes we would set off for the tourist city, where the big hotels and the museums and prospects offered a vision of the cosseted, historic St Petersburg experience, but here at the edge of the northern suburbs, where Lenin had hidden, here, on this magnificent piece of ruined real estate, was a strange enclave of aspirational hobbyists. A gleaming Range Rover sat amidst the shit and some New Russians were unloading their picnic hampers.

We picked our way through the bomb-site and its rubbish towards the gate. The compound had a small wood in one corner, dotted with more mysterious heaps. Access to the crumbling facilities was jealously guarded. When we got to the gate we could see that access was also literally guarded. Boy sentries in camouflage fatigues touting sub-machine-guns manned a barrier.

'The boat will be quite safe here,' Vladimir explained. But as we left the Trade Union Country Club and its badly groomed premises and went out into the city, we all felt slightly relieved.

37. Catherine the Great

What was left of the day in St Petersburg passed in a bleary, sleep-deprived haze: the bus to the Admiralty, the walk down Nevsky prospect, the Hermitage, the crowds of sailors in their dinner-plate caps and the women in their old-fashioned day frocks. We tottered past them, swaying slightly in a dream. Past the zig-zag sweaters and the cardi combos, the furbelows and the bulky leather jackets, the leather flat-caps, the laces with little fur tippets and the seventies patch-pocket, belted safari jackets, all striding around unabashed.

Four years previously I had stood in Red Square on an early March evening and looked on, goggle-eyed, as the rush hour began. Huge crowds washed across the great open spaces of Moscow. Tidal waves of people scurried home. I could see why Russian thinkers had been obsessed by 'the masses'. If the masses had only kept to the back streets, or discreetly sluiced across bridges like London's Waterloo, perhaps the intelligentsia of Russia would never have considered harnessing their power at all.

This soup of humanity absorbed five Englishmen easily enough.

After months of visiting Scandinavian cities which promised the imminence of utter global uniformity, we had finally set down in Oz: part Emerald City and part stronghold of the Wicked Witch of the West. The cracked pavements, the rubbish, the collapsed transport system and the beggars reminded us of home, but the mix of palatial extravagance and market-trader glamour was, at last, somewhere excellently different.

But the magnificent architecture of the Italians and French, who had flocked to the city to make their fortunes and left the fancy-cake palaces, the colonnades and the monuments, blurred into an impression of pale pink and apricot under fuzzy skies. We had arrived and just wanted to sleep. The only solution was to trudge on. We were stalled by the utter impossibility of seeing everything in three days. So we resolved to see nothing.

There is too much history in the short history of St Petersburg. It is a city that has been ruled for 200 years by megalomaniac hobbyists with bottomless purses. Catherine the Great was the Elton John of her day. She shopped for her country. She collected buildings like other people collect Beanie Bears. 'The more you build the more you want to build,' she is reported to have said. 'It's a sickness somewhat akin to being addicted to alcohol. Or perhaps it's just a habit.'

She might have said 'just one of my habits'. She collected everything else as well: pictures, statues, ghastly bright green marble urns and soldiers. She actually collected collections as a way of speeding the process up. And so did subsequent tsars and empresses, obliged to increase the cornucopia of imported important objects with more important objects of their own. Along came the Bolsheviks. They stole a few collections, to keep up, and added works of art from their conquests in Eastern Europe, plus a completely new set of must-sees, like 'The Communication Workers Palace of Culture'.

Swaying in the middle of all this, suffering from sea-lag, cultural nausea swept over me. Could I skip the Marble Palace? What would people say if I had to admit I had passed by the Blok Museum, never got to the Gramophone Museum, missed out on the Engineer's Castle? Sod it, I would have to come back and look at it properly some other time.

We did the only safe thing to do in this metropolis of unbridled acquisition. We went shopping.

In Gostiniy dvor, an apartment store that dates from the eighteenth century, we watched New Russians kit themselves out with black leather trench coats while their admiring girlfriends, in shiny plastic boots and lacy stockings, looked on. Each floor was an extended passageway that wound along different levels and past uncoordinated staircases, like Gamages, or those dead department stores in London suburbs where yellow cellophane in the windows indicates nobody ever changes the window displays.

Gostiniy dvor was lined with independently run stalls, selling furs or lighting fittings or sports goods. One natty place sold second-hand machine-guns, another, miniature lead models of the Beatles.

Bob was bent on looting Russia. 'It's too late,' I told him, 'all the Soviet militaria crap has already gone to the Portobello Road. They actually make Lenin buttons in the factories now, simply to sell to the tourists. And don't get a gun, please, Bob.' But Bob was already gazing longingly at the interlocking Brezhnev dolls and fingering the pilots' uniforms at the street tourist markets.

We arranged with Vladimir to take a ride into the southern suburbs to a flea market and, early the next morning, wandered in a dusty cinder field, down the carefully demarcated paths between the car-boot rubbish laid out in the dirt. Massive pylons crossed a washed-out landscape of broken factories and vast housing boxes. Lines of shabbily dressed people shuffled up a littered bank, past the remains of fences and abandoned buildings into the market, looking for what? Half the stalls, manned, like car boot sales all over the world, by unshaven men in broken glasses wearing three layers of coats and peculiar hats, sold rubbish, while the other half sold utter rubbish. There was the last drawer in the flat, emptied out and laid on a blanket, in the hope that someone needed half a broken pair of spectacles, a cracked watch without a strap or a single shoe. (The single one of a pair seemed to be a recurring marketing opportunity.)

Perhaps all these punters who stared at the goods so intently were, indeed, looking for the other stirrup or the missing bit of their handle. Several stalls offered electrical parts: transistors, knobs and wiring, clearly from the same radio, snipped and cleaned and laid out side by side on a square of dirty cloth. Could the component parts of a broken radio possibly have more value than the whole? There was no hope of riffling through a cardboard box of junk in search of some lost treasure. The box itself would have been a prime exhibit; the staples removed, straightened out and sold separately.

The place was insanely crowded. It was more crowded than the

Winter Palace that we visited in the afternoon. The passers-by looked at the single copies of faded magazines with missing backs, or the decapitated and limbless plastic dolls, more fervently than the spectators in the museum looked at the priceless ormolu-encrusted commodes. But they didn't want the old radio valves or the glassless motorcycle goggles. Who possibly could? This was a market of despair, a market of hopeless inertia.

If there was Soviet memorabilia, it was broken, feeble stuff. Sometimes the face of Lenin or Stalin stared out from the heap, but with a chipped cheek or a smashed nose. Baines bought a hideous china owl clock. But the indefatigable Bob had to admit defeat.

'You see,' Vladimir told me, 'candidly, there are some things that we all believe were better under the old Soviet system and some things that have got worse. Hospitals, education and the public services are all much worse.'

'And better?'

'Personal freedom. People can make their own way. There is no sense of fear. And it is possible to travel.'

'To leave Russia.'

'Yes.'

Baines's friend who worked in the Hermitage had put us in touch with Catherine, so, at the 'stage door' of the Hermitage, we waited at the bottom of a set of steps, in a vestibule panelled in oak, while curators and scholars scurried past clutching briefcases to their chests.

Catherine, our free guide, took us on a brief tour of a collection that it has been estimated would take seven years to look at in any detail. She had originally come to Russia to work as a nanny in the Embassy. One day she was told that the personnel department thought she was a spy. The rumour became so insistent that she felt obliged to confront a senior official. He smiled at her. 'Yes, Catherine, we know all about you.'

She was shocked. 'What on earth makes you think I'm a spy?'

'You learned Russian.'

'Yes, I learned it for my job.'

'Yes, but you learned it remarkably quickly, didn't you?' And he smiled knowingly again.

She tried to assure him that it was eagerness, not indoctrination, but never felt they were convinced.

'They were very charming,' she said, 'but I felt I was being watched all the time.' Since the other side was also convinced she was a spy, she ended up with far more status than she might otherwise have deserved: a double non-agent nanny.

Linguistically equipped, she had looked for another job and that's how she came to be appointed to the museum, helping to organize the exhibitions in Somerset House, which, in a series of cramped rooms in London, attempt to give some of the flavour of the Winter Palace.

'You were at the opening of it, weren't you,' she said.

'Yes.'

'We saw your name and wondered if you were some secret expert on Russian art.'

'No, no. It's just the charity circuit. One of Somerset House's benefactors also helped out with the Hackney Empire.' We felt conspiratorial, solving our little mystery, far from home.

Her next assignment was to ship artistic coals to Newcastle. Some English art was going home: Wright of Derby, Joshua Reynolds and other painters admired by the Enlightenment Russians. But the five rooms in Somerset House could never really capture the spirit of the magpie hoard on the banks of the Neva. It was the overwhelming volume of posh junk that impressed. We stumbled along behind Catherine as she strode across the acres of parquet, stopping to talk about the pieces, about the tsars, about the painters, and leading us on and upwards past thousands of paintings, clocks, urns, commodes and jewels to the upper floors, where six rooms unfold into the stark simplicity of the Matisses and Vlamincks and Van Dongens, all collected on the eve of Revolution by wealthy Russian businessmen.

Like the Gaugins in the Pushkin Museum, they were shocking. The Matisses were so fresh and alive, so new, that they seemed to say, 'Look, here is a clean, clear, bright future for the twentieth century.' They opened shutters into light after the heavy brocades and gold-encrusted fustiness of the 'treasures' we had walked past. Free of the pomp and servile craftsmanship that had created the rest of the expensive brocante, they seemed democratic and universal and leap-frogged the entire revolution, denting the accepted chronology of the last hundred years. How could they have come from the same world as Lenin?

Vladimir had arranged for us to meet up with his friend Mischa, appropriately, given Bob's bear collection, a dealer in militaria. They were waiting on the embankment. Mischa was in his fifties, thin and long-haired. He spoke in a soft, distracted way, taught classical guitar and lived in the 'Golden Quarter'.

A stone staircase took us up to his tenement, past heavy, leather-covered doors and crumbling grey plasterwork. An enormous stove by the entrance fed cumbersome radiators on each floor.

Mischa was restoring his flat. 'It is very difficult, very difficult, the pieces must be found with great care. I go looking for the right wood for a frame or floorboard or a fireplace.' A distracted Dostoyevsky intellectual, he was dressed in a panama hat, corduroy trousers, grey suede lattice shoes, a stripy banker's shirt and a cravat, like a member of the Bonzo Dog Dooh Dah band, but he seemed very burdened.

'Many of these apartments are owned now by New Russians and they just want everything new, with mirrors and black leather walls.' He shook his head as he unlocked the door. His apartment had high ceilings and the wallpaper was stripped in most places. A fridge had been propped up against one wall on an improvised pallet. The floor was made of rough boards and some parts of the wall had been cleared of old plaster and the interleaved lengths of ancient wattle showed through. Wiring hung out of the cracked gaps. Every surface was piled with boxes. There were tottering heaps of trunks and neatly arranged piles of navy clothing. Mischa began casually opening boxes of insignia, cap ribbons and gun sights and passing them to Bob.

This was the second flat he had renovated. Here was a familiar

London figure: the speculative gentrifier. 'Originally all the Russian people were given houses according to their status and then with Perestroika they were allowed to buy and sell them, but this area is very popular with foreigners and when I am done then maybe I will sell the house and move on to somewhere else.'

Bob emerged from the room next door wearing a submarine officer's reefer jacket and a woolly hat.

'This is real leather,' said Mischa. 'An ordinary sailor would have one of these. You see, plastic.'

He presented a glossy catalogue which sold nothing but Russian army surplus. It was printed in America and was backed by a website. I was taken with the battleship binoculars, mounted on stands and the size of small artillery pieces. Never used, they could be supplied in their original boxes for £3,000 each. 'Now you can own a piece of Russian military precision engineering that you will treasure for ever.'

Mischa told us he could get anything in the catalogue at a very reasonable price. In fact, he was a middle man for the American producers. He showed me a beautifully made set of heavy Perspex parallel rulers and a slide rule, both presented in lacquered boxes and rather lovely. But I sensed that we were scavengers at the tail end of a bargain hunt. Other looters had been here before us and the real kitsch had already been hoovered up and transported away.

Bob, undeterred, had everything in the flat opened up and laid before him. His negotiations were to last two days and he eventually returned to the boat with his hat and his coat, a high-altitude oxygen helmet and a rolled-up painting of a parrot, chopped from its stretchers.

'You know what,' he told me later in London. 'I sent the picture of the parrot to be reframed and they told me that it had been painted quite recently.' He was more puzzled than angry. Even Bob recognized that it wasn't a very good nineteenth-century painting. 'So why bother forging it?' he asked, bewildered.

38. The Black of the Monster Lagoon

The rush hour had started and we hailed a taxi on the embankment. The Peter and Paul Fortress was directly across the nearest bridge.

'You take?' Bob said, adopting a slight Russian accent.

'What's that, Bob? You think he's going to understand you more easily if you talk to him in bad English? He doesn't speak English.'

Waving a self-important hand, Bob gestured at the meter. 'How much?' The taxi driver shrugged. The rest of us were sitting in the humid interior, but Bob was not keen to hire the man until he had a price. There was the peep of a whistle and, a few seconds later, a policeman jogged up and leaned in the other window. He wrote out a ticket for parking in a red zone, while Bob continued to bargain with the driver from his side of the car.

Alexei, the taxi driver, might have turned and pointed at Bob. He could have remonstrated with the cop. But this wasn't New York. He took the ticket and drove off silently, in an advanced state of despair, holding up his ticket for me to see, groaning under his breath and muttering.

'Look what you've done now, Bob,' said Baines. 'The man is going to kill himself.'

'It was his choice to pick us up. I was just saving us money.'

When we stopped, I paid the fare and the parking ticket too. A heart-warming act of spontaneous generosity which failed to cheer up Alexei. He slunk further into depression and then off into the traffic.

In the eighteenth century foreign visitors were struck by Russian stoicism. St Petersburg was a city of appalling disease and grinding poverty. Sixty out of every 1,000 people were expected to die every year, because they lived on top of a festering cesspit. Crime was inevitable and punishments were draconian. Things got considerably worse in the nineteenth century. Dostoyevsky himself was thrown into the dungeons on the island we were now visiting (commanded by one of Nabokov's great-uncles, as it happens). He was kept in solitary confinement in a cell that regularly flooded with the sewage-laden waters of the Neva.

Executions were so commonplace that the people on one side of the town could hardly be bothered with the beheadings taking place on the other. The visitor from London, used to high levels of public interest in this sort of thing, put it down to the Russian ability to absorb suffering. And, by any account, St Petersburg has been a city of suffering. But it seemed to me that many of the Russians we met, like the taxi driver, seemed to be less stoic than self-dramatizing.

The babushka, the grim old lady, was still everywhere; a Russian solution to age-concern. It seemed inconceivable that any of the pretty girls of St Petersburg could turn into those unsmiling gargoyles in the kiosks, but, in fact, the youngsters took their apprenticeship in surliness hugely seriously. It was learned behaviour, just as much as the 'have a nice day' in McDonald's is learned behaviour. Mischa the militaria-salesman had worked hard at his act too. He was disdainful of his own people. Victor, in Tallinn, had been piratical and roguish, Vassily moody and wan. It occurred to me that the only other people with a similar need to dress up and swagger were the Germans and the British. The Danes, the Swedes, the Lats, the Estonians and the Finns had their drunkennesses and their flamboyances, but they were practical, modest people: real stoics, in fact. It was the ex-imperial nationals who seemed to need to play-act.

Like late guests for a city wedding, we scouted the exterior of the Peter and Paul Cathedral, looking for a door. An audience of about fifty tourists had settled in the nave, surrounded by the tombs of the Romanovs, to listen to the St Petersburg Male Voice Choir.

Chris had been a choral scholar at school. He wanted to listen. Charlie came inside too. Bob and Baines sat on the step to have a fag, but as the dinner-jacketed choir began to sing, they crept in, like extras in a Hollywood musical comedy, faces rapt, stumbling over the stools, transfixed by the air-wobbling transcendency of the singers.

This cathedral was famous for not being Orthodox but Protestant, but the music was ritualistic and magical. Stravinsky, though not religious, always returned to the Mother Church to experience the wavering melancholy of male voice choirs like these. These singers, each of them called forward in turn to give a solo, seemed to be able to feel the volumes above them and, with minimum effort, waft harmonies, to hover and pulse in the vault. It is said that this beauty was once the only thing that kept the peasant serf sane.

It helped to remember this when I went for a shower in the River Club blockhouse the next morning.

I'd been for a run in the park on the other side of the river on Krestovsky Island, crossing over a bridge two-deep with anglers, and pounding along the crumbling, littered paths through the wooded hinterland around the Kirov Stadium. There were couples down by the river bank. Further in, I spotted a large and fierce dog, so I hauled a right and headed further into the brush, to disturb a man taking a piss. I waved cheerily, and veered left into a couple making the beast with two backs under a hedge. Now rivalling Spring-heeled Jack for sprightliness, I sprinted back towards the river-bank across a small plank bridge. It shattered under my weight and I plunged both feet into some form of sewage rivulet.

So, carrying the massive gaoler's key to the shower, I followed directions up the crumbling concrete stairway into the dark interior of the club. The facilities were truly ghastly, a ghastliness which had only been achieved, it would seem, by extreme deliberation. There were six or seven different types of tiling randomly spread around the interior, a number of which had fallen off in despair. A gruesome pool of green-tinged liquid sulked in one corner. The lavatories had no seats and the cubicles looked as if there had been one of those fights in them – you know, where Joe Pesci takes hold of a man's head and smashes it several times into a handy partition. The dents had even made the graffiti indecipherable. There were things screwed in randomly. Lighting fixtures which didn't work any more, but still had bare cables hanging down, were fixed on the peeling walls. Someone had attached a mysterious shelf somewhere up near the ceiling, miles above my head. Every tile was cracked, some were mere fragments of pottery, held together by a string mesh. A brown stain had worked its way up the grouting and over the tiles to about waist height. The exact shade of brown is difficult to describe without associations I'd rather not explore, but it exactly matched the brown colour of the pipe-work under the sinks. Under-sink plumbing is the stuff of nightmares at the best of times, but this was especially arresting, because it seemed to have exploded. The pipes had furred up on the outside with layers of scrofulous rust. They had swollen up to five times their normal size and now hung in the gloom like suppurating sausages.

I stood paralysed for about five minutes. Where could I put down my clothes? The prospect of crossing the floor in bare feet and climbing into the shower tray, which seemed to have doubled as a paint tray, and was disfigured by splashes of lurid green, was too much. Even touching the shower curtain seemed an act of foolhardy bravado. I found a dry bit, stood on my towel, then scampered to the shower. The chrome handle was pitted and green. I gingerly turned it and there was a hissing followed by a dribble of hot water. I tried pulling the cracked plastic sliding door shut, but I felt I might inadvertently heave the whole structure down, so I soaped myself, standing stock still under the miserable dribble.

It was still easier than trying to shower on the boat.

We planned to leave in the late afternoon.

By the time we had cleared immigration it was getting dark. We passed through the sea gate and into a wind that was just beginning to froth up the waters. By midnight we were at sea and, for the first time in three months, directly heading towards Ipswich.

The St Petersburg traffic churned past us in the shipping lane. Through the night and the early dawn the wind, inevitably, shifted steadily round so that we had to pound into it, but eventually, free of the shipping lanes, and past the island of Gogland, we turned north and drove on a tack across the Gulf, towards Finland.

We went looking for a sheltered route, through the inner islands, that could take us all the way to Helsinki out of the heavy seas. For the next four hours, we rushed towards the shore, an invigorating, surging sail. At six-thirty in the evening, twenty-four hours after leaving the Sea Terminal, we were swooping and bounding past outlying rocky mounds into a wide bay, flanked by low granite islands, topped with straggly pines and bright green shrubbery, glowing pink in a low evening light.

'Where did he come from?' Bob pointed.

A powerful launch had suddenly surged up alongside. It had a bright green hull, grey superstructure and whippy aerials. It pulled across so closely that its wash crashed into our bow wave and threw a sock of water over Chris.

Everybody started shouting. The skipper of the boat was wrestling with his wheel. Both of us were travelling fast. He had slowed to match our speed and was dipping and wallowing, a wave's trough away, but edging closer all the time. We were two grinding bits of machinery, two pumps or pistons, crashing towards each other at different rhythms.

Baines, Bob and Charlie were waving and yelling, but not as much as the man on the aft deck of the coastguard launch. He was already red in the face from screaming at us. He had come up on our windward side. He was now so close that if we turned up into the wind to slow us down, we'd hit him. If I turned the other way, he'd get closer, so I struggled to spill some wind, letting go of the sheets, trying to slow us down before they tried to board us. Bob was holding out his palms like Marcel Marceau pushing the imaginary boat away. And the man was still shouting.

'Where are you going?'

'Helsinki!' Bob shouted back.

'No, no, you must go to the island.' The sails were flapping and we were slowing, but it made hearing him difficult.

'What island?'

'You must clear immigration at the island!'

'We thought we would go on to Helsinki!' I offered.

This did not meet with his approval. The Finnish coastguard was straining at his tight green uniform.

'No, no!! You must proceed to the island! Now. Immediately!'

We were still some way off-shore. The mainland lay 5 or so miles ahead, through an increasingly complex maze of uninhabited islands. Apart from a lighthouse on the summit, there was nothing to distinguish the island he meant, until we came around a point to reveal a secret, totally unexpected natural deep water harbour, filled with bureaucratic vessels.

'Look at that. Dr Helsinki's secret island lair,' said Chris.

The patrol boat was already moored to a jetty. The man who had shouted was standing at the end of it, directing us to pull alongside. It became obvious close to that he was a mere boy, in his early twenties. He had even become rather shy.

'Just here, if you could. Thank you. Where are you from?' He took our proffered rope.

'Britain.'

'Oh, yes, I am afraid all boats must check in here.' This was bizarre. He was hardly the same man. Had he taken a pill? Gradually we realized that he had mistaken us for Russians. He must have thought we were illegal immigrants, making a dash for the shore.

Baines squinted about. 'Will we be all right to stay the night up here?'

'No, not here.' The coastguard looked concerned. 'Have you a chart?' he asked. 'I will show you.'

'Er . . . no.'

He looked puzzled by this admission. (Those crazy English, eh?) I brought out the Admiralty chart's fifteen quid's worth and he chewed his lip. I gestured at the envelope-sized electronic gizmo and he nodded distractedly.

'It will be difficult to navigate through the islands with this,' he said eventually. 'Wait a moment.' He went back to his own boat and brought up two sizeable folio ring-bound books. 'These are the charts for the next sixty miles towards Helsinki.' He opened them at random on a frightening exercise in cartography. A splash of colours resolved itself into green blobs of land, yellow of shallows and white of water, all spattered together: the Jackson Pollock of maps.

'You must take these,' he said.

I demurred.

'No, no, these are our old ones. We have been issued with new.' I sensed that he was atoning for his bulging neck muscles earlier. Besides, some sort of map was probably rather essential. So we thanked him and searched out the only thing we could give him in return: a small bottle of rubbing-alcohol vodka. He looked at it with alarm, his neck muscles began to bulge again. And, holding up his hands, he literally backed away down the pontoon.

Before he turned back into the Incredible Hulk, we slid out of the secret lair towards the mainland, without even the faintest idea where we were. The slabs of the pine islands grew blacker, and the misty blue of their surrounds got bluer. And eventually there was more land than water, so we thought we must have got to Finland. It was a Caspar David Friedrich dusk. We felt like raiders scouting a new world.

In what was almost the last of the light, we negotiated a channel and slunk into a yacht harbour behind a great fortification, on an island. There were no other boats, but we noticed some form of scout camp further up the shore. Twenty or so kids were lighting fires and squatting, as if ready to start banging pots and singing in unison at any moment. Baines wrinkled his nose and stepped ashore to hook up to electricity.

'What's that over there?' Bob was pointing further up the channel. There were lights twinkling in the murk.

'That must be a town or something.'

'It's something,' I said, looking at the chart. 'There doesn't seem to be a town.'

'It's a lot of lights,' said Bob. 'Could be a restaurant or a club.'

'I don't think so.' Damn them. They made me do this. 'It's not going to be the King's Road. I mean look where we are. This is a wilderness. We'll be fine here. Lovely, peaceful . . . nothing. Peace. It's what we came for.'

'Apart from the boy scouts,' said Chris.

Baines came back. 'I've tried breaking into the electricity supply, but they've shut it up for the season.'

'We could go over there. They've got plenty of electricity there.' Bob pointed at the lights a couple of miles away.

What the hell. There was still the merest glimmer of daylight behind the pines. We took in all the warps, pushed off, crept through the complicated buoyage of the fjord in the pitch dark, and, an hour later, motored up to a large and well-lit cement factory.

'I'd rather not tie up to the cement wharf, if that's OK,' I said steadily.

Our new charts indicated that there was a tiny yacht harbour just inside the crook of the factory and we crept in across a shallow bay at one-year-old-baby-crossing-a-carpet pace, touching frequently with the centreboard and feeling our way in to the pontoons.

The following morning I was trying to get out to the roadway by climbing over a locked gate when a man came down to his 10-foot motor-launch. He started back with horror. 'Is that your boat?' he asked.

'Yes,' I replied.

'How did you get her in here?'

Undina was a good three times the length of any other floating object in the harbour and seemed to straddle the walkways like the *Ark Royal*.

'Oh, round the end of the cement wharf and past that island.'

'That island. The island there. You were lucky.'

'We've got a centreboard.'

'Ah. You are very enterprising.'

'I don't think so,' I replied, and sagged, 'more sort of easily persuadable, really.'

39. Island Hopping

'I was in this fetish club in Berlin . . .' I was trying to negotiate a route through the islands on the electronic chart and concentration was difficult, but I gathered that a colleague had invited Chris to a club, which, to his anguish, turned out to be a kinky one. 'I felt such a fool,' Chris said, 'because I had left all my usual stuff at home. I had to go in these pants.' He was still lazing around the deck in his skimpies. 'Ordinarily I have a fetish mask I wear,' he went on, 'with a zip down the front, just in case I'm recognized.'

We were passing through by far the most exquisite scenery we had yet seen on the journey. No, more than that. The most exquisite scenery we had seen, ever. The southern coast of Finland, the northern coast of the Gulf, was dotted with over 80,000 islands. And every one was beautiful.

The border had moved back and forth along this fragmented shore many times in the last 1,000 years. The Swedes had been beaten back home by Peter the Great. For 300 years Finland had been part of Russia. (During the Crimean War, a British fleet had been sent to bombard Åland, which was way out to our west.) Russia had only let go of this wonderland, where the tsar had yachted, in 1917, when the Finns negotiated their independence with Lenin.

We snaked past reed beds, close to rocks, in and out of channels. We twisted between high boulders of granite, running alongside bright patches of green reed, periodically breaking out into sudden wide sounds, crossed by larger boats.

'There was this bloke by the door who seemed to be wanking for hours and hours.'

'How long were you there, then?'

'I don't know. Oh, I see. Oh, all night, I suppose, but it was a little bit off-putting, because the corridor was rather narrow and you had to sort of get by without ever getting in the way.'

By the terms of the slimy Ribbentrop–Molotov agreement, on the eve of the Second World War, the Russians had been 'given' Finland, as a sphere of influence, by the Germans. They invaded in 1939. To the north of where we were now, up in Karelia, in a freezing, vicious winter war, the Finns miraculously held off the Russians for 100 days. But, with no one to support them, and in temperatures of minus 40 degrees, they had been forced finally to agree to the Peace of Moscow. The tiny country lost 25,000 people, and a lot of territory, but it did halt the Red Army, a feat so worthy of everyone's admiration and respect that it is disturbing to realize that Finland ended up on the wrong side at the end of the Second World War. During their fight for independence, they had looked to Germany for help. As a result, they narrowly avoided becoming a post-war satellite, as the Baltic states did. They remained free, but had to pay huge reparations to Russia – $226 million by 1938 prices.

We had decided on a passage marked with a '4', which meant there was never less than 4 metres of water. There were others marked '3', '6' and '10' and they ran for hundreds of miles, intersecting each other, or heading off north to cities way inland, or plunging south, to an open sea we hardly even glimpsed. The whole area was alive with potential. Like a smoothly edited travelogue, it continuously fired visions of exquisite beauty at us. Nothing was grand or magisterial. Everything was proportionate. It was totally exhausting.

'Look at that!'

'God, how lovely.'

To begin with we drew attention to the little humped boulders, flecked with lichen, the deeper woods, the crooked pines surmounting an islet, the cleft in the rocks, the turn in the channel, but then we ran out of awe. And there were hundreds of miles of this to go. From here until we left Åland, a week of constant motoring later, the engaging, mysterious, unfolding, sliding-screen, revelatory, ever-changing spectacle never let up.

Finland's entire history, like that of so many of the small countries of the area, had been driven by a wholly justified fear of its neighbours. The disputes, the civil wars, the blood-letting, even the internal political geography were caused by the aggressive policies of Russia, Germany and, before them, Sweden. During the post-war period, the cost of reparations motivated the Finns to industrialize and, ironically, this was the foundation of a thriving capitalist economy; but the 'special relationship' they had with Russia gave the Cold War a new word: 'Finlandization', as used by American hawks, meant a Western European country too sympathetic to Russia. With liberalization, in the 1980s, the Finns wanted to clear their name, and so they sent for Melvyn Kenneth Smith and me.

Yes, us two chirpy Brit sketch-comics played a small but, we like to think, vital part in the post-war history of plucky Finland. I played a smaller part than him. He played Santa Claus. I was just 'interviewer'.

Ronald Reagan was coming to Europe and he intended to visit Finland. They feared that the Great Communicator, like rather a lot of Americans, thought that Finland was still part of Russia, and they wanted to demonstrate that, though not allied with Nato, Finland was a free, Western-type place, with the right ideas and good toilets. To do this they decided to show him a short film on the plane on the way over.

The Finns had taken to *Smith and Jones* in a way that probably baffled the BBC. When we were shipped over to begin work on this important propaganda, we were embraced by restaurant owners and stopped the traffic in urinals. Naturally, ever since, I have had an affection for Finland. I remembered smiles from stunning elfin girls with white blonde hair. I remembered bear-hugs from massive stoker types in hotels. I had assured the others on *Undina* it would be like going home, and I was excited to be now threading through the islands to Helsinki, but I hadn't expected it to be quite so beautiful on the way.

'Why do the British go to the Grand Canyon, get on an airliner to fly to Australia to look at Ayers Rock, or visit the Seychelles, when they could come to these extraordinary islands?' I asked.

'Yeah, yeah,' said Bob, lighting another cigarette, 'but, tell me, Christophe, do you go to these fetish clubs in London too, or what?'

40. Another Beautiful Hut

In Helsinki, we decided to berth ourselves at the prestigious NJK Yacht Club. What was effectively the Royal Yacht Squadron of Finland sat on its own little rocky island right in the middle of the capital's main harbour. It looked down on the whole of the Helsinki waterfront, and the whole of the Helsinki waterfront looked up to it.

Like ''Awence', Peter O'Toole arriving at the Officers' Club in Cairo, I rolled up the pontoon with a studied gait, towards the club verandah, past people in suits, standing on the lawn in the evening light, drinking aperitifs, who stared at me. 'Bob,' I called to my dirty man, 'do you want to come along too?'

He loped after me. The clubhouse was the second building we had met from the Finnish-folk-awareness period: another lovely, soaring hut. We adopted a 'travellers, weary from expeditioning' demeanour and clomped into a hallway adorned with trophies and sepia pictures of sleek yachts with big sails. 'Halloah,' I called (a little nineteenth-century, I grant you, but greeted with silence anyway). We faced an impressive dark wood staircase, sweeping away ahead, which bifurcated and passed back over our heads. It was brown and polished, not unlike Bob. It debouched into a room of opulent magnificence: white tablecloths, gleaming silverware, sparkling crystal. Acres of ornate fenestration led on to balconies that looked out across Helsinki. Men in yachting caps and blazers glared at us from walls lined with trophy cabinets.

As we stood, reeking slightly, in the warm evening air, a girl went past in a white mess coat. I stopped her. She was obviously a waitress but seemed perplexed that we had arrived by boat. 'Is there anyone we can talk to?' I asked. 'The harbour master, captain, commodore?'

'Yes, yes,' she said. She was holding two plates of crayfish and sauce in her hands and gave one of them to Bob, so that she could wave her free hand expressively. 'He's just ashore but he'll be back.' Then she took the plate back and carried on through a swing door.

We were waiting at the dockside when the club tender came in and Lief got out. He was club-tight, self-contained, beer-bellied, possibly ex-naval, with a walrus moustache, and certainly not open to blandishments, nor to Bob.

'Are you the commodore?' Bob asked. Alas, Bob's woeful ignorance of yacht club hierarchy was strutting about and waggling its plumage.

Lief looked nonplussed. I intervened.

'We've just come in.'

'Ah, the boat from Britain. Yes, welcome. We do have a mooring for you,' he said.

'And you are the commodore?' Bob persisted. Lief looked a little shocked, as he might well do. I was shocked myself, and, later, I tried to explain to Bob that the commodore was likely to be a member of the Finnish telephone communications aristocracy with banking connections. Lief was the harbour master. Bob was relieved we hadn't met the commodore.

The Union Jack was run up on the mast. 'There aren't many visitors here at the moment, it's the end of the season. Some from Sweden, they've booked the sauna from seven.'

As well as the sauna, there were showers, washing machines, electricity and even (a first for us) a vacuuming point. Alas, we carried no vacuum cleaner.

Later, Nina, our waitress explained the NJK set-up. 'They come over, from businesses, and have their dinners here and then drink brandies and start singing songs.' The club had a lucrative sideline as a yacht-club theme-evening for city functions. We felt obliged to do our duty as a yachting exhibit, and had our evening meal there.

In our little private room, next to the balcony, constantly interrupted by business people walking through to smoke cigarettes, we sat, ate reindeer and chewed over Christophe Pant-boy's love affairs. He was feeling chipper, having achieved a lifetime's ambition of shagging three separate women in one day, for the second time.

'That's two lifetimes' ambitions,' Baines said.

'Yes, but the first time was better, because they were total strangers.'

'Don't you think that any of these women might have been expecting some sort of continuing engagement?' I decided to adopt a high moral tone to disguise my obvious envy.

'No, no, they weren't looking for a long-term relationship.'

'Hardly possible with two others waiting outside the door,' I said.

'Two of them already had boyfriends,' Chris said reasonably. Implying, of course, that Don Juan offered pleasures unavailable to these deluded women.

'Marvellous,' we all agreed. We sat in silence for a moment, projecting studied indifference. Bob gobbled down some smoked reindeer.

'I had five in one day, once,' he said finally.

'Well,' I said, 'that's absolutely magnificent Bob,' trying to imagine the great sloth of Peckham putting himself to such trouble.

Chris blustered, 'Well, you surely aren't using your total of five to downgrade my three, I think three is a pretty good achievement by any standards.'

'Yes,' said Bob, 'but not as good as five.'

I never found out if my film with Mel was a hit with Ronald Reagan. It was eventually shown on Christmas Day on Finnish TV; I suppose that, if nothing else, it proved that Finnish Christmas Day programming was in need of modernization. For a while we would continue to get invitations to work in Finland, but nothing quite as nationally significant again. Now I realized the moment had passed. I was no longer a local hero. The oily smear of light across the water after our dinner was placid and imperturbable. Boats wallowed in the washes of motor-launches and ferries. Robert swathed his head in a towel and sauntered determinedly to the sauna. 'We've barely been here three hours,' Chris said.

'But it's hot,' said Bob. 'I checked.'

We sat and steamed. It was hot enough to blanch a broccoli

floret, and turned Baines bright pink. Robert draped himself across a plank. 'You're supposed to stay in for an hour,' he said, 'or at least whack in and out. Get hot, get cold, get hot again for an hour.'

'How do you know that?' asked Baines.

'It's in Bob's big book of facts,' said Chris. Chris was going home the following day and we were going to miss him. On the way back to the boat I started suggesting some people to replace him, joining us for the last leg of the trip.

'That's charming,' said Chris.

'No, no, no one will ever fill your pants on our boat,' I said mollifyingly, 'but . . .' and I mentioned the name of an actor I had sounded out about his interest. 'I'm not sure if he should come though,' I went on. 'He's done a lot of yachting, but he's very keen, and I hate boat pedants.'

Chris nodded and looked at me sweetly. 'Yes,' he said, 'you only really need one per boat, don't you?'

41. Hunting, Shooting and Fishing

Never go back. In 2002, Helsinki itself was a bit of a disappointment. But at least I'd now seen the point of the country. Helsinki reminded me of Harrogate. It was larger, but similarly confident of its own old-fashionedness. The town itself, which I'd liked and still liked for its mild orderliness, was perfectly all right. But we could see why Helsinkites escaped on the Estonian ferry. Helsinki was prosperous, expensive, of middling size and neuter. Tallinn was wild. But we'd seen all the houses hidden in the woods, on the islands, and now we knew what the Finns really lived for.

A week later, in Turku, for example, we were eating in the seventies, Kardomah-Coffee-House ambience of a hotel restaurant, and we asked the girl serving us whether she had a house on an island. She laughed. 'No, no,' she said. 'I could not afford a house on an island. They are for rich people.'

'Sorry,' I said. 'It's just there are so many we assumed that everybody had one.'

'I dream of owning one,' she went on. 'At the moment I have to make do with my house by a lake.'

The city was becoming an irrelevance to us, now, too. So we went to the hunting and fishing shop in Union Street.

Everybody wants to fish off boats. Bob particularly so. In the Caribbean they have a special plastic lure hanging on the side of the game fishing shop. It's pink and orange and the size of a massive squid and it is positively irresistible to holiday-makers called Bob. ('Have you got anything more colourful and off-putting to fishes, at all?') But the shop in Helsinki was a serious backwoodsman's destination. There were dazzling outfits, not merely for camouflage, but designed to make you disappear completely: stealth-duck-hunters' cloaks of invisibility. How about a complete green mesh net bee-keeper's outfit, with extending prongs, so that you could walk about the forest under a mobile marquee of mosquito-netting? Out there were elk and bear, and the walls were lined with weapons for disembowelling them, pans for cooking them and clothes for impressing them. But it was fish we were after. We suddenly fancied the possibility of dragging a free supper out of the water.

Bob and I had only achieved this once before. Sailing downwind from Antigua to Barbuda, we had set a line to trail many yards behind us, attached to that squid made of day-glo plastic. We forgot all about it until we came to anchor and then hurriedly pulled it in. Inconveniently, given the circumstances, there was a long fish, with a row of sharp teeth, thrashing on the end of it. After we had struggled with it, we cooked it and it was delicious. Bob telephoned a friend. 'It had a blue sort of back . . . yes. I see.' He switched the phone off. 'Well he says it was definitely a barracuda but we shouldn't have eaten it because they give you mercury poisoning from nibbling things on the reef.'

In Helsinki we swaggered up to the shop assistant with the confident demeanour of practised time-wasters. 'These moose . . .' Bob began, pointing in the direction of the photos behind the bloke, of men in flappy hats cradling guns with their feet up on large dead mammals. 'Are they easy to find?'

'Did you want to hunt elk?'

'Well, I'd quite like to see one.'

'There are many elk in Finland.'

'Round here?'

'Not in Helsinki, no, but further north, yes, many.'

'Right, but what about along the coast? Are we likely to see an elk sort of coming down to the water to have a drink or anything?'

Since eating a grilled elk chop in Tallinn, Bob had begun to yearn for an encounter with the gentle giant of the woods.

'Not really, no.'

'How about bears?'

I interrupted. 'What my friend is working his way slowly towards is fish, actually. We want to do a spot of fishing.'

'Lake or sea?'

'Sea,' said Bob promptly, 'though actually we might get across to a lake or two, if there's a chance of spotting an elk.'

'No. Look we are going from here to Åland by boat and we just thought, you know, if we were to stop for the evening in a secluded bay, would this be a good time to catch fish?'

'Of course.'

The salesman was enthusiastic about our trip. He was highly enthusiastic about the time of year and the time of day. He was overcome with enthusiasm about the fishing possibilities.

'Because, you know, we're not fishermen,' I explained, perhaps a little redundantly. 'We are rather keen on actually catching something. We don't just want the sitting-around bit.'

'Sure, sure,' said the guy, nodding violently. He was a reassuringly hip figure with a funny beard and floppy hair. 'Believe me, you'll catch something. You're on a boat. That's great. The best way. Where you're going, there are hundreds of fish. It's the ideal season.'

'Hm . . .' This sounded just, well, too good to be true. I felt I ought to be just a little sceptical. 'What sort of fish, then?'

'Salmon! Pike!'

'Big fish?' asked Bob.

The assistant held out his arms and indicated a fish that would feed a family of four for a couple of months.

'And these are easy to catch?'

He reached behind him and started pulling down a rod. It was about 12 feet long. 'You would need a reel,' he said and put a piece of hand-tooled precision engineering on the counter. It looked complicated, and more than that, it looked expensive. 'At dusk they come after almost any fly,' he continued.

'Whoah. Hold on a minute.' I took the reel out of Bob's hands. 'I'm not sure we want to learn how to fly-fish at this late stage in our careers. We're used to rather less demanding fishing.'

I was thinking of our trolling. After the barracuda success, naturally, we had decided to troll on the way back from Barbuda. Bob had cast the ineffable plastic squid and the weights over the side, but he forgot to tie the end of the fishing line to anything on the boat and, as we powered out of the bay, with a stiff trade wind in our sails, the whole lot spun out of the reel, over the stern and into the sea.

'Aren't there any fish that can be sort of hooked up?'

'Sure, sure. You mean bass.'

'Sea bass?' I had eaten sea bass in expensive restaurants. It was very good eating.

'Yes. One minute, tops. You put the worm on the hook on the end of the line and throw it over. I guarantee you will have a fish on the end of it in one minute.'

There was a pause. Something unspoken hung in the air. In the end, I spoke it.

'A minute?'

'Yeah.'

'Bass?'

'Yeah. Listen, if you don't catch a bass, then telephone me, I will come and catch one for you myself.'

Well. We were overcome with admiration for this young man. He deserved a medal from the Helsinki Rotary Club. He was salesman of the decade. He was implying that the bass-fishing business was so easy, it demeaned the rest of the shop. This seemed to be just stopping short of offering us a barrel and a pistol. We could hardly reach for my wallet quickly enough. He found us rods. Not only that, he found us telescopic rods that could be truncated to the size of a walking stick to be stored away with the rest of our junk. He reached behind him, opened a fridge and brought out an ice-cream-sized tub of earth, within which, he assured us, resided a colony of earthworms, as delicious to the bass as the bass would be to us. In awe of this man, we scurried around the shop and bought an armful of useless accoutrements, just to demonstrate our gratitude. Clutching our new gear and waving merrily, we sallied out into Union Street eager to face the wild, blue, Finnish yonder.

Nobody had come out to join us for this leg. In the end, we were just the three of us again. I wanted to finish the trip, before some sort of residual guilt surfaced. What were we doing anyway, plugging onwards? The children were back at school. The season was over.

I went to bargain for reindeer skins in the market with Bob ('I want to give them away for Christmas') and then on to the covered food hall alongside the old fish dock, where he bought more reindeer, in tins. ('Their faces, when I give them Rudolph instead of turkey.') But by six o'clock, I was relieved to get out of Helsinki and cruise through the islands to somewhere new. I felt more secure, travelling on, and after a couple of hours, we tied up to a jetty in a peaceful neck of the waters.

The waterways were dotted with these pontoons designed for four or five boats. Without facilities, they were just a mooring buoy and a plank to get ashore: a stopping-off point for the night. It was dusk as we came in. There were a few other little boats around. There was a club which was closed for the winter. Some people in maroon fleeces were lighting a fire on the shore.

'Look at the fish!' said Bob, suddenly.

I peered over the side of the boat, and tensed. The water was alive with fish. Like carp in an overstocked moat, fish were coming up to the surface by the side of the hull and sticking their mouths out of the water.

We almost turned and shouted at the people on the shore, 'Look at this!' But they must have seen it all before. They were busy with their barbecue.

'What's the matter with the fish?'

'They're after the mosquitoes!'

The place was thick with gangly insects. We should have bought ourselves the complete bee-keepers' outfit, while we were at it, but never mind the bugs! In a state of trembling excitement, we fumbled for our extending rods.

'They're still coming,' said Baines.

Now the fish were jumping out of the watery deep, offering themselves up for supper. There were silvery flashes all across the surface. It was like that bit when the missionary falls in the Amazon and the piranhas get him.

'Wouldn't you be better off with a bucket?' Baines asked.

Bob came on deck clutching the can of worms. I took off the lid and prodded around in the earth. 'Go on.' 'Yes.' They were unlikely to bite, I realized that. But all the same. They seemed to have scurried away to the bottom of their tub. I hauled one out and it wiggled horribly. I stuck a hook through the front of its knobbly end and after several false starts got the worm on the hook by thrusting it straight up the shaft until the metal showed through its slightly translucent skin. Never mind if the fish feels any pain. Impaling worms was a bad business.

Around us, the humps of islands turned violet as the night came on. The channels were dotted with the lights of commuters hurrying home in little boats.

We had pretty little red and white floats and we lowered these into the water. Nothing happened. We pulled up the rod.

'Drop it further from the boat, they can see us.'

'Of course they can see us. They're practically jumping up on deck to get a look.'

'Yes, but they can see that we're trying to catch them.'

This was patently absurd. What sort of fish were these? Educated fish? Did they go to fish school and get instructed not to go near to the delicious worms dropped from the sky? It made no difference.

'Lower the worm,' said Baines. We lowered the worm. The float bobbed.

'There we go.'

I pulled it in. The fish had eaten the worm. They had nibbled whatever wiggled straight off the hook, leaving a section untouched, in case it brought their sensitive mouths into contact with the sharp end. Altogether, the fish ate a dozen worms. In between eating the worms, they came to the surface and mouthed for more. Obligingly, we fiddled for the bait. With great care, we prepared a long succession of worm kebabs. The fish got their supper. The worms got eaten. The only real bites we got were from the mosquitoes.

Thirty minutes passed and, rather than thirty bass, we had nothing, and it was dark, and the fish went away.

'Shall I give him a ring?' said Bob, reaching for his mobile. 'He must be only twenty minutes away by car.'

'No, no.' I felt it was unfair. 'They probably weren't bass anyway. We'll try again tomorrow.'

We didn't. Unlike Arthur Ransome, who seemed to find several hours a day to sit amongst the reeds, smoking a pipe, fishing and writing in his note book, we were hurrying on. Besides, Ransome didn't have a computer and an unconnectable mobile phone modem to occupy his every waking moment. And, let's face it, he probably knew how to fish.

42. Aground

That night the unexpected happened. It rained. It rained for eight hours; thrashing on to the deck, not with a constant drumming, but a pitter-patter pit, pat, pat, spatter, pat, spatter, patter: a dish-washer noise. I lay in the darkness rolling my eyes. The dripping around me intensified. Damn. God! And I jerked upright, put on the light, feverishly patting around me with the flat of my palms, expecting tell-tale silver dribbles all over the bedclothes. But the tissue wodges tamped into the cracks were performing their super-absorbent duty. I was dry. I was dry! I settled back and lay awake with leak-paranoia instead, until it got light.

Dawn came as a grey, wet blur. I believed I'd lie there all day, listening to the sloppy, insistent drizzle, but at about nine o'clock it suddenly stopped and we crawled out into another gleaming day, to leave Penticaana, through a still morning, threading between the islands in a white mist.

We were using the charts we'd bought in Helsinki. Like the coastguard's books, these were massive, floppy folios. Each page turned laid out a new wallpaper pattern of islands. The route was feverishly complex.

'How many thousands of posts, growing apparently out of the sea, are to be met with round the shores of Finland? Millions we might say,' wrote Mrs Ethel Tweedie, author of *Mexico as I Saw It* and *Through Finland* in 1896. They were still there: countless buoys. Any wrong turning, any muffed identification, any inattention would stick us straight on a rock. So I left the pencil with its point on the last recorded position. Glancing down, I hoped I could instantly see where we were. I scrupulously made a pencil cross on each and every mark we twisted past. And, after a while, it became satisfying. Heading west, we moved smoothly along the books, the pages turned over every ten minutes. 'That's another fiver gone,' I would announce.

We put up the sails and slid into a narrow sea-canal between two wooded banks. Beyond the trees, we spotted shy country huts. Unlike in Denmark, these routes didn't bring us to a neat market town or village. Instead, we travelled through a continuous pattern of hidden suburbs. It was all remarkably discreet. Sometimes only a flagpole indicated a house. (There were national flags for sale in hardware shops, next to kitchen towels and the boat paint.) Unassuming little jetties clambered across the rocks to meet the water. Sometimes there were hammocks or a few cane chairs on the rocks. Occasionally, boats buzzed past at great speed, on their way to these tidied-away homesteads.

Bob took over and I pointed at rocks; how close we passed to humps and eddies as we sailed down the Barrowsund, a channel marked by perfect round islands, topped with trees. Creeping to the edge of the channel, at 6 knots, I put the engine on but didn't engage the gear. Bob was learning to luff up to the point of stasis, then pull back. 'You can go the other side of the port marker,' I pointed out, peering at the electronic chart.

'Oh, easily,' says Bob, meaning he could get the boat to sail there.

'No, no. I mean, you can,' I told him, meaning there was enough water for the boat to float there.

He pointed slightly into the wind as we drifted past. We were approaching narrows. After some creeping and fussing, it was obvious we were not going to sail through. There was no room to tack between the high rocks on either side. The land had risen up like a mini canyon and I put the engine into gear so that we could motor between them. Bob had the chart at his side. The paired, suddenly larger, red and green buoys led us a little south and round.

I had been using the electric navigation system as a back-up, in case we faltered. I looked down to concentrate for a moment or two. When I glanced up again I noticed a big red buoy passing about 20 feet away to our port. For the last six hours, since we were effectively leaving Helsinki, we had been leaving red port hand markers to starboard. In fact, we had left about 600 red markers to starboard and this was by far the biggest we had seen. 'Shouldn't we be on the other side of that?' I asked Bob.

We hit the rock before Bob could actually say, 'We're fine.'

There was a sudden juddering crash; a violent, grinding banging underneath, and the whole of our world was humped upwards. We didn't stop just like that. The entire boat bounded forward like a car hitting a ditch. One, two, three, four jerking, painful, lifting, loud smashes.

Baines, below, was thrown bodily out of his seat. 'Hey, look out!' he shouted, a little redundantly, sprawling in the bilges. I registered an image of Bob teetering, grasping at a handhold, with a look of outraged surprise on his face and I grabbed at the gear lever. The engine was driving us forward. I yanked it back into neutral. But the sails were up, and as we leaned and turned, the wind banged into them and the whole boat 'oofed' and yawed. We had been doing 6 knots and even with the wind full in the sails, we came to an utter dead halt.

The boat was sort of shuddering and quaking from the impact, though, and I could see that the wire that pulled up the centreboard was hanging, horribly slack, meaning the blade had been pushed upwards. No granite spike was poking up through the hull, so I leaped away, on electrified appendages, whipping the ropes holding the boom off their cleats, letting the mainsail rattle out as far as the wind wanted to take it, shooting to the jib and letting it fly, flapping and cracking, trying to stop any possible further forward motion.

'What's happened?' asked Bob somewhere behind me.

'We've hit a rock, you twat!'

Did Baines say it? Or me? Probably both of us. I hung and dithered for a fraction of a second, trembling and nauseous, and then looked over the side, but she was stationary. There weren't any waves. The water was smooth and unruffled. The boat was fixed, with all sails. Stuck, like a flash photograph. There was nothing to see in the Prussian blue water which still, perversely, lapped at the boot line, as if we were floating.

I scrambled to the mast like a panicked animal and let the sails down. Baines put the engine into reverse, pushing the throttle, and I ran to the side, but nothing. The depths at the stern swirled and burbled. I stared intently at the shore. Then at a buoy and the shore. Was there any movement at all?

'I don't like the sound of the engine revving like that.'

'Never mind the f . . .' But we slowed it anyway. The buoys and the trees on the sunlit shore stayed precisely related to each other. We were simply marooned, pinned on a rock in a gorgeous spot, a lovely cove, on a lovely, lovely day. It was like being frozen in time.

'Try forward,' said Bob.

'We don't want to get further on to it. I think we might have to try and get off the way we came on.' I tried to envisage what we might look like underneath. I hoped the rock had been washed smooth by the water.

'OK,' I said defiantly. 'Let's . . .' and the 's' hissed out. There were ways of getting boats off mudbanks, but this . . . 'Bob, get out the dinghy.'

'We'll never pull her with a rubber dinghy.'

'No, we'll take an anchor and try to kedge her off.'

'Right. How does that work?'

'We put an anchor over there and pull.'

Baines came up from below. 'I've got the floorboards up all along and there doesn't seem to be any hole.'

Bob was looking vaguely at the lockers.

'That one. And pass me the sail ties.'

I pulled on the main sheets, hauled the boom in to the boat, and tied up some of the mainsail. Bob started pulling all the junk out of the locker and piling it on the deck.

'We could try this!' I said. 'Baines, can you get up on the boom?'

'On the boom?'

'Up there.'

'OK.' He struggled up and sat astride it, like a worried jockey.

'Now we'll push it out, you see.'

'Right.' He clutched at the sail.

'And then the extra weight on the end of the boom will lean the boat over. If we lean it over to one side then the bottom might lift off and we can slip back.'

'I see.'

We were just dangling Baines, who weighed about three stone, over the edge of the water to no particular effect, except to make him whimper, when the little boat came past. It was a dory, a small family runabout, and it was filled with a family. They drove past staring at the boat with the heaps of junk on deck and a short bearded man sitting on a spar.

'You are on the rock, there,' shouted the father, who was sitting upright at a steering wheel.

'Yes.'

He slowed his engine and bobbed towards us. His wife and children looked pityingly on.

'The channel is this side.'

'Yes.'

'Could you try and pull us off?' Bob said. I restricted myself to turning slowly towards him.

'Oh, I don't think we would be strong enough for that,' said the man with understandable restraint, moving his runabout a little further away.

A large white motor cruiser, the sort I generally denigrate, came throbbing round the corner. A man and his wife were standing at the controls on a plastic balcony about 20 feet above the deck. The dory man drove over towards it and, pointing at us, spoke in Finnish. The white boat frothed at its stern and gingerly approached closer.

'I can try to tow you!' shouted the man.

'Yup. Thank you. Right,' I shouted back.

The towrope, last used back in Kent, was somewhere in the back locker. Waving and gesticulating, as if we feared they might all run away when we weren't looking, Baines and I opened it and plunged in head-first. We dragged out everything. Funnels, bags of sail covers, buckets, brooms, jerry cans, the folding chair, fenders, boots, a wet suit and heaps of Bob's bloody shoes all joined the rest of the chaotic mess that Bob had dragged out earlier. In about two minutes, almost every single item we had ever had on board was lying on the deck. I dropped head-first into the locker, legs waggling like a duck, and grabbed hold of the heavy towrope, which had been carefully folded away, but now, with a heave, came out in a bundle. Baines and I tore at it, kicked it into its coils and then unwound it, passing it behind the mast and over the fairleads and down to the dory, which carried it across to deep water and the motorboat.

'OK,' shouted the man. He looked down at his control panel and twisted something. The boat heaved. The ropes tightened like wires. The water churned around the stern of the motorboat.

Nothing.

We signalled to the family runabout. 'We think we need to get off and get into your boat.' But the father held up a hand.

The motorboat had started to move in a circle, to try and pull us off from a different angle. We ran from side to side, like modern dancers simulating panic, trying to tip it up.

'We'll have to get a bigger boat,' shouted the dory man eventually, unmoved by our choreography. But now the motorboat was turning us sideways, grinding across the top of the rock. The motorboat was swivelling the boat and the ropes were pulling hard across the fixtures on the stern. All the strain of the movement was being held by the ensign staff. It was clearly going to snap it off. I bounded aft to get it out of its holder.

'Don't!' Baines was shouting at me. 'Don't! If the rope parts, it could whip back!'

An image of sailors cut in half by lashing cables came to mind. I abandoned the national colours to their fate and scurried back to the others. The boat groaned and the ropes creaked. All three of us elbowed each other out of the way to get as far as possible from the stretching, twanging hawsers at the stern, scuttling, like the Three Stooges, right up to the pointed end of the boat. As we got there, we tipped the whole boat up an inch or two, and with a sudden, smooth rush *Undina* slid backwards off the rock and settled calmly in the channel.

She lay, floating serenely, in deep water.

I looked at the others and then around. Then I looked over at the motorboat. I lamely raised a hand.

'Thank you!' I shouted. 'I think she's off the rock, now.'

'No, it's nothing,' said the motorboat skipper. The dory was already disappearing and the children were waving back at us.

'Please, please accept this!' I said to the motorboat man and his partner as they handed us back our towrope. We passed them a bottle of cheap Russian champagne. They didn't really want it – neither did we for that matter – it was horrible stuff and I couldn't see much to celebrate.

'Well, we're off, anyway,' said Bob, after they'd gone and as we started to heap all our junk together and stuff it back in the lockers. 'No harm done.'

I breathed heavily. 'I'm not sure,' I said finally. 'I find it difficult to imagine that we crashed into a rock under full engine and with all the sails up without dislodging something underneath.'

Baines pulled up the floorboards and we shone a torch over the greasy black depths of the hull, peering at the frames, and noticing beads of water and trickles of slime. Mind you, we'd never looked quite so intently at it before and as far as we knew it always leaked slightly.

'We'll have to get her out.' I said gloomily.

'Oh, I don't think that'll be necessary,' Bob said authoritatively.

'Don't you, Bob?' I turned to look at him.

He shut up. I think my tone had been a little tense. 'One way or another we're going to have to check and see whether we've done any damage,' I said melodramatically.

'I can get my wet suit out,' said Bob.

We started the engine.

The scene turned greyer. We crossed an open sea passage and turned north into the islands. Reedy banks and plumped-down islands crowned with twisted firs passed us by, cafés and mooring sites, for day-tripping motorboats, all deserted, mostly empty, until we came to Rossund. It was a ferry point, where the inhabitants of the islands left their cars and went on by boat. There were fifty or sixty cars, but we saw no human beings of any kind.

As we tied up to the side of the ferry landing place, Bob turned
to me.

'It must happen all the time,' he said.

I nodded vacantly.

43. A Pecking Order

The boat next door lay in the early sun with all its hatches open.
They had come in late the night before, and, pleased with themselves, had banged about and hollered at three in the morning,
so, at six a.m. on Sunday morning, I pissed more widely across
the intervening water, belched extravagantly, and farted for good
measure.

We were about to leave Hanko, famous for mud, saunas, stoves
and dynamite, where we'd spent the night after a bruised interval
pressing on through the islands. Bob had threatened to take on
all-comers in a Thai eat-all-you-like buffet, we'd toured the
wooden houses amongst the pine trees and gone to bed grumpily.
It had been a subdued day, but staggeringly beautiful, none the less.

Hanko was on the corner of Finland, at the far end of the Gulf.
We were going to turn slightly north now and make for Turku,
the ancient capital, which was hidden behind a maze of islands
beyond what appeared to be a missing part of the world. On any
throwaway map of Europe – an airline route plan, say, or a road
map, or a Scandinavian Gourmet Delights guide – where we were
about to go did not exist. From Hanko to Åland, near Sweden, is
commonly presented as 'sea'; just a blue, blank nothing. There is
sea, but in reality it laps thousands of separate dots of island. As
much land as water, the Turku Archipelago is the hard-pressed
cartographer's nightmare. It was exciting to be heading for somewhere so topographically complex that it was expedient not to
draw it. I dimly recalled that I must have decided, sitting in a Suffolk
shed, that we wouldn't go there. I had no Admiralty chart of the
area. But I wanted to go there now. There hadn't been any cranes
in Hanko. Turku might have the facilities to haul us out so we
could inspect our damaged keel.

I folded in the boarding steps from where I'd left them hanging in the water, after a hopeless plunge into the harbour the evening before, to inspect our damage: pushing down through the deaf water and forcing my eyes open, to look at the blurred, swollen whale's bottom of *Undina*. But, even with my eyelids gaping wide and my white hands paddling down, it was icy cold and too murkily green to be able to see anything at all.

We hadn't sunk in the night, and we'd managed a full day's sail, so we decided we might as well keep going.

We struck out across the bay. The sea was denim blue. The islands were still preposterously pink. The buoys were big plastic noodles sticking some two or three metres out of the water. They glowed red and green in the early light in a pristine archipelago. There was no visible rubbish – no plastic bottles, frayed rope or extruded polystyrene, no beer, Coke, or Omo bottles, no bags or plastic shoes. Not even driftwood nestled amongst the rocks or sat stranded on the hundreds of bare rock islands. Three times in the next few hours, I watched as a single white feather blew across the mottled surface near to us, the only visible detritus in the landscape. A startled pair of swans and five well-grown cygnets stood up on their boulder and looked around, but didn't take off. At one point, a wagtail came and landed dextrously on the actual arrow of our wind vane, on the top of our mast.

The course required only the slightest adjustments, but they occupied us totally. We had to follow a twisting channel. Each change was confirmed by leading marks. Sometimes they appeared behind us, sometimes ahead. We would spot a square of slatted wood, 10 feet wide, on derricks, painted with a yellow stripe. At a distance behind it, perhaps half a mile, maybe only a few hundred yards, there would be a taller twin, painted similarly. When the yellow marks made a straight line, we were on course. Keeping this extensive navigation system going, for the benefit of a population of 5 million people, must partly account for the Finns being amongst the most heavily taxed people in the world.

After lunch, Bob told me about a dream he had had the night before. 'I was standing with my mother and a block of flats comes striding towards me.'

'A block of flats?'

'Yeah, with metal legs. It was spurting shells, which burst and turned into giant spiders and wriggling things. "The unforgiving worm," my mum said.'

Robert dreamed actual Hollywood scenarios. He had no stress or paranoia about work or status, not even about sticking my boat on a blasted rock, just run-of-the-mill, apocalyptic nightmares from *Star Wars*.

The passage in to Turku was a wondrous thing. The last sound, the final approach, was 10 miles long and a mile wide. The banks were lined with boathouses and villas and the occasional fishing hut stacked with wood. High up on a rock, a group of children watched us pass. Open motorboats impertinently overtook us. We came to some form of esplanade, a municipally planted park, and then, suddenly, face to face with a Silja ferry, of liner dimensions, coming the other way. It seemed to block the entire creek.

'It's not moving, I can't see a bow wave,' said Baines.

But it was, and we hovered in a short cut until it passed through and out to the Baltic.

I had a voice-over scheduled in Helsinki the next day and left Bob and Baines to inquire after a crane in Turku. From the train, a parade of neat towns glowed in the autumnal sun. Finland was a place of stones, by the roads, in the fields, in hummocks under stands of birches. The Finns squeezed in amongst, alongside, on top of and behind their landscape. It was only a few days into September, but I was feeling faded and touched with decay myself. In a few weeks it would be winter.

Finland was, after all, defined by its snow. 'Look at the down-pipes,' Baines had pointed out the night before, when we had walked into the strangely bare city of Turku. 'They don't reach the ground because of the ice. The snow must build up that high.' Patches of the ground in gardens and in parks had that flattened, bare look from heavy falls. The entrances to apartment blocks were close-sealed and lino-covered.

The night before, the centre of Turku had been a ghastly, naked square lying under a black sky made darker by lurid neon signs. It was a car park. Bob pointed to a row of planters with faded, dying trees in them as we walked by on our way to watch *Austin Powers, International Man of Mystery*. There were syringes lying in the mud.

'This feels like Canada,' said Baines, 'though I've never been there.'

In Helsinki, the sound engineers who were helping with the two-word change to the script were modern Finns. 'We never lived through the bad times, so we're prepared to take risks,' they told me.

Their parents had lived in fear of the Russians but the new generation was growing up with a different mental landscape altogether. 'The guy who was in here before you,' said Hari, and indicated the studio, 'he has only two rules in life. One is never to go to Russia or meet any Russians.' I never found out what the other rule was. 'It's just racism,' he concluded.

He took me to his computer and showed me a website. He and his mountain bike club were going to central Estonia soon. There was a photograph of a farmhouse in a field they were going to rent.

'See,' he pointed to the bottom of the picture, 'eight hundred hits for this one property.' I wondered whether it might just have been members of his club looking at the place over and over again, but he told me it was the Finnish people in general, and their rage for all things Estonian. 'The ferry only takes eighty minutes. I'll be there this weekend.'

'Looking for what?' I asked him.

'Looking to look, to explore. It was possible to go before independence, but there was only one ferry and everybody was spied on.' The one major hotel where Finns were forced to stay had had a whole floor dedicated to bugging equipment, 'listening out for clues, anything, and all these sexy girls working the lobby, you know.'

But the Finns didn't think of the Estonians as their fellows. Hari laughed. 'Oh, no, they're too Russian. People don't think they are really Scandinavians like we are.' He went into the familiar routine. 'The Danes look down on the Swedes, who look down on the Finns, and the Finns look down on the Estonians, and the Estonians

look down on the Latvians. And the Lithuanians, I'm afraid, are
right at the bottom.'

And everybody still feared the Russians, if not for their military
intentions, then most certainly for their criminal intentions. 'Near
the border,' he went on, 'there is trouble with the gangs coming
over, and the problem is that the Finnish police just aren't used to
it, they don't have any experience of this sort of crime.'

I shared my waffly notions with them. How the imperial powers
seemed the corrupted modern nations, and the small countries of
the Baltic seemed ordered and cooperative to outsiders. They, for
example, were good, patriotic Finns. I praised them. Their identity
as Finns was important to them, not tarnished by the post-imperial
shame we Brits have.

'What do you mean?'

'Look at all your flagpoles and your flags. It's sometimes easier
to spot habitation on the islands because of the flagpoles than the
house hidden in the woods.'

'But in the end,' said Hari, 'perhaps this is because we don't have
as much respect for the flag as you do for the Union Jack. It's just
decoration for us, you know.'

Baines had sorted out a yard to lift the boat. We were lucky. All
the Finnish yachts were going to be hauled out on dry land in the
next few days. The yard across the harbour had hired a massive
crane for the purpose and was prepared to get us out for a couple
of hundred quid before they started work.

'So . . .' the yard manager and the crane driver looked down at
the boat, 'where should we put the straps?'

This was a good question. The crane had two lengths of webbing
hanging down from its hooks. They were slid underneath the boat
from either end and then the whole thing was simply lifted up.
But where should they be put? I could scarcely remember the
underwater outline of my own boat. It might be a sensible idea to
put them as far apart as feasible, but I knew that she had a long keel,
and if we put one of the slippery thongs too near the front,
presumably it might slip up the sharp nose and the whole boat

would drop off the sling and crash back into the water, a prospect too horrible to contemplate.

I telephoned home.

'Darling, somewhere on my desk, there are some photographs of the boat when she was hauled out in Kent . . .'

'Oh, hello. Where are you?'

'Eh? Oh we're still in Finland. I think they're in a pile to the left of the pencil mug . . .'

'Is everything going all right?'

'What? Yes. Well sort of. Are they there?'

'I'm coming out to Stockholm to meet you.'

'That's great, great. Only they're just about to . . . hold on . . . Baines! Hold it just a minute!'

Jo found the photographs but they gave nothing away. They were all taken from the wrong angle. Except in one, where the two straps seemed to be rather closer to the middle and further back down the boat than one might have expected.

'I'll be arriving on the ten-fifteen plane . . .'

'Yes. I'll ring you back.'

I ran over to the dock and adjusted the webbing straps and the crane pulled *Undina* up.

'Ah, that's right. I remember now,' I said to Bob. There was something vaguely unnerving about staring at what had been hidden beneath us for so long. But it wasn't a case of peering up an old lady's skirts. The boat was built like a knife.

I photographed every inch of the hull, particularly where it flattened out. The steel housing had been squashed a little flat, but nothing seemed out of place. In fact, the hull looked almost as clean as when we had put her in the water, three months before. We had been travelling all that time. There were no barnacles.

'Oh, dear, look at this.' Baines was standing, stooped and squinting, by the stern, peering at the propeller. I joined him. While there wasn't any visible damage from the impact, there was certainly another, probably unrelated, problem.

The propeller shaft ran along the bottom of the hull from the engine, near the middle of the boat. Then it came outside, through a complicated arrangement of glands and fixtures. The last one, the stern cutlass mount on the outside of the boat, had become detached. It hung on the shaft, its holding screws gone. Over the last months we had experienced a great deal of vibration from the engine and it must have shaken the whole thing free. More than that, it had worn away the socket it was supposed to sit in and washed out all the heavy grease that was packed in there to seal it from the water. It hung limply out of a hole in the back. Even Bob and I could see that this was not right.

Baines excelled himself. We were escorted to a magnificent Finnish hardware shop, with the clean, spacious dignity of an art gallery. I felt for him. He was in a hardware paradise. Even as we sorted out the perforated metal straps and self-fixing screws with which he was to achieve the lash-up of his life, he would stop before a pair of anodized bolt cutters or a set of carbon wrenches and finger them gently with admiration and awe. Thank God we had proper business to attend to, otherwise we might never have left.

The managers of the yard were patient and helpful, considering that we'd negotiated to haul out the boat for a quick look and then spent the entire morning repairing something else altogether, and we were back in the water by noon.

In C. S. Forester's Hornblower stories, there was always a chapter where Hornblower took his boat off to some deserted island and spent months building a battery on the shore or chopping down trees and making himself a new mast, and we felt a certain adult satisfaction in having undertaken something as major as lifting our entire accommodation out of the water, fiddling about with it, and sticking it back in again. So much so that, ten minutes later, we stopped at a pleasant yacht club under some yellowing trees and ate an extravagant lunch.

44. The Islands Were Closed

As I walked up towards the harbour office in Nasby, deep in the non-existent islands south of Turku, a small, battered red car bounced down the steep hill to the pontoons. 'Did you see us coming?' I asked the driver.

'No, no.' The harbour mistress unlocking her darkened shop and office was a neat, blonde woman. Her nine-year-old daughter had come with her and she stood watching us both, leaning back on the ice-cream chest freezer with her arms folded. 'I just came down here to shut up everything.'

'Oh, you're closed.'

'Yes, the season is over, and tomorrow, we go away.' It was nearly dark. There was a strange purple light shining from behind the pines that lined the fjord.

'Right, so there's no electricity?'

'No.'

'No showers?'

'No.' But she was an island person and considerate. She paused for a moment, jiggling her keys on the desk. 'I will open the shower and you can lock it up yourself,' she said finally. 'I could put up the electricity for you, no one will take it, and the toilet is open, I'll show you.'

Outside, she took me to the red barns, built against the cliff, for the facilities. 'Oh, you have a big boat,' she said.

Baines was sloping towards us, carrying his cables. 'The harbour mistress is going to Tallinn on holiday,' I told him.

'That must be a complicated journey,' said Baines.

'Three ferries, and then we're in Turku and the train.' She shrugged.

'So where shall we recommend in Tallinn, Baines?' I asked him. We had been there only a month before – no, wait, three weeks before. Was it? No, barely that. She watched us as we stood there trying to work it out. Apart from putting ourselves aground and rushing around St Petersburg and Helsinki, what had we done? Little but skirt the edge of the northern world. But each day seemed to wash out the last, and it felt like a huge stretch of time. Helsinki and the NJK were like something from a few years back. Tallinn was another life. And we could hardly think of anywhere in particular to recommend.

The next morning glowed like a picture in *National Geographic* magazine, with 1950s Technicolor backwoods and an Ektachrome sky. I walked up, past a supermarket and a builder's merchants into a village with no more than about four or five domestic houses, but with a library, a bank, a church, a hall, a school, a hospital and a massive fire station, and the Black Pirate, an evil-smelling pub which opened at ten.

The inter-island hub appeared shut, but, in fact, everything was open for business. They were just hiding. The owner of the Black Pirate looked mortified to see us, as we duck-walked through his curtained saloon across a carpet which stuck to our feet. Bob cosied up to the bar, complimenting him on his wall-paintings of guillemots. The owner pointed out they were penguins. He painted murals of a fantasy Caribbean all winter long. The rest of his dive was decorated with chainsaw carvings of bears.

There were six clouds in the sky with a rainbow in it as we sailed on. Bob sat there and periodically said, 'Oh yes, this is, well . . .' and then, after a while, only 'Ha!' and 'Oh!' and 'Ah!'.

We had become sea-cowboys in this wilderness, three gnarled pan-handlers in the Yukon, with a boat rather than mules. After weeks of guests (Pant-boy, Charlie the cabin-boy, Jo, the kids, Rebecca and Matthew) we were alone, just the three of us again and, what's more, everybody else in Finland seemed to have pissed off too. We worked up the sort of wary tolerance that Randolph Scott, Yul Brynner and Jack Elam might have had (that is, not much at all) concentrating on stewing up beans, humming and tending the critter, but mainly just moving on and squinting.

When Baines sidled up and told me we were in danger of running out of gas, 'fer cookin' the vittles', I was mildly sceptical. As far as I could see, there was no real danger. But, like the Wild Bunch, we'd run out of things to do, except ponder the immense diversity of Nature and squabble, so Baines put on his most serious engineer's voice. 'I think we'll have to get hold of a new cap and distribution system for the gas.'

Bob was in immediate agreement. 'Yes, that's a good idea, we must.' I avoided their eyes. This was just boredom. Baines was itching to disassemble the entire gas system and rig one of his Heath Robinson lash-ups, I could tell. And, for some reason, I resented the irrelevance of it.

'I'll just get it done, shall I? We might run out of gas, and then we can rig this up,' he said.

'No, no,' I snapped, brusquely, my father again, treating the two of them like twelve-year-olds. But then, in my defence, your honour, they was behaving like twelve-years-olds. They wanted to play gas now, and I'd been forced to harden my heart against all forms of inane frivolity. So I had to shoot 'em.

When we got to that evening's anchorage in the even more remote Skelige Island, six or seven ferries from Turku, I made a half-hearted effort to sort out 'the problem'. Perhaps because she was further out in the islands, the Skelige harbour mistress was even more solicitous for our welfare than the Nasby one.

She went to fetch her car and drove us half a mile to knock up a large woman in big trousers, who waddled about, peering into cages, reaching for a staggering variety of gas bottles and fittings. None of them matched our requirements. We thanked her and turned away. 'Do you think she makes her own gas?' Bob asked, quietly.

It took quite an effort to persuade the harbour mistress to go back home and look after her children. But she reappeared half an hour later with an electric stove. Then she offered to let us come and cook in her kitchen. Bob seemed keen. But I had to reassure her that we would survive the night.

In the early evening, Skelige was lit with a Samuel Palmer gold. It was a three-road island: one fork in the middle, and three branches that went nowhere. We strolled up into it, now like the baddies in *High Noon*, over the rolling hillocks and past the huge, Nissen-hut stones, through coppices laden with cob nuts and between the outlying buildings of three farms, but we saw no one. The gas lady and the harbour mistress had gone. At one point, far away, we spotted a farmer, but he glanced at us and hurried indoors.

'Perhaps he thinks we want to steal his gas,' said Bob.

Åland, reached the next day, was the furthest outpost of the Finnish Archipelago and the end of wandering. It was a large island, big enough to register on every map. Thirty miles beyond it, across the open sea, lay Sweden and the approaches to Stockholm. People spoke Swedish in Åland, but they had elected to become part of Finland.

Every sailor we met went 'ahhh' when it was mentioned, but it seemed they weren't going 'ahhh' about the main town Marie-hamn. They must have been going 'ahh' about the island and all the other islands around it. Mariehamn was an unprepossessing grid of twentieth-century shops, offering various ways of enjoying yourself somewhere else. There were mountain bike shops, canoe-ing shops, hiking shops and great outdoors shops. The fishing shops displayed photographs of men in baseball caps hugging dead fish. (After you'd spent hours dragging a mammoth salmon from the river, you spent some time cuddled up with it and then got a photographic record of your relationship.)

We had entered Åland by the back door, coming across a 6-mile-wide inland lagoon to a tiny canal across an isthmus. It was blocked by a swing bridge. We looked up at the control tower. There was no one in it. We drifted in front of it. There was a big blue sign in Finnish.

'What do you think it says?'

Bob squinted at it. 'There's a number. Ten. It must open at ten past.'

'Or ten o'clock,' said Baines.

'Well, it wouldn't open just once a day, would it?'

No. But ten past went by and it didn't open. In the end, mysteriously, it opened on the hour. The number we had seen referred to the month it changed its opening times.

We tied up in a marina on the shallow side of the island. The ferry companies operated out of Åland and in the winter they stored their unused boats there. These were in winter storage already. It was 12 September. The weather remained calm and sunny, but I wanted to press on. We had one more obstacle to confront before we could relax in the shelter of Swedish waters. This was no great leap, a mere 30 miles of open water, but it was off Åland, out in the mouth of the Gulf of Finland, that the *Estonia*, an Estonian-registered ferry, had foundered in a storm.

'The crew used her badly,' Ola told me later. 'She was not designed to go into those huge waves and they were supposed to slow down, but they pressed on and the crashing of the waves on the bow doors burst them open.'

Everywhere we went in that late season, there had been little reminders of the disaster. A monument on the end of the eastern Estonian Islands. Willi, the Estonian Customs man, had been called out, but it had been too late to help anyone. A Dutchman we met early on in Denmark had mentioned it too. He and his wife had been to St Petersburg on a sister ship. As they sailed past the very spot where she sank and everybody drowned, it was pointed out on the tannoy.

The *Estonia* may have been going too fast, the bow doors may have caved in, but what sort of a storm was it that could overwhelm one of those huge boats? The weather was preternaturally good at present. But the longer it lasted, the more it seemed to be shortening the odds. Surely, like a stretched rubber band, the whole thing would suddenly twang back with the force of a huge tornado. And then what chance would a little boat like ours stand? In a few months, no more than ten weeks, this whole area would be frozen solid, but now the trees were all crinkled and dead, not from the usual effects of autumn but from the effects of the unnatural heatwave. The weather, let's face it, was curious for this time of year.

And the *Estonia* had gone down on 28 September, a mere fortnight away.

45. Swedish Neutrality

What a fuss. As it happened, we crossed without incident, in billowy seas, and, by the end of the morning, were slipping through the outlying islands of Sweden. It was grey, it hadn't been grey for six weeks; over forty days of unblemished blue sky. Now the light made the granite banal.

Eventually, the broken land closed in. The route became riverine. We were still 60 miles from Stockholm, but mysterious structures started appearing on the banks ahead. At first, I took one of these things to be a glamorous public building, perhaps a university, or an award-winning electronics factory, but, as we got closer, I could see that what I had assumed were regular formations of windows, in strict geometric form, some fine example of modern Swedish design, were the lattices of walkways and the gangplanks of drive-on ramps. It was a ferry park and as ugly as sin close to.

Now there were houses amongst the trees: less scattered and more exuberant than Finnish lodges. Clearly, land was beginning to be at a premium around here. The houses were more visible. They were grouped into settled areas. Less part of an organic landscape, the houses were 'in' rather than 'of' the scenery. We were approaching a city, but unlike the Thames or the Humber or the Hudson River, the population here had noticed, early on, that these islands were an asset. If there were oil refineries and big things with chimneys they'd hidden them somewhere else. The approaches to Stockholm were charming, neat and suburban, much like the Swedes themselves.

Overnight in Vaxholm was like tying up in Thames Ditton or Weybridge. The Friday-night rush hour was just ending. The bars were full. Unlike Helsinki, where we'd occupied a sort of quarantine island, here we were, in the middle of ordinary prosperity. We could slip on a cloak of invisibility for the first time in months.

We blew on in the next morning, through dinghy races, river buses and ferries. The dragon backs of wooded outcrops continued to undulate past on either side, but now they were decorated with show-off houses and whole suburbs. Suddenly we were right in the middle of Stockholm, mugged by traffic and tourists.

We found a berth between the Vasa Museum and the fairground, next to that now-familiar anomaly, a Swiss yacht.

Jo had flown over to join us. God, I'd missed my wife. There are some traveller-writers, disciplined men all, whose principal delight, as they light off for the territory, appears to be the clack of the garden gate behind them. But I've always preferred Eric Newby and his attachment to his wife Wanda. I'd seen all these wonderful things in the company of a couple of blokes. I'd had to be jokey and cynical for days on end. But I'd really wanted to sit and say nothing with my wife. Circumstances meant that she hadn't been able to come for a lot of it, but now she was joining us for a week. I was ecstatic. She arrived at the dockside and I opened the door of the taxi and greeted her with all the exuberance and passion I could command.

'Oh, hello. Everything OK?'

We went and discreetly held hands across the gravad lax in the nearest place we could find for lunch. This was in the Vasa Museum. The principal, indeed, almost the only exhibit was an entire sixteenth-century ship, built originally as a showpiece for the Swedish King by a Dutch boat builder. The *Vasa*, a huge sailing boat, had fallen over unexpectedly and sunk. I shouldn't go to these places. They only increase my latent sea-anxiety. The boat had only gone about 200 yards when a bit of breeze heeled it over, water came in the open gun ports, and the whole lot went down to the bottom of Stockholm harbour. It says something for the depth of the gorges between the islands, which are no more than a few hundred yards wide, that the ship was completely lost for the best part of 500 years before somebody decided to have a go at getting it out. They had built the Vasa Museum to house the wreck.

It is odd to think of the Swedes as a warrior people. After all, the Swedish model, periodically brought to the table of civilized debate, is a neat and well-planned one, with little trees and plenty of taxes paying for advanced social services. But after the Danes had raped and pillaged their way to Vladivostock – sorry, traded their way to Vladivostock, invading Gotland (to sell cheese presumably), building a massive fort which became Tallinn (to establish a few Celtic jewellery stores) and driving their long boats right the way through to the Black Sea (for the purposes of swapping Danish open sandwiches for furs), the Swedes in the seventeenth century decided they'd have a go. Under Gustav II, admired by Napoleon as the equal of Hannibal, Alexander and Caesar (a dangerous criminal in other words), they went foraging around the Baltic, extending as far as Novgorod, and joined the Thirty Years' War. For two centuries, the Swedes were a great European power.

For now, Jo and I went to stay in a cool hotel. There was a row of buttons in the gloomy lift marked 'Funk', 'Hip-hop', 'Jazz' and so on. I studied them. Our key said number seventy-four. Which music was that? 'Rap'? I made a face, counted seven and pressed the button. The music changed to rap.

'The floor numbers are over here,' said Jo, pointing to the other side of the lift.

Because the hotel was cool, the room was grubby, smelly and tiny, and the only thing I wanted, after the boat, was a bit of space.

46. Swedish Manoeuvres

We could have closed a loop now. Nynäshamn, the southern ferry point for Stockholm, lay some 25 miles ahead of us. We were only a short sail from Karlskrona, where we had been in July. Instead, we were going inland, by the Göta Canal. We were going to avoid the exposed coast and put our nautical trust in the mountains. But we had our own encounter with the mighty Swedish navy to experience before we did so.

The sun was a faint glow in a grey sky. A shivery breeze blew out of a cold-looking horizon, humpy with islands. Out of Dalorö, south of Stockholm, we hauled up all the sails and slid along at 3 knots. The sounds were largely deserted, and as the wind increased during the morning, we sailed into it, tacking down between the islands of Muskö and Utö, not intending to try to get far that day, and still no real distance south of the capital. We were happy to move sedately on.

Naturally, each tack took us close in to the shore, trying to carve a little more off our distance. As we skirted in on the port tack, I noticed that, in front of us, there was a half-hidden, deep entrance between the rocks. There were yellow boards to either side of it. We had no idea what they said, but they were clearly warning us not to enter.

'Ah!' I said over-dramatically. 'That must be the entrance to the secret hidden Swedish naval base; underground hospitals, machine-gun nests, missiles, and what-not.' I had been warned about this place in Dalorö, by Steppan. With his under-chin beard and comical distraction, Steppan had been like one of the tortured, angular Swedes standing on black mountains in pictures in the Atheneum in Stockholm, except that thankfully he had his clothes on. He was a boat builder and wanted to inspect *Undina*. He had run a finger with a broken nail over my charts and pointed out the dangers of the route ahead. 'I saw red and green buoys and went ahead,' he told me. 'But then a patrol boat came out and escorted me away. It's silly, really.'

Naturally, we reached for the binoculars and peered into the piratical chasm in the rocks, but there was nothing to see, though we were, by pure happenstance, about to sail straight into it, if we didn't turn about. So we did turn about, and 200 yards off the mysterious entrance we flapped around and headed off for the other side of the channel some 2 miles away.

The Swedes had always taken their defences seriously, especially in the 1970s and 1980s. In Karlskrona, half a floor of the Maritime Museum was given over to the 'incident' of 1981 when a Russian Whiskey-class submarine had been discovered amongst the rocks just north of the town. In fact, much to the embarrassment of the Russians, it had been discovered on top of the rocks just north of the town – the captain had taken a wrong turning in the dark and put himself aground. (It can happen surprisingly easily, in my experience.) There was great excitement amongst the Swedes, who offered to help to tow the stricken vessel off. They managed to bring a tug alongside and, using a hidden Geiger counter, found that the submarine had nuclear potential, something hitherto strenuously denied by the Russians. The Red Navy were left with red faces, but, more than that, it rather tended to confirm the hawkish, paranoid tendency in Swedish politics. They had been claiming that Russian submarines were operating all through the archipelago. There were even submarine-sail sightings in the middle of Stockholm. As a result of the incident, strategy was tightened up, the Swedes paid even more taxes and the right wing got a bit of a boost.

I didn't feel I wanted to put the whole system to the test. But, eventually, of course, we had to tack again and we headed across the intervening miles back towards the mystery island and the hidden naval base once more. This time a good deal further south. The chart was dotted with warnings and purple lines. On the C-Map a pattern of illuminated bombs came up. But I realized, with a little start, that, completely by accident, we were heading straight into another entrance to the top secret lagoon.

'Er, I think we should come about again, soon,' I said to Bob.

'We've still got quite a lot of water under us.'

'Yes, but there are only two major entrances on this side of the secret island and for some reason we have sailed right into the middle of both of them.'

'There doesn't seem to be anybody about. Who's going to know if we go in a little further, pop straight out and carry on?'

'Well, honestly. They'll be watching us on the radar, probably.'

'They could be watching us from over there.' Baines pointed south.

Some 4 miles away, there was an interesting shape hugging the grey water. I looked at it closely through binoculars. It was a warship: a nice modern big one too, with mottled camouflages in an appealing blue, grey and black.

'Ready about then!'

The ship continued to hold its station and we laboriously zig-zagged our way further south and towards it. A Chinook helicopter passed over. We could see it some miles further on, out to sea, hovering for long periods.

'Well, there we are,' said Bob. 'It's obviously there doing something with the helicopter.'

Obviously it was. And, now, inexorably, we seemed in imminent danger of tacking into the side of a top secret Swedish warship. I mean, that's the nature of tacking. The wind decides your course. One zig had taken us well to the stern, but now as we came about, it looked very much as if our zag would take us close to the bluey-black behemoth.

'Oh, good!' said Bob and Baines. 'We'll get a close-up look at it.'

'Yes, but they might not like us doing that.'

'Why not? We're their allies.'

'No, no, They're not part of Nato. And you . . .'

I looked across at Bob. He was sitting at the helm wearing

his cold-weather gear: his new Russian submariner's reefer jacket and his new Russian submariner's hat, with flaps, which were blowing about in the breeze. He looked convincingly like a Russian submariner in need of a shave.

'They won't be able to see us,' he said.

'See us,' Baines snorted. 'They'll probably be radioing us to complain about our choice of music on the stereo, with all the equipment they have on there.'

'Actually, can I complain about the choice of music? Have we got anything else except Groove Armada?' said Bob.

'And with the sort of binoculars the modern navy can afford, they'll be studying your uniform with intense interest, Bob.'

Bob started singing a feeble fake Russian song. It was clear they weren't going to let us get too close, anyway. The stern of the boat foamed again and it moved back a couple of hundred yards.

'There's no sign of activity at all,' said Bob.

He was wrong. Looked at more closely, through our own binoculars, not very expensive or state of the art, I could clearly see a crew hanging out on the flying bridge watching us. We sailed a good half-mile in front of their bow. Then their guns swivelled.

'Well, look at that,' said Bob, 'the gun has turned round and is pointing right at us.'

I looked. Unbelievably, K23 had turned its forward armament in our direction. I reached for the binoculars again. The men on the flying bridge had all disappeared.

'It's obviously just the captain having a little joke. What shall we do?'

'Run up a white flag,' said Baines.

Recently, the Russian archives have been opened. It has been possible to take another look at Russian intentions in the Swedish Archipelago. Yuri Andropov was asked at the time of the Whiskey incident how he would react if the Swedes had more openly challenged some of the sightings. He replied, 'It would suit us very well if the Swedes used live ammunition against the intruding submarines.' This was a bit of a stumper, but it has now been claimed that most of the foreign submarines were, in fact, British or German. It is said that Nato was so concerned about the capabilities of the Swedish armed services, that they had engaged in secret operations to test them out, by smooching around in their own submarines. Margaret Thatcher herself gave her agreement to their deployment. It is alleged.

In 1995 the Swedish navy admitted that most of the signals were of unarmed minisubs. And conspiracy theorists like to point out that twelve naval officers publicly attacked Olof Palme for his politics four months before he was assassinated.

47. The Canal of Doom

For 1,000 miles we had gazed on fir trees. Every rock, every hillock, every island, every shore, every knoll, every-bloody-where had bristled with the unrelenting pine. Lumber is us. We had become sombre ourselves. Sombre, gloomy, thick and bristly. So it was a shock to come to Mems, at the entrance to the Göta Canal. Beyond a neat, miniature stone-built gate and a placid lock, the waterway ran off through a rural, fat, pale green land. The autumn sun glowed on mown meadows and faded ash leaves. There were cows, hay ricks and an aura of bucolic fruitfulness, but, as far as I could tell, no taxi rank.

Ryanair, conveniently for us, flew Stockholm-bound passengers to an airport a long way south of the capital, 30 miles from Mems. Eventually we found a taxi. Jo was going back to England, Patrick, an actor, was coming out. I was apprehensive. No voyage was so rough, no berth so small, no quick trip to the shops so mundane, but Patrick had the appropriate costume. He had once helped me with a charity performance in Windermere. We got back to Euston, after a Sunday-working-on-the-line Virgin Rail journey. Shortly before we arrived, he had disappeared. He stepped out further up the platform in a primrose blouson, navy draw-string pants and canvas hat: his splendid 'alighting from the train' gear.

At the airport I fretted. I expected a trunk and bearers at least, but we almost missed him at the change-over. He had managed to restrict his luggage to what he was able to carry in his hands. 'Well done, Patrick!' I said.

'What?'

'Lovely to see you.' And it was. He was the best sort of friend: an old friend.

I was glad to be at Mems. We had made it to the canal with days to spare. Another week and it would have closed for the season.

By the time our own Thomas Telford had finished helping build it for the Swedes in 1808 (although the statue in the canal town, Motala, is of a Swede, who seems to have taken all the credit), the railways had come and rendered the whole thing obsolete. It rendered itself obsolete quite effectively for most of the year, anyway, by freezing solid as soon as the winter came. But we were nearing the end of September. It was no time to be yachting in the Baltic. The ditch across the middle of Sweden would do, and it was reputed to be exquisitely beautiful as well.

We passed through Sweden's scenic potential on the way to the airport, swooping and dipping over a humped agricultural landscape, with enough natural boulders, lumps of rocks and, yes, brooding pines to add a wild edge. On the way back, Bob was lighting a fag and suddenly coughed with delight.

'An elk!' he cried. 'Oh yes. In the headlights up at the edge of that field.'

'Are you sure it wasn't a sheep?' asked Patrick.

'There are too many elk,' said the driver. He was utterly unexcited. 'You have to be careful at night, you know, you can just drive into them, in the road.'

'Can we do that later?' asked Bob.

Eena, who was our lock-operative, and rather beautiful, was waiting for us in a woolly hat and lifejacket, the next morning. She went over to the Göta Canal shop – a hut on the bank – and ceremoniously unlocked it. I stood by, while she sorted out some maps and instructions. I owed her £800 already. It was what they charged for the canal. I bought a bundle of ropes, an extra fender and a chart, but her credit card machine wasn't working. 'You can pay at the next stage,' she said with Swedish practicality.

'Thank you, Eena.'

Bob was in the corner collecting teddy bears in blue jumpers and polo shirts, covered with Göta Canal logos.

'Would you like to go back to the boat and get breakfast? We'll be leaving soon,' I suggested.

'When I've done my shopping,' he replied.

We would have to show off our infamous mooring skills to the world – well, to Eena and the other canal straggler who was making the journey with us: Morton the Hunter, from Norway. 'I just want to do one thing,' I said, stopping Bob on the return to the boat. He looked at me like Sergeant Wilson used to look at Captain Mainwaring.

I gave him the bundle of rope I'd just bought. 'Now, show me you can throw a rope.'

'Why?' he said.

'Because none of us can throw ropes.'

Bob regarded me steadily. 'I spent hours trying to lasso that pole in Denmark, remember.'

'Yeah.' I did. I thought that proved my point. But Bob thought he had acquired the wrangling skills of a Calgary Rodeo hustler.

'I discovered that you mustn't throw it all, you have to keep some back,' he said.

'Just throw it!'

'You bastard!' He threw the coil of rope from some ten yards away. It sailed across and hit me in the face. 'See!'

Behind us, Eena was unlocking the cover of the gate. Morton was moving up towards the lock. Patrick came up on deck wearing a striped blue pullover, short chinos and some sort of burnt orange smock.

'We all need practice,' I went on.

Baines stood ready to throw, theatrically wincing, 'because of his bad arm'.

'What arm?'

'I've got a bad arm.'

'So have I. A frozen shoulder,' said Patrick.

'Yes, OK, Patrick.'

The rope went vertically straight up into the air, coiled around itself and landed back on the deck.

'Well, let's not bother with this now,' I said encouragingly. 'They're opening the gate.'

Morton smiled and waved, as we let him go first in his 20-foot wooden motorboat. It was a pretty little clinker-built, varnished thing. He was a carpenter. 'I have taught myself all the trades, you know, building. I have all the . . .'

'Tools?'

'No . . . for exams.'

'Certificates.'

'That's right. It means I am an independent man. I can work wherever I want in the world, you know. Portugal.'

He had a great admiration for Portugal, partly because of the liberal democracy and enlightened political climate but mainly because of the weather. He intended, at some point, to live and work there, 'because I can build my own house and do everything'. While he was thinking about it, he had bought himself this new boat, for fishing, and was taking it home to Oslo with silent Jorg, his crew, who did all the rope work. Unlike us, Morton happily admitted he knew nothing at all about boats. He had been intending to go through the canal the day before, but had arrived at Mems and confused the entrance to the canal with the entrance to the river. He had motored 5 miles up to Söderköping by mistake, believing it was the canal all the way until he got there. We were impressed. This was the sort of mistake we expected to make ourselves.

There was another boat on the other side already, a big boat made out of cement with a hand-made pilothouse and a bald, smug sort of skipper squiring two short, fat ladies. He was waiting to go on, and the fat ladies were looking impatient.

One member of the crew needed to be on shore, to take the ropes and pass them back to the boat. Bob volunteered. We were, at this stage, going upwards, eventually by some hundreds of feet, but to begin with by a mere twelve. Baines readied himself.

The observant would have noticed that Bob, with his recently acquired skill for throwing ropes, had placed himself in the receiving position, whereas Baines, who lacked Bob's aptitude, and, apparently, had something wrong with his arm, had placed himself in the throwing position. But then, we were many things, but rarely observant.

We motored in. It was deep-sided. Baines drew himself up to his full height, swung his manky arm and, with a low moan of pain, threw the rope to Bob. Bob missed it. It fell back into the dock with a splash.

The boat was drifting away from the side of the lock, into the path of Morton from Norway, who was watching us, the experienced mariners, with intense interest.

I made a short observation. It was intended to galvanize the pair. Both of them looked at me. Baines gathered the rope, threw it again. Bob decided to put his cigarette in his mouth, in order to free both hands. This time he caught it. We shouted encouraging support. Bob pulled a bit, then knelt, with the end of the rope in one hand, and fiddled with a large metal ring on a bolt. He carefully adjusted his fag from his hand to his mouth, examined both ropes, eventually chose one of them and started pulling it through.

'Bob!' I shouted. He looked up, like a man disturbed while doing a particularly difficult crossword. 'I think it might be better on a ring further forward.'

He looked around. 'Oh, OK,' he said. He spent a few minutes unthreading his rope, moved on vaguely, spent a few more minutes rethreading it, grunted with satisfaction and in a leisurely manner dropped it back to Baines below him. He stood up and wiped his hands.

I breathed out with a low noise. 'OK. Now we have to do the stern!'

Bob looked around and lit another fag. He cracked his knuckles.

After a few more minutes of threading and debate, we were tied up. We turned to Eena, who was standing on the lockside. There was a sort of weird, glazed expression on her face.

'All right?' shouted Bob.

Morton, Jorg, the fat women and the smug captain all seemed fascinated by us. Eena eventually blinked, shook herself, as if waking from a coma, and turned away to press a button. The lock gates behind us hydraulically rammed themselves shut, nearly catching on our ensign pole. There was a gurgling. Vast gouts of water eddied and swirled, and the boat rose up a few feet. We were through the first lock. Only fifty-eight more to go.

Eena seemed rather keen to press on. She pointed to a little black car. 'That's my grandmother's car, the one with the big dent. I ran into one of these.' She pointed to a granite bollard. 'A bollard,' we chorused, forgetting, for a moment, to marvel at the Swedish command of nuance and vocabulary. 'Yes, a bollard. Anyway, I'll see you at the next lock, won't I?'

'Yes, of course, Eena.'

We joined the back of a convoy and pootled on at about 5 miles an hour. A short while later, she shot past, in a cloud of dust.

'She's a doctor – well, training to be a doctor,' said Patrick. 'She's off to Stockholm on the three o'clock train this afternoon, to go drinking with her friends.'

'Three o'clock?' I looked at my watch. It was half past eight. 'Well, she must be expecting to get through all these locks quite quickly.' There were eight locks and six bridges that day. But we were moving along. At least we were for a while.

Söderköping was the next lock. Patrick had just been showing me his new Adolfo Dominguez yachting shoes. He suddenly jumped ashore in them.

'We'll only be a few minutes in the lock, Patrick!'

'I know, I know. Just going to get some milk.'

'Is that wise?'

'Breakfast.'

'Keep the boat in sight!'

It took about sixty seconds for the lock gates to open. Morton went straight in. After a moment's hesitation, so did we. Bob improved his rate of rope and ring identification, and we were through in minutes, basking in Eena's approval. Morton and the other boat chugged off around the corner, moving swiftly on to the next lock. I dithered. 'Er . . . just a moment.' I found my mobile phone. 'Where are you?'

'The supermarket was a bit of a distance,' purred Patrick.

'No, no,' I said. 'Forget the shopping, just get back to the boat. If we miss the next lock, Eena will leave us to freeze here in a lump of ice through the winter.'

There was a roar. Eena screeched up in her grandmother's car. She leaned out of the window. 'Are you stuck?'

'No, no,' I bleated. 'Er . . . We were just getting a spot of breakfast.'

Eena looked perplexed.

'I'm sure he'll be here in a few minutes,' I said, looking down the canal path.

'I could bring him in my car.' Eena was looking at her watch again.

'Would you?' I said. 'Would you, it would be most awfully kind of you.' The fenders squealed, we pushed off and motored on.

'It's supposed to be a 5-knot speed limit,' said Baines.

'She said we should go as fast as we can,' I told him.

'Doesn't she care about the bank erosion?'

'Not at the moment.' We pushed up to our limit of about 7 knots. 'See, look at that. This boat used to do 7.2 knots under motor but all this Russian militaria is weighing us down.'

The banks were lined with chestnut and oak trees, tinged with the faint yellow of early autumn. Our dirty brown wash rose in a wave and surged along. Ducks squawked and flapped out of our way. We came around a bend and the other two boats were already slowing down in front of a swing bridge ahead of us. My mobile rang. 'Ah, Patrick . . .'

'Where are you?' he said.

'About three miles further down the canal.'

'What?'

'No, it's OK. You can get a lift with Eena.'

'Oh. Can I? Oh yes. No. That's all right then. I can see her little car.'

In five minutes, he stepped down on to the boat with milk, bread and a packet of Swedish meatballs in a plastic tub. 'Pretty girl.'

'Yes.'

The bridge swung upwards.

'Actually, I've got an idea.' Patrick put the supermarket bags on the cockpit seat. 'Why don't I go with Eena in the car up to the next lock and I can meet you there and be ready to take the ropes and things?'

'Fuck off.'

'Oh, because . . .'

'Fuck off!'

'It would be quite simple . . .'

'Go and make the breakfast.'

'You're only jealous.'

'Yes.'

Patrick went below to make an excellent breakfast.

We progressed in stately convoy through the Göta Canal. After several more locks we were getting moderately efficient.

'Not according to Eena,' said Bob.

'How do you mean?'

'Well, she thought we were being a bit slow.'

'Slow, us? But we're going just as fast as the other boats, aren't we?'

'We're always the last in.'

'We have to be the last in, Bob, we're at the back of the queue.'

Some bridges swung up, some trundled backwards. After a morning spent waiting for traffic lights and working out the system, we had reached Lake Roxen.

'Goodbye,' said Eena breathlessly, as she hurried out of our lives, to get her train to Stockholm.

We were parked by a place straight out of an American film, under the shade of a tree on a huge dirt car park. The owner of the café imported bespoke cowboy boots from the Philippines and sold home-made brushes.

Eena told us that we had to cross Lake Roxen and wait for the night at the other side, so, in the middle of the afternoon, we set off, a motorized crouton in a bowl of pea soup. There was not a breath of wind. The water was thick with algae. It was so still that

the wake spread out in a ridge stretching behind us and off to the
bank about a mile away. Gradually, the lake widened. Far to the
south we saw a big town with spires.

'That's it,' said Bob. He was waving an electric mosquito racket
at the swarm of 6-foot-long gnats trailing in the exhaust fumes.

'What?'

'Berger, the town.'

'No it's not.'

'Well, it could be.'

'It must be,' said Patrick.

I looked at the map. 'No, no. That's er . . . well I don't know
what that is, but Berger . . .' I looked at the map again, '. . . it's got
about three houses and it's somewhere ahead, directly west.'

'That's west-ish.' Bob and Patrick were leaning over the side,
peering intently at the distant prospect.

'That's south.'

They continued to keen after the phantom Berger, until tiny
Berger itself became just about discernible in the corner of the lake
straight ahead.

It was a group of houses, a low lake wall of stones, some swans
and a ladder of locks. We tied up to a wall at the bottom of the
ladder and Bob and I walked up the steps of locks, rising past grass
slopes under big trees. After counting six, we came to a pool with
canal boats and pleasure craft. Five more locks went on beyond
there. 'We're going to be in Berger most of tomorrow, then,'
I said.

The showers were locked. The tourist restaurants at the top of
the ladder, where a main road crossed the canal, were all closed. It
was cold and grey. The boat rocked against the fenders. The fenders
squeaked, and the lake water was black and freezing.

'That other place we saw wasn't far away, though, was it?'

A taxi driver took us to Linköping for an excellent meal. Bob
leaned over the wine-list. He had once dealt in bin ends for his
friends, going to Christie's and buying job-lots of wines, some
without labels, or their caps, or deformed bottles, and got huge

bargains, which he then divided into boxes and sold on to people. During these transactions, he told us, he'd learned that Château Haut-Brion was in fact an Irish-owned Château: it was the French pronunciation of O'Brien.

'Bollocks!'

'It's true.'

'Oh, yeah? This is like that stuff about the Pope.'

'What stuff?'

'You said that the puff of smoke from the Vatican was the cardinals burning the dead Pope's genitals to prove that he hadn't been a woman.'

Bob looked amazed. 'You're not saying that's not true?'

'What was that other one?' Baines leaned forward. 'About koi carp being trained by the Japanese.'

'You've obviously never shared a bath with koi carp.'

'You should bring out a book: *Bob's Book of Unbelievable Facts*.'

'I should. Excuse me.' Bob was smirking at the twenty-year-old wine waitress.

'Leave her alone, Bob. She's not going to know, is she?'

But we were in Sweden. The wine waitress had been to college for three years to study wine waitressing. She was a trainee mistress of wine and had a reference library and an encyclopedia which she brought to the table. 'No, I'm afraid it doesn't say anything about this. It seems to be Haut-Brion,' she told us firmly.

'Well, there we are,' Bob said, after she had gone to another table.

'What?'

'The encyclopedia only went back to the mid-eighteenth century. Undoubtedly this Irish business had all happened before then.'

48. The Ride Across Lake Vättern

We felt we were being sucked down the narrow canal now, down towards the end. It was cold the next day. Meyruga was our new mobile lock-keeper.

There was something absurd about a sailing yacht gradually inching into the middle of Sweden. To get to Gothenburg we were going to climb over ranges which were mountains rather than hills. Sometimes, curious onlookers stood with their bicycles and watched us pass through their inland villages in our fisherman's clothing, with bemusement.

We were informed, in the severe handbook of canal etiquette, to switch off our engine inside the locks. So, as we entered the ladder, we did, and began manhandling the boat through each gate and on into the next walled box. We got one rope from the stern, one from the front, and then heaved, as the lock gates opened, manfully wrapping the warps across our backs, tottering forward as the boat suddenly gathered way and then, unmanfully, scrabbling with our feet to stop the massive thing going further than we wanted.

'Is that a beard, Bob?' Patrick stood with his arms up in surrender, looking for somewhere to wipe off the rusty slime from a ladder.

'I thought I'd see what happened.' A grey Axminster had begun to bristle over his chin. Patrick had arrived with a Worsted in full sprout.

'Of course, the saddest thing is that it comes out white now,' Patrick went on.

'Well, it doesn't look white.'

'Ah, that's thanks to "Mandrake". It's a two-can preparation,' said Patrick. 'You don't want to slap it on, just apply it gently.'

'Good God, Patrick!' Bob said.

'I knew you would be unsympathetic. It's not camp, it's my profession.'

'No, no, it's just that it's so effective, I'd never have guessed. How do you deal with the roots?'

As each lock filled, we rose 10 feet, then another. At the pool in the middle, we stopped and took a shower. Then on, until we reached a plateau; through fields, more locks and more bridges, even over a motorway at one point, more ramps of locks, more double locks. There was a sense of relentless progress. We were chugging on into the very heart of lovely, lovely Sweden.

By half past three we were close to Motala: the only boats on the cut, just us, and Morton in his little wooden ark, bobbing and swaying in our wake. The country passed by in endless variety: ash groves, rocky cuts crowned with juniper, low marshy wastes, stands of mountain ash and forests of fir. Birds of prey flapped out of branches and away from tree to tree, keeping their distance from us and then circling back.

'Was that an eagle?'

'Well, it must be.'

'It's a crow.'

'Oh, come on, Baines, use your imagination: a fish buzzard, at least, a canal harrier!'

'It was a Morton's vulture,' said Bob authoritatively.

These were places that were not exotic enough for Lunn Poly or dirty enough for Paul Theroux. They were fat, comfortable, ordered places, but sometimes so exquisite, so golden in the pale glowing autumn sun that it felt sinful to be there. After weeks of coast, it was restful to be sweeping gently through the heart of the countryside on a brisk autumn day. The last time I had been out like this was when I was at school, the season of short trousers and waiting at bus stops and going out to play football. The rest of my life I must have been indoors on autumn weekday mornings. We felt like we were bunking off.

Baines clumped down from the foredeck, folding away his mobile phone. 'That was my sister.' By coincidence she was sailing too. 'They're just going through the Suez Canal.'

'Any locks there?' asked Bob, now keen to investigate the sluices and locks of the world.

'Yes, I suppose so. They're worried about pirates.' Off Somalia and Aden, yachts are frequently chased by gun-wielding brigands in speedboats.

'Have you got a weapon aboard?' Patrick, who shot regularly at Bisley, inquired; as if there was a gun cupboard he had missed, somewhere, which we could break open in emergency.

'Certainly not,' I replied. 'Anyway, when Peter Blake got shot in Brazil recently, it was precisely because he had a weapon.'

'Ah, but you have to know how to use it,' said Patrick.

'No, no, more than that, surely,' I said. 'You have to know you could actually bring yourself to shoot another man dead. If you come from Hampstead and not the mouth of the Amazon, you might be capable of pulling the trigger, but your scruples would stop you.'

Patrick laughed. 'I think I'd be able to shoot a person dead. I've done it in enough mid-season mini-series, after all.'

Ironically, now that sailing was impossible, the engine was giving trouble. It was sensitive to the slightest change in torque. Any alteration in pressure, and a horrible juddering would seize the entire boat.

'What I think it is,' said Baines, 'is the folding propeller. One of the blades is canting in and it becomes asymmetric.' He would sit by the throttle control, listening out for the slight change in note that told him the thing was about to go nasty on us, and if it went, throw the engine into reverse and then straight into forward as if to catch the machinery unawares and coax it into operation, but it was a grinding, squealing procedure. I could feel the cogs crashing and the gears heaving into each other and protesting in pain.

Bob and I sat at the bow, thinking over the incredible distances we'd covered. 'Can you even remember Helsinki?' I asked him. He pulled his Soviet surplus reefer jacket closer around him. 'It's like when I was a child,' he said finally. 'I always thought that you lost any sense of time because everything was filled up, because it was all new. I suppose we've become the same.'

Meyruga abandoned us in Motala. We were told to cross Lake Vättern and wait overnight on the other side. The canal had been designed to take advantage of Sweden's network of inland lakes. Vättern was 30 or so miles of grey water, it would take us four hours to cross. The other side was way ahead, below the horizon.

We slithered from a little creek and out, on to the vast lake. As we left we could see rainstorms roaming across the waters like black ghosts. The sun was going down through a translucent watercolour of lurid, scudding cloud. The land was gradually blanked out by a white mist of drizzle creeping across the dark lake, past the conifer islands, wrapping them in gloom. It was atmospheric, to say the least. In fact, it was the atmosphere. We were inside a demonstration of the earth's vaporousness.

Morton had been worried about this stage of the trip. He was the one with the GPS. (Naturally, our electric chart didn't cover this bit and we had to rely on paper.) But he asked us to lead the way. The dodgy engine ran smoothly enough, but we started to creep ahead, so we stopped it and hoisted the jib. Now we matched Morton's pace, sailing out towards a half-way island, lashed by white breakers, with the little wooden motorboat rocking and wobbling behind us.

Far to the south-west, the sun set in a kind of postbox of cumulus: a somnolent, silent explosion. It dipped down and, for a few minutes, blazed on the underneath of the ranks of clouds, as if they were a low-vaulted roof; a tunnel of fire leading us towards our silhouetted destination. It was an improbable, apocalyptic vision. It was all just a little portentous. And, God, it was getting colder. We hunkered down.

As we approached the furthest bank, the inevitable happened. A moonless, utterly dark September night suddenly fell, and we were left, peering at a shore on which a hundred lights of some lakeside town began to twinkle, wetly, in the black.

I felt a familiar tingle of helplessness. It had been a long time since we had had to rely on simple, paper navigation and it was a strange shore. Many of the lake buoys were not lit at all. I was unprepared. I hadn't expected it to get dark before we got there, or, certainly, not so quickly and now it was raining quite heavily. It was difficult to see.

The lights to guide us in were all in front of that shore ahead. How far off were we? The canal was now an improbably tiny thing somewhere in the total wipe-out. And what was that huge, red light over to one side?

As usual, the street lamps, and the domestic lighting, cluttering the edge of the blackness, were more powerful than the navigation lights. Everything was twinkling. The waves were high and we were heaving through a freezing wind. After five minutes of peering through raindrops on the front of the binoculars, I finally worked out that the big red light was a filling station. The lighthouse marking a rocky point was dead ahead. We had certainly gone far enough towards the western shore. I told Baines to turn hard to starboard, to take us north and parallel to the coast. He did, but not the 45 degrees needed. I waited, but we weren't coming on to the bearing. I asked him to turn to starboard again. Again he did, but, perhaps, 5 degrees, and still not enough. Bob was below hunched over the chart. It was too wet and dark to bring the thing on deck. We were rocking about.

'Baines,' I said. 'We have to head north until the lighthouse light turns green. Then we will be past the point. It'll be safe to proceed west and into the shore again.'

We motored on for a few seconds. 'It's not going green at all,' said Baines.

'No, no, turn a bit more north.' I gave him the bearing again. Reluctantly we swung, bucking around. Eventually the light went green. 'There,' I said. We were safely to the north of the cape it marked. 'Now there should be a much smaller entrance light in the west.' It was somewhere in the mess of street lights on the shore. It marked our way in. I just caught it, an improbably tiny twinkle ahead. It was also flashing green.

'There! You see it?' I asked Baines.

It was another beacon, much less powerful than the lighthouse, but the same principle: one light with three colours arranged in a triangle. It was a simple enough system. If the light showed green we were too far to the right of the channel. If the light turned red we were too far to the left. If it shone a pure, steady white, we were on target.

At this juncture, though, we had slightly overshot. Rather than risk cutting any corners, we now needed to veer back to the south, so that we could follow the zig-zag into the channel. Keeping an eye on the light, I told Baines to turn to port, or south, again. We hardly turned at all. He swung the boat less than 3 degrees. 'No, swing more.'

'I can see the light,' he said, vehemently.

'I know, but it's still green, so we need to turn to port.'

'Come on!' he said loudly, 'Come on! Let's have this out, let's have it? If you turned round you can see that I have already turned this boat to port!' I did turn. He was tensed at the wheel and nodding vigorously.

I was taken aback. But we had been heading for this. Since Bob had put us on the rock I had taken absolute control and refused to trust them with the simplest of duties. Now I seemed to be directly contradicting what I had already just said, and we were having a 'we're-all-grown-men' spat.

'We're not on course yet. Turn harder to port,' I snapped back. I seemed to prevail. Baines pulled the wheel round and we rolled through the choppy black waters.

Suddenly Bob yelped, 'Is that a buoy?' He shone his torch. A blank pole loomed up, just a few yards away, topped by two conical markers. We veered away from it, missing it by yards. It marked an underwater rock.

We now knew exactly where we were; just outside the hazard and only just in the channel. We had turned to port enough. We fell silent.

Closing on the shore, the wind dropped. The lake became a pond. Crawling forward, in a moody silence, we shone torches into the darkness, flashing on unlit buoys and calling out directions. Some fifteen minutes later, we tied up, out of the wind, against the wooden frame of the long entrance dock to the canal. The first swing bridge was brightly lit and lay a few hundred yards ahead.

Morton moored up behind us and came sauntering up the towpath. 'You went right along the route of the GPS,' he said. 'You knew where you were going, then.'

Later, on the bank, heading off towards the main road (it was still only eight o'clock), Baines apologized. What did I do? I grunted something. There didn't seem any point in the two of us hugging and making up. In any case, that would be impossible for me. I had sunk into a childish mood of self-righteousness. For the time being, I settled back into my role as the big ape at the back of the cage, morosely squatting on a rock and occasionally scratching myself, while the smaller apes ran around jumping on the tyres and throwing bananas. Baines and I would settle into a wary, mutually respectful distance for a while. We were near the end of the trip. That's what had prompted the whole affair, after all.

'I think you should all congratulate me,' Patrick announced out of the darkness. 'I have found us a restaurant and they've prepared a table.'

49. Boiled Pony

Would Captain Scott have gone to restaurants? (Had there been any in Antarctica, of course.) I doubt it. I suspect home-prepared seal blubber was essential to his sense of adventure. He seemed to hanker after the tang of boiled pony. After all, he had planned to eat his equine transport from the get-go. This was not something I could justify or arrange. (Quite apart from the fact that we had dozens of unopened tins of ham sitting in a hole under my bed.)

We rarely ate on board in the evening. We were dismally attracted by the bright lights. As a result, we endured hardships that Captain Scott could never have imagined. We left perfectly good anchorages at dusk, to clamber through bramble thickets and over scrap-heaps in search of restaurants. Apart from a frightening Chinese meal in Norköping, we ate remarkably well. Sild in Sweden. Elk in Tallinn. Reindeer in Trollhättan. The only difficulty lay in making our collective mind up where to go.

My preferred strategy was to walk around the entire city, usually three or four times, until, by peering in through windows and staring at the menu and indulging in a sort of mystic communion with the table ware, some force compelled me in. The others were relatively patient with me, but only because they were equally fussy.

The next afternoon, a Saturday (although the days of the week had become meaningless), after crossing the great, silent lake of Vixen, a superb vinyl-topped pond, surrounded by forest, we were suddenly stopped in the middle of nowhere.

We hadn't expected this. As far I was concerned, this was a three-day trip, which would see us out of the Göta Canal system. But as we passed through a swing bridge just after twelve midday, and were sweeping on to the next lock. Bob pointed out a van keeping pace with us on the road that ran beside the canal.

'Isn't that today's lock opener?' he said. 'He seems to be waving at us.'

He was. He was waving frantically and slewing all over the road. We slowed. He screeched to a halt.

'We are finished today,' he shouted.

'No, no,' I shouted back. 'We have to get to Lake Vänern.'

'Tomorrow!' he shouted, put the little car into a three-point turn and roared away in a cloud of dust.

After passing through some of the most exquisite scenery in Europe, we were now abandoned in the only ugly bit on the whole canal – a dull town made up of a suburb of bungalows. It was three in the afternoon.

Patrick was optimistic. 'We'll go into town and find a hen party.'

Bob was chewing on a string of licorice. 'A what?'

'It's Saturday night. There is bound to be a party of lovely Swedish maidens celebrating a forthcoming wedding.' He had been studying the map. 'Mariestad,' he announced. 'Fifteen miles by car. There will be something there, I ween.'

'It doesn't look much bigger than the place we are in now.'

The place we were in now had exhausted its possibilities within three-quarters of an hour. It was a two-supermarket town and they both closed at two in the afternoon. It was so quiet that we watched a man get out of his car and go to the cash machine, leaving the engine running and the door open. Though what he wanted money for we couldn't guess. We enjoyed walking round one supermarket, but missed the other by five minutes. So we went to Mariestad to eat something. For the first half hour we wandered the freezing streets exercising a variety of theories.

'Where's the station? There's always something near the station,' said Patrick. We couldn't find the station, because it wasn't on a railway line.

Bob pointed to the local version of Blockbusters. It was crammed with people. 'That's what they do. They get a video and go home to eat pizza.' We pressed our noses against the window. 'Do we get to sail near here? We could drop off the DVD in the morning.'

We walked on towards a light at the end of the street. It was indeed a café. 'I have a rule. I never go into a café when the only people in it are the staff and they're sitting at the table, smoking,' said Patrick sagely. 'We should try up that way. I feel it in my bones.'

His bones were not entirely reliable. We stopped in a pub. I watched sporting disasters on the big television. Bob came over with a strange gleam in his eye. Unbelievably, there was a hen party sitting at one of the tables. A woman in a wheelchair was getting married the next morning. She was wearing her bridal hat and veil for the benefit of her two middle-aged friends.

Bob leaned over the bar. 'If we wanted to eat in this town tonight,' he said, 'how would we go about doing it, then?'

The large barman looked back at him. 'You would eat here,' he said.

'Oh, you can eat here?'

'Yes.'

'Yes,' said Bob. 'But what is the best restaurant in town?'

'This is the best restaurant in town,' said the barman.

'OK,' said Bob. The menu painted on a board behind the barman offered thirty different varieties of pizza. Bob didn't believe him. I did.

Ten minutes later Bob came over to where we were sitting in front of the big television. 'Well, I got to work on him,' he said. And he's given me the name of a place down by the lake, but he doesn't know if it's open at this time of the year. We'll have to get a wiggle on, because it's past nine already.'

So we set off. It was very quiet. I protested that the lake was unlikely to be up the hill, but Bob reckoned that we had to go over the hill to get to this place. We passed a hedgehog walking down the pavement.

'If we followed the hedgehog,' said Baines, 'we might at least get some milk and bread in a saucer.'

'Aha!' said Bob. He was pointing off to the left. 'I told you we would be all right.' Half-way down the street was a big pink sign. It was flashing neon and said 'Zoo'.

'What do you think?' said Patrick. 'A club? A sex bar? I knew the Swedes wouldn't let us down.'

We walked down towards it. It was a zoo. Or, in fact, a pet shop. But it was heartening because it indicated a residual grooviness. There were people here who liked the idea of buying pets from a shop that pretended to be a zoo. On the other hand, perhaps they didn't know what zoo meant. We certainly didn't. We thought it meant some sort of bizarre sexual entertainment.

We turned the corner, briskly, because it was cold, and walked straight into a restaurant. It was some sort of disused bank. There were torchères on the wall. The maitre d' was wearing a Nehru collar. Young people in good black clothing were sitting at widely spaced tables in the sort of discomfort that promised earnest modern cooking. Patrick, himself dressed in his finest linen blouson, Adolfo Dominguez draw-string pleated-front wool pantaloons and Romeo Gigli banded wool top with a little dog-ear collar, looked pleased with himself. This was a definite possibility.

We trooped in behind him. Bob was wearing the same grey pedal pushers that he had worn since Haapsalu, a filthy shirt covered in nude mermaids, oh, and a pair of aviator glasses, white clogs and his Russian reefer jacket, I was wearing a torn fleece and an oilskin and Baines was dressed as a rock-festival de-rigger.

No, they didn't have a table. No, not even if we had come off a boat from England that was working its way across the Swedish canal system. No, that table was reserved. No, there was nowhere else in Mariestad they would recommend.

Patrick blamed Bob. 'They took one look at you and turned us out.'

We left him still negotiating with the man in the Nehru jacket and moved on to an Italian up the road. It had a spare table and was as indifferent to the state of our clothes as it was to its own cooking.

It was busy. Next to us by the pillar was a big black American and a woman in a shell suit. Beyond the pillar were two long tables pulled together and, seated round them, eating spaghetti, were approximately thirty identical blonde girls aged about eighteen, giggling and chattering. While we sat and waited to order (and for Patrick, who was still up the road), one of the girls got to her feet and made a passionate speech. The others applauded and hugged and lavished kisses on each other and then a tall, grizzled gentleman, who looked a lot older than us.

The waiter was laying out knives and forks and a basket of six-year-old bread. Three more girls across the restaurant jumped up and embraced each other with squeals.

'They are football girls,' he said.

'Eh? Sorry, what?'

'Football girls who have won big match here for Mariestad. Champion football team. They come to make party.'

'Yes.'

Patrick came in. He was unimpressed with the restaurant, but seemed to forget his earlier disappointments. We had difficulty getting him to concentrate on ordering the food.

'You know what that lot are,' I said, noticing his gaze wandering. 'They're a girls' football team.'

'Yeah, yeah.'

'No. They are, Patrick. Patrick, would I lie to you? That is an entire team of girl football players.'

'They're not. You don't get me like that.'

'No, Patrick. We're not lying. They are female footballers.'

'Heh, heh, heh. You won't get me. They're not.'

There was the sound of a chair scraping back loudly. The large black guy on the table next door suddenly got to his feet and towered over Patrick. 'They're a football team, OK? Soccer. They kick balls around. You know?'

Patrick smiled weakly. 'OK. Yes. I'm sure.'

He was a soul singer from Gothenburg called J.B. After their initial shaky meeting, he and Patrick formed a distinct bond. Before we left the restaurant Patrick had made an arrangement to go and see J.B. earn his living in a dance hall next to the bus station.

The next morning I asked Patrick if the football team had put in an appearance.

'No,' said Patrick gravely. 'But the hen party did. She was a sweet girl, sweet.'

50. Revenge of the Elk

I had expected the equivalent of an Alpine lake, but the vast, dark, inland sea that was Lake Vänern seemed never to have been tidied up, or dotted with bland housing. The shores were a wilderness of forest. There were a few distant industrial chimneys and the odd dainty town. A castle gleamed whitely on a distant hill. But it seemed completely and utterly remote, only traversed by the occasional cargo ship. At the bottom, in a corner, a drain, the Trollhättan Canal, the exit to the sea, led to Gothenburg.

Our trip would end there, I'd decided. We had to find a yard. I was not going to take the boat out across the North Sea in October. I was going to leave her for the winter. We were tired of travelling. 'Let's hurry across Vänern.' But we had underestimated the sprawling monster. It was too far. We were forced to stop overnight.

We had finished the last stage of the Göta Canal on the Sunday morning. 'You were the quickest I've ever seen,' said the lock-keeper, gratifyingly. We drank our bottle of Russian champagne, by way of farewell to Morton, and then onward, onward, hard sailing, out into the blank, cold lake.

It had not been cold up until now. I mean, we thought it was cold, but then it got 'cold'. A film of wet condensation lay over the varnish. Grey drops poppled on the dorades. Fingers were unable to do the ropes. Layers of clothes went on: vest, thermal fleece, another fleece, big jacket, huge gloves. 'I'm still cold,' I moaned.

The first 'harbour' on the wooded shore was a dinghy park. So on, to another night entrance, another difficult-to-identify buoy, finally spotting the posts, port and starboard in the gloom, with everybody melancholy and quiet. We were low. We just wanted to get done. Eventually, we tied up at the end of a giant quay under a lonely industrial complex, where I worried that somebody was going to moor up, not notice us and crush us to bits.

Patrick calmed me down. 'I have just the thing,' he said.
'What?'

He opened a locker. 'The meatballs!'

We settled down to an evening of winter-comfort food.

The Trollhättan Canal was a far more serious waterway than the one we had left two days before. If the Göta was for narrow boats, Trollhättan was for wide ones. Large freighters and tankers came up to Vänern from the sea. It was no cosy tourist route. We didn't have to book in advance, it never closed. But in consequence we had no handy little booklets or instructions.

We came down upon the entrance, through the lake, on a gorgeous day, like a wary gun boat. All pairs of binoculars in our possession (that's two, and one was fuzzy in one eye) were trained on the canal, sizing up the massive road bridge at the entrance. The Trollhättan Canal was all bridges. We were in Sweden's industrial hinterland, criss-crossed by railway lines and motorways. There was no little person in a Noddy car running on in front of us and opening obstacles on cue. We had to radio ahead and announce we were coming and hope we didn't appear presumptuous, holding up the throbbing arteries of the Swedish economy while we sauntered down to the coast. But the bridges opened all right. Miraculously, they opened. Even without reaching for our radio, we could see the glinting windscreens and the tailbacks forming, and several thousand tons of road lifting up for us. We passed through. Then the massive gantries of a railway bridge swung open unbidden, and we passed through them too. There was no delay. We hardly slowed. We waved feebly like a jogger on a zebra crossing. In fact, because Trollhättan was part canal and part river, we began to go faster, riding on the current. Three hours later, we finally reached the first locks (after several more important bridges, including one which yanked the entire railway up two massive towers on either bank). The locks were quite gigantic, big enough to take a 150-foot boat, and deep enough to drop us way below the height of our mast. Here we paid our dues, while we waited for the lock to clear another boat below us, and then we dropped like a lift.

It was to be our last night on the move. We stopped by a little grove of horse chestnut trees overlooking a quiet stone quay.

As we walked the 'love path' to the town of Trollhättan (surely not literally the troll's hat place), we followed the course of the old river, which cascaded down past more failed locks, iron-age cairns and a beautiful gorge. After a visit to an Irish pub so that Baines could have a pint of Guinness, we went to the Hilton for a grim bar-snack. We had broken the only rule of the trip for the second time: 'Never take gourmet advice from an Irish barman.' But as we marched up the steps and into the bar lined with pale wood, we had another end in mind.

Bob stopped a passing waitress. 'I understand there is an elk for sale here,' he said.

'An elk?'

The south-eastern shores of Lake Vänern are elk country. There are reputedly more elk in the woods than anywhere else in Scandinavia and we had hoped to see gigantic herds of the graceful creatures, wading in the shallows and bellowing at the moon, but we were disappointed. The coast was too far away, the trees too dense. Having left the rural middle, we were back in pine country. But Bob had been told by the Irish barman that there was a stuffed elk for sale at the Hilton.

'Oh, wait,' said the waitress kindly, 'I think I know what you mean. In reception.'

It was a big and shiny hotel. Saab made their cars in Trollhättan and the hectares of marble were clearly polished by the expense accounts of the factory. We passed along a corridor panelled in orange wood. And there, standing in the window, was a complete stuffed elk. His nose was a long, sensitive, goofy proboscis. His eyes, though glass, were wan. He stood on ridiculous legs, thin and over-extended. He looked the least harmful large creature it was possible to conceive. Morton had finally decided to eschew his hunter existence (his rented forest and champion hunting dogs) after an epiphanous sunset moment the year before, when he had shot one of these clerical beasts, and instantly regretted it. I noticed that between the elk's delicate cloven feet there was a little card, so

I bent to examine it closer and, as I did so, I skewered my forehead on the pointed branch of his antlers.

I stepped back with a yell. The receptionist got to her feet. Bob reached for an anti-macassar from the back of a well-designed banquette seating unit. He stuck it to my forehead, to try and staunch the flow of blood. Baines reassured several Japanese car engineers that I was merely hysterical, while I rocked back and forth, apologizing to everybody. After a while the pain subsided. I sat back, breathing heavily.

'I'm sure we could have it shipped,' Bob said. 'It would look good in your barn.'

It was a Ridley Scott setting for our final morning. The sun shafted through a thick mist, which filled the river gorge like a big bucket of dry ice. Waking at eight, we drank coffee and waited for the birches on the far bank to shimmer golden through the fog. Patrick had plans to visit the Saab exhibition centre. He'd been a celebrity driver for Saab.

'I'm a friend of "On The Roof" Carlson,' he said.

It all sounded interesting, particularly the reconstruction of a Saab hitting a stuffed elk. But we wanted to get the boat to Gothenburg. So we left him in Trollhättan, where he could catch a bus to join us later, and just the three of us – Baines, Bob and Griff – cast off into the wavering river. We could just about see the further banks. The fog had coagulated into a large, pink-edged blob of vapour, hanging in the ravine.

'Deer!' Bob pointed to the bank. There were two deer watching us from a sparkling field by the water's edge. A second later, a fox. Another came and joined it briefly. They pricked their ears in our direction and bounded off. The current was pushing us now. We could suddenly move at a speed over 8 knots. *Undina* veered slightly from side to side in the eddies. The sun shone, the clouds were a superb, frosty, pink-tinged hue. Pairs of cormorants waited until we got alongside them and then launched themselves, dropping down until their wing-tips fluttered on the water, stretching their long, dark necks to push forward their beaks, circling away and across the river, round and behind us, back to their original perch.

Mini-mountains, red barns, the occasional white church with baroque grey spire-top. The flash of a car reflected on the nearby road. We went through a lock to a chorus of approval from a school party. 'That's why he said welcome,' I said.

'What?' said Bob.

'When you talked to him on the VHF, the lock-keeper said welcome,' I said.

'He was very enthusiastic,' agreed Bob.

'Because he had something to show the kids at last.'

Bob and Baines played conkers, sitting down, and, every now and again, Bob let out a howl, as he missed and whacked his kneecaps. Baines had a technique. He had clearly been a whiz with conkers, and he still was. It was a first term in the playground at break, sunny autumnal day experience. The fresh air brought back chapped knees and red cheeks.

I watched from my usual position, aloof, the daddy, plonked at the helm. And watched ruefully as the self-draining cockpit filled up with the white, squeaky, bitter fruit of the broken nuts.

At the last opening bridge, outside Gothenburg, there was no preordained, magic opening. We slid towards it, backed up and turned in the current. The lights remained obstinately red. They refused even to go to white and red, the signal that told us we had been acknowledged. After all the speed and rush, after all the headlong charging on, all the strict schedule and the early starts, it was as if Gothenburg was unwilling to let us finish and be done. As we turned upstream, we saw that a large blue freighter was coming up behind us, and they were only going to hold up the traffic once. As she came alongside, the bridge opened and five minutes later we tied up in Gothenburg, outside the Opera House, where Ola worked. It was finished.

51. The Cold Box

But it wasn't finished. We went back to Sweden in early October. Gothenburgers slithered through the rain across slimy streets in puffed coats, and ran for their scalding saunas. We, by contrast, were going sailing.

I had expected to deliver the boat to a yard for the winter. 'It's a few miles north,' Ola had told me, 'but Martinson can deal with it.' I had telephoned.

'So. Ha, ha, you are John Cleese.'

'Er . . . no.'

'John Cleese is a very funny man.'

'Yes.' It is better to agree in these circumstances. I assumed we would return to the subject of the boat at some time. Though we might have to take a detour around Benny Hill.

'I like Benny Hill too.'

'Good. Good. Yes. He's dead of course. And John Cleese doesn't have a boat.'

'No, but he is a friend of yours?'

There had been a measure of expectation in the voice.

'Yes, a very good friend. We almost live together. In fact, Mr Martinson, I can assure you that, were you to look after my boat, my very good friend John Cleese of English Comedy may very probably, at some unspecified time, pop over and be funny in your boatyard.'

I had sent a fax which listed the work that needed doing: the hull, the decks, the cabin sides, the leaks, the engine gearing, the broken stanchion, the scuppers, the lockers, the varnishing, the painting, the electrics, the mast, the fiddles, the heater extensions . . . Oh dear. I could have gone on, but I stopped. I added a postscript. 'Of course, I understand that you may not be able to do all of this, this season, but we will need to attend to the more urgent stuff.'

Mr Martinson's reply had been addressed 'TO THE CAPTAIN
OF UNDINA'. This was above a rough, hand-drawn map of how
to reach his boatyard by road. Underneath was a scrawled note,
underlined and in capitals: 'THE BOAT IS PHILIP RHODES.
EVERY SEAM IN THE HULL IS OPENED!'

I finally managed to talk to him when I went back to Gothenburg
the following weekend. I had planned to hire a car and visit his
yard. But the sun was still shining. The high was still stationary. I
had half decided that I would simply motor up and leave the boat.

'But I just need to check that you will be able to do the work.
Why can't you deliver it until June, Mr Martinson?'

'Your boat is very beautiful.'

'Yes, yes, that's true.'

'We can put her here in store for the winter.'

'Yes, and will you start the work at once or does it need to wait
until June, then?'

'Bring the boat.'

'Yes . . .' Something, I feared, was not quite straightforward here.
There was something of my former Portuguese landlord about Mr
Martinson. He shared Mr Nicolau's selective English-language-
incomprehension-during-moments-of-straight-talk-about-neces-
sary-repairs.

'How much of the work could you do by then?'

'We can store the boat.'

'Yes. And the work?'

'We do that next year.'

'Next year. You mean January . . .'

'No, no.' Mr Martinson abandoned himself to hearty laughter.
Clearly, at boat-building school, he had taken the special course in
'dealing with owners' inquiries'. He paused, to wipe his eyes, I
assumed. 'November.'

'Next November!'

On past form, I now assumed that he was going to go on to tell
me that he knew that this would be disappointing to me. But he
had a different approach.

'You take the boat and sail in Sweden in July, August. Sweden is very beautiful. The best for sailing. And then bring to me for varnish.'

'I see. So you wouldn't do any of this huge list of work, at all, before then?'

'No! Impossible!' Did I detect that Mr Martinson had suddenly let a sharp edge creep into his tone? I was clearly expecting too much. 'For work you must reserve in May or June! We do work in November, next year. You understand!'

So, after all that, he was offering to store the boat, at special exorbitant rates, admittedly, but he had no intention of doing any work on her before the end of next season. I was unsure why that meant I couldn't have it back until June. Perhaps only an extraordinarily extended length of storage would make it financially worthwhile for him.

We abandoned all plans to take the boat to his yard. Instead I faxed and telephoned Denmark.

In truth, I had always meant to take the boat back to Peter Heller in Kastrup near Copenhagen. What had stopped me, at the last moment? It was partly the sheer slog of travelling another 150 miles down the Kattegat in autumn. No, I'll correct that. It was mostly the sheer slog of travelling another 150 miles down the Kattegat in autumn. I also secretly knew that his place was not really a wooden boat yard of the traditional type. But I have to admit what had originally decided me against going back to Kastrup was Mr Heller's avowed commitment to his incredible, patent German varnishing system.

It was a concoction dreamed up by the same engineers who had developed the everlasting house paint. And Peter Heller was a convert. He had shown me the gleaming, glassy Riva he had restored using it. To my eyes, it hardly resembled a wooden boat at all, so luminous and smoothly was it glazed with this novel plastic covering. But he loved it. At the very prospect, his eyes gleamed with passion, though not, perhaps, as shinily as the Riva.

I was worried that he intended to completely encase my boat in his flexible polythene. The two hatches he had done earlier in the summer still shone beneath their cocoons of sealant. But they seemed rubberized, unreal, glassy: the wood glowing through like a laminated menu, as if from the bottom of a deep pool. It just wasn't natural. But he was extremely keen on it.

'You will not recognize the boat,' he had reassured me, ominously. 'And this will stop the leaks too. It forms a seal, which is flexible.' He had had a hinged flap of wood in his pocket, and he had flexed it in front of me.

And quite apart from recognizing my boat, would I recognize my bank account? The system required a careful preparation of the wood and meticulous sanding. After all, go too hard at it with your machine, and the rubber might just flex itself off, seize up the working parts and then go slithering down the road, roaring and gnashing its teeth and frightening children. Many man-hours were required to apply it, and many man-hours were not a cheap option in Denmark, with its progressive minimum wage, high taxes and expensive men. But I had had enough. I wanted to put *Undina* into hibernation. I telephoned him.

'Yes . . . we can do it.' His voice dropped. 'And we can make sure it is all done with the varnish, like the hatches.'

'Yes.' My God, he didn't waste any time. 'Well, we'll discuss the extent of the varnish, later,' I replied. 'There are many other things which will need doing.'

'I understand . . .' I could hardly hear him now. 'And the inside can be made completely beautiful.'

'Indeed. So if we were to deliver it next weekend . . .'

'Yes . . .' There was a pause. His voice was now a mere croak. 'You can drop the keys with my wife.'

'You aren't there yourself?'

'No, no,' he explained. 'I am currently in Sweden,' he whispered. 'I am hunting moose and birds.'

'Oh, I see.' He was clearly pushing his way through the brush, a gun in one hand, his mobile in the other, even as we spoke. 'Any luck?'

'Not so far.' I fancied I could make out the crackling of little twigs. 'We have been very close to a mummy and two babies.'

'OK, well don't let me interrupt you now,' I told the Bambi

killer. I felt his laudable concern for business might make it difficult to stalk game through the Swedish wilderness, anyway. Perhaps he'd adapted his ring tone to a duck call.

We finally pulled out of the Gothenburg marina a week later. I identified the strange white blobs floating down around us as snowflakes. The air and the land and the boats had taken on a grey, yellowish sheen, not unlike Mr Heller's magic varnish. Some large ships were coming up the river breasting the frosty grey sea, with bow waves of a terrifying icy-white. A ferry bustled through the cold, hanging sea mist. But it was clear that there weren't any other sailing boats around. We were the only ones mad enough to go out in what we English would identify, to all intents and purposes, as a bleak, snowy day in the middle of winter. It was a first, for me, anyway.

It was 140 nautical miles to Copenhagen. We might easily expect to make the trip in twenty-four hours, and since the prospect of a night on a frozen boat in an empty, shut-up, rocky harbour was not alluring, we had elected to keep going, and do the whole leg in one hop, through the night.

'If we leave after lunch,' I told Bob, we can, at least, guarantee to arrive in daylight. I don't fancy trying to get the boat into Copenhagen in the dark.'

Bob had telephoned three days before and asked about the boat. I casually mentioned I was going. He immediately wanted to come. I admit, I had hesitated. Surely the ancient seafaring nation of Sweden could provide somebody equally incompetent? Bob and I had been reduced to 40 miles of silence between platitudes. We were tired of each other.

Besides, I had already secretly betrayed Bob. I had asked Ola to join me. Ola was a sailor. Ola had his own boat. He was there already, he didn't need return tickets and hotel rooms, and Ola was unlikely to cover the boat with boiled sweet wrappings.

But Ola, not surprisingly, had experienced a little difficulty in finding any other willing crew. My son, George the Unready, was also coming, but we needed four to effectively man *Undina* through a night. Loyal Bob, amusing Bob, patient and long-suffering Bob was ready, as always, to drop absolutely nothing at all and come with me. How could I have ever thought of leaving him behind? So, for the last time, I ordered an extra plane ticket and a hotel room and told him to meet me on the train to Stansted. The next day, Ola text-messaged me that he had found someone else. Per was coming too. We were five.

Per was a tough-looking bloke with a shaved head and an interest in meditation. He worked in the backstage crew at the Opera House and, so Ola told me, had sailed a lot.

An hour further south, we were still amongst the islands, follow-ing a channel just inside the westernmost outcrops of Sweden. Ola pointed out some painted huts perched on a barren crest.

'They were built at the beginning of the last century for the poor people of Gothenburg,' he said.

'As permanent homes?' I asked. It seemed inconceivable that anyone would require the needy to take up their council housing on a desolate blank rock.

'Oh, no,' said Ola, 'as summer homes.'

Then just as the open sea loomed and the last urban scatterings of the city's islands fell way behind us, we turned sharply round a wall of rock and into a little natural harbour. In front of the harbour was a small, enclosed pen with three massive fuel pumps.

Ola had rung ahead. The attendant in salopettes and a T-shirt waved from behind his glass door. He had come down specially to open up for us, but stayed inside now. We filled up with water and diesel and I paid him by card.

'Where are you from?' he asked, peering out at the boat.

'England.'

'Hey! You've been sailing around Sweden.'

'We've been all the way to St Petersburg.'

'And now you are going home?'

'Just down to Copenhagen. We must put the boat to bed.'

'Yes, yes.' He shut the till and locked it. There were unlikely to be any other customers. I stood for a moment. It was warm in his glass booth. The others were stamping their feet on the concrete quay.

'We'd better go.'

'Yes, OK. Bye, bye.'

I swung open the glass door and stepped out. The door shut with a finality that I liked. Outside, the air was sharp at the back of the throat. Salopette stayed looking at us from behind the glass as I crossed to *Undina*. He was still standing watching as we left harbour, a lone sailing boat heading off at the end of October into the Kattegat on a rapidly darkening night.

At least the weather forecast was with us. 'Three to six metres per second,' Ola had text-messaged me the day before. 'Starting from the east and gradually turning north.' This was excellent. The east wind would come off the land and we were travelling southwards, close in to the indented, rugged shoreline.

With an east wind there was no danger of being blown on to a lee shore, and there was no open sea to allow waves to build up. It could blow as hard as it liked, but six metres a second, somewhere in the region of a force three, was a light soufflé, a fresh breeze, that would give us enough power to zoom home.

As we turned out from Douro and hauled up the sails, it was clearly gusting up a little higher than that. There was a deal of flapping and flogging in the sail and, when we came round and took the wind on our beam, we dug in and quickly charged up to 8 knots, near to our maximum speed. We went bounding down towards the buoys that marked the furthest reaches of the Gothenburg entrances and sluicing past the last seamarks of the channel on an exhilarating reach. Well, it was blowing stronger than they'd promised, but this was later than we had bargained for. It was an unpredictable time of year. The faster we went, the sooner we got there. I wanted this over.

There was no glamorous sunset. It just got dark. A black, wild night replaced the lowering grey. All mist and haze was blown away.

Soon we were enclosed in a jet environment, tossing and leaning into a foaming anthracite whirl. Immediately around us, the impenetrable darkness of the water reflected the eerie glow of our own navigation lights. Looking ahead, from the wheel, I saw *Undina*'s heavy bow smash into and through the seas, sending a continuous glittering white foam swirling away into the blackness.

As we got used to the dark, and the bucking motion, we could almost feel, rather than see, the divisions of the horizon and the sky and the darker clouds above it. We moved forward through the world in our own crashing, freezing circle of commotion.

Ola was wearing his red all-over suit and white rubber Wellington boots. His face poked out through the balaclava effect of his hood. Ola, George and I had taken the first night watch, starting at six, relieved at midnight.

Per and Bob had gone straight to bed, not just to rest (although Bob liked bed at almost any hour except the early morning), but because, already, it seemed the only possible response to the ghastly, iron grip of the cold.

What had the sun been all day? A weak, feeble, flickering fluorescent tube somewhere behind a screen of cloud. But, now it had disappeared, we realized that it must have been a five-bar gas fire. Without the grey miasma of the daylight it was seriously cold.

I was wearing a pair of thermal woolies, a forty-niner's underwear, a tracksuit bottom and a large pair of bibbed waterproof trousers on my legs. My socks were especially thermal, and my feet resembled small winter-coated rodents. Encased in knubbly wool, they were inserted into the latest fibre-woven sea boots, lined, gusseted and reinforced and reaching almost to my knees. On top of my ol' gran'pappy's lambswool vest I had pulled a T-shirt. Over that I had dragged on a tight fleece and then a large Victoria Wood 'you can't guess how fat I am in this' orange extra-fleecy fleece. Only then had I reached for my fleece-lined mariner's 'storm-force-rugged-southern-ocean-all-weather-lurid-yellow-reflective-tape-covered-plastic-breathable' oil skin. That went on top of everything.

You know when you walk out in the middle of winter wearing just your indoor clothes and stand for a few minutes, waiting, and you know how you start to shiver in the night air and then jump inside gasping, 'Ah, ah, ah! God! It's cold!' Outside, at night, in the Kattegat, it was just like that. Despite all my clothes, I might as well have been wearing a T-shirt and jeans.

When Per finally took over four hours later, he had put on so many layers that he couldn't get the available lifejackets around his middle. I tried to help him, but by then my fingers were senseless frozen tiger prawns.

I was puzzled by this. Earlier that day, I had bought two pairs of 'helmsman's gloves' made by 'Gill', one of the chief and most extravagant of advertisers in the yachting press. 'Waterproof and windproof' and costing £30, the gloves, it would appear, were, in reality, designed to absorb the water and hold it against my skin, ensuring that the icy, lashing wind could further reduce the temperature of my fingers.

Given that a steady, sleety rain was now hammering out of the night and a continuous flung spray was crashing over and across the deck; given that *Undina*'s nose was often buried in the crest of a wave which then continued, as a mini tidal wall, to race across the whole deck towards us, and then subsume the cabin roof, the spray protector and us, the human constituent, before being swallowed into the blackness astern; given that this was a night when there was no definite point where cold air finished and cold water began; I was surprised that they didn't advise me to take off their scientific marvels and store them in a safe, dry place.

But there was no time to care for my gloves. There was only time for a sort of dull, throbbing resentment, like a sore. The weather was clearly worsening. Instead of staying in the east, just as it had done, on every leg of this trip, the wind was inexorably heading round in front of us.

'This wind is veering south-east!' I shouted at Ola. He nodded. Talking, communication, the chatter that usually accompanies cold nights on open boats, seemed an extra effort, too difficult. We were sharply heeled, making over 8 knots. The seas were rising up and we were cutting into them at colossal speed. *Undina*'s deep shape meant she rode into the night with the dignity of a pendulum. But it was a big swing. George reached for a bucket and was sick. He felt immediately better, but I let him lie in the berth immediately below the cabin entrance, wedged into the side of the hull by the angle of heel and wrapped in a duvet.

For me the motion was the one unchanging charge. I liked the roller-coaster lift and drop and the fierce momentum of the boat under sail. It took me entirely by surprise when Per, preparing to come on deck at the watch's end, suddenly stepped to one side, bowed like a courtier and politely retched into a bucket. Ola, who had been up there with me for those long four hours, just as unexpectedly quietly excused himself and vomited over the side.

Had I felt sick, I feared I would have collapsed into a slough of self-pity, because, despite the onward rush, in every other respect, this was sailing as an extended experience of utter discomfort.

Any progress required careful pre-judgement. The next move forward had to be calculated and then executed with dash: swinging forward on the uprise, grabbing at a handhold, moving the feet to the next ledge and tensing against the downward crash of the boat. As the night wore on, dash came in shorter supply. Just staying put required acute concentration. There always seemed the danger of being pitched out and over the side.

I had to go forward and fiddle with the sails. Ola, who was not used to the fittings and the fixtures of my old-fashioned rig, but was perfectly experienced in handling boats, was better on the helm. He took the wheel. I braced myself. My turn.

I took hold of two big winch handles and heaved myself up on to the side decks, bent double to hold the grab rail with one hand, and, timing my forward rush with the plunging of the boat, dragged myself up the deck in a series of lurches.

I yanked my safety line up behind me, braced myself against the pounding deck and yelled back at Ola.

'Ola! Let the mainsheet go!'

He did and the back of the sail, instead of holding the wind, now flew loose. The thick wooden spar of the boom rattled ferociously, violently, as if wanting to shake itself free of its bronze attachments, clanking and banging at them; a banshee of anarchy.

The boat surged on, heeling, bucking, driven now solely by the foresail. I reached around the mast and, with fat thumbs, pulled at the brake of the halyard winch until a shrill, metallic whirring, clearly audible above the racket, brought the sail dropping down a few feet. I needed to drag it down further. I had to get more down. Somewhere, there was a cringle, a metal, hooped eye about an inch across, about four feet up, somewhere on the front edge of the sail. Groping, I got a wet bulbous finger through it, pulled, leaned down, feeling with my other hand for a short-length rope.

I undid the rope, pushed the hook through the tugging cringle in my other hand, heaved on the rope and retied the loose end to the cleat.

Bracing against the tossing, I shook my head to loosen water. I spat out salt and, timing myself with the rising and falling of the boat, applied both hands to the winch. I leaned into it with as much strength as I could in order to pull the top of the sail back up the mast and tighten its front edge at its new, lower height. I turned it. The boat crashed on. I turned it again. I pushed and yanked for one final effort. That would do.

A great mass of sail-cloth now danced and plunged in a wet, flapping, shapeless bag under the boom. Ducking, I shouldered it away, fumbling helplessly with wet gloves and cold fingers, cursing and spitting and wiping at my eyes. I manoeuvered myself upright, and peered along the length of the boom, yanking at ropes in turn, until I had the one I wanted. And all the time the boat bounced on, the wind roared and the sail whipped and flogged like a mad thing.

I squeezed one set of freezing toes into a hatch corner on the slithery deck and leaned back on the rope. The pain in my foot reassured me that my toes had not frozen solid. The gloves gave no grip on the rope in my hand. I worked at the boom winch handle: yanking forward and pushing back, yanking forward and pushing back. With my other arm I pulled at the rope, but the sopping braid was slipping on the winch, so again I unslotted the handle, wrapped another two turns to increase the friction, slotted it back and again heaved and yanked. Heaved and yanked, heaved and yanked, and finally began to feel the pull of the winch as it gripped and wound the rope attached to the far end of the sail, down to meet the end of the boom.

Breathing heavily and straining at it, worried that I might lose it after all that work, I tied off the rope, water oozing from within its coils as it tightened on the cleat. It was done. I clumsily jerked my way back to join Ola.

'OK?'

'OK.'

I'd been up there less than five minutes. There had been no danger. Ruefully, I reflected that if the wind blew up more I would have to go back soon and do it again, for another reef.

Ola tightened in the mainsail. The flapping stopped. The boat picked up speed again. For a while I teetered, exhausted and shivering, under the protection of the spray hood. Ola was hunched at the wheel. His head was down against the wind and rain. His eyes were fixed on the dim light of the compass binnacle.

I read the speed across the ground on the Navman. 'Seven point six knots,' I told him. Then I stood and, raising my head back into the cold wind, took stock of the blackness.

There were dozens of ships, most of them passing on an invisible road a mile or so further out to sea. They were heading, like ourselves, for the tiny channel, 80 miles south, that passed between the island of Sjælland and the mainland of Sweden. On one side was the Swedish Helsingborg and on the other the Danish Helsingør (Elsinore). We had to go through there and so did they. And, disconcertingly, travelling in the same direction, some ships seemed to hang around our tail for hours.

'It's because we're moving so quickly. Some of these boats aren't going much faster than us,' shouted Ola. I nodded.

And at one point, from behind, there suddenly came a blinding glare of bright light. I had to shield my eyes to look into it. What was this? A coastguard boat? How close was this huge and alarming light? It was a freighter, still a good half mile behind us, concerned to identify these feeble navigation lights or that tiny blip on its radar, and which had now turned a powerful spotlight on us. They were, presumably, startled to see a small sailing boat cruising down the Swedish coast in the middle of a freezing autumn night. Anyway, without any other form of communication, they switched off, swung slightly out of their way and passed us by, a mile out.

By eleven, on checking the battery charge, I could see that, even with scrupulous rationing, the heater had drained the power from the first main battery. There was another fully charged battery. But we couldn't risk switching straight to that. We needed, whatever happened, to ensure that we didn't lose all power, otherwise we might not be able to start the engine. The engine was a vital resource, not just to move us around, but also because it charged the batteries. We could restore battery power with the engine. Without it we were dead: possibly in more ways than one.

I turned the ignition and switched it on. There was a distant churning and the lights and instruments died. Alas, there wasn't even enough power in the number one battery to start the engine. And now I had stupidly used up what little trickle remained. It didn't matter. I switched to the other battery and the engine fired into life. The lights returned. We reset the instruments. But there was something missing. One system had found it all too much. The heater just refused to come back on.

There was a little illuminated control panel for this thing. The lights on it had flickered back. So something was there. I sat and pressed the minuscule buttons. After five minutes I had managed to ensure that the boat would be heated between six in the morning and eleven at night on odd days in March 2007 and would switch itself off for the whole of 1997, but failed to get it to come on and put any heat into the cabin for the present. After completely covering an extensive electronic calendar with separate little black blobs, underlinings, thermometer symbols and minute centigrade numbers, I even went so far as to search for the instructions.

Of course, it was useless. With time and fingers of rodent-like proportions I could ensure chilly air on my mother's birthday in five years' time. What I could not do was switch it on now. Nothing was happening at all. The lights were on but there was no heater home. More bizarrely still, though, I gradually discovered that I couldn't switch it off. This seemed ergonomically impossible, but there it was. Despite a complete absence of any warm and comforting air, there was a motor whirring.

'It must be the fan system!' Ola shouted at me through the howling wind and over the roaring of the engine.

I had supreme confidence in Ola's diagnosis. He was, after all, the technical director of the Gothenburg Opera with direct responsibility for the installation and running of the most complicated computerized stage machinery system in the world.

'What should I do?'

'I don't know. I never trust anything electrical,' the director replied.

'I can't switch it off!' I shouted. 'Even though it's not working.'

Ola looked too cold to deal with this. He made an uncommitted groaning noise.

We left it. It continued to cool down for the next fourteen hours. After we had closed the boat up for the winter and shut everything off, the fan ran on, unable to instruct itself to stop.

'I have a solution to this,' said the technical director of the Gothenburg Opera. He lifted a locker lid, reached inside and ripped out the wiring. The whirring faded.

But that was miles ahead. For the time being, our watch was ending. For four hours we had sat there in the dark. For four hours we had hung on against the pitching and yawing. Now the others came on deck to take over. They were dead on time and wide awake. It had got too cold to lie in the cabin. They preferred to be up. We didn't joke or cheer. We grunted, shivered, drew their attention to the ships around us and went below ourselves.

I filled in the log before getting to my bunk. Everything across the chart table was wet. In adverts for boats, plump blokes sit upright in tartan shirts, sleeves rolled up, wielding a pair of dividers and smiling benignly at the camera with a cup of coffee at their elbows and a minuscule map in front of them. Here in the middle of the night, wedged against the vertiginous pitch of the heeling cabin and peering at a chart by the light of a single red bulb, I despaired as the water from my own waterproof clothing ran across the chart. The pencil wouldn't mark our position on the sopping paper. The dividers and the parallel rules clattered about and the mahogany glistened with drips.

Some hours before, Per had originally intended to sleep in my fore-cabin. He had emerged a few minutes later. It was wet, apparently. When I looked, there was an oxbow lake in the middle of my bed. The upholstery had the consistency of a recently dunked digestive biscuit. Great rivulets were running down and across the deck above. My duvets and pillows, for which I'd lugged the covers through Customs, were monstrous wet sponges.

Per took all this philosophically. I didn't. I railed. I moaned. I banged my head. Despite our work, our fixing, gluing, varnishing and rubberizing, despite the fact that Baines seemed to have spent half the summer with a tube of mastic in his hand, trailing loops of black goo across the teak decks, waiting for it to go off, kneading it and plugging and sealing, despite the repairs and the careful stopping, we might as well have been sitting in a cardboard box in a shower. I shut the cabin door on the whole sorry mess.

As I pulled myself into the weather bunk, I cursed this stupid boat, with its stupid wooden decks that would never hold out water, and its stupid, over-designed modern features that couldn't survive in its stupid, old-fashioned structure. Was I prepared to just go on spending money to keep this stupid bit on the side in cosmetic repairs only to find that she would let me down in any crisis? Above the racket of the engine, Bob was loudly complaining because the speed of the boat had fallen to under 5 knots.

From where I lay, I could feel what was happening. He was swinging the boat into the wind, until the wind got behind the sails and stopped her dead, then, having discovered this himself, he was swinging her back on to the wind where she was blown almost over on her beam ends, then steering off our set course by 20 degrees to recover and then repeating exactly the same operation over and over again. Should I get up and get him to let Per helm the boat? It had taken me five minutes to lever myself into the bunk. There was no danger. We would simply add another four hours to our journey. I couldn't be bothered. I was too cocooned in a blanket of self-pity. An hour later Bob gave up his unequal struggle, put the engine into gear and motor-sailed the course he'd been set.

I rocked in my wet hutch and dozed until four in the morning. Ola and I took our watch. Per and Bob had furled the gennaker. The wind had come round further to the south. We were bashing into choppy seas. There were 18 sea-miles to go before we reached the narrows and relative shelter.

'Surprisingly, it's not so cold,' were Bob's words as he scurried to get below.

It wasn't. The south wind, as one might have expected, was warmer. We had to hang on to get into the lee of Denmark and we were nearly there. But, like all approaches to land, the hours seemed to creep past while the shore and its lights came no closer. We had flown across the sea and charged down the coast, but this final stage, rounding the point of Kervoeren and crossing into the sheltered waters of the Helsingør Strait, took all our watch.

At six it began to get light. We had crossed the paths of all the ships and were now well over on the far shore, out of the main lanes, and into some shelter from the wind, as a cold, blustery day gradually made itself known: an ordinary day for the merchant shipping fleet all around us. Just because it was October and the yachting people had all gone, there was no diminution in their business. Tugs, coasters and ferries roamed around the narrows, banging into a lumpy sea.

But at least it was possible to change my footwear. Sitting bent double in the fore-cabin I yanked at my boots. I was wheezing with the effort. They finally overcame their vacuum with a loose, wet 'thwock' and my red and blue fingers fumbled to roll off my socks. For a moment I sat with one wet sock in each hand. I towelled my feet like new-born baby pigs, cradling them, padding at them, wrapping them, nursing them until the stinging pain of contact began to fade and the paradoxically hot searing pain subsided.

It was a measure of the incapacitating, enervating discomfort of the passage up until now that none of us had thought of food. Usually, night on a boat is a running buffet. Biscuits, chocolate, soup, more biscuits, biltong, more biscuits, sweeties, pork pies, snacks and biscuits are passed around every five minutes, but the last eighteen hours had seemed to concentrate all attention into a direct physical struggle with inertia. Steering the boat, at least, focused the body and the mind into a single operation. On such a cold night the act of just sitting on a tossing boat, neither talking nor doing, not pulling in sails nor attending to the navigation, but just sitting, closed in, wasting no energy, fighting the rising grimness of the cold, had become an act of will in itself. All of us had sat, when not at the wheel or standing looking into the battering seas, totally immersed in the business of nothing.

But we should have eaten. God knows, we had stocked up with enough delicacies before we left Gothenburg. I lit the stove. I found a pan and a packet of chicken soup. I opened a cupboard and tossed chocolate biscuits to Ola.

'Griff! Griff!'

Ola was calling from the helm.

'Griff, could you take the helm for a moment or two? I think I must change my boots. My feet have gone very cold.' Ola's old, white Wellington boots were as useless as my brand new 'sea-master footwear'. We swapped places.

The soup helped. The biscuits helped. But by the time Bob came on deck, my mind had locked into an exhausted, frozen toffee. I was up on the cabin roof, taking in the main. My fingers were raw. I stared at him with marblized eyeballs, finished trussing up the sail and lowered myself below. It was daylight but it was colder than ever. I poked ineffectually at the controls of the heater, as if, by some miracle, it might reinvigorate itself, took off my shoes and jacket and thrust myself into the bunk. It was wet in there but my body generated some heat. When I turned back the covers four hours later I was startled to see a cloud of grey vapour, a human mist, lifting and swirling off my chest into the freezing atmosphere of the cabin. Like a cheap effect in a play, I was swathed in my own personal morning fog.

I dragged myself out of bed, flung on my jacket and pushed my feet into my shoes and hauled myself up into the light.

We were skewing through a very lively sea. The wind had blown up to a good force six and had become icy cold again.

'It's blowing from the west!' I said disgustedly.

'Ya, ya,' said Ola.

In fact, the wind turning west over the land had saved us a good deal of further discomfort. This was a very powerful breeze indeed. Ugly towering heaps of cumulus were scudding across a strained sky. We were close under a long row of giant windmills that marked the southern edge of Copenhagen approaches. Their propellers were whizzing round above us like demented mixers. A Dutch sea painting come to life, lighters and barges were skewing down grey, luminous waves topped by breaking white crests. A ferry pulling out towards the Baltic sent a long streamer of smoke before it. But now we were sheltered enough by the Copenhagen shore. The wasp black and yellow of a middle-ground buoy came scudding towards us, marking where the channel split to take traffic up to the south harbour. I pointed ahead.

'There!' Ola followed my finger. 'That's the green.'

'Ya, ya. I can see the port too.'

There were two little sticks to mark the entrance to Kastrup marina. And beyond them, towards the glittering shore, where yellow-leaved trees were feathered by the shocking breeze, there was another pair. We turned and crossed towards them.

Ola gave me the wheel and we teetered in towards the heaps of stone that marked the entrance. Even now the wind was catching the boat and threatening to swing her off course. For a second or two, just outside the eastern arm of the entrance we touched, but we just as quickly lifted off and swooped, on a dirty wave, into the sudden, still calm of the marina.

It was still crowded with boats. Their aluminium masts gleamed in the low, stark morning light. Their rigging set up a humming and rattling in the wind, like muted applause, and the sudden change in our conditions brought the others up on deck.

We turned and swung into the bay where we had lain before. I used the engine to turn her and let the wind blow her back a bit, until we were pointing into the mooring, opened the throttle a bit, and squeezed in. We tied up.

In the next berth along from us, there was a boat called *Perdita*. She was wooden, probably built in the 1930s, with a neat, deep mahogany cockpit and a long, curved sheer. She had a low coach roof and a row of oval portholes, bronze winches and a pretty canoe stern. She probably leaked. She would be cramped underneath. She would be uncomfortable and impossibly expensive to maintain.

I stood looking at her for a moment or two.

'What a beautiful boat,' I said to no one in particular.